STUDIES IN PUBLIC COMMUNICATIONS

A. WILLIAM BLUEM, GENERAL EDITOR

THE COMMUNICATIVE ARTS
An Introduction to Mass Media

STUDIES IN PUBLIC COMMUNICATIONS

MASS MEDIA AND COMMUNICATION
Edited by Charles S. Steinberg

THE LANGUAGES OF COMMUNICATION
A Logical and Psychological Examination
By George N. Gordon

TO KILL A MESSENGER
Television News and the Real World
By William Small

INTERNATIONAL COMMUNICATION
Media, Channels, Functions
Edited by Heinz-Dietrich Fischer and
John Calhoun Merrill

The COMMUNICATIVE ARTS
An Introduction to Mass Media
By Charles S. Steinberg

STUDIES IN PUBLIC COMMUNICATION

THE COMMUNICATIVE ARTS

An Introduction to Mass Media

by Charles S. Steinberg, Ph.D.

COMMUNICATION ARTS BOOKS

HASTINGS HOUSE, PUBLISHERS • NEW YORK

For Hortense

First Edition

Cloth Edition ISBN: 8038-1151-9
Text Edition ISBN: 8038-1152-7

Library of Congress Catalog Card Number: 68-31692

Published simultaneously in Canada by
Saunders of Toronto, Ltd., Don Mills, Ontario

DESIGNED BY AL LICHTENBERG

PRINTED IN THE UNITED STATES OF AMERICA

Contents

Preface

THE PHENOMENON OF mass communication marks the third major technological revolution in the history of man. It may also evolve into the most significant one from a social and cultural point of view. The invention of printing, in the Fifteenth Century, changed the course of man's destiny by making it possible for all men to become literate and by opening a great new vista of opportunity through universal education. The Industrial Revolution, in the Nineteenth Century, transformed man's way of living in society and resulted in the development of an urban civilization with all of its discontents and paradoxes of poverty and plenty, comfort and deprivation, work and leisure. Both phenomena were precursors, culturally and technologically, of the great communications revolution of the Twentieth Century. Print was the first step in a series of transformations that began five centuries ago and are still continuing today. Steam was the second, providing the sources of industrial power which made for speed, accuracy, mass production and distribution, along with more efficient means of transportation.

Mass communication—the means by which print and electronic media bring education, entertainment and information to millions—is the significant technical accomplishment of this tumultuous century. In terms of sheer technological magnitude, the achievements in mass communications range among the most brilliantly effective of man's scientific endeavors. And they are but a harbinger of what is still to come. Having joined sight and sound in the medium of television, communications scientists have now brought toward successful fruition computer technology, community antenna, global communications by means of satellite, lasar beams, picture telephones, and other achievements which will evolve out of both basic and applied research. Never in history has man been able to communicate with such technical proficiency, accuracy and speed.

As with most successful technologies, however, the results cannot

ix

be evaluated solely on the quantitative criteria of science. All technical phenomena have social, cultural, political and economic consequences. The social and cultural consequences of the communications resolution are only beginning to be felt and evaluated. The power and reach of mass media have made instant communications possible almost everywhere, but they have not resolved the semantic roadblocks to effective communication between men and nations. The impact and effect of mass media, and the way in which they interact with society, is still to be studied with a greater degree of empirical success by social scientists. The potential of mass communication for education has just begun to be realized. In the wake of communications technology must come an appraisal of its social consequences and its cultural potential.

This book describes the development of the media of communication primarily as cultural and social phenomena. It does not attempt an exhaustive history of the media, for the history of each of the communicative arts is a volume in itself. But the basic historical and technological developments of the mass media are discussed against the background of their social and cultural significance. Man's first steps toward communication are described, followed by a discussion of the process of interpersonal and mass communication. The major efforts in the development of each of the media forms the background for an evaluation of the impact of mass communication on public opinion and a discussion of the overriding problem of freedom, control and responsibility in mass communication.

It was felt that to interlard the pages with a multiplicity of footnotes and peripheral comment would serve no useful purpose and would prove cumbersome. References made in each chapter, however, are documented in the complete bibliography. At the same time, the bibliography is selective, rather than exhaustive. Here, again, it was felt that a carefully selected and relevant bibliography would be more useful to the reader than a long, exhaustive and essentially irrelevant list of every book under the sun.

The author wishes to express his appreciation to those who were good enough to read part of the manuscript and, in particular to Laurence Laurent, Television Critic of *The Washington Post* and Adjunct Professor-Communication at the American University; Professor Robert Blanchard, Chairman, Department of Journalism and Communication, The American University; Herbert Kamm, Associate Editor of *The Cleveland Press*; Lawrence Holcomb, Professor, Department of Communications, Emerson College; Leonard Spinrad, Director of Corporate Information, CBS Corporate Affairs; Arnold Becker, Assistant Director of Research at the CBS Television Network. Appreciation is due also to Miss Sherley Abrams, Librarian in the Special Projects Department of CBS News, whose assistance in aiding the author to locate source material was particularly helpful.

Introduction

IT IS EVIDENT that the mass media, in exercising their informational as well as diversionary functions, gain increasing influence over the processes by which men arrive at those decisions that govern the social contract. Upon these media may rest the responsibility for change, and perhaps upheaval, in both the policy and organization of our basic social institutions—in government, in education, in our courts and laws, and in all those agencies and systems by which social stability is perpetuated, progress assured, and individual liberty guaranteed.

The mass media are, without question, persuasive instruments in the social aspect of man's struggle for self-liberation. They select and bring to waiting multitudes a constant flow of detail related to those fruitful dialogues of differences and concordances upon which free societies thrive. It inevitably follows that what information is transmitted, and the nature of transmission, will dictate the direction and intensity of change in all other institutions within society. Each of the mass media, in varying degrees, in different ways, and in distinct presentational methods, brings us to confrontations with ourselves as social beings. By doing so, they not only shape our collective hopes, aspirations and futures, but extend to us a new and deeper understanding of the quality of our existence.

By all reasoned measure, then, the major function of formal education in the field of communication is to come to grips with the great public media of this century. If the range of interests in media education must be linked with all areas of life where technology has entered and influenced human communication, the study of public media *as media* must still be central to inquiry and to teaching. Regrettably, media study in the university has yet to attain a maximum level of effectiveness. Educators have tended to accept two basic approaches to mass media studies, neither of which is wholly satisfactory.

First, various traditional disciplines within the humanities and the social sciences have sought to incorporate mass media "appreciation" or "critical" studies into their own curricula. This practice has many proponents, and is currently also in vogue at secondary education levels. The result of such thinking has been damaging to all concerned. The teacher or student with an interest in the media discovers that he is isolated from the rest of the academic community and those rich reserves of research and scholarship which might help him achieve a broader understanding of the media. Since the media cut across all lines, no single department or academic unit in which they are treated—perforce as merely one aspect of the discipline—can offer the student a holistic view. Indeed, this approach has in the past produced many teachers who actually enter mass media departments with little real knowledge of the field. The student, of course, is equally deprived. His outlook upon media is limited by the critical analysis of the psychologist, sociologist, historian or literature professor, and nowhere are their respective viewpoints and approaches drawn together.

An equally unsatisfactory approach to media study in our colleges and universities is the creation within a "communications" complex of strong but separate units which focus upon specific kinds of media (newspaper and magazines, radio and television, motion pictures) or one *function* of media (theatrical, instructional, journalistic, cinematic) if not to the exclusion of other media or functions, at least to their detriment— and the detriment of the student. The approach tends to overspecialize the student—locking him into a career that may not even exist after ten more years of technical innovation.

It is useful, therefore, to strike for an approach to media study which is more germane to the student's needs—a program wherein he studies media *qua* media in a curriculum which is informed by the discoveries and revelations of both the humanities and social-sciences. For if we carry from the hectic 60's a single impression of what students want, it is that they seek greater breadth and depth of understanding about media role and function. Gone are the days when a student waited until his year of Ph.D. residence before he was told that the behavioral sciences had something to say about television, or that newspaper reporting, microphone technique, acting and film-making all were merely different aspects of the same creative human activity. A beginning text which sets the mass media into such broad perspective is long overdue, and for this reason *Studies in Public Communication* welcomes this important work by Dr. Steinberg.

A. William Bluem, Ph.D.
Professor
Newhouse Communications Center
Syracuse University

Mass Media and Society

COMMUNICATION began when primitive man discovered, with a sense of awe and wonder, that he could reach out and influence and even modify other men's behavior. And this sense of wonder prevails in this age of sophisticated technology where the electronic miracles forged by science enable men continuously to find new ways to interact with each other, not only in face-to-face communication, but across the horizons and under the sea and from the great void of outer space.

Interpersonal and tribal communication evolved over many centuries into instantaneous national and global communication and, in this second half of the Twentieth Century, into the phenomenon of radio dialogue and televised transmission between men in space centers on earth with men in orbit and literally out of this world. The science-fiction marvels of Jules Verne and H. G. Wells, once the great stimuli of schoolboy imagination, have been rendered commonplace as science, having reached the moon, contemplates the intriguing possibility of communication with men in space ships on distant planets.

Having discovered the dynamics of speech, man ultimately sought for a meaningful dialogue. The long, slow process of socialization and acculturation began—a process which has undergone a continuous modification over the centuries with the rise and fall of civilizations. Verbalization developed into writing, and from written language there evolved print media and sophisticated means of audiovisual communication, phenomena which comprise the most forceful and distinguishing characteristics of this technologically-oriented civilization.

The temptation to telescope the achievements of the centuries is one of the least rewarding results of the development of writing and printing. The need for brevity and the restrictions of time and space unfortunately make it necessary to condense the history of man's long, arduous and still-continuing struggle to communicate effectively. Long before the development of the mass media, indeed centuries before any formal communication was achieved, an unusual species of nature's creatures became known as man. The exact time and place of this momentous evolution has not been recorded with certainty. But with the emergence of man came the gift and the power to communicate, and eventually, as the science of semantics describes it, the ability to use verbal, and ultimately written, symbols to represent the world of things. Man established a primitive kind of speech first, and later developed the ability to represent ideas in drawings on stone and cave, finally learning to read and to write. This ability to read and write was a fateful occasion in the evolution of mankind. For verbal communication is limited, even though word of mouth was long employed to carry on the folk tradition from generation to generation. As a result of writing, the pageant of events became part of a pattern of history and culture. A residue or pool of knowledge developed, as man found ways to preserve those events called "history" by means of writing and printing.

These developments in communications, however, were neither sudden nor quixotic. They occurred only through a long process of accretion in time. The earliest manuscripts were limited necessarily to the few who could read, and those who had attained this distinction were able to participate in politics as a minority estate. But the human being is a gregarious creature, and it is this sense of socialization which has distinguished and set him apart from lesser creatures—the socializing function and something beyond. The additional factor—the something beyond—is the ability of men to communicate with each other and among diverse social groups. This communicating tendency is what has made social cohesion possible and which has resulted, ironically, not only in the rise, but also the fall of many great civilizations.

Man as Communicator

No history of mankind, regardless of the point of view from which it is narrated—historical, sociological, anthropological or philosophical—can be told without the implicit recognition of the fact that man is a communicating creature. The development, the structure and the transformations that characterize society are permutations in the chain of communications. Print brought literacy and education to the masses. Radio and television bring mass entertainment and instantaneous "breaking" news to the millions. The phenomena of a print-oriented culture and, subsequently, of an audio-visual one are the two seminal developments in the evolution of mass communications. Communication, reduced to the basic and most functional level, involves a chain reaction between individuals and groups, a social counterpart to the constant interaction of stimulus and response which occurs between the organism and its environment. Man communicated before he learned to use language, but it was language, and man's adeptness (and paradoxically his curious ineptness) in employing it, which made socialization possible. Communication, which forged new bonds among men, also proved disruptive when men failed to surmount the semantic roadblocks they themselves had structured.

As little is known of man's appearance on earth, so less is known about his fateful leap into language. Certainly man learned to talk before he learned to write, but the origins of both are shrouded in historical half-truth and apocrypha. Whether man learned to speak from lower animal forms, or whether speech came eventually from his own howls, grunts and grimaces is a matter for fascinating conjecture. Speech may have come when, after centuries of evolution, man's brain had reached a stage of development that indicated it was ready for this monumental step. Early efforts at verbal communication were certainly accompanied by grunts and dance, mimetics and gestures. But the gift of speech did come eventually to man, and with it the emergence of socialization and civilization.

It is understandable, if egocentric, of English speaking peoples to believe so earnestly in the importance and the integrity of their language. But the sobering fact is that relatively few speak and write this language when compared with the millions who communicate in the many Asian tongues. Nor is it true, as the uninitiated naively believe, that English was one of the older languages. When, a century ago, scholars of linguistics began to look into the origin and history of language communication, they discovered several thousand living languages, as well as a multiplicity of tongues, like the Phoenician, which were long dead. Many of these languages, whether they developed in proximity to each other or remotely, bore a general family relationship, however tenuous. The oldest were, of course, the Semitic languages, such as Hebrew. The English language developed much later, partly from the Indo-European group which, in turn, came from the original Latin, and partly from the Germanic. Of the ancient languages few have managed to survive the centuries, but the Hebrew used in the State of Israel today is virtually identical with the Hebrew of the ancient tribes of the Old Testament. These language developments belong more appropriately to a discussion of the history and social impact of the manuscript and the book.

Although our knowledge of the rise and fall of civilizations is based primarily on written records, man first communicated and transmitted his social and cultural tradition from generation to generation by means of oral language. The contribution of the ancient bards to the history of civilization is a significant one and proved both pragmatic and romantic until the development of writing. Early man also devised other methods to satisfy his need to communicate, as some primitive men still do today, in his ability to draw signs on the walls of paleolithic caves. Eventually, as the history of printing and book-making show, the written word appeared, and with this revolutionary development came man's first genuine effort to record for the future his aspirations, thoughts and deeds, his laws, his medical knowledge and his religious beliefs.

Man began by means of signs and ideograms, and eventually he recorded the phenomenon of his existence on paper. This was one of the miracles of the ages, this uncanny art of preserving in permanent form the lessons of history and the roots of culture. With the development of more sophisticated means of communication, man was able to move out of the rut of primitive living and to develop codes of laws, systems of epistemology and metaphysics—in short, a culture and a civilization. With this sophistication came ultimately the unfortunate discontents of urban civilization, the problems of mass education and the challenges of new ways of preserving knowledge through the techniques of automation and information storage.

The art of writing bifurcated along two paths, the Western and the Oriental. Each reflected different beliefs and diverse ways of life in widely divergent script. The first tentative effort to put thoughts and words on paper occurred in the Third or Fourth Century B.C., although archeologists have discovered some earlier evidence in pictographic drawings. The Fourth Century B.C. saw the first use of the wedge-shaped cuneiform characters by the Sumerians, a method in which pictographs and ideographs were used to represent meanings. As this early cuneiform script took on a phonetic character, symbols began to represent external objects and this wedge-shaped style of writing was disseminated by the Babylonians and the Syrians. At about the same time, the Egyptians were developing their own hieroglyph style which was also ideographic or pictographic in form. But the hieroglyph style was a complicated one, involving literally hundreds of characters and the script was restricted in use to the educated, priestly caste. The famous Rosetta Stone, found during Napoleon's campaign into Egypt, is the key to the two styles of Egyptian script—the hieratic used by the priests and the more popular demotic style.

In the Far East, the Chinese were developing their own complicated style, involving hundreds of signs and characters, while from Greece in the Aegean came the origin of the Graeco-Roman alphabet which forms the basis for the development of Western civilization. Through trade routes, this alphabet passed originally from the Phoenicians to the Greeks who added vowels to it. Thence it passed on to the Etruscans and the Romans, finally becoming the basis for the contemporary languages of the Western world by means of the dissemination of Latin by the church.

In every instance, language became a communications medium and something more. It became identified with a way of living and at the same time it served to reflect the mores and culture of society. Even today, particular segments of a society, living in different parts of the same country, tend to be identified by distinctive variations in language, as in the sectional dialects of the United States, the dialects indigenous to different parts of the British Isles, and the variations in speech and idiom in the various regions of France, Italy, Spain and the Soviet Union. But these are local variations that tend to fortify the conviction that the ability to communicate by means of language—oral and later written— was the magnificent step that transformed man from primitiveness to sophistication, that gave man the opportunity to use his intelligence and his imagination in new and fascinating directions.

Communications Technology

Modern man, for better or worse, is the product of a series of major developments in technology, but each social transformation was essentially a revolution in the art and science of communications. The advent of print moved civilization a step beyond the beautiful, but necessarily limited, range of the illuminated manuscript into a new world of literacy and universal education, of broadsides, newspapers, books, magazines, electronic journalism, teaching machines and computers. The Nineteenth Century Industrial Revolution, with the harnessing of steam for power, made printing both cheap and expeditious, so that almost everyone could share in the cornucopia of education and knowledge. And the Twentieth Century carried the communications revolution forward with the development of radio and television and the growth of information technology and instantaneous global communication by means of orbiting satellites. Each of these thrusts forward in the development of modern communications carried in its wake potential benefits for mankind, at least some of which have been realized superbly. Communications technology has increased the opportunity of education for those who were intellectually disenfranchised. It has made information available quickly and cheaply to the masses. It has offered, through the instrumentality of the televised debate and the radio and television news and public affairs program, a unique opportunity for citizen awareness of, and participation in, the process of government.

While its positive contribution have far outweighed its negative ones, the revolution in communications has not been without its residue of problems. The technological feat of global communications has not reduced materially the semantic roadblocks to international understanding. The speed with which information is gathered and disseminated does not always lead to comprehension and knowledge. But the institutionalization of the media of mass communication has resulted in unprecedented opportunity for the democratization of educational opportunity through the speed with which information is gathered and conveyed and through the new techniques by which knowledge may now be preserved on microfilm, video tape and other devices of information storage and retrieval.

These new techniques, which use the science of communications technology, have given rise to a host of theories concerning the nature, structure and function of communications. The techniques of quantification of data and the growth of the behavioral sciences as an area for basic and applied research have given rise to considerable speculation and, indeed, some controversy, among students of communications as to the role of mass communication in society, both as an art and a science. But the development of communications technology has been so rapid that the technicians have moved ahead of the more reflective pace of the scholars, so that modern man finds it difficult to grasp and to harness the results of his scientific achievements. The techniques for gathering, storing and supplying information are miraculous and sophisticated, but man's grasp of the psychological and sociological implications of the communications revolution are still secondary to his technological expertise.

Thus, diverse theories of communication have been developed to encompass and explain the social implications of scientific achievements in such areas as radio and telecommunications and in the newer areas of information technology. The mathematicians offer a structural theory in terms of integers and quantification of communications data. Older disciplines, such as psychology and sociology and newer areas such as semantics, offer alternative, but related, ways of understanding the development and functions of mass communications. But each approach to the phenomenon of mass communications is predicated on the basic agreement that the entire life process of contemporary man is one of human interaction through the communicative arts. The life of man, from waking to sleeping—and, indeed, during sleep—is one of continuous exposure to communications stimuli and of response to those stimuli. All human behavior, in essence, is communications behavior. When the process of communications is so structured as to reach a great many people, as in the media of newspapers, radio and television, the channels of transmission become media of *mass* communications.

The Mathematical Theory

Of particular significance in the newer concepts of mass communication is the theory of the mathematicians, as articulated by Norbert Wiener and Claude Shannon, among others. This theory applies the concepts of engineering and mathematics to the process of communication, with particular emphasis on linear transmission of communications data, or content, from sender to receiver. The mathematicians believe that inherent in the mathematical theory of communications are certain relevant psychological aspects such as feedback, as well as the development of automatic control systems (cybernetics). The mathematical theory identifies communications with social and behavior control. While man has communicated by a variety of methods—dance, drama, gesture, art, music—the mathematicians are concerned with the basic science of transmitting data through electronic devices from source or sender to receiver.

What, then, is the significance of the mathematical theory? One significant aspect of the theory is to be found in the conviction that the *meaning* of the message, or content, is materially affected by the accuracy or deficiency of the modus operandi of technical transmission. Noise, for example, can interfere with and affect the *meaning* of the message, as in the case of static on radio and television. Hence, the eagerness with which the Iron Curtain countries try to jam radio transmission from abroad. The obtrusiveness of noise, according to the mathematicians, is even more significant than semantic roadblocks to effective communications. As the message is relayed from the sender, through the transmission devices of the media and thence to the receiver, it must be clear of noise or interference.

Precisely what relevance the mathematical theory has as a theory of meaning in mass communications still remains to be established. For the semanticist, however, the concern is primarily with the *meaning* of communications content. And for the sociologist and the social psychologist the process of communication, particularly in the mass media, is studied from the standpoint of influence on opinion and behavior. For, in the final analysis, all communication, whether primitive sign language or sophisticated mass media, embraces both meaning and behavior. The difficulty with the mathematical theory of communications is that it tends to denigrate legitimate semantic implications in favor of an approach that is concerned basically with "transmission" or pure technology. If communication is to be consummated successfully there must be some agreed logic of language, some basic consensus as to common and accepted meaning. And for meaning to have meaning, so to speak, there must be some agreed upon method of studying the relationship of signs to each other, to things in the external world and to other people involved in the communications chain. Communications must provide a shared experience by more than one individual in order to make sense out of what William James and Walter Lippmann have termed the booming, buzzing confusion of the world, out of the welter of opinion and fact, emotion and reason.

While only the two respective nervous systems of a given sender and receiver interact, mass communication involves a vast nexus of nervous systems, a kind of universal "extension," as Marshall McLuhan has phrased it, of each of our nervous systems. Paradoxically, McLuhan has argued that the growth of the mass media has been atavistic in the sense that television, for example, actually has tended to push man's horizons back to a type of communications environment which is basically tribal or semi-primitive. But the problem is not as naive as McLuhan would have it. Modern man simply finds it difficult to bring his sociology and psychology up to the level of the scientific achievements of the technological revolution. Technology is moving ahead so rapidly that it threatens constantly to leap far beyond man's ability to keep abreast of it. The demand for information is voracious and the techniques for information gathering are available, but the utilization and interpretation of data are still traditional from an epistemological point of view.

The fundamental process of human communication is deceptively simple. Basically the communications situation can be resolved into the scheme of who says what to whom about a given subject. And this semantic simplicity would pose no problems if all human communication were reduced to such comments as, "it will rain tomorrow" or even such denotative statements as "that is a car." But human communications deals not only with facts, but with ideas; not only with direction or information, but with emotion. And, as one goes higher in the levels of abstraction to such statements as "all college students are nonconformists," communication and meaning become a more complicated affair. It is precisely because communication in a mass society is complicated that it has generated varying theories as to its function in human affairs from the philosophers of logical syntax, the psychologists, the mathematicians, the sociologists, the anthropologists, and more recently, the psychiatrists with the evolving theory of "therapeutic communication."

A Functional Process

Communication has been defined in a variety of ways by students of mass media. C. I. Hovland calls it, "the process by which an individual —the communicator—transmits stimuli (usually verbal symbols) to modify the behavior of other individuals—communicatees." H. P. Fairchild, in the *Dictionary of Sociology*, defines communication as "the process of making common or exchanging subjective studies . . . usually by means of language, though visual representations, imitations and suggestions . . ." Warren Weaver terms it "all of the processes by which one mind can affect another."

It should be noted that each definition observes communication as a *process*, for it is precisely that—a dynamic and functional interaction between individuals and among groups which takes place in a social environment. For the interaction to occur certain essentials must be present. There must be the sender of the stimulus, or the communicator. There must be a receiver who may be a single person or a vast receiving audience. And there must be a message, or communication content. Some sociologists believe also, with E. L. Hartley, that a communications situation is not fully consummated without some specific effect resulting from the causal relationship that sets the communications process in motion.

This communicative process need not be verbal, although most communication, and particularly mass communication, occurs on the verbal level. But non-verbal communication such as writing, or even gesture without speech, can be equally effective. Indeed, great novels and fine poems provide a most stimulating and effective communications setting. And simple speech is often greatly enhanced in its effect by appropriate gesture, inflection or intonation, particularly in the theater, the motion picture or in the television close-up. Non-verbal communication involves signs which do not employ spoken language. Richard Wagner, in the operas of the Ring of the Nibelung, for example, uses periods of silence punctuated by gesture to convey meaning, although the orchestra does serve as an active participant in the Wagnerian music dramas. But the importance of non-verbal communication must not be overlooked. Japanese and Chinese drama employ dance, mime and gesture as powerful communicative forces. The motion picture, before sound, conveyed cognitive, emotive and directive meanings solely by silent action, gesture and facial expression. To view these motion pictures today in such a setting as the Museum of Modern Art, and then to compare them to the contemporary sound movies, is to realize how powerful non-verbal communications can be.

Whether communication is to be verbal or non-verbal—or a combination of both—depends upon many factors, but primarily upon the exigencies of the communications situation, as Hartley and Hartley point out. Each situation in which the individual finds himself elicits a particular form of communication, either verbal or non-verbal. Furthermore the communications setting determines who says what to whom and under what circumstances. Interpersonal communication may involve stimulus and response between two persons, among several people, or among large, heterogeneous groups which comprise the true mass communications audience for television or radio.

What occurs in each of these communications situations is a two-way street, a constantly flowing interaction between organism and environment. A simple stimulus may result in a series of chain reactions, the consequences of which may appear to be surprisingly out of proportion to the simplicity of the original communique. Because communication is so powerful and dynamic a force, those who use it—particularly in the area of mass media—quickly discover its potential. It is precisely because a medium like television is as powerful an entertainment and informational force that it has attracted the attention of politicians, and psychologists, educators, parents, and any number of varied special interest groups.

John Dewey's description of interaction between organism and environment may be projected to encompass what occurs in the area of both interpersonal and mass communication. Direct vis-a-vis interaction between one individual and another becomes a mass phenomenon when a vast multiplicity of people are involved in the communications process. An original communication stimulus in the form of a message from one sender may result in a simple, naive stimulus-response syndrome; or it may involve a long chain of responses in a heterogenous and undifferentiated audience of a mass medium. In either case, there is "feedback" of some kind and degree. The political debate on television, if it does not result in immediate reaction, is ultimately reflected, in terms of impact and effect, in how people will vote. Thus, whether between two persons, among a group, or in the macrocosm of the mass, the individual learns quickly that verbal communication is a powerful instrument for information and persuasion.

One of the delightful and enlightening aspects of early childhood psychology is the speed with which the child learns how powerful a tool language can be and how dramatic verbal stimuli can become. Words, accompanied by facial expression, gesture and intonation, are exceedingly effective in their ability to get things started and accomplished, in their tendency to elicit sympathy, empathy and responsiveness. Part of the whole painful and fascinating process of socialization and acculturation is the power of language to bring forth positive—and desired—responses. Symbols take on meaning, words stand for things and, ultimately, for concepts. The child becomes a part of the fabric of society by learning that communication is a two-way street, an interminable, but nevertheless necessary and efficacious, way of living successfully in one's environment. When this social structure breaks down, neurosis, or even psychosis, are among the lamentable possibilities that may ensue. But, in a "normal" situation, there are basic, if not entirely satisfactory, criteria, for determining the success of communication. The pragmatic viewpoint states, simply, that communication is successful if it elicits the reaction or response one hopes it will bring forth.

Non-verbal communication, of course, may also be successful, but its success is not so pragmatically immediate, although it may be more lasting and effective in the long run. This is clearly delineated in the effect great social, literary or scientific documents have had on those who do not hestitate to pronounce that a masterpiece may have changed their thinking and even the course of their lives. Whether verbal or non-verbal, however, communication is complete and successful only when the receiver indicates by response that he "understands" the message or when he responds to it, either overtly or implicitly. Communication is not only a biological or psychological process. It is a social process as well. Unless people communicated effectively, one with the other, society could not function successfully.

Since communication is a social process, it has to do not only with information, but with direction, persuasion and emotion, as well. Personal influence is closely involved in any communications situation and, indeed, some social scientists believe that political debate and propaganda to a mass audience may be considered to be successful only after personal influence—the exchange of verbal stimuli between individuals —has become operative. Cooperation and consensus in society stem from successful communication. Scientific research and development are not possible without effective communication. And the thrust of history, which becomes part of man's whole residue of knowledge, is possible only because sophisticated techniques of communication enable man to provide a storehouse of historical data.

Communication, then, is not only mechanical or technical, but a dynamic and functional process by which men interact with each other and pass on their successes—and their failures—from one decade to another, from one generation to another. As McLuhan has pointed out in another context all communication involves our nervous systems. Verbalization is, in itself, the ultimate expression of neurological activity involving the brain and central nervous system. The process of communication not only extends our nervous systems into the environment, but also sets up a mode of interaction between one nervous system and another. Each draws on the nervous system of the other in a series of stimuli which become responses and responses which become stimuli. In this process, communication is consummated successfully and patterns of culture are transmitted from individual to individual and from one generation to another. All of the media—books, newspapers, radio and television and magazines—play a part in this process. And, despite the disruptive qualities that occur when communication is unsuccessful—as in the breakdown of dialogue between East and West—communication provides the one best hope for human understanding and cooperation. Indeed, it may become the last best hope for the successful survival of man in the age of the missile and the hydrogen bomb. For communication is, at best, a healing or therapeutic process, because it can generate understanding and cooperation. It can make it possible for men to relate successfully to each other within a given culture or society.

Communication Is Constructive

What successful communication does for individuals is both intrinsically therapeutic and socially effective. It enables man to relate to others without neurotic anxiety or defensiveness. It tends to give a sense of form to man's environment and a sense of proximity to other social creatures. It allows for interaction and adaptation, for comprehension and exchange of point of view. Clearly, when any of man's adaptive tendencies breaks down, psychological problems result. This is why the psychotherapist works so persistently and arduously to bring his patient to that point of release of tension where verbalization becomes feasible and therapeutic. For language is the basic tool of communication, expanding and contracting, limiting or delimiting man's relationship to man and to his social environment. Communication is imperative to successful living in a civilized society. When communication breaks down there is always the possibility of human breakdown.

The concern of many thoughtful statesmen is not that war might happen because of an act of human deliberation, but because of some inexplicable breakdown in the technology of communication. Much of the revolt of the cities and the urban riots of the mid 1960's were a result of failure to communicate between black and white, between youth and older groups, between capital and labor, and between the underprivileged and the political authority. The disruption of activity on the Columbia University campus involved a total breakdown in channels of communication. The United Nations is an example, however tenuous, of world effort toward peace and understanding through communication. Language barriers, of course, set up considerable difficulty in successful international communication, because the process of a meaningful dialogue is made more difficult. Even when the language is indigenous, as in English, there are semantic roadblocks that make communication difficult between sections of the United States and even between the English speaking peoples. When, under any circumstances, communication breaks down, the results are moral and social turbulence. Motives are suspect, antagonisms flare and cooperation becomes impossible. The function of effective communication is to provide a way toward understanding and cooperation between individuals and among the diverse groups that comprise a society.

Despite the sophistication of modern technology, communication frequently leads to misunderstanding and semantic impasse. The barriers between the Soviet Union and the United States override the miracle of technology, the "hot line" and the availability of instantaneous international radio and telecommunications. And barriers persist precisely because they are both ideological and semantic in character. One of the very causes of lack of rapport and understanding among one group and another, or one nation and others, is the fact that each tends to attach different meanings to the use of language. Symbols have diverse meanings to different peoples, and the process of symbolization becomes further complicated by differences in language and idiom. The study of the process of communication seeks to clarify meanings, to find and consolidate areas of social rapport, rather than to accentuate differences and antagonisms.

Unfortunately, neither the science nor the art of communication has reached a juncture in development where scientific method is sufficiently successful to overcome these barriers to effective interaction. Groups differ from one another and, despite similarities, each has its own realms of discourse and its own value systems. Communication is successful when it brings about a consensus, or an accommodation, among these divergent groups. The ultimate success of inter-group and international communications will depend upon the success with which empirical or scientific study can be brought to bear on the whole process of verbalization. At the moment, only the physical scientists appear to speak the *same* language, while the social scientists still argue over meaning and implication.

For these reasons, among others, social scientists are devoting an ever increasing amount of attention to the communications process. Because communication conveys meanings, it is a complicated affair. Its appeal is informative and directive, as well as aesthetic and emotional. Those who offer simplistic panaceas for mass media, such as television, often fail to take into account the fact that communication is a multi-faceted phenomenon, involving numerous shades of meaning. Society contributes to the process of communication from many areas—technical, economic, administrative and artistic. A newspaper or a television program is the result of a multiplicity of efforts, involving creative talent, sales techniques, production facilities, advertising, promotion and electronics. And these represent only the "sending" side of the communications nexus, for communication is not complete without both a receiving audience and the transmission of content or message. In mass media, the audience is heterogeneous. Indeed, there is no single mass audience, but rather a multiplicity of audiences, or publics, which coalesce into the mass. The public for mass media, particularly in a democratic society, is not monolithic, but variegated and pluralistic.

The substance of communication is selective. The communicator, whether individual or mass, tends to select out content that will cohere with his system of values, for all communication is normative. The communicator operates from a sense of norms or values which are unique to him, and the receiver also filters the communication content through his own system of value judgments. In the area of mass media, the larger the audience, the greater the variety of social, ethnic, economic and political stratifications. Furthermore, each of the media, while directed toward a mass audience, tends to reach these audiences in different ways and under different sets of psychological and social circumstances. The movie audience differs from the television public. The radio public, while a mass audience, is composed of housewives, motorists, and other diverse segments of the same ultimate whole.

Mass communication, then is a multi-faceted phenomenon. In a functional sense, one speaks of mass communication in terms of media which are capable of reaching a vast number of people simultaneously. Such media include radio, television, newspapers and wire services, national magazines, motion pictures and, to some extent, books—particularly the paper-bound volumes. Even though a television program may be viewed as a private affair at home, the fact remains that what is being broadcast also reaches millions of persons in millions of other homes from coast-to-coast. And the distinguishing features of any mass medium, and particularly television, is that it not only reaches many millions simultaneously, but also that it carries an advertising message to these millions at a given "cost per thousand" viewers. Even beyond these characteristics, however, is the fact that mass media cost relatively little to the consumer, for the investment in a television set is comparatively slight in terms of the amortization one derives from years of use.

Mass media are not only effective in an economic sense. They are also *affective* in that they deal with material which is almost invariably emotional, and frequently aesthetic. The media appeal to the audience need for emotional gratification, and their success depends in good part upon the success with which this human need is met. A particularly successful motion picture or television program, in this affective sense, is one in which there is implicit rapport between the value judgments of the communicator and those of a majority of the audience. For in the last analysis, communication is a two-way street. The mass media influence the audience, but the audience also exerts considerable influence, both implicit and explicit, on the media. Communication is never free from value orientation. And, while it should strive for extensional orientation, all communication content reveals the influence of the communicator. Each newspaper, for example, has a character, a bias or point of view which is singularly its own. All purveyors of mass media are affected by value judgments which, in turn, have been formed by multiple environmental influences—the home, the school, the church and other social institutions. But the receiving audience also has a point of view which is occasionally expressed harshly and overtly, but is also present in many subtle ways—the selection of one movie over another, the tuning out of a given program, the cancellation of subscription to a particular magazine. The communicative arts have become an integral aspect of human experience. Aesthetically as well as economically and socially, communication is at the very core of contemporary mass culture.

BIBLIOGRAPHY

Bauer, Raymond A. and Alice Bauer. "America, Mass Society and Mass Media." *Journal of Social Issues*, Vol. XVI, No. 3, 1960.

Berelson, B. and M. Janowitz. *Reader in Public Opinion and Communication.* Glencoe, Illinois: Free Press, 1950.

Casty, Alan. *Mass Media and Mass Man*. New York: Holt, Rinehart, Winston, 1968.

de Vries, Leonard. *The Book of Telecommunication*. New York: The Macmillan Company, 1962.

Emery, Edwin, Philip H. Adult, and Warren K. Agee. *Introduction to Mass Communications*. New York: Dodd, Mead & Co., 1960.

Fabre, Maurice. *A History of Communications*. New York: Hawthorn Books, 1963.

Harlow, Alvin F. *Old Wires and New Waves: The History of the Telegraph, Telephone, and Wireless*. New York: D. Appleton Century Company, 1902.

Hartley, E. L. and Ruth E. Hartley. *Fundamentals of Social Psychology*. New York: Alfred A. Knopf, 1952.

Hobhen, Lancelot. *From Cave Painting to Comic Strip*. London: Max Parrish and Co., Ltd.

Hovland, C. I., Irving L. James and Harold A. Kelley. *Communication and Persuasion: Psychological Studies of Opinion Change*. New Haven: Yale University Press, 1953.

Jacobs, Norman, ed. *Culture for the Millions: Mass Media and Modern Society*. Princeton, New Jersey: W. Van Hostrant Co., Inc., 1959.

McLuhan, Marshall. *Understanding Media: The Extensions of Man*. New York: McGraw-Hill, 1964.

O'Hara, Robert C. *Media for the Millions*. New York: Random House, 1961.

Peterson, Theodore and Jan V. Jenson and William L. Rivers. *The Mass Media and Modern Society*. New York: Holt, Rinehart and Winston, Inc., 1966.

Reisman, David, et al. *The Lonely Crowd*. Garden City, New York: Doubleday and Co., Inc., 1953.

Rosenberg, Bernard and David Manning White. *Mass Culture*. Glencoe, Illinois: The Free Press, 1957.

Schramm, Wilbur, ed. *Mass Communications*. Urbana: University of Illinois Press, 1949.

Seldes, G. *The Great Audience*. New York: Viking Press, 1950.

Smith, Alfred G., ed. *Communication and Culture*. New York: Holt, Rinehart and Winston, 1966.

Steinberg, Charles, ed. *Mass Media and Communication*. New York: Hastings House, 1966.

Verne, Jules. *From the Earth to the Moon*. Translation, L. Mercier and E. E. King. New York: Scribner, Armitage and Co., 1874.

Weiner, Norbert. "Information, Language and Society." *Cybernetics: or Control of Communications in the Animal and Machine*. New York: John Wiley and Sons, Inc., 1948.

Wells, H. G. *The First Men in the Moon*. London: G. Newnes, Ltd., 1901.

White, David Manning and Richard Averson. *Sight, Sound and Society*. Boston: Beacon Press, 1968.

Wright, Charles. *Mass Communication: A Sociological Perspective*. New York: Random House, 1959.

Yu, Frederick T. C. *Behavioral Sciences and The Mass Media*. Russell Sage Foundation, 1968.

Symbols and Things

COMMUNICATION in any context, interpersonal or mass, is an integral part of the discipline of social psychology. The structure, the basic matrix of the human interaction which comprises a society, is essentially a juxtaposition of individual and group relationships. Communication in a functional sense involves inter-relationship, an application of John Dewey's concept of experience as interaction between organism and environment. As interpersonal communication relates two or more individuals in terms of interaction between sender and receiver, so mass communication requires a reciprocal relationship between medium and audience. In each area, the functional effectiveness of the message, or communique, depends upon certain relevant factors—cooperativeness instead of disruption and lack of cohesion (for communication functions at optimum to enhance social cohesion and cooperation) and the subsitution of accommodation or rapport for antagonism or resentment. In every case of successful communication one may expect interpersonal and group cohesion and understanding. Communication which fails almost always results from semantic impasses which involve confusion of symbols and the things they represent, or a confusion of various levels of abstraction.

One of the factors which contributes to lack of understanding between individuals and among groups is a confusion of meanings attached to the process of symbolization. For symbols, as the basic tools of communication, convey different meanings not only to different people, but also to nations which employ diverse languages. The discipline of communication, as a facet of social psychology, attempts to eliminate the differences and weld together the areas of agreement—to find a basis, in short, for cooperation. Communications study and research, as a behavioral science, attempts to treat available data empirically and to test tentative hypotheses in terms of their application to concrete human experience. How well equipped the social sciences are to test these hypotheses empirically is debatable when compared, for example, with the more accurate techniques of the physical sciences. But theories are being studied, developed and applied, particularly in the basic area of semantics, which attempt to confront communication in terms of the application of language to reality.

Man lives in an atmosphere where symbolization—the use of signs to represent things—is constant and unrelenting. Communication is a symbolic process which involves both verbal and non-verbal language. How this process of symbolization functions in a social situation comprises the science of semantics. In this sense, communication attempts to bring order out of an essential disorganization, to integrate social, political and cultural concepts and to pass on a historical and cultural tradition from generation to generation. But the conveying of a cultural tradition is an epistemological process which involves the application and acquisition of knowledge, and it is through communication that knowledge is acquired and transmitted. Communication is a behavioral process which involves both verbal and non-verbal language. And language, oral or written, is a means by which knowledge is acquired and transmitted. The process of communication makes history possible and meaningful.

Man's Symbolic Environment

Alfred Korzybski, whose contribution to the study of semantics was original and far-reaching, pointed out that "man's achievements rest upon the use of symbols." This process of symbolization, a linguistic structure in which words stand for things, is inherent in, and essential to, human communication. And it is the tendency to confuse words and things, or symbols and the things they stand for, which is at the root of much of our semantic difficulty—a difficulty which extends into politics and economics, into sensitive problems of race and religion, into every area where man interacts with man in his social environment. Symbolization, or representation, is neither optional nor fortuitious. It is this symbolic process, however artificial and contrived it may seem to be, which makes communication possible and pragmatic. The structuring of a symbol-system, relatively scaled in terms of degrees of importance, allows human communication to take place successfully.

Communication is symbolic. But the word "tree" is not the same as the flowering, green phenomenon one sees in reality. The word "dog" is not the same as one's own terrier, Spot. If the confusion were allowed to exist, how then define the Spanish term "perro" which *represents* the same thing, but is *not* the same word as "dog"? And, if the symbol "dog" stands for one's own terrier Spot, does it also stand—in every discrete particular—for one's neighbor's collie, Trigger? Obviously, it cannot, for Trigger is not Spot and Spot is not Trigger, and yet both are represented by the same word, "dog."

These linguistic dilemmas are relatively simple, even when one extends the process of symbolization to more abstract concepts such as the meaning of the American flag, the insignia of the doctor or the lucky rabbit's foot. Even beyond these are the rich symbolization of religious ritual, and the aesthetic symbols of art and music. A painting by the Flemish master, Van Eyck, is fully comprehended for its beauty and meaning only if one understands the symbols of fidelity which highlight the consecration of a marriage.

Beyond the symbolism of ritual, there are problems of greater complexity, particularly in the area of social psychology. Among the more confusing and perplexing of the many symbols impinging on contemporary man are those which deal with the explosive subject of racial equality. Prior to the Supreme Court decision on desegregation, the plight of the Southern black was clearly symbolized by the signs which separated "white" from "colored" in railroad stations and on public transportation. More recently, the civil rights marches in Washington and the South and the wearing of working man's denims by the Reverend Abernathy at the funeral of Robert Kennedy were symbolic gestures designed to arouse the conscience of society to the plight of the underprivileged.

Essential to effective and comprehensible communication, therefore, is the understanding of the process of symbolization which gives meaning to communication. Our use of language, in which the words used stand for things in the "real" world, is basically an externalized manifestation of a stimulus which occurs within the central nervous system. The whole process in which thought results in verbalization is a stimulus-response phenomenon. But, as Wendell Johnson pointed out, verbalization is not an end in itself. It is imperative that a distinction be made between language and reality, between "words and non-words" if we are to communicate effectively. Unless the relationship between words and the things they stand for is clearly understood and delimited, effective communication is thwarted. Confusion reigns when symbols are identified or "merged" with the things symbolized, when we mistakenly believe that the word "table" is the very same as the table which stands before us. Indeed, what we perceive of the world is never perfect and it is always limited by the imperfections of our perceptive mechanism, our sense organs. Man, despite the optimism of modern youth, never really "sees it as it is," but sees, at best, vicariously and with limitations. Our brain and nervous system allows us to see, move, feel, think, but never perfectly and frequently—as S. I. Hayakawa has stated, only with the aid of artificial devices, such as the microscope, to help sharpen our sensoria.

It is precisely because we are limited in our perception that we rely on our tendency to abstract and to indulge in generalizations. Based on our past exposure and experience, we come to identify objects in the world of things by names which stand for these things. In this process of abstracting, man distills out certain distinguishing and similar features in other dogs, cars or men; and goes on finally to attach the generic name or classification to the object perceived. What this process involves is literally the abstracting of similarities and the leaving out of differences, such as the different colors or sizes or shapes of cars, dogs or men. Korzybski urged that language and reality accommodate to each other when man adds index numbers to dogs, cars and man such as dog [1] (blue) dog [2] (brown) man [1] (short) man [2] (tall). For each dog, each man and each car, while the same, is also uniquely different from all other dogs, men and cars. How vital these distinctions are can readily be seen in such complex use of language as "Communist" or "Jew" or "Negro" where stereotyping minimizes effort but, at the same time, condemns all in one sweeping generalization.

The deceptively simple process of symbolization, a method of representation common to all men, is essential to the complex process of human communication. Language, in which words stand for things, is a verbal externalization of what is occurring in the central nervous system. For the syndrome of thinking, and verbalizing that which is thought, is fundamentally a process of stimulus and response. And what is uniquely important, indeed what is vital to effective and comprehensible communication, is the realization that there is no relationship between the symbol and the thing symbolized. "Tree" is not the tree one sees in the garden, but a verbal representation of it. A uniform does not make every policeman good, strong, dependable or brave. A black skin does not indicate one's employment as being a Pullman porter or cotton picker. Semantic confusion is the inevitable result of identifying symbols with things symbolized. Despite the temptation to identify them, they are not one and the same.

One of the most tantalizing temptations of the communicator—and therefore a cardinal temptation of all of us—is to depend upon the symbol and accept it for the thing, so that one tends to attach far greater significance to the symbol than the thing symbolized. The Sunday churchgoer is not necessarily a man of probity or piousness. Unfortunately one of the semantic difficulties with the mass media is that they simply inundate mass man with words and more words, symbols and more symbols. S. I. Hayakawa specifically cites the dangers of accepting maps for territories. It is possible, indeed it is beguiling, to draw elaborate maps only to discover that there is no corresponding territory in the world of things. It is as though man constructed a perfectly beautiful and geographically feasible map of a continent that simply did not exist.

Apart from its speculative or aesthetic quality, the map is utterly meaningless. Since we cannot fit any discoverable or tangible territory to the map, we run into practical difficulties. The "intentional world" of symbols is confused with the "extentional world" of things. As Walter Lippmann put it, the things in our heads may not be verified or exemplified in the extensional world, for there is a difference between our intentional world and the real or extensional world. Mass media, on occasion, have been accused of limning false maps in our heads which bear no relationship to territories in the extensional world.

Nevertheless, man relies on verbalization as a way to sane, and rational and comprehensible communication for, in the words of Aldous Huxley, "words have the power to mold men's thinking, to canalize their feeling, to direct their willing and acting." What we think, how we think and ultimately how we behave is determined in large measure by words. Man strives to solve problems, as the meeting between the United States and Soviet officials at Glassboro revealed, by communication. It is upon rational communication that man's survival may ultimately depend, for men who find ways to communicate effectively and intelligently tend to cooperate. Even when language fails or semantic roadblocks occur, man still has recourse to communication by other methods—by art, by graphics, by print. These non-verbal methods, too, can be instructive or directive or emotive.

One of the more powerful tools for the communication of knowledge is print. It was the momentous invention of print which brought about the beginning of the age of mass communication. For print enabled man to understand his institutions and to record and transmit his cultural heritage and traditions. Communication, whether oral or print, is the binding substance of a civilization. Man's capacity to learn, grow and survive depends largely upon his effective use of the techniques of communicating with other men. But it is these very techniques which give rise to linguistic and semantic dilemmas.

Meaning Is Functional

One of these central problems involves definition and meaning in the use of language. In the universe of languages, the essence of communication is meaning. But meaning, contrary to the capricious use man makes of it, depends not upon what the dictionary prescribes, but upon function. The use to which man puts words, and the tenacity with which he insists that their ultimate referants be extensional, is directly related to the success of his efforts to communicate effectively. The accepted word for certain four-legged creatures in English is "dog." The same four-legged creature is called "perro" in Spanish and "hund" in German. In a sense, then, the creature has no "real" name, for the terms we apply are simply symbols which stand for the four-legged creature we are discussing. But even to say that each of these words which stand for the thing—dog, perro, hund—refers to a four-legged creature is not enough, for four-legged creatures which are not dogs abound in the world of things. Furthermore, even if the word were extensionally defined by denoting or pointing out a particular dog, the problem would be only partially simplified, for while this dog can now be defined operationally, there are still many other defining factors left out—the age, sex, size, color, and breed. Nor does this dog stand for all dogs, for each dog is an entity and, as Korzybski has stated, our efforts to define should really take into account the fact that dog [1] is different from dog [2] and dog [2] is different from dog [3]. And so on.

Venturing into more abstract areas, it can readily be seen how misdirected is the kind of thinking that calls *all* college students activists, all Jews Communists, all blacks militants or all Scotsmen stingy. Dictionaries are frequently indispensible, provided they are used properly. They are both cnnfusing and meaningless when the reader accepts dictionary definitions as hard and fast, without seeking further to find referants in the world of things. For the best the dictionary can do for us is to define words by using more words. Even for so simple a term as "a domesticated carnivore, Canis Familiaries, bred in a great many varieties . . . any animal belonging to the same family, Canidae . . ." the dictionary goes on to list twenty-four variations, each more abstract and less denotative, until we come to the following: "put on the dog—U.S. slang. To assume an attitude of wealth or importance; put on airs."

Each of these definitions is utterly meaningless, unless a way can be found out of the forest of abstraction into an area of discourse where words can be described in terms of function. And one way to make meaning more meaningful is, wherever possible, not merely to describe by more words but to point out precisely what we mean by seeking a functional or operative illustration in the world of things.

Meaning, ultimately, depends upon the arbitrariness of a prior definition—although definitions are useful as a starting point. In terms of function, there is no "real" meaning to dog which may mean a pet in New York, a worker in Alaska or food in Vietnam. Meaning has no meaning except in terms of function or use. And only by working in an operational environment which does not confuse words and things can man work himself free from the tendency to confuse levels of abstraction. Meaning, in large measure, depends upon social use or function. Our ultimate test is pragmatic or empirical. As convenient as the dictionary may be, unsophisticated use of it simply confuses words and things and obscures meaning in a hail of words and more words. The dictionary speaks of things only by using words to describe them. When we come across a defining term which we do not understand as, for example, that a dog is a "carnivore," the best we can do with the dictionary is to look up carnivore and so on ad infinitum until we reach a point either of linguistic exhaustion or of extensional verification. To describe "wealth" as "affluence" or "affluence" as "wealth" is to obscure rather than to enlighten. Our best and last hope in the search for meaning is empirical.

Unfortunately, man is all too frequently beguiled by the sound of words and more words, and tends to slide into a semantic quicksand from which there is no extrication. Political demagogues tend to attract followers who succumb to the "tyranny of words." This emotive and directive use of language was the stock in trade of the German Minister of Propaganda, Goebbels, during World War II in which all who were with the Hitler movement where "true" Germans while all others were "non-Aryan" and "Communists." More recently, and in another context, the inability to get a meaningful dialogue started between student militants and the college administrations is fundamentally a semantic impasse, a confusion as to the meaning of such terms as "freedom" "inquiry" and "democracy." It is difficult, for example, to equate the phrase "Students for a Democratic Society" with many of the procedures indulged in by those involved in 1968 and 1969. The "rightness" or "wrongness" tends to become confused in a welter of words where such abstractions as "democracy," "communism" and "freedom" become fixed or frozen, and attempts at meaningful dialogue are frustrated. Even in an academically oriented environment levels of abstraction become confused. Polarization into black and white thinking results, so that the issue cannot yield to meaningful discussion.

Abstraction is a useful excuse in mathematics, formal logic and much of general philosophy, but at a more mundane level, where practical problems must be resolved, meaningful language which gets things done can only come about through function. "Black power" is a powerful emotional phrase and its implications are puissant and formidable, but its meaning can only be tested pragmatically. One might develop a fascinating exercise by citing any number of such concepts and testing them, where possible, operationally. Was World War I fought "to make the world safe for democracy?" Do we "have nothing to fear but fear itself?" Is "our country right or wrong" a morally justifiable idea?

Unfortunately, man's limitations are such that society will always, to some extent, be trapped in the quicksand of abstraction. Progress in effective communication is a slow and tortuous one in which awareness of semantic impasses is the first step toward finding the principle of reality. Some, such as the schizoid personalities, may never extract themselves from the linguistic morass, although psychiatrists such as Dr. Juergen Reusch believe that mental illness is directly related to one's inability to communicate meaningfully and rationally and that mental health can be achieved through "therapeutic communication." But semantic confusion is not confined to the schizophrenic. There are those who devote their lives to research and teaching such aesthetic disciplines as music and art without discussing, by concrete, operational example, particular compositions or paintings. Similarly, it is possible to construct an entire course in ethics without reference to the perplexing and agonizing moral dilemmas that confront individual men in a mass society. Through the less difficult device of rationalization, man learns to accept common stereotypes as a slothful way of minimizing effort. Thus, in this society, the struggle for school integration becomes a struggle between "blacks" versus "whites" where an infinite and complex variety of meanings are eliminated in order to reduce the problem to one of hard choice. In this process, connotation and denotation become confused, the intentional black teacher becomes identified with the extensional individual at a particular school and in a particular set of circumstances. This kind of confusion would be absurd if it were not tragically illustrated by the phenomenon of some Japanese generals in World War II who were reported to have told the Nazis that they regretted they had no Jews to persecute as an example of their fidelity to their military allies.

Stereotyping is not only semantically unjustifiable. It is socially and individually destructive. One has only to consider the far-reaching effects of an easy acceptance of such words as "wop," "nigger," "mick" or the kind of stereotyping that once prevailed in motion pictures and stage plays to realize how simple it is to confuse words and things. Words have a dynamite of their own in their potential for social and psychological destructiveness. An individual who has been in a plane accident will react with utter neurotic anxiety to the very use of the word "flying." One who has been bitten by a dog may become terror-stricken by the most casual use of the word, "dog." The power and the "tyranny of words" underscore the crucial importance of effective communication in the life of man. Communication becomes effective and meaningful when man becomes aware of the difference between words and things, between connotation and denotation, between intentional and extensional meanings, in short, as Hayakawa states it, between the maps in our head and the actual territory they purport to represent. For there is a difference, implicit and explicit, between the way man talks and writes and the way man behaves.

Language As Communication

Language, if it is to be meaningful, has a purpose. Originating as a cerebral stimulus, it provides a stimulus, in turn, which travels from communicator or sender to communicant or receiver. Man's use of language, consequently, varies in thrust. It can be, variously, cognitive or directive or emotive. Language can be used for sheer information, as in many newspaper stories, in expositional writing or in factual reporting. Despite the overlay of opinion and propaganda, a good deal of newspaper copy is purely reportorial, informative and factual in nature. Scientific information belongs in this category.

Language is also directive, as when it calls categorically for a specific mode of action. And it is emotive when it affects man's capacity to feel as well as to think. While man tends to point with pride to his ability to "stick to the facts," the truth is that there is little in our interpersonal dialogue or in our channels of communication that does not present fact with an overlay of judgment, direction or emotion. Feeling and emotion are expressed non-symbolically, but they are also expressed verbally. Freud's purpose, in psychoanalytic therapy, was to dredge repressed data from the subconscious by verbal free association until a kind of catharsis through communication was achieved. But equally for those who do not need therapeutic communication, language can be helpful in providing an outlet for directive and emotive impulses. This is essentially what is meant, in terms of modern communication, by the Aristotelian concept of tragedy as providing a catharsis for man's emotions of fear and pity—an indirect and less painful way of expressing anger or frustration.

Not all communication is meaningful, and it is dubious whether certain nonsense syllables we are prone to use can be communication at all. The chanting at political rallies, the whoops of attacking armies, the grunts and grimaces in front of the mirror and even the ridiculous attempts of adults to "speak" the language of small children are all non-symbolic uses of language in which the non-symbols stand for non-things. The language of diplomacy, in its studied effort to avoid embarrassment and yet to observe social amenities, too often tends to be suspect in terms of meaning.

Connotative use of language is both informative and emotional. Denotative, or extensional, use of language is always verifiable in the world of things. A young woman who describes her date of last night as a "wolf" is using the term connotatively. Its meaning is not factual, although it may be both informative and emotional to other girls. Connotative use of language also tends to be euphemistic as when physicians describe a patient as having "expired."

Directive language, used more frequently by parents, teachers, clergy and politicians, involves an attempt to make something happen, to provide a course of action. It implies a thrust, a step into the future. Some of the great essays and addresses, such as Lincoln's on the slavery issue, employed language in a directive, as well as an emotive, sense. Presidential candidates who promise specific courses of action, if elected, use language in this futuristic and directive sense. Advertising, promotion and public relations appeals are also fundamentally emotive and directive in nature, although the message frequently is ostensibly presented as fact or information. While the world does not end if the advertised deodorant does not accomplish what the reader is led to believe, directive and emotive use of language can lead to more serious and complex problems when applied to such areas as civil rights, religious prejudice or economic disparity. When meanings become confused and emotions run high, cooperation becomes impossible, truth and falsehood become confused and communication not only ceases to be efficacious, but becomes powerless. Directive language, regardless of context, carries with it the implicit ethical obligation to deliver what is promised. This obligation is one of the seminal responsibilities of the media of mass communications, and one which is critically involved in questions of taste, obligation and in the effects of mass media.

As Supreme Court Justice Hugo Black has stated, dissent on the campus—including the kind of dissent that involves directive language —is vital to a free functioning academic community. But there are conditions and limitations to dissent in any area which include the caveat that normal channels of communication be maintained. For when dissent is accompanied by physical activism, which precludes a comprehensible and rational dialogue, patterns of law and codes of ethics also tend to become disruptive. In situations where this occurs, an academic society cannot function intelligently because the channels of communication remain closed instead of open. It is ironic that, while communication and fruitful dialogue should provide an example for much of society, the environment of the contemporary university has not proved immune to semantic roadblocks and confusion of levels of abstraction.

It will be noted that the cries of the dissident have been emotive and directive, rather than cognitive, in connotation. Their appeal has not been to rationality, for to state that the present system is "undemocratic" and to fail to use democratically-arrived-at means of communication in order to bring about desired change, is to close all doors to reasonable dialogue. This kind of thinking narrows down to either/or alternatives, or choices between black and white. If one is not for us, it says, one is against us. The truth, however, is,—as in most controversial areas in social intercourse—neither black nor white, but gray. The solution lies not in polarization, but in a weighing of all possible alternatives and the reaching of tenable, pragmatically operative conclusions, forged in the crucible of the kind of fruitful dialogue which makes communication possible and successful.

Society lives by a nexus of agreements, arrived at through intelligent use of words. Some of these agreements are legal, some are moral, some are economic or political. But society, in any of its various manifestations, could not function in a viable way if agreements were not openly arrived at through man's use of his ability to communicate. It is true, of course, that the use of language does not provide the last word. The problem of police power or campus militants may not be resolved to everyone's complete and universal satisfaction by dialogue alone. But communication is ultimately a far more potent weapon than non-verbal force, because coercion simply prolongs an agonized situation and postpones the time when covenants of one kind or another must be forged by communicating. The distinction between words and things was illustrated when the police, popularly known as "New York's finest," were called in to restore order on the Columbia University campus. Certainly, to the students with whom they fought, the police were anathema rather than an exemplification of the "finest." Perhaps, as various reports subsequently revealed, this directive and emotive use of language might have been avoided to a great extent had some of the ground rules governing the crisis been established through an early effort at communication. Words are not always restorative or ameliorative. They should be given a fair trial, however, in the area of social relationships before resorting to other methods of nonrational behavior.

Some critics of the mass media have advanced the viewpoint that so-called "two-valued orientation," which tends to divide problems into the good guys versus the bad, or to see all problems in terms of only two alternatives, is a result of the very content of the media. According to this point of view, student activists and other social militants leave no room for rational communication, because they have absorbed the tendency toward either/or thinking through the example of the media of mass communication. But the media themselves operate in such fashion that they tend to reflect society. If Korzybski's concept of "two-valued orientation" is to be found in the media it is because this kind of unhealthy communications attitude is to be found in many segments of society. Political campaigns advanced the notion that those who were not for us were against us long before television came on the scene. The Soviet Union and Red China advance it currently in all areas of human discourse, particularly in literature and the arts. Indeed, the controlled press of the Communist state can function only in terms of a two-valued system, because it cannot suffer the empiricism of extensional verification.

A Pluralistic Society

If this kind of orientation is found in the Communist world, however, it is not too much to hope that it can be avoided in a free environment through the instrumentality of effective communication. In a democratic, pluralistic society—whether on the campus, in politics or in the arts—the objective should be a rationally defined one in which not one, but many, points of view are listened to intelligently. In this way, through rational discourse, the channels of communication are kept open. And, when these communicative channels are open, one encounters all of the advantages of an open society in which there are many alternatives, many criteria and many values. As a result there are a multiplicity of choices. The way to consensus and agreement is by communication in which alternate paths may be explored in a spirit of inquiry. In such a sane context, problems of integration versus segregation, of black power versus white backlash become amenable to an exchange of viewpoint through dialogue, rather than a choice of either one or the other. Dean Rusk made this clear in a televised hearing before a Senate Committee when he stated that certain questions could not be answered either be simple affirmation or simple negation, but called for additional discussion under circumstances which would permit a more flexible exchange of viewpoints.

Korzybski emphasized that two-valued thinking has academic merit in the thought that is applied to logic or mathematics. It plays no productive role, however, in a social context. Language which deals with problems of economics, politics, race, color and religion cannot be used effectively if it does not leave room for the kind of thinking which weighs a multiplicity of values, which is, in short, not monolithic, but pluralistic. Democratic ends cannot be achieved through either/or thinking, whether in a mass medium such as the newspaper, on the college campus or in the political arena. Our dialogue—the use of words as a means to an end— must be so oriented as to allow for the free expression of many alternatives. Our communication must use language in a way which allows, at some point along the line of argument, for extensional verification. This kind of operational definition of communication, as Anatole Rapoport has stated, enables us to "bring the thing defined or its effects within the range of one's experience." Weight or length have meaning only in terms of actual measurement of an object in the world of things. This is a functional or operational definition which makes communication effective and meaning meaningful. The foes of the New York City Board of Education may have had good reason to be critical, but they did not advance their goal of eliminating the Board by refusing to go beyond such statements as "we must get rid of the bureaucracy." Pressed for further extensional discussion, one vocal opponent stated that the "bureaucracy" (never defined) must go because "*all* members were psychotic."

This language, however effective in arousing emotional reaction, is meaningless unless it submits to empirical verification. It demonstrates still more ominously the danger of confusing symbols and things. The insistence that "bureaucracy" must be eliminated, without further effort to identify in terms of function and verification, is that Wendell Johnson called "deal level abstracting," a kind of Freudian fixation at one level which blocks any further growth toward mature thought. It is an example of what Walter Lippmann meant by our tendency to confuse the pictures in our heads with the varied confusion of the world outside.

The kind of verbalization that calls all teachers psychotic is, of course, neither logical nor cognitive. It is an example of the emotive use of language whose purpose is to eliminate all, instead of *some*, teachers who may, indeed, be psychotic. While this use of language can be emotionally effective as verbal charges, hurled in the context of a debate or public forum, it is also to be found in the print media. Newspaper editorials and even slanted news articles and columns of opinion are replete with emotive and directive thinking. And it is peculiarly relevant, and often effective, in drama, poetry, and literature where allegory, simile, metaphor, alliteration, and onomatopoeia abound. Indeed, it is because of the wide variations in idiom that barriers to effective communication exist between nations employing different languages. One of the challenging hurdles for the translator of foreign works of literature is to maintain the idiomatic flavor of the language and still make the translation palatable and effective in terms of communicative literature in the English language. How, for example, does the translator communicate the quintessence of such peculiarly American phrases as "to run out of gas," "run it up the flagpole," "milk it dry" or "gut feeling" in another language? It is precisely these, and more serious, semantic difficulties which thwart intelligent communication between nations in one corner of the world with those in another.

Of course, literature, like music or painting, need not be factual, for the great truths and insights gleaned from masterpieces can go far beyond the cognitive and still yield a kind of transcendental truth, an illumination which is more powerful and more moving than any factual account. Yet, there are times when a straight newspaper account or a television newscast of the facts can be more effective as communication than art. No novelist could improve, in terms of drama, on the stunning and graphic description on television (through the device of pure information) of the plain facts of the shooting of President Kennedy or the direct verbal account of the toll of a battle in Vietnam. Indeed, it is the very drama of this kind of factual reporting which also shows the significance of feeling and emotion as expressed in the novel or the stage play. Coleridge's "willing suspension of disbelief" expresses the precise effect which dramatic masterpieces may have on the reader or viewer. Coleridge's "suspension of disbelief," like the Aristotelian purgation of the emotions of fear and pity, provides not only a vicarious experience, but also a symbolic way of relieving neurotic tension through communication. Language becomes a psychological device through which tensions can be verbalized and communicated empathetically. The psychotherapists have shown that accumulated tensions trigger neurotic anxieties. One of the functions of verbalization, or of symbolic representation in terms of drama or the novel, is to drain off tensions. In this way the communication arts enable man, and society, to maintain equilibrium and balance. If art forms, as Marshall McLuhan believes, are extensions of our nervous systems, then literature, drama and poetry, in print or on radio and television, can serve as excellent modes of therapeutic communication. There are therapists, such as Dr. Juergen Reusch, who believe that *all* communication provides, at least to some degree, a relief of tension. And John Dewey saw in the communication arts a healing influence in the life of man, because they function to create order out of chaos and flux.

Value Judgments and Roadblocks

Unfortunately, communication is not always rational or ameliorative. Because of the tendency to confuse words and things, the communicative act often confuses, rather than clarifies, issues. Those whose business it is to bring about opinion or attitude change, as in the case of the public relations practitioner, quickly realize that there are enormous difficulties involved in the successful completion of such an effort. One of the difficulties of advertising and public relations as instruments of persuasion is that people who are exposed to the message, or communique, are not blank tablets. They come with a set of values, and they tend to accept that which coheres with their value system. Their behavior is institutionalized. In the shifting sands of international affairs, language difficulties accentuate the communications barriers to effective communication. From the work of Sigmund Freud and Harry Stack Sullivan one learns the difficulty of communication and interpersonal relations, not only in the abnormal personality, but in normal circumstances as well.

Communication is interpreted by the audience and its individual components basically in terms of one's value system, psychological set and social and educational orientation. The psychoanalysts believe that these factors are formed in infancy, in a non-verbal period, and are carried over to the time when verbal communication begins. Freud and his followers believed that verbalization through free association was a communicative process in which the individual externalized repressed material which was striving to be released from the primitive area of the id. Since these ideas inevitably find expression in overt behavior, specifically in anxiety neuroses, they are best resolved through free verbal expression as a therepeutic procedure. Even in the so-called normal individual, however, communication faces barriers, because ideas become fixed and intractable, attitudes become frozen and rigid and refuse to yield to change.

These impediments to clear communication are not difficult to explain. The individual, by virtue of past experiences, has developed his own frame of reference and set of values. Learning has taken place, and a set of values has taken hold as a result. What has been absorbed in this process of acquisition of knowledge tends not only to enlighten and orient, but also to predispose to certain responses when stimuli occur. Positive or known experiences tend to elicit positive responses, while unfamiliar stimuli may bring about negative responses. That which gratifies the ego is accepted. That which does not bring about ego gratification tends to be rejected.

Therefore, despite McLuhan's conviction that the medium is the message, the content of communication cannot be ignored. Precisely what is communicated, as well as the manner in which the message is conveyed, have an important bearing on its effect on the receiver. If positive response is to be hoped for, some empathy must take place from sender to receiver in order to help lower barriers to effective communication. Communication which is so couched and conveyed as to arouse resentment or antagonism is neither efficient nor successful. It fails to elicit positive affective attitudes.

Even under optimum conditions, where the most careful public relations is operative, the barriers to communication are not easy to hurdle. Beyond the semantic impasses, there are psychological barriers, erected as a result of many years of conditioning, and a stubborn tendency to accept one point of view and no other. These barriers made any communication with a good part of the South virtually impossible when the question of desegregation was raised. The more insulated the group, the more alien any new idea will appear to it. For individuals and groups, as well as nations, try desperately to preserve values and convictions which they have long maintained and hold precious. Social attitudes affect not only the sender and the receiver, but the nature of the message and the manner in which it is communicated. Change of any kind becomes a threat to established patterns, particularly when the individual is usually not consciously aware of the basis for his attitudes and beliefs.

It is the very difference in social groups, the stratification of areas of society, which make communication so difficult between child and parent, between campus rebel and the administration. Age, for example, is one parameter for evaluating the so-called "generation gap," for much of the failure to communicate stems from a struggle by one group to maintain status quo as against the desire of the other group for immediate and cataclysmic change. In a very literal sense, different groups fail to communicate because they do not, indeed, speak the same language. "Democracy" means one thing to the educational administrator and quite another to the students demanding administrative change. Words do not mean the same thing to all people, nor are ideas which involve change accepted without struggle. Because ideas do not cohere with past experience, ideas which are new are frequently rejected out of hand as either absurd or radical. And when impasses of this kind develop, communication simply becomes blocked and frustrated. What has been learned in the past becomes an important building block for future experience. Our social structure, to a great extent, tends to perpetuate barriers to communication which find their bases in age differences, sex differences, as well as in economic, political and religious differences. Man finds it most comforting, from an ego standpoint, to communicate effectively with those whose experiences are similar, and with whom he can most readily relate or identify.

The mass media, despite the conviction held by some that the media are restrictive and perpetuate cultural lag, can accomplish a great deal in the eradication of at least some of the barriers to communication. The stereotype of racial and ethnic types no longer appears in motion pictures. The Children's Film Festival series on the Columbia Broadcasting System network, for example, emphasized man's common interests and humanity by revealing how communication can lower barriers to understanding. Communication as a result of the broadening scope of the mass media, is beginning to flow more freely among various groups, although the barriers to truly effective communication are not easily destroyed. The tendency to identify with one's own social stratum to the exclusion of other groups is undergoing a slow but effective erosion as a result of many of the liberating influences of motion pictures and television. Mass media are beginning to show, at least, how the other half lives.

Yet, despite the scope of media as purveyors of information, values do not change without a struggle. A good part of the battle over school desegregation and decentralization stems from lack of communication and understanding between the student, with one set of values, and the teacher with another set of different values; between the value-system of the blacks and the value-system of the whites. In the television program "Hunger In America," the rigidity with which individuals can cling to outmoded thinking was revealed in the comment by a state official that the fathers of impoverished children simply ought to go to work, because the state had no obligation to feed these hungry youngsters. The advocates of black teachers for black students believe firmly that white teachers cannot understand the Negro child and, therefore, cannot communicate effectively with him simply *because* the child is black and the teacher is white.

There are, nevertheless, conditions under which effective communication can be facilitated. Among these are the mass media—the newspaper, radio, television, motion picture, magazine and book. But social change still lags behind these miracles in technology. It is possible to convey pictures and messages instantaneously by satellite transmission and to talk to the Russians almost immediately by phone, but when concepts are not commonly agreed upon, barriers remain and fruitful discussion remains frustrated. The technical apparatus for affirmative communication remains to be matched by the social apparatus. Through such media as telecommunications, for example, opportunity is provided for a broad exchange of experience, for an eradication of stereotypes and for a common approach not only to the problems, but also to the potential of mankind. The past decade is proof of the fact that institutions are amenable to change. Problems in communications are not insurmountable if they are approached extensionally or functionally. Rigidity and conformity yield slowly to a system of communication which abandons either/or thinking and recognizes that there are many values and many choices available.

Man's communications behavior, to be successful, must be inquiring or empirical, instead of obdurate. Meaning is not something rigid or fixed by a prior definition, but is a result of function. Language has meaning in its appropriate context, and symbols are not identical with the things symbolized. The communicator must be careful to distinguish between cognitive, emotive and directive statements. Stereotyped thinking may minimize effort, but it is lazy and dangerous to conclude that all politicians are crooks, because one politician has absconded with public funds, or that all doctors are immoral because one doctor has been apprehended for selling narcotics. Communication is not an isolated or purely academic exercise. It is a dynamic, social phenomenon, an instrument both informative and aesthetic, and a powerful agency of social control, as well as a means of social progress and change.

BIBLIOGRAPHY

Burke, Kenneth. *Language in Thought and Action*. New York: Harcourt, Brace and Co., 1949.

Chase, Stuart. *Tyranny of Words*. New York: Harcourt, Brace and Co., 1938.

Gordon, George N. *The Languages of Communications*. New York: Hastings House, 1969.

Hayakawa, S. I. *Language in Thought and Action*. New York: Harcourt, Brace and Co., 1949.

Hayakawa, S. I. *Our Language and Our World*. New York: Harper and Brothers, 1958.

Jesperson, Otto. *Growth and Structure of the English Language*. Garden City, New York: Doubleday and Company, 1955.

Johnson, Wendell. *People in Quandaries*. New York: Harper and Brothers, 1946.

Korzybski, Alfred. *Science and Sanity*. Lancaster, Pennsylvania: The International Non-Aristotelian Library Publishing Company, 1933.

Laird, Charlton. *The Miracle of Language.* Greenwich, Connecticut: Fawcett Publications, Inc., 1953.

Morris, Charles. *Signs, Language and Behavior.* New York: George Braziller, Inc. 1955.

Ogden, C. K. and I. A. Richards. *The Meaning of Meaning.* New York: Harcourt, Brace and Company, Inc., 1953.

Pei, Mario. *One Language for the World.* Devin-Adair, 1969.

Rapoport, Anatole. *Science and the Goals of Man: A Study in Semantic Orientation.* New York: Harper, 1950.

Sapir, Edward. *Language: An Introduction to the Study of Speech.* New York: Harcourt, Brace and World, 1949.

Whatmough, Joshua. *Language, A Modern Synthesis.* New York: The New American Library, 1956.

3

Who Says What to Whom?

THE STUDY OF mass communication, because it is so closely identified with the techniques of sociology and psychology, is subsumed under the heading of the behavioral sciences. Because accurate methods of measurement and of empirical research are difficult to apply to the mass media, the communicative arts do not lend themselves readily to the quantitative methods of the physical sciences. The exponents of the mathematical theory of communications and the logical positivist school of philosophy have attempted to apply quantitative techniques to mass communication, but the volatile and unpredictable nature of communication does not make it amenable to strict scientific method. Communication is a dynamic process, best tested in the crucible of experience, with all of the volatility which that experience involves in terms of human behavior.

The classic description of the communications process has been in terms of one variation or another of a series of basic and sequential events: who says what to whom, through what channel, under what circumstances and with what effect?

On the face of it, however, this description is deceptively simplistic. While it seeks to encompass the whole process of communication from exciting cause to ultimate effect, it leaves out a number of extraneous factors which color the whole process. In particular, it leaves out the likelihood that communication does not involve one single response to stimulus, but that a multiplicity of responses will occur. Further, determination of effect is difficult, particularly in mass media such as television which reach large, heterogeneous audiences, because there is virtually no means of measuring accurately overt or direct response. Factitious events, such as competing stimuli and other environmental

34

factors, also intervene in a communications situation. The stimulus-response phenomenon is not direct and uncluttered and there is, further, an inevitable time lapse between the originating stimulus and the eventual response.

Audiences tend to respond to the stimuli of mass communication against a background of many adventitious factors. The personality or "set" of the communicator is one such factor. The kind of message or content is another. The technical proficiency (the presence or absence of noise) of the channel is still another. Finally, the receptivity of the receiver is vitally involved in order to complete the chain of communication. Every recipient strives to avoid unpleasant stimuli, and leans toward accepting the pleasant and responding in terms of his own system of values. Indeed, situational factors are themselves of significance, such as the relative calm and comfort of the environment at the time the communication takes place. Significant, too, are such questions as to whom the stimulus is directed, i.e. one or more persons, as well as the social and economic status of the group within the larger framework of a given population. In a so-called "other-directed" society, response to mass media is influenced strongly by status and approbation within the peer group. Those who pride themselves as being members of the intelligentsia, for example, are reluctant to admit that they watch, and frequently enjoy, certain popular television programs. This makes a study of the effects of mass media all the more difficult. As the late Dr. Gary Steiner found in a study of viewing habits, there is a wide disparity between what people say they watch and what they actually view on the television receiver.

The Nexus of Communication

Communication, in its most direct manifestation, involves a message —or content—which travels in a stimulus-response pattern from sender to receiver, or from communicator to communicatee. In a communication-oriented society, however, the pattern does not end there if, indeed, it can be said to end anywhere. Although it may be punctuated by periods of silence, the chain of human communication is continuous. Where circumscribed communication between individuals and among groups ends, mass communication takes over in a relentless flow of stimuli. When man finds surcease from the welter of verbal stimuli which virtually inundate his environment, he is still subjected, to some degree, to non-verbal stimuli. Even if man were to want to, it would be difficult to find the environmental solitude which was available to him a century ago. Mass media have the capability of interrupting man's sleep in order to bring news of some cataclysmic event in a shrinking world.

Those who send the messages—the purveyors of communication content—through the mass media magnify and extend the microcosm of interpersonal communication to meet the peculiar needs of the macrocosm of mass communication. What is communicated, if it is more than nonsense syllables or a non-meaningful nod or "good morning," is communicated with intent. The intention is to inform, to direct, to affect the listener and, implicitly or explicitly, to elicit response which may, in turn, serve as a stimulus for further communication. Even communication which is purely emotional—a cry of rage, accompanied by a blow or a grimace—has intent and effect. In the world of advertising, communication is both explicit and implicit. It combines an overt "pitch" to buy a brand along with the illustration of "beautiful people" who use the brand to their romantic satisfaction. But in advertising and public relations, in particular, the intent of the sender is only effective when the audience responds to the stimuli by the overt act of buying the product.

The advertiser, however, because his message is carefully tested through the elaborate machinery of research, communicates with an acute awareness of precisely the response the message is supposed to elicit. But most communication is not scientifically planned and executed. As Eugene L. and Ruth E. Hartley point out, communication content, like Freud's analysis of dream content, has both a manifest and a latent aspect. There is that part of our verbal communication with which we are familiar and aware, the manifest or obvious content. And there are implications, or latent content, of which we have no awareness. Man is not always consciously aware of the intent that lies below the surface of his verbalizing. Nor is meaning always what it purports to be. Manner, tone, expression and inflection color verbalization and can add, or detract, from the impact. A motion picture producer who would brook no dissent from his subordinates showed them a new film and asked an assistant what he thought of it. The subordinate cannily replied, "That was *some* picture." Obviously the meaning of this statement, when analyzed, is ambivalent. It may have indicated great praise, or it may have been a way of begging the question through the ambiguity of language.

It appears, then, that "pure" communication is not sufficient to convey adequately various shades of meaning. What is of paramount significance in the comment cited above is not only what was said, but how it was said and under what circumstances. The prior experience and the opinions formed of each other by both communicator and communicatee color the meaning and thrust of what was said about the film. What the sender intended his comment to mean may be interpreted by his superior in one way, but by his colleagues—who may be privy to his "real" thoughts about the film—in another. In this situation, the sender obviously had a fairly specific idea of the personality of the receiver, and his comment was couched with the intent of provoking a hoped-for response. This ability to find out something of the nature of the audience is helpful in bringing about desired effect. Political speeches are invariably drawn up with some prior knowledge of the audience in mind. The chairmen of the board of large corporations usually meet with stockholders after a thorough briefing about what questions might be expected, along with appropriate answers to them. By gearing the message to the needs, wants and aspirations of the audience, the communicator can establish the kind of communications atmosphere which helps to bring about the reaction and response he is seeking.

At the same time, the audience—individual or mass—also comes to the communications situation with some preconceived ideas and some value judgments of its own. Directly or indirectly it does not confront the sender as a *tabula rasa* on which the message is indelibly inscribed. The audience has a mind of its own, and it comes rather heavily laden with opinions, stereotypes and judgments which are not easily discarded. Whether one likes it or not—and frequently in spite of earnest disavowal of prejudice and genuine efforts to come unencumbered—the receiving audience still reacts to the sender in terms of mental short-hand. And the sender bears the same semantic burdens as the receiver. These stereotyped responses are unfortunate, because they tend to color one's thinking and response in a communications situation.

In an ideal circumstance, all agents involved in the communications process would be aware of the dangers of stereotyping, of the tendency to confuse symbols and things and of the ambiguity inherent in high level abstracting. Ideally, they would have sufficient insight into the psychology of each other to understand how attitudes and opinions have been formed. They would have gathered sufficient knowledge of each other to make some tentative estimate of what response might conceivably be forthcoming to stimuli. For communication is only successful if attention is paid to it. Communication, whatever the context, is unsuccessful if it does not elicit response; and affirmative response is more likely to be forthcoming if the sender has some prior working knowledge of the attitudes of the audience, so that what is conveyed will draw a response. In the mass media, and particularly in the advertising area, the more that is known of the audience attitudes, the greater the chance that the response will be positive. The audience for books, movies or television tend to distill out of the content of the medium those values which cohere with their own system of values, so that what is seen and heard becomes absorbed in, and congruent with, their own interests. Emotional, as well as cognitive factors have a great deal to do with coloring the interests and attitudes of the audience, which is why propaganda is almost always heavily laden with affective appeal. Not only what is communicated, but the manner in which it is communicated, has a relevance to its ultimate effect.

Various parameters have been established to determine communications feedback, but there is still much to be learned of the cause and effect relationship of communications stimuli. How an individual or an audience will respond to communication depends upon a number of variables. Value judgments are of great significance. What the receiver has learned from previous perceptive experiences, as well as his background and orientation, color his response to stimuli. The stimulus which is familiar in context tends to bring about a more favorable response than stimuli which are unfamiliar or alien. For the audience reacts quite naturally on the basis of previous experience and prior conditioning. An individual who appears dressed as a policeman, but is in reality a thief, will tend to be accepted as a policeman until the shock of recognition reorients the conventional audience response. Indeed, communication which has no relevance at all to the audience's previous experience may fail to elicit any response whatever. The meaning of verbal symbols, despite our goal of a universal language, varies with, and is to a large measure determined by, the experience of the audience. And this experiential background is difficult to change in both normal and abnormal individuals. Each political administration tends to move slowly in suggesting change, because it wants to prepare the public for such changes. No better example illustrates resistance to change and the frustration of communications barriers than the effort to change black attitudes toward whites and vice versa.

The greatest challenge to communications is that of hurdling barriers—psychological and sociological—so that different individuals of different cultures and experiences can find a way to common understanding. Despite the ubiquitousness of telephone, radio and other instruments of instantaneous communication, the basic problems to comprehension and rapport remain cultural ones. Differences in connotation and meaning which are prevalent in the United States are magnified when one tries to find a common semantic atmosphere for communication with countries of totally different language and culture. Even the experts find difficulties in choosing the "right" words, for what is condoned in one society may be considered immoral or outrageous in another. The tendency to simplify *all* experience in terms of one's own experience leads to an equally strong tendency to reject that which does not cohere with one's own values. But what is particularly difficult for successful communications is that one may reject the value system of another without realizing that, while different, it may still have a rationale and validity of its own.

Communication As Interaction

For these reasons alone, it is important not only that the communicator have some knowledge of the background of the audience, but also that he learn to couch the message so that it will have some relevance to the value system of that audience. Communication, if it is to be successful, must be purposeful. The sender ought to determine with some degree of candor and precision what it is that he wants to say, how he wants to say it and what effect he hopes it will elicit. A considerable part of journalism functions to persuade, as well as to inform. The greatest novelists were more than story-tellers, for they had a point of view. The polemicist and the philosopher hope to gain converts. Communication is not only informative, but emotive and directive as well.

Those on the receiving end of communications stimuli, however, react with their own selectivity. Built-in prejudices heighten emotional response, trigger directive activity and color even pure information with an affective overlay. The audience's reaction to communication tends to be subjective to a very great degree, for the viewer, reader or listener—consciously or otherwise—distills out of the communique precisely that content which will mesh most comfortably with his own interests, aptitudes and his educational, social and religious background. The audience's point of view is partly a response to the communication content and partly a mixture of its own variety of goals, drives and anxieties. It is precisely because of these factors which affect the nexus of a communication situation that the message should be as free as possible from both ambiguity and noise. Clear transmission under optimum conditions must be matched by a genuine effort to be meaningful, to speak in terms which the audience can understand.

Both sender and receiver, in other words, influence and interact upon each other. Neither one conveys or accepts a message which is free from the attitudes of the other. A good part of the functions of opinion research aims to provide those who communicate with relevant information about the habits of the audience, so that the message can be fashioned and directed with those habits in mind. Communication content is influenced by the style of the communicator, and it is interpreted in terms of the attitudes of the audience. While the fact that the receiving audience interprets content in terms of its own social attitudes is profoundly true, it does not eliminate bias and stereotyping. Thus, messages concerning civil rights were transmitted against a background of stereotyping which marks all Blacks as lazy. The crisis in the Middle East is colored by attitudes toward the Jews and Arabs.

These attitudes toward communication content may defy the laws of logic and reason, but they are nevertheless very real in terms of our emotional response to words and things. In international communications the philosophy of one's country right or wrong may be patriotically justified, but it does not always cohere with the facts in a particular situation. The semantic failure is a lack of realization that admission of errors does not in any logical way diminish one's patriotism and, indeed, may enhance it. The British and American plays of the 1930's made much of the opprobrium attached to the word "foreigner." The term itself was enough to bring about the conventional stereotyped response from audiences already conditioned to equate "foreigner" with a person whose moral and political habits were less than palatable.

Because of the extraneous factors which color communications, it becomes particularly hazardous and difficult to arrive at any precise evaluation of the effect of mass media. Neither the sender nor the receiver can escape from the restricting influence of attitudes and conditioning. Only by overcoming our own learned reactions can we accept content without bias of one kind or another. But this is patently impossible even in the best of all possible communications worlds. To an extent, we engage in solipsism. How each individual viewer or reader reacts to a situation depends upon each respondent's individual perception. As much depends on what he rejects as upon what is accepted. The audience not only brings attitudes formed from past experience, but also a particular frame of mind at the time the communication is being transmitted. Communication frequently "means" precisely what we want it to mean. The ear has a habit of shutting out what it does not want to hear, as the eye tends to pass over what it does not want to see. Pure communication is next to impossible to achieve.

In directively motivated communication, such as prevails in public relations, errors of commission or omission are not fortuitous. Slanting of content is a frequently encountered transgression. The easy bandying of famous names in order to make the audience identify with them, or to give the impression of endorsement, is a common device. The careful selecting out of pertinent data to alter the meaning of content is frequently done to buttress an argument which would otherwise be specious. Name calling, directly or indirectly, has strong emotional connotations. The manner in which words are chosen or omitted from content tells a great deal about the communicator and his objectives.

The catalysts which convey the message between sender and audience are media of communication. What is conveyed from communicator to audience is content. The message is the stimulus which functions to elicit a response, either overt or implicit. As both sender and audience act in terms of previous training and experience, so communication content itself is also not pure message. What is conveyed is influenced by both intrinsic and factitious factors. The mathematical theorists believe, for example, that noise alters content. Furthermore, pure content is altered by its very transmission from sender to audience. The immaculate idea that began in the nervous system undergoes inevitable change as it is externalized, conveyed and received by the audience. There is no communications situation which is not affected by the personality of the sender, the attitude of the receiver and the nature of the message. Because man is the target of an infinite variety of communications stimuli, the best he can do is to make an effort to reduce complicated statements to the most simple common denominator in the world of things.

The basic factor in the human communications chain is content which may be verbal or non-verbal. Human interaction makes communication possible and this interaction involves a message of one kind or another. Since communication is symbolic, it can only function effectively when the sender chooses appropriate symbols which will convey meaning to the receiver within a specific frame of reference or realm of discourse. Because symbols are used differently and have different meanings in diverse circumstances, it is important not only to choose symbols carefully, but also to avoid confusing symbols and the things they represent. Man cannot eliminate facial expression, attitude and other emotive factors which color communication, but he can strive for agreed-upon ground rules as to the relationship between words and things, between the connotative and the denotative worlds.

Words stand for things, experience and feeling. Words are particularly effective when both communicator and audience are on the same verbal wave-length which, unfortunately, is often not the case. Words mean different things to different people, and communication content is modified in order to cohere with one's experience. Words color, and are colored by, emotional and other factors alien to their "pure" meaning and to the intent of the communicator. The tendency to confuse the word with the thing it stands for—although it is critical to agree that they are *not* the same—is at the root of most of our semantic confusion. Children in the South learned their attitudes toward blacks long before they saw their first Negro. This identification of word and thing is also at the base of the difficulties between the so-called "free" and "non-free" worlds. In the negotiations with Hanoi, the Americans did not understand the Asian concept of "face" and the North Vietnamese had no philosophic or linguistic parallel for the American concept of democracy.

Verbalization

If these difficulties were restricted simply to verbal communication or to oral dialogue, they would not be impossible to hurdle. The settlers of the American colonies were able to communicate eloquently with the Indians by means of gesture and sign language. But communication, particularly in the diplomatic area, is written and, therefore, formal and stylized. Words and more words complicate grammar, and syntactical complications ensue. This toughness of language, oral as well as written, is illustrated in the difficulty which even skilled writers and speakers encounter in translating the neurological phenomenon of thought into intelligently expressed and comprehended symbols. This is why so many writers and debaters speak of the pain and frustration of verbalizing thought. They know what they want to say, but have difficulty in externalizing thought and making it overt and intelligible. Actions, in some situations, do indeed speak louder than words. Since words are not things, they can do not more than symbolize or represent. They are transformed in the act of externalizing and are distilled again through the crucible of the medium and the personality of the receiver. One of the problems of psychotherapy is getting the subject to verbalize emotion.

Perhaps the purest communication is the stream of consciousness style of writers such as James Joyce, for this purports to express directly and without inhibition the basic thoughts that stir in the subject's mind. But stream of consciousness verbalization does not have meaning in the sense of any pragmatic relationship between sender and receiver. Its meanings are literary and arcane, and subject to the putative opinions of the literary scholar. In more mundane communication, words serve as a conveyer of meaning between communicator and audience. Most verbalization operates to get something done, either immediately or at some future time. Words, in a sense, both substitute for and express what we think. Since mind reading is best left to those gifted with extra sensory perception, the most practical tools man has to express his thoughts, hopes and aspirations are words. Yet, despite the fact that, in a communications-oriented society, man is inundated with words, language suffers limitations. Thoughts are not easy to express and one frequently hears the plaintive comment that there are simply not enough proper words available to say precisely what one wants to say.

The problem is complicated particularly because words simply refuse to be the same as things. "Cat" is a word, but the cat one sees on the window sill is not the same as the word. It is the thing the word stands for. This distinction is relatively easy to explain, albeit difficult to accept, for man confuses words and things during every day of his communicative life. But the matter becomes quite complicated when language becomes connotative. This language makes it difficult to find a counterpart in the world of things. How, for example, denote "democracy" or "generation gap" except either by using more and more words or defining in terms of function? That which can be described and illustrated is denotative, or what Korzybski calls extensional. But concepts, inferences and expressions of emotion are intensional or connotative. They cannot be explained by any physically defined object in the external world, but only by using additional words. A cat can be denotative. But to call one a demogogue is a more complex affair. There is no demonstrable thing called "demogogue" which can illustrate what the word stands for. Only words and more words can be used by way of explication. Even "cat" becomes complicated when couched in such a context as calling someone "a cool cat" or a "hep-cat." The meaning here is connotative and illustrative of the emotional overtones in language. Demonstrably, to be described as "dog tired" is meaningless, except that we have agreed to attach a certain emotive meaning to the phrase.

In short, the world of things differs from the world of words. Which is the "real" world is both a moot and largely unanswerable question. The world, through our use of language, is an elaborate system of symbols which stand for things. And we put language to use either to inform, to direct or to convey or elicit emotion. Frequently a combination of the cognitive, directive and emotive is involved. The trained and perceptive audience will be able to differentiate between the cognitive and emotive uses of language—a decided boon to those who would reveal the activities of the propagandist.

For any communication to be complete there must be at least two persons involved—a sender and a receiver. In mass media the receiving audience is both vast and heterogeneous. But, in either case, communication is neither complete nor successful unless there is an implicit and mutual agreement as to the ground rules. There must be, in other words, some community of interest between sender and receiver, a sense of shared experience. A good deal of communicating which seems to make sense, simply fails the test of verification in the world of things. Most political addresses, for example, suffer considerably when subjected to the process of moving down the ladder of abstraction. A great deal of discussion of the "law" during the widespread campus unrest of 1969, for example, demonstrated graphically the difference between law as a moral and humane concept against the presence of police moving in on faculty and administration buildings to evict students by physical means. A fruitful dialogue can occur only when those involved agree that what they are talking about must be brought out of the clouds of abstraction and down into a universe where discourse is intelligent and some ultimate consensus is possible. Since student activists used "academic freedom" in a totally different frame of reference from the administration's use of the same phrase, successful communication became impossible, because neither could agree upon a mutually acceptable basis for discourse. Efforts at discussion were either turned aside or turned into a debate. Since debate simply accentuates polarization, no common ground could be established unless questions of "rightness" or "wrongness" were eliminated in favor of an attitude of mutual trust and exploration. One of the reasons for man's failure to resolve so many problems in an urban society is that the problems are dealt with by means of verbal abstractions, instead of by seeking concrete referants. As long as polarization exists between the "rebels" versus the "establishment," the semantic barriers tend to harden until all communication becomes blocked. This kind of frustration is what leads to physical force, instead of an accommodation through dialogue.

Words are not only not the same as things. They have different meanings when used in various contexts. A "fair" lady is not the same as a "fair" mark. Words differ in terms of the situation in which they are used, and the word is unique in its application to that situation. Words are rarely absolute and almost always relative to the particular circumstances and context of their use. An "activist" has one connotation when it describes a surgeon who believes in getting a new operating room established, but it means something different in describing an individual who incites others to riot and civil disobedience. Meaning derives in large measure from context.

The Medium as Message

A unique theory about meaning and communication content has been advanced by Marshall McLuhan. The theory states, quite simply, that the medium itself is the message. Because it challenges most of the conventional wisdom which has prevailed in communications study, because it would eliminate the triad of communicator-message-communicatee, the theory invites examination. McLuhan advances the theory that to understand media, certain basic assumptions must be accepted, chief among which is the categorical statement that "the medium is the message." Media are extensions of man's nervous system, and by media is meant not only the conventional channels such as radio and television and the newspaper, but a host of other modalities such as the wheel, clothing, the motor car, the bicycle and weaponry. Indeed, the invention of print was not truly a step forward for modern man, for it brought him out of the cohesiveness of a tribal society into a period of social fragmentation. Man may ultimately be saved by electric technology through which society will achieve a new, creative global consciousness.

Media, like radio and television and the press, are either "hot" or "cool," meaning that they call for high participation or low participation. And the most satisfactory contribution which the new electric technology, which is pure information, can make to modern society is to provide a means for man to regress into the more coherent society of the tribal era in history. As for the impact of mass media, apparently they do not produce effect in the sense that most behavioral scientists understand this concept. Since the medium is the message, as an operational or practical fact, content—what is communicated—is consigned to limbo. The medium itself provides the message in terms of its sheer technology. Print, as a medium, is fragmented and anachronistic. The phonetic alphabet was a disastrous invention of man, but there is hope that electric technology will return modern man to the sophisticated innocence of tribalism. Through a kind of Hegelian thesis and antithesis, man will achieve a "synesthesia" of all of his senses. The thesis states that tribal society was integrated, functional and individualistic. The antithesis of this is the emergence of print which de-tribalized man and fragmented society. Finally, in the Hegelian synthesis, the new electronic technology will return man to the naive wonders of a tribal era. Human society can anticipate a brave new world in which our nervous systems will become extended so completely into the electronic technology that, ultimately, man will simply transfer his consciousness to the computer.

McLuhan's theory of the media generates some perplexing problems for the conventional wisdom. The classic concepts of communication do not apply. Since content is consigned to limbo in favor of the medium as message, it makes little difference whether television carries Shakespeare or situation comedy, whether programs are deemed benign or violent.

And, since the medium, rather than content, comprises the message, problems of effect and feedback are equally insignificant. By a "technological extension of consciousness" man would have no moral values with which to concern himself, for he would develop a "servo-mechanism" toward a computerized society. Man is then confronted with what Rene Dubos called "undisciplined technology." The new, non-print world can do without literature or the press, for man "does not need words any more than the digital computer needs numbers." Literature and language—the basic stuff of art and of communication—will be transcended by a "general cosmic consciousness."

Paradoxically, however, McLuhan has expressed the conviction that a medium like television demands a "creative participant response." But this response must be to the medium itself and not to what it conveys, for man needs no longer concern himself with the creative or moral implications of mass media or with value judgments about them. Unfortunately, this separation of form from content is artificial, for in the communicative arts, form and substance are inseparable. Furthermore, a philosophy which resigns itself and consigns man to become a "servo-mechanism" of electric technology is spurious and self-defeating, for it truly ignores the social and ethical implications of mass communication. The effect of mass media is irrelevant if the medium, rather than communication content, is the message. It is not only the media which have revolutionized the way in which media are used. Who says what to whom under what circumstances and with what effect cannot be delegated to the computer alone to determine. The alternatives and the value judgments inhere in man.

Few will dispute the contention that electric technology has had a far-reaching impact on modern society. But what is disputable is McLuhan's apparent conclusion that the use of mass media—the "how" of mass communications—is neither good nor evil, neither moral nor immoral, for it has no relevance to content. Media are not extraneous factors. They *are* ourselves. Man's sole identification with communication is as a servo-mechanism in a computerized technology. This is not, at best, a happy thought. At worst it relieves the communicators, particularly the mass media, of any genuine responsibility for what is communicated and precludes any serious effort to analyze the impact and effect of mass media in a democratic society.

McLuhan's theory, however provocative, is more significant for what it omits than for what it includes. The medium is not the message, although there is little doubt that the mass media, by the very act of transmission, do have considerable effect on the message. Nor has man quite become an appendage of the computer. There are audiences for mass media, and they are clearly discernible in the way they shape up and in their behavior. Man lives in a constant flow of communications stimuli, for the mass media impinge on every aspect of his existence. And man can employ media to a degree never thought possible when the newspaper was hawked by itinerant newsboys. The politician no longer needs to stump the country, addressing relatively small crowds from the platform of the railroad train. A candidate, in the television broadcast, can reach a potential of many million viewers simultaneously. The contemporary newspapers, operating with the advantages of wire copy and automated production techniques, reach about sixty million readers daily. Since the advent of the paperback book, many millions who seldom purchased hard bound volumes have become book readers. The motion picture rebounded briefly from its lean days following the introduction of television and reached a very sizable audience.

Media and Audiences

Despite the fact that these are mass media, they vary to some extent in their audiences. Magazines and newspapers, in particular, have large blocks of special interest readers. Motion picture audiences are more selective than they were before the advent of television. Book-oriented audiences are not necessarily television audiences, while readers of magazines like The Atlantic and Harper's probably do not watch television as avidly as non-readers of these publications. Even in a mass mass medium like television, the audience is not homogeneous and tends, to some extent, to select what it views. Selectivity is also evidenced by the newspaper reader. Some readers buy newspapers for sports, funnies, and ads, while others turn primarily to the news columns and to editorials. Radio audiences listen primarily for news, sports and music because of the circumstances of television and because radio listening has become identified primarily with automobile driving. In an age where mass media such as television are criticized for lack of cultural diversity there is, paradoxically, a greater audience for books and fine music than ever before.

Generally, the behavior of mass media audiences reveals considerable cross fertilization. The audience for one medium tends to seek exposure to other media. As Lazarfeld and Kendall have shown, those who were radio fans tended to be movie fans also. According to the Magazine Advertising Bureau, readers of one magazine are inclined to read several magazines. And while research shows that audiences place greater credibility in television news broadcasts, there is still a great demand for the newspaper as a source of information.

Television is, of course, the medium which reaches the greatest cross-section of the public. The medium is so geared that its thrust is to reach the largest possible viewing audience. Books and magazines, on the other hand, tend to attract those with fairly comfortable incomes. From a demographic standpoint, the contemporary film has become unusually attractive to the college-age public. Television, depending on the kind of program it presents, appears to attract viewers in three basic age groups: those between childhood and eighteen, between eighteen and forty nine, and forty nine and over.

Despite the fact that mass media have been scored for pandering to a least common denominator of taste, the public must be selective if only because it is literally inundated with communications stimuli. Most television viewers have a choice of three VHF channels from which to select a commercial program. Motion picture audiences, at least part of the time, have several options open to them. The newspaper reader need not read everything in print, despite the fact that a good many cities publish only one daily paper. The book audiences are clearly selective readers. And the audience for any one of the media will select in terms of his own value-system, educational background and economic and social status. Wilbur Schramm has delineated a basic principle of selection. It is, simply, the path of least effort or least resistance. Because the media are readily available, the public selects them in terms of its own respective social and cultural backgrounds.

The public responds to mass media not only because they are ubiquitous. People read books and newspapers, attend movies and watch television for a variety of valid reasons beyond sheer availability. People read newspapers for information, but also for entertainment. Human interest, a sense of security, grist for the conversation mill, keeping up with the peer group and even a genuine desire for knowledge are motivating factors in the use of mass media. Magazines, for example, offer many values to women readers—social, educational, economic and personal. Despite the increasing volume of research material, however, there is still much to be discovered about why people use mass media, why one medium is preferred to another. There are perplexing questions relating to the effect of mass communication, for this area, as well as the question of choice of media, involves a need for still further research into the basic role that media play in the lives of those who are exposed to them, the needs they satisfy (or fail to satisfy) and the way in which media affect and reflect value judgments.

BIBLIOGRAPHY

Berlo, David. *The Process of Communication.* New York: Holt, Rinehart and Winston, 1960.

Cherry, Colin. *On Human Communications.* New York: John Wiley and Sons, Inc., 1961.

Crowley, T. H., G. G. Harris, S. E. Miller, J. R. Pierce and J. P. Runyan. *Modern Communications.* New York: Columbia University Press, 1962.

De Fleur, Melvin. *Theories of Mass Communication.* New York: David McKay and Co., 1966.

Dewey, John. *Art as Experience*. New York: Minton, Balch and Company, 1934.

Dubos, Rene. *The Dream of Reason*. New York: Columbia University Press, 1961.

——. *So Human an Animal*. New York: Scribner, 1968.

Freud, Sigmund. *The Basic Writings of Sigmund Freud*. New York: The Modern Library, 1938.

——. *Introductory Lectures in Psychoanalysis*. Authorized English translation, Joan Riviere. London: Allen and Unwin, 1952.

Galbraith, John K. *The Affluent Society*. New York: Houghton Mifflin, 1958.

Hartley, E. L. and Ruth E. Hartley. *Fundamentals of Social Psychology*. New York: Alfred A. Knopf, 1952.

Johnson, Wendell. *People in Quandaries*. New York: John Wiley and Sons, Inc., 1948.

Katz, Elihu: "The Two Step Flow of Communication: An Up-to-Date Report on an Hypothesis," *Public Opinion Quarterly* (Spring, 1957), pp. 21, 61–78.

Lazarsfeld, Paul F. and Patricia L. Kendell. *Radio Listening in America*. New York: Prentice-Hall, 1948.

McLuhan, Marshall. *Understanding Media*. New York: McGraw-Hill Book Co., 1964.

Peterson, Theodore, Jay W. Jensen and William Rivers. *The Mass Media and Modern Society*. New York: Holt, Rinehart and Winston, 1965.

Pierce, J. R. *Symbols, Signals and Noise*. New York: Harper and Row, 1961.

Rapoport, Anatol. *Fights, Games and Debates*. Ann Arbor: The University of Michigan Press, 1960.

Ruesch, Jurgen. *Disturbed Communication*. New York: Norton, 1957.

Reusch, Jurgen and Gregory Batesm. *Communication, the Sound Matrix of Psychiatry*. New York: W. W. Norton and Co., 1951.

Reusch, Jurgen and Weldon Kees. *Nonverbal Communication*. Berkeley, California: University of California Press, 1956.

Schramm, Wilbur. *Responsibility in Mass Communication*. Harper and Brothers, 1957.

Shannon, Claude E. and Warren Waver. *The Mathematical Theory of Communications*. Urbana, Illinois: University of Illinois Press, 1949.

Smith, Alfred G. *Communication and Culture*. Holt, Rinehart and Winston, 1966.

Steiner, Gary. "The People Look at Television in *A Study of Audience Attitudes*. New York: Alfred A. Knopf, 1963.

Sullivan, Harry Stack. *Interpersonal Theory of Psychiatry*. ed. Helen Swick Perry and Mary Ladd Gavel. New York: Norton, 1953.

Weiner, Norbert. *Cybernetics*. New York: John Wiley and Sons, Inc., 1948.

Wiebe, G. D. "Mass Communications," *in* E. L. Hartley and Ruth E. Hartley, eds. *Fundamentals of Social Psychology*, pp. 159–195. New York: Knopf, 1952.

Wright, Charles R. *Mass Communication: A Sociological Perspective*. New York: Random House, 1959.

4

The Phenomenon of Print:
The Book

No HISTORICAL SURVEY of the development of the book as the chief beneficiary of the invention of printing could dramatize the impact of this
cultural milestone more vividly than a simple recital of the growth of
book publishing in the United States where thousands of hard cover,
and millions of paperbound books, are published each year. In one year,
1967, American publishers brought out more than 50,000 volumes.

Prior to the development of printing by movable type, books were so
few in number as to reach only that circumscribed audience which could
read—essentially the clergy and the paltry number of political and
intellectual elite. Medieval manuscripts, however magnificent, were
painstakingly wrought by hand by the monks, working diligently and
silently in the *scriptoria* of monasteries. The invention of printing revolutionized the entire fabric of civilization, ultimately making literacy and
education available to the masses and opening the way to the resultant
development of mass media. The book was the first, and it is still the most
culturally significant dividend of print.

The amazing growth of book publishing continues each year, despite the gloom of pessimists who assert that the popular communicative
arts have stifled the desire to read. The printing and publishing of books
witnessed an increase in 1968 of more than five per cent over 1967.
Among these some 2,800 works of fiction (1,822 new books and 989 new
editions); 17,000 non-fiction (11,048 new books and 6,077 new editions);
2,000 textbooks (1,630 new books and 574 new editions); were published. In addition, 7,000 paperbacks were published (4,056 new and
2,675 new editions). This is a far cry from the limited number of medieval
manuscripts extant before the invention of printing.

It is significant that the three great revolutions in the history of modern civilization were technological and that each affected communications. The first was the invention of printing by means of movable type which made both literacy and universal education possible, and paved the way for a community of world scholarship based on scientific research. The second was the Industrial Revolution of the Nineteenth Century which brought about a total upheaval in man's way of life, resulting not only in momentous changes in transportation and communication, but also in its economic and social implications for man in the new, urban society. And the third was the communications revolution of this century, exemplified by techniques of electronic technology which not only made the world smaller in terms of man's ability to speak to man, but also posed the tenacious problem of a poverty of international understanding amidst a plethora of new electric gadgets which provide the hardware, but not the content, for the transmission of information and ideas.

It was print, however, which produced the intellectual base for future developments in the history of human communication. For without print, man would still be struggling to convey knowledge by means of techniques so circumscribed that relatively few could be reached by them even in the course of a lifetime. Without print, universal education would be a virtual impossibility and mass media would have been an infinitely less useful technology. There is an interconnection, or interaction, among the media which has its origin inevitably in the invention of printing. From print, from the early books, man drew inspiration for later developments in the communicative arts.

Man's First Efforts to Communicate

Books, however, did not originate full-blown. Since printing with movable type is based on the alphabet, one must turn to the origins of communication, to the first efforts man made to reach other men by the use of symbols. It is almost certain that man first communicated with his fellow men not by verbalization or oral language, but by the emission of some kind of primitive sound or grunt accompanied by—and unintelligible without—gestures or sign language. This primitive method was obviously not satisfactory for acculturation to take place, and man necessarily turned to other symbolic ways of expressing thought and intent. The earliest examples of this method which scholars have discovered are the cave drawings of the Paleolithic Age. Largely drawings of animals, the signs, or pictographs, were obviously a means of communication. There are, in fact, remote corners of the world where this primitive method of communication is practiced today, although the spread of transportation and communication are eventually erasing these contemporary remnants of the Stone Age. In any event, these early drawings are considered by many scholars a naive form of communication, although the pictographic techniques themselves did not develop into writing. Just how the phenomenon of writing occurred is not known, but it is clear that, over a period of time, man learned to identify signs or symbols with objects in the external world. Eventually, too, man learned to connect symbols with abstract ideas and, ultimately, to convey his thoughts not only orally, but in writing. An ancient civilization such as China still clings to ideograms to represent thought, although this complicated mode of expression is slowly being modified as China undergoes cultural, economic and political change.

The one momentous step that made modern Western language—oral and written—possible was the gradual development of phonetics, a process which encompassed several centuries and which was one of the seminal cultural achievements in the history of man. Phonetic writing meant the use of symbols to represent things. Its development was slow because, among other reasons, those who enjoyed special privileges saw to it that phonetics were very much circumscribed for use only by the economic and religious elite. Entrenched interest and cultural lag were as indigenous to the ancient civilizations as they are to the modern world, but inevitably phonetic writing became popular. Symbols began to represent sounds which, in turn, were employed to denote specific objects in the world of things.

The early Egyptian civilization used both ideograms and phonetics as devices of communication. Although the Egyptians gradually developed a phonetic system, it was a most abstruse and complicated one, employing hundreds of symbols. But other nations of the ancient world were also at work. In Babylonia and Mesopotamia methods of phonetic writing were being devised to replace the ideograph. From its original use on caves and stone, the pictographic style developed into the phonetic. Other modes of communication besides stone were employed, including tree bark, animal skin and, in Egypt, where no hard stone material was available, men wrote on tablets made of clay. This style was known as the cuneiform, because the writing was wedged onto the clay tablet by a stylus. Official documents, such as the laws, were painted in this manner. At the same time, the Egyptians were beginning to use sheets of papyrus on which they wrote with a brush-type of pen, using a combination of red and black ink so that the scribe literally painted the words on the papyrus. Called "rubrics," because of the red color used, the style was originated by the Egyptians and later adopted by the Greeks and Romans.

This discovery of the use of papyrus marked a great step forward in the development of writing as a means of communication. The papyrus plant supplied the basic raw material which was so constructed as to absorb the black and red painting, applied by brushes made from a kind of reed. The sheets were appended to each other in the form of a foot long scroll, or roll. Unfortunately, the material was delicate and rain tended to wash away the colors. That papyrus was preserved at all owed largely to the dry, desert-type climate of the country. Used for many centuries in the ancient world, papyrus was eventually replaced by parchment which came into general use about 500 A.D. Parchment was derived from the skin of sheep and is used today basically for diplomas ("sheepskins") and occasional official documents. It absorbs writing from a broad point pen and gives a unique appearance, quite different from the painted-on style used on papyrus.

The Discovery of Paper

It was the development of a paper substance which was both practical and inexpensive which, as much as the printing press, made possible the development of popular education and the proliferation of learning in the Western world. At first vellum was used, but the need for a cheaper and more feasible substance led to the development of paper as the staple used to feed the new and hungry printing presses. Paper came into use by the Western nations from the East where the Chinese first introduced it in the First Century A.D. While Chinese ideographic writing had been accomplished on bamboo or silk, neither proved efficacious, and paper was invented by one Ts'ar Lun. From China, the use of paper moved to the Middle East and thence to the European nations of Italy, Spain and Germany. It was not used in England until the Sixteenth Century and did not appear in America until the end of the Seventeenth Century. Curiously, the use of paper served a religious missionary purpose, for the Chinese used it as an expedient method of disseminating the idea of Buddhism to the peoples of Asia. By the Tenth Century, paper had replaced papyrus in Egypt where, as a result of the dryness of the climate, it could be preserved easily. Much of the knowledge which modern scholarship has yielded about ancient civilizations owes to the remarkably good condition in which early documents have been preserved. It is a curious paradox that the Western world did not employ paper for several centuries after its development by the Chinese. Literacy was at a low estate, parchment was the writing method of choice and books were neither plentiful nor in demand.

Ultimately, however, it was the remarkable juxtaposition of printing and paper which made possible the enormous explosion of knowledge which followed the introduction of printing during the periods of the Renaissance and the Reformation in Europe. First made by hand, paper eventually was mass-produced by machines, first in France and subsequently in England. Today, a wide variety of paper stock is available to printers, ranging from stock which is very cheap to extremely expensive in quality. A glance at a number of magazines, newspapers and hardbound and paperback books indicates the broad spectrum of quality in paper available to the modern printer. There are published each year a number of beautiful limited editions of books designed to serve as permanent library items and printed on fine linen stock. On the other hand, newspapers tend to yellow and decay relatively quickly as opposed to the rag stock in use during the colonial period. As a result, a newspaper such as *The New York Times* prints a rag edition of each issue in order to assure the preservation of "all the news that's fit to print" for future generations.

The Alphabet

But paper and print could only have been invented as the result of the prior development of the phonetic alphabet, which was based primarily on verbal language, and which was employed in the earliest examples of written communication. Scholars such as Douglas C. McMurtrie, have gathered together what knowledge we have of the development of the alphabet from the sparse information which is available. Thus, it is pieced-together evidence at best and largely speculative. The term itself, alphabet, derives from the first two letters—alpha and beta—of the ancient Greek alphabet which, in turn, may have derived from ancient Semitic sources. It is known that some form of alphabet existed among the Phoenicians who may have been responsible for the acquisition of a phonetic alphabet by the Greeks. Here, again, the evidence is apocryphal. The alphabet may have originated in Egypt, Crete or Babylonia, but the evidence in each case has not been established. Meanwhile, students of linguistics continue to search for origins through the discovery of tablets or stones with symbols carved on them. The Semites or the Egyptians may have derived the idea of writing from each other, but there is evidence to establish that early writing did occur in the Sinai Peninsula. This early style may also have influenced the development of the Phoenician alphabet, passed on to the Greeks until, ultimately, the phonetic alphabet became identified with the modern English system of writing. From a strictly logical standpoint, the twenty-six letters of the alphabet are paradoxically illogical. There appears to be no rhyme or reason that certain sounds, representing verbal or written language, should arbitrarily call for specific letters while other sounds, almost identical in nature, demand the use of totally different letters.

Historical evidence reveals, in fact, that some early civilizations used relatively few phonetic symbols while others employed literally hundreds of symbols. The Semites appear to have used few symbols, as evidenced by the Moabite Stone which was discovered in the Nineteenth Century. The Stone, which records an ancient battle, is now on display at the Louvre, in Paris. The Phoenicians, according to scholarly evidence on tombs and sarcophagi, had a rather well-developed system of writing. It is probable that, at about the Eighth Century, B.C., the Greeks derived their alphabet from the Phoenicians, for it is known that both nations exchanged goods through commerce. Since the Phoenicians first colonized the Aegean, the alphabet probably was adopted from the Phoenicians by the Greeks. An inventive people, the Greeks not only adopted the alphabet but added two innovations which are commonplace in the Western world today. One was the method of writing from the left side of the page. The other was the use of alphabet letters to represent the vowels a, e, i, o, u. This introduction of vowels was a major contribution of the Greeks to the modern language alphabet.

The Semitic style of writing, still used by the contemporary Hebrew and Arabic worlds, runs from right to left on the page and has a complicated system of syntax and grammar, quite different from either English or the Romance languages. Evidence from ancient stones, coins and tombs indicates that the Semites at one time used the Phoenician alphabet, before developing a style of their own which has endured into the contemporary world.

The Western world turned to the Greek phonetic alphabet, and the first nation to use it was probably Italy, although there is no evidence extant to show how the alphabet reached the Mediterranean area. It may conceivably have come by way of the Etruscans, a people who developed an alphabet at an early date. The Romans absorbed a considerable culture from the Etruscans, including the Etruscan method of writing, and from the Romans evolved the alphabet currently in use by the English speaking peoples. Manuscripts of poetry by the Romans reveal the use of large block-type capital letters, ultimately giving way to a smaller type lettering which was written on vellum. Unfortunately, and largely because of the constant ferment of civilization as a result of invasion and conquest, the writing of books was confined almost exclusively to the manuscripts produced in the monasteries and cloisters. Despite invasions by the Germanic tribes, however, the great Roman contributions to law remained and a semblance of culture survived through the church. In Ireland, the smaller "uncial" type of writing developed by the Romans was adopted through missionaries, such as Saint Patrick. And in the monasteries of Ireland were produced some of the most beautiful of illustrated manuscripts, including the world-famous Book of Kells. The missionaries carried their script from Ireland to England where, having found a civilization decimated by invasion, they brought writing and culture. Fortunately, despite the barbarian invasions, there were voices of enlightenment such as Charlemagne who, as historians point out, provide an enormous incentive to scholars and to the development and preservation of a cultural tradition.

Each passing century produced changing styles of script. The large block capitals of the Romans changed to a smaller "uncial" style and thence to a smaller or "miniscule" type of writing. Ultimately there evolved the modern lower and upper case alphabet which, since the development of printing and the publication of books in quantity, become fairly constant both in printing and in handwriting. Prior to the invention of printing, however, books were handwritten or handlettered. The first efforts to put together a manuscript in book form occurred at about the Fourth Century A.D. In this process, several sheets were bound together by rolling parchment in leaves which were then juxtaposed one to the other and fastened together. These so-called "coden" manuscripts were handwritten. After the barbarian invasions, the making of books was restricted to the monasteries where the monks, working in scriptoria, laboriously produced the illuminated manuscripts which exemplify so beautifully culture of the medieval period. This era produced some of the most magnificent books in the history of mankind, both in design and illumination. Indeed, it was the copying of priceless volumes, including both the works of ancient Greece as well as the Bible, which made these priceless treasures available to modern civilization.

The Invention of Printing

The book, as we know it today, could not have become the indispensable communicative art which it is were it not for the invention of printing, perhaps the most notable creation ever devised by man. Certainly the invention of printing by means of movable type changed the face of civilization in a way accomplished by few other developments, and many scholars consider the advent of print the most important cultural explosion in world history. Without print, the Industrial Revolution of the Nineteenth Century and the electronic revolution of the present would never have occurred. The development of printing by means of movable type brought in its wake a great surge of cultural activity that ultimately brought man from illiteracy and ignorance into literacy and enlightenment. Popular democracy could only have come about as a result of the effect of print, for it was from the impact of print that the book, the magazine and the newspaper developed and ultimately, the phenomenon of journalism on radio and television.

Although the invention of this revolutionary process is generally ascribed to John, or Johannes, Gutenberg, there is no categorical proof that Gutenberg actually invented the printing press. Gutenberg, born in Mainz, is known to have moved to Strasbourg in the middle of the Fifteenth Century where, with two associates, he began experimenting with a device which was to become a printing press. The positive evidence available, however, does suggest that Gutenberg probably was the first to use movable type. Scholars have determined that a fragment of an early poem entitled "World Judgment" may have been the earliest example of printing with movable type. And scholarly evidence points further to the fact that the individual who most probably was engaged in early experiments in printing was Gutenberg. The "World Judgment" poem appears to have been printed a few years before the production of the famous Gutenberg Bible which is considered historically the first official book produced by print in Europe.

McMurtrie does not believe that the forty-two line Gutenberg Bible was actually printed by Gutenberg. Although Gutenberg was undoubtedly involved in its production, it was probably completed by his two associates, Fust and Schoeffer. In fact, although the forty-two line Bible is famous as the first official book printed in Europe, there are a few copies available of a thirty-six line Bible which was produced exclusively by Gutenberg. It was Gutenberg, therefore, with Fust and Schoeffer who generated the revolutionary development of print, the result of which began with the first production of printed books in Mainz. Some scholars believe that there were others who experimented with print at about the same time, but history indicates that Johannes Gutenberg, in the Fifth Century, was the first to print with movable type—a development that made possible an extraordinary communications revolution which began when books could be produced for the masses.

Because of the military and political upheavals which shook Europe in the Fifteenth Century, many of the German printers migrated to other countries. In this way, the art of printing developed in France, Spain and Italy. Various German printers left Mainz, for example, to work briefly in a monastery before moving on to Rome. Others introduced printing by means of movable type to Switzerland and France where, for example, Lyon became an important publishing center. Some worked to produce a series of volumes for use by scholars at the Sorbonne. Venice, in particular, as a commercial center, boasted a flourishing printing and book publishing industry. Such craftsmen as Nicolas Jensen, a Frenchman, and the famous Aldus Manutius brought out books of brilliant type design and went far beyond the primitive typographical efforts of Gutenberg. Manutius, in particular, combined fine typography with an excellent selection of books, including editions of the works of Aristotle. Thus, did the book publishing industry contribute to the remarkable revival of classical learning which characterized the Renaissance.

Evidence reveals that the first volume in the English language, brought out by William Caxton, was not printed in England but in Belgium. Caxton, a name not unfamiliar to students of English literature, went from London to Belgium and eventually came to the service of the Duchess of Burgundy. At that time, and under the encouragement of the Duchess, he translated into English a volume entitled *Recuyell of the Hystroyes of Troye*. Caxton then undertook to publish copies of the translation and, as a result, he became the first to publish in the English language. Returning to England in 1476, Caxton set up his own print shop where he brought out, among other books, an historic and famous landmark in English printing, the Caxton edition of Chaucer's *Canter-*

bury Tales. Caxton's contribution, when compared to the typography that was being accomplished on the continent, was not aesthetic but historical in significance. His books were not fine printing, but he did publish some of the major literary works of the period, such as the Chaucer edition. This is his claim to fame in the history of both literature and book-making in England.

Throughout Europe, however, the intellectual quickening engendered by the Renaissance, along with the fact that printing was available and books could now be produced, resulted in an outpouring of volumes, particularly of the Bible. The publication of books became an integral part of the excitement of the revival of learning in an age of discovery and of intrepid exploration. Printing helped bring about the transition from the philosophy of the medieval era into the new and exciting cultural perspectives of the Renaissance. Printing flourished, particularly on the continent where some of the most beautiful of books, such as the *Book of the Hours,* were produced. These volumes were for the most part superb examples of fine typography, as were the many notable reproductions of the classics of Greece and Rome which were printed at that time.

The works of certain bookmakers stand out as landmarks at a period when the whole spectrum of the arts was flourishing. Christopher Plantin on the continent and John Baskerville in England are notable examples, although removed from each other both in location and in time of production. Plantin was French, but worked in Antwerp to escape religious persecution. He started a publishing business in the Sixteenth Century, bringing out editions of the classics and engaging in printing books as well as in publishing them. Because a prayer book which he published did not adhere to the religious and political convictions of the authorities, Pantin went to Paris where he published many magnificent examples of fine printing. His plant became the greatest and most productive in all of Europe, publishing among many other volumes the famous Polyglot Bible which read simultaneously in Greek and Latin as well as in Chaldean and Hebrew. It ran to eight volumes when completed, and its ornamental title page announced that it was a publication of the sacred Bible in Hebraice, Chaldean, Graece and Latine. Plantin was one of the great contributors to the development of the printed book.

In England, the great name in printing was John Baskerville who worked in the Eighteenth Century. Beginning as a clergyman and teacher, Baskerville eventually turned to printing as a hobby. Since he was amply provided for and needed no sponsor, Baskerville was able to experiment painstakingly at perfecting the art of printing fine books on fine paper. He succeeded in developing a new kind of paper and a printing process never before used either on the continent or in England, finally bringing out an edition of the works of the Latin poet, Virgil. Successful with this effort, he then turned to an edition of Milton's

Paradise Lost which was, again, beautiful in terms of lettering, color and print. Baskerville's work is not flamboyant, for his objective was clarity and beauty of line. He paid great attention to layout and spacing, and the type face he invented became famous and is used widely today.

Baskerville's work produced what was probably the finest and clearest bookmaking of any printer in Europe. His style and tyopgraphy were adopted by the famous Didot printers in France, and Baskerville also influenced another famous originator of type face, Giambattista Bodoni, and Italian printer, whose typography is also widely used in contemporary book design and printing. Bodoni's work, however, was also influenced stylistically by the Far East. Most Eighteenth Century printing on the continent was both ornamental and flamboyant, but Bodoni's work reflected a more classical approach to the art.

Print in Colonial America

The first printing presses in the American colonies were established in the Seventeenth Century in the State of Massachusetts. But long before the settling of the colonies, there is evidence that printing was done in a Spanish settlement in Mexico. Indeed, historians believe that printing of some kind was accomplished in the New World even before print became popular in Europe. The purpose was to print religious literature for the clergy with the intention of bringing Christianity to the New World. In the early American colonies one Jose Glover, an English curate, sparked the setting up of a college and printing establishment with a press he had brought from England with the assistance of Matthew Day. It was Day who established a printing press at Harvard College and who issued the Book of Psalms in 1640. Day's work was carried on by Samuel Green who brought out several books printed in the Indian language and were designed to convert the natives to Christianity. Green also published the first American edition of the Holy Bible, printed in Indian and English, and encompassing both Old and New Testaments.

Unfortunately for the printing of books, as well as of newspapers, the coercive force of political authority was very much in evidence in the colonial period, and the authorities decreed that printing presses could not be established outside of Cambridge. Despite authoritarianism, however, printing and publishing were accomplished, albeit under difficult circumstances. It is not often recalled, for example, that one of the colony's first printers and typographers was Benjamin Franklin, America's Renaissance man. Franklin's brother had established a print shop in Boston where the first bona fide newspaper was published. But the paper, *The New England Courant*, was soon indicted by the authorities. Franklin went to Philadelphia where he secured a position with a local printer and thence moved on to Boston. Ultimately, he returned to Philadelphia and set up a publication called *The Pennsylvania Gazette*.

Franklin also published his famous *Poor Richard's Almanac* which has become an early American classic.

The establishment of the printing press in America served two purposes. Primarily, the availability of books and pamphlets made it possible for some form of communication and cultural exchange to exist between the Old World and the new. At the same time, books and newspapers provided a source of opinion and information which were truly American in flavor. The first presses in Boston were followed by publishing ventures in New York, Philadelphia and Baltimore. Indeed, it was the printing of some unflattering comments about Governor William Cosby, of New York, which resulted in the imprisonment of John Peter Zenger. Andrew Hamilton defended Zenger in a trial which is famous for having established the principle of a free press in America.

Most of the presses in the New World produced both books and newspapers. But book publishers, as well as newspaper editors, had to be most cautious about what they printed, because printers were licensed and virtually all printing presses were under government supervision and control. There was no First Amendment to protect publishers who had to be careful not to rub the authorities the wrong way. It was only after America had become truly independent that freedom to publish became a reality. In the Twentieth Century, when more books are published—and read—than ever before in this country's history, the publisher and printer enjoy a unique freedom restricted only by the laws of obscenity and libel. The courts again and again have upheld the right to print and publish books as a basic freedom under the constitution.

Not only are there an unprecedented number of hardcover books being published, but the paperbound book has revolutionized publishing by bringing the classics, educational volumes and reprints of popular fiction and non-fiction to more readers than ever before. Books which heretofore were available only in bookstores are now sold on a popular basis in drug stores, airline and railroad terminals and other popular consumer locations. There is still, however, a dearth not only of bookstores, but of libraries, when measured against the enormous growth of literacy which has occurred in this country, and particularly in the past two decades.

While the original purpose of book publishing, as a medium of communication, was essentially the transmission of knowledge, in recent years book publishing has had its aesthetic side as well. The medium of books is the basic mode of communicating man's cultural heritage from one generation to another—an achievement so commonplace today that its momentous contribution to civilization is taken for granted. But there is also the cultural aspect of the book as a communicative art, in which some of the most beautifully printed and bound books are issued in limited editions. From a practical viewpoint, however, the objective of the book publisher is to bring books inexpensively to the masses. Since rising costs of production have made the hardcover book an increasingly costly item, the millions of paperbacks in circulation literally have made the book a medium of mass communication.

BIBLIOGRAPHY

Aitken, G. A. ed. *The Tatler and the Spectator*. London: 1898–99.

Berelson, B. *The Library's Public*. New York: Columbia University Press, 1949.

Blades, William. *William Caxton*. San Francisco: Winsor Press, 1926.

Bouchot, Henri Francois. *The Printed Book, Its History, Illustrations, and Adornments, from the Days of Gutenberg to the Present*. Trans. Edward C. Bigmore. New York: Scribner and Welford, 1887.

Burns, Aaron. *Typography*. New York: Reinhold Publishing Corporation, 1961.

Cowley, Malcolm, ed. *Books That Changed Our Minds*. New York: Doubleday, Doran, 1939.

Enoch, Kurt. "The Paper-Bound Book: Twentieth-Century Publishing Phenomenon" *Library Quarterly*, University of Chicago Press, Vol. XXIV, No. 3 (July 1954).

Franklin, Benjamin. *Poor Richard's Almanac*. Boston, New York: Houghton Mifflin and Co., 1886.

Goudy, Frederic William. *Typologia*. Berkeley: University of California Press, 1940.

Isaacs, George A. *The Story of the Newspaper Printing Press*. London: Co-operative Printing Society, 1931.

Johnson, Alfred Forbes. *Type Designs: Their History and Development*. London: Grafton, 1959.

Johnson, Henry Lewis. *Gutenberg and the Book of Books*. New York: W. E. Rudge, 1932.

McMurtrie, Douglas. *The Book: The Story of Printing and Bookmaking*, rev. ed. New York: Oxford University Press, 1942.

Wings for Words. New York: Rand McNally and Company, 1940.

Meara, Frank Sherman. *John Baskerville and the Baskerville Press*. New York, 1925.

Oswald, John Clyde. *A History of Printing and Its Development Through Five Hundred Years*. New York: D. Appleton and Company, 1928.

Steinberg, S. H. *Five Hundred Years of Printing*. Hammondsworth, Middlesex, England: Penguin Books, Inc., 1955.

Thomas, Isaiah. *History of Printing in America*, 2 Vols. Worcester, Massachusetts: Isaac Thomas, Jr. (first printing), 1810; Albany, New York; Joel Munsell, 1874.

United Chapters of Phi Beta Kappa. "The Future of Books in America," *The American Scholar*, Vol. 23, No. 2 (Spring, 1954).

Waples, D., B. Berelson, and F. R. Bradshaw. *What Reading Does to People*. Chicago: University of Chicago Press, 1940.

5

The Newspaper:
A Changing Institution

THE NEWSPAPER as a mass medium has undergone a metamorphosis over the past twenty years comparable in at least some respects to that of the movies and the magazine. And the basic stimulus for change again has been the tradition-shattering appearance of the newest mass medium, television, on the American scene. It is true, as Raymond Nixon's studies showed many years ago, that newspaper publishing was tending toward greater concentration of control with fewer competing organs long before the advent of television. Television, however, wrought still further changes, not only in the business and advertising side, but in the character and purpose of American newspaper journalism. Where at one time the terms "press" or "journalism" meant specifically the newspaper, they have come to have a far broader connotation. There is now a distinction between print journalism and electronic journalism.

Television news coverage has forced changes and adjustments in newspaper coverage of the news. And, while television has no review policy toward the newspaper, print journalism has had a field day evaluating the social, political and aesthetic performance of the television medium. Yet, tradition is a stubborn phenomenon, and newspaper journalism at its best still believes that it maintains a character and stature which remain unchallenged even in the face of the development of excellent electronic journalism. The great newspapers, albeit only few in number, still lay claim to being the aristocrats of the mass media.

The inexorable effect of social change, as well as competition and supplementation by television, has given a new look to newspaper journalism. The stereotyped cynical reporter of "The Front Page" or the movies has retreated before a new kind of journalist, professionally trained, better educated and far more sensitive to and perceptive of what is going on in a changing society. There is still an effort to inject color and human interest into journalism, but the flamboyance of the tabloids and the once bitterly competitive newspaper rivalries have given way before a growing sobriety and a greater degree of what might be called consciousness of change. The long-term results of the Industrial Revolution and the development of a highly mechanized and mercantile society made newspapers more efficient organs. No longer, in the main, tied to one political party as its mouthpiece in print, the newspaper functions as part of a vast complex of mass production and distribution. More impersonal by far than in its early days, the press has become a gigantic industrial and social institution. Finally, where at one time there were cities with as many as seven or eight papers—New York once boasted fourteen—most cities now have no more than one or two daily newspapers.

Yet, the newspaper business is sanguine about its future. A 1969 federal report from the U.S. Department of Commerce indicated "an explosion in the interest in, and need for, the printed word, reflecting our rapidly growing and better educated population and the increasing complexity of an advanced technological environment." The American Newspaper Publishers Association, in its annual meeting in April of 1969, reported that more cities in the United States have daily newspaper service than in 1945—1,500 papers in 1969 as against 1,396 in 1945. The ANPA, listed a total of 1,753 dailies, four more than in 1945. Although there are only 45 cities with "commercially competing local dailies," there are 1,298 cities with daily newspapers and a grand total of 4,879 competing "media voices." By this is meant any separate ownership of two or more newspapers, radio or television facilities. Of the 202 cities with only one media voice, most were near large urban centers and many published weekly papers as well. And, in 1968, newspaper advertising rose by 6% to exceed the five billion dollar mark for the first time. In addition, and for the first time in many years, there was an increase of 25% over the previous year in journalism school graduates and a record enrollment of more than 27,000 students was reported by the 124 colleges which offer courses in journalism.

For most of the 1960's, the newspaper industry was beset by long and crippling strikes by printers, delivery men, type-setters, newsmen and other of the various newspaper unions. Some newspapers were unable to publish for several months, and many able reporters found employment in other media, such as radio and television. The installation of automated techniques resulted in union demands which publishers, already facing increased production costs, were either reluctant or unable to meet. The result was the passing of such large-circulation papers as New York's *World-Journal Tribune* which had already been amalgamated from three papers: the *World-Telegram*, *Herald Tribune* and *Journal-American*. Over the past year, however, the pressure from labor has not been motivated so much by a fear of automation as of rising costs and extensive inflation. The newspaper industry has finally reached a plateau after years of union-management turmoil, but the truce is still an uneasy one and is buttressed primarily by the fact that print journalism is enjoying unexpected economic prosperity. New procedures of automation have resulted in more accurate, and speedier, typesetting, production and distribution. Raw tape is now fed into a computer, corrected and then fed into a linecasting machine.

Contemporary print journalism, undoubtedly reflecting the student and the black revolutions, the problems of an urban society and the precarious state of world affairs, operates from a base of broader responsibility than at any time in the history of the American press. Newspaper journalism has become institutionalized, but it represents a power structure which reveals greater awareness of its obligations in a changing society. The growth of graduate study in all of the mass media, the emphasis on research in effects of mass communication and the publication of scholarly journals such as *The Columbia Journalism Review* and *Journalism Quarterly* has given journalism a more acute recognition of its obligation as a medium of both information and of interpretation of the news.

The more responsible and better educated reporter is not the only change which has taken place in American journalism. The itinerant newsprinter, who traveled from city to city in an earlier day, has all but disappeared with the development of linotype. The "tramp" printer has been transformed by the introduction of new typesetting methods into a unionized industrial operator. Automation, considered until recently the major menace to all who work in the journalistic profession, has not proved as malignant as the trade unions believed it would be. A working journalist today may be a newspaper reporter or editor, a member of the editorial staff of a national magazine such as *Time* or *Newsweek*, or a member of the news department of a television or radio station or network.

The Beginnings of Journalism

At its inception, however, the rise of journalism was identified solely with print, and the newspaper was a direct consequence of the development of the printing press during the Renaissance. The revival of classical learning during that period and the happy circumstance of the development of printing by means of movable type gave an enormous incentive toward literacy on the part of the large mass of the uneducated and the illiterate. A native literature developed in many countries, and the art of reading and writing passed from the minority elite to the common man. This transformation, however, was more evolutionary than revolutionary. From William Caxton's first printing establishment in England in 1476, more than a hundred years elapsed before the appearance of regularly printed pamphlets for the dissemination of news. But the profession of journalism was a result of the printing press, as well as of the growing industrialization of society. Print itself was largely responsible for the development of the modern industrial state as, conversely, industrialization gave impetus to the development of journalism. And, beyond the economic impact, print had a momentous cultural effect. Through the tangible products of print, man had a new and resourceful tool available to preserve in concrete form and pass on a vast cultural heritage from one generation to another. It was possible, as nationalism developed, to produce and transmit a national literature, a common set of hopes, dreams and aspirations of a given society, reflected particularly in its journalism.

Until the Twentieth Century, print journalism enjoyed a splendid status as the one significant medium of mass communication. This century, however, saw the development of other media for the masses. The motion picture was followed by radio and by television, each with a unique ability to entertain as well as to inform. In addition, the development of journalism as a truly mass medium resulted in the concomitant development of new methods of persuasion. Techniques of public relations and publicity, of promotion and advertising were a consequence of the use of journalism as a medium of persuasion as well as of information. Journalism no longer stands unique and alone. It has become part of a vast and intricate universe of mass communication which includes newspapers, magazines, books, radio, television and motion pictures, as well as the corollary activities of advertising and public relations and propaganda. These techniques use the media, particularly the newspapers, radio and television, as instruments to relay affective or directive language that is aimed at modifying behavior. And they are particularly significant because mass communication can now reach millions of listeners, viewers and even readers with essentially the same message. This implicit power to persuade and inform, as well as to entertain, places mass media in the position not only of reflecting social mores and values but of influencing them as well.

There is, however, something curiously paradoxical about the concept of the press and other agencies as mass media. For no medium, however powerful its reach, communicates with all of the people all of the time. As audiences for newspapers and television tend to seek out and select media, so media tend to select out their audiences. It is only within this context that, even under a process of mutual selectivity, modern media still reach millions. Thus, the phrase "mass communication" takes on meaning. But the meaning and impact, despite the millions of readers and viewers, is still limited to a given audience at a given time. Even within the specific frame of reference of a particular medium, such as the newspaper, the reader selects out those news stories, features or editorials which attract him because they cohere with his own interests and value judgments.

The First Newspapers

The beginnings of journalism in America emphasize this principle in a rather oblique way. Although a printing press—the first one—was established at Harvard College in 1638, it did not produce a newspaper because there was no apparent need for one. The colonists, selecting what was of primary concern to them, were quite satisfied to glean whatever news there was by way of reports from England. But the basic desire of the citizens for information, even though selective and value-oriented, existed as far back as the great civilizations of ancient Rome where a single informational sheet known as the Acta Diurna was publicly posted for the edification of the citizenry. This, of course, was not a newspaper in any sense, nor can any of the sundry informational devices that appeared be called a newspaper until after the invention of printing in the Renaissance. The crowning achievement of the invention of movable type was not only that it made books more readily available, but more significantly that it made newspapers possible by creating a revolution in the field of education. The newspaper made information available to the masses quickly and inexpensively and for the first time in history. Its result was to stimulate a general desire for literacy. An interest in information and a desire for news were implicit in a civilized society. It was inevitable that this basic need for news would be satisfied by newspapers once the technical facilities for providing them were developed.

At first, the need was accommodated by broadsides and essays which were not newspapers in a modern sense. But eventually, informational organs were published which were to develop the clear characteristics of a newspaper. They were not sporadic, but published at regular intervals so that the public could look toward obtaining them regularly. They were printed in quantity and were available either by subscription or direct purchase at extremely modest prices. And they purveyed the basic grist of all journalism: news or information.

It was not until the Eighteenth Century that bona fide newspapers of this kind appeared in England. Historical evidence reveals that the origin of the modern newspaper was not England, but Germany at the beginning of the Seventeenth Century. Newspapers subsequently were published in several countries on the continent and in Sweden, with the first English publication brought out in 1621. Immediately, however, print journalism as a mass medium—even in a relatively restricted market—was bound to create problems for the ruling elite who not only governed but who could also read and write. The result was a licensing system established under Henry VIII which stipulated that no printing shop could be established without the official *imprimatur* of a representative of the crown. It was but a step further to the setting up of a Stationers Company which ultimately exercised authoritarian control, as well as direct censorship, of all print material, especially the newspapers, which was intended for distribution to the public. There were remissions in, and objections to, this kind of government control, in particular John Milton's publication of his trenchant criticism of restrictions on freedom of the press, *Areopagetica*, but the road was uphill until well into the Eighteenth Century. In 1688, during the reign of William and Mary, there was a diminution of government control over print and the beginnings of a genuinely free press in England. But there are critics of journalism today who remain convinced that a form of censorship still exists in many countries through subtle pressure, while the idea of a free press in China and the Soviet Union is, of course, impossible of achievement under present conditions.

Unlike the electronic media, the modern newspaper did not burst on the scene full-blown. Journalistic efforts at first were tentative and a century elapsed before print journalism as it is known today was established. In 1621, a single news sheet called a "Coranto" was published in England. The Corantos dealt exclusively in foreign affairs, reflecting the primary interest of the colonists in news from their original homeland. This was followed by publication of daily news sheets called "diurnals" and, eventually, by the printing of four-page journals which were to develop into the newspapers of today. The earliest diurnal on record appears to be a sheet called *Diurnall Occurrences*, published by one John Thomas in 1641. By 1665, with the appearance of the *Oxford Gazette*, later to become the *London Gazette*, England finally could boast of a regular newspaper which was distributed twice weekly. The Eighteenth Century saw a marvelous efflorescence of literature in England, distinguished particularly by the essays of Addison and Steele, Daniel DeFoe and Dr. Samuel Johnson. Each contributed in no small measure to the development of modern journalism, although DeFoe was identified particularly with the growth of the concept of print journalism in terms of coverage of current events that comprised the substance of news. It was the happy circumstance of essayists of the calibre of Johnson and DeFoe, along with the rise of a growing and mercantile middle class, that created a genuine demand for news. This demand resulted in the publication, in 1702, of *The Daily Courant*, the first daily newspaper to appear in England. *The Daily Courant*, under the aegis of Samuel Buckley, was in every sense a *news* paper, a journal which was printed regularly and which was based on an accurate rendition of events in the news that might be of interest to the middle class reading public. It came as close to being fair and impartial as any journal which had appeared until that time.

The Press in America

The American colonies at first were interested primarily in news from England, but as a society began to develop there was generated a genuine desire for information of local significance. The first American newspaper was published by an individual who had fled England, because what he printed created such difficulty with the authorities that he was forced to leave and come to the colonies. Unfortunately, he was to fare no better in America. This journalist was Benjamin Harris who, in 1690, published the first newspaper to appear in the colonies. It was called *Publick Occurrences Both Foreign and Domestick*. This publication is considered the first bona fide American newspaper, although there had been various news sheets or broadsides, printed on one side of a sheet and bearing such titles as "The Present State of the New English Affairs." Harris ran true to form in the colonies. Because the press was licensed, no printing was permitted without official sanction. Harris' anti-Catholicism, which had created his original problem in England, was evidenced in the first American newspaper. Because Harris had no official license to publish, and particularly because he was critical of the colonial government, *Publick Occurrences Both Foreign and Domestick* was put out of business. As a result, Harris returned to London where he began still another publishing venture.

The second regularly published newspaper in the colonies was the *Boston News-Letter*, published in 1704 by the Boston postmaster, John Campbell, and printed in the shop of Bartholomew Green. This sheet created no problem, because Campbell, as postmaster, operated under official license and took pains to state in print that the *Boston News-Letter* was published by permission of the government authorities. Campbell's newspaper eventually ran into competition when, in 1719, William Brooker brought out the *Boston Gazette*. Brooker had succeeded Campbell as postmaster and he, too, published under authority. It was the shop of Bartholomew Green, incidentally, which not only printed the *Boston News-Letter*, but which also served as one of the few print shops in existence during the early colonial period.

The style of early colonial journalism was crude, as might be expected. Literacy was not widespread and printers were neither men of learning nor journalists in anything resembling the contemporary meaning of that term. It was not until the journeyman printer as publisher was succeeded by genuinely independent newspaper editors that a style which can be called truly journalistic developed.

One of the early editors who revealed a touch of literacy was Ben Franklin's brother, James, who published the *New England Courant* in 1721. This newspaper was a cut above its contemporaries in that it was literate, flavorsome and carried articles of genuine human interest to its readers. It was also outspoken. This was, by far, the most literate paper to appear to date, and it came under Franklin's direction because of a complicated business tangle between John Campbell and Bartholomew Green. The *Courant* thereafter became the third newspaper to appear, in competition with the *Boston Gazette* and the *Boston News-Letter*. It was Franklin's *New England Courant* which showed the first spirit of inde-

pendence against the rigid authoritarianism of the licensing system and
which printed material critical of colonial rule. Ostensibly, Franklin undertook a campaign in print against researches that were underway to
develop a vaccine for smallpox, a disease that was epidemic at the time.
Actually, the campaign fulminated against the pompous and insufferably
disciplinarian attitude of Cotton Mather, a clergyman who demanded
unquestioning obedience to authority, both in his addresses and his
pamphlets. Mather fought back through the instrument of rival newspapers, but Franklin's editorial crusade had established for the first time
that a newspaper was not a passive journal, but a genuine medium of
communications with a powerful ability to reflect and influence public
opinion. James Franklin was an editor with a point of view, a tough-
fibred journalist who did not succumb easily to authority and whose
strong position contributed significantly toward freeing the press from
the shackles of censorship. It was in the *New England Courant* that
Benjamin Franklin's felicitous articles, signed by "Silence Dogwood"
first appeared.

When James Franklin was thrown into prison because of his criticism of the administration, Ben Franklin, through a legal maneuver, was
able to assume the position of editor of the *New England Courant.*
Benjamin Franklin was America's Renaissance man, the true "man for
all seasons." But his journalistic distinction rested primarily on his contribution as a charming essayist. After taking over the paper, he continued
to contribute urbane and entertaining pieces under the pseudonym of
Silence Dogwood and, in 1729, brought out the famous *Pennsylvania
Gazette* in Philadelphia. This publication and Andrew Bradford's *The
American Weekly Mercury,* a rival to the *Gazette,* were the first newspapers to appear outside of New England, and the *Pennsylvania Gazette*
proved, under Franklin's direction, to be one of America's fine early
newspapers. It was, as might be expected, literate, pointed and sophisticated in character—a distinct improvement over the perfunctory journalism of the period. In 1725, William Bradford, father of Andrew and
the official printer of New York, published the *New York Gazette,* the
state's first newspaper. In 1733, the *New York Weekly Journal* appeared
and became one of the first colonial newspapers to defy the authority of
the British Crown and to take an editorial position in favor of the demands and dissatisfactions of the colonial people.

The Zenger Case: Partisan Journalism

The *New York Weekly Journal* was edited by John Peter Zenger
whose name is synonymous with the battle for freedom of the press in
America. History has probably credited Zenger with greater glory than
he merited, for his case was more a symbol of press freedom than a concrete accomplishment, but he does serve a function as a symbolic representation of a free press. It was Andrew Hamilton's brilliant plea on

Zenger's behalf which became the basis for the eventual re-evaluation of laws of libel and the concept of free access to obtain and print the news. Several years before the Zenger case, William Bradford had championed a free press and had threatened to move his paper if harassment continued. His son Andrew and, to some extent, Benjamin Franklin also pleaded for greater freedom to publish. But Zenger's involvement was, ironically, inadvertent. Zenger was convinced that an attack in print should be made on Governor William Cosby because of Cosby's high-handedness as an administrator. A combination of circumstances, including Zenger's criticism of Governor Cosby for allowing units of the French navy to move into New York Harbor, caused Cosby to request that his chief justice, James Delancy, institute proceedings against Zenger. Finally, in 1734, Zenger was arrested on a charge of sedition. In a case that became a considerable *cause celebre*, Zenger ultimately found a brilliant defense attorney in Andrew Hamilton who decided not to deny what Zenger had published, but to base his defense on the fundamental issue of a free press. Zenger, therefore, could not be guilty unless what he printed was, indeed, seditious. To be libelous, Hamilton argued, must include seditious and malicious falsehoods. Zenger was acquitted and the idea of a free press was established philosophically, if not operationally. Libel laws were not changed for the next half century, but at least the *principle* of a free press was finally structured in America. Eventually, with the First Amendment, this principle was to become incontrovertible fact.

In the latter part of the Eighteenth Century, as the country moved closer to independence, the press began to play a more partisan role both in influencing public opinion and in reflecting that opinion. The press also developed into a strong political influence. The struggle of the Colonies for freedom was aided considerably by certain segments of the press while others took up the defense of the Crown. Franklin's *Pennsylvania Gazette* crystallized the philosophy behind the Colonial struggle for independence. But the Crown had its journalistic advocates in the *Boston Chronicle* and the *Boston News-Letter*.

By the middle of the century there were approximately thirty newspapers published regularly, five in Boston alone. Although there was the beginning of a trend toward bona fide editors, most newsmen were still publishers or booksellers. William Parks, with his publication of *The Maryland Gazette*, brought out a far superior newspaper than had heretofore been published. Parks also brought out *The Virginia Gazette* at Williamsburg where his quaint print shop still stands as a permanent exhibit of the printing establishment of the period. The news in most publications contained information of political developments abroad, with particular reference to the impact on the Colonies. Strong positions of pressure were taken by newspapers which inveighed against the colonies or against England. The press, however, was still cautious not to offend political authority. It was the passing of the Stamp Act in 1765, considered highly inimical to the functioning of a free press, which evoked the wrath of many newspapers against England. More papers began vehemently to argue the revolutionary philosophy.

Many papers found it difficult to remain in business and more than half of those which were established failed to survive. But the development of journalism as a growing profession was not to be restrained, because the demand for news was growing. A mercantile class was developing and, with it, the continuing growth of educational opportunity and literacy. As news created a demand for literacy, so a growing literacy acted to spur a hunger for information. This increasing interest in news led ultimately to the establishment of *The Pennsylvania Packer and General Advertiser* as the first daily newspaper in the United States. Originally printed three times a week in Philadelphia, it acceded to a public need and established regular publication in 1784. Philadelphia, Boston and New York each boasted three newspapers in print during the last quarter of the Eighteenth Century.

Although many newspapers did not survive the Revolution, those which did survive served as a cohesive force in galvanizing public opinion. And the interest in news engendered by the crucial period resulted in a better quality of journalism. Particularly notable during the period were such journalistic figures as James Rivington and Isiah Thomas. In New York, Rivington's *New York Gazetteer* was a violently partisan newspaper which espoused the cause of the British Crown. As publisher and bookseller, Rivington managed to create news to such an extent that the colonists temporarily put him out of business. Rivington did attempt, however, to include both sides of the Whig-Tory dispute and, during the war, he changed the name of his paper to the *Royal Gazetteer*. At the same time, Isiah Thomas published with Zechariah Fowler a newspaper called the *Massachusetts Spy*. The product of a first-rate journalistic intelligence, the publication made an effort to present fairly all conflicting viewpoints. And it did so with uncommon literacy and color. Thomas also published several magazines and hundreds of books, including a history of printing in America. He was a fine craftsman as publisher and printer. The *Massachusetts Spy* remained in publication until the beginning of the Twentieth Century. Throughout its years of publication it was a superior journalistic enterprise which did an exemplary job of reporting the progress of the struggle for independence.

Tom Paine, although not a newsman in the literal sense of that term, was in many ways, the supreme journalist of the American Revolution. Uneducated and not particularly literate, Paine was a self-made writer and a natural polemicist. After contributing articles to the *Pennsylvania Gazette* magazine, Paine wrote his famous pamphlet, *Common Sense*, in 1776 followed by several of his *Crisis Papers*. Each of these remains a classic of revolutionary fervor, revealing Paine's enormous gift for espousing a cause in which he believed ardently.

Journalism in the New Nation

The tone of news after the War of Independence was both political and economic. Foreign affairs predominated, and domestic coverage consisted basically of reports of political speeches, government proceedings and news of mercantile interest. The average newspaper reader belonged essentially to the commercial or mercantile public. The beginnings of the editorial appeared, and newspapers were now published by editors rather than by the old printer-journalist. The so-called "penny dreadfuls," because they began to include a more sensational kind of copy which high-lighted police news, murders, rapes and suicides, also originated. Paradoxically, the editorials stressed ethical principles and espoused a stringent morality. Subscription sales gave way to newsstand circulation and the newsboy became a popular figure on the American scene. The press began to carry advertising, which served to defray costs, but the ads were not of high calibre, either in terms of copy or layout.

There was an interim period immediately after the war, however, when American journalism was most undistinguished. The quality of the editor improved, but overt propaganda and partisanship still were much in evidence. George Washington, unlike Jefferson, neither understood nor trusted the press. Like many of his successors as President, he complained bitterly about those journalists who attacked him in print. There was a bitter political schism between Federalists and Republicans, between the advocates of states rights as against a strong central government. Alexander Hamilton published the *Gazette of the United States*, a Federalist newspaper, while Thomas Jefferson appeared to be the motivating spirit behind the *National Gazette*. The paper was edited by Philip Freneau, the "poet of the Revolution," who articulated the Jeffersonian philosophy. Freneau, writing under the name of "Brutus" attacked Hamilton vigorously and engaged in a series of journalistic jousts with one John Fenns who came to the defense of Hamilton.

One of the most vitriolic journals of the period was *Aurora*, later called the *Philadelphia General Advertiser*. Published by Benjamin Franklin Bache, it was viciously anti-Federalist. Washington's reaction to bitter criticism was to give his farewell address exclusively to a Federalist publication in much the same way that President Lyndon Johnson's announcement that he would retire was given to the press without the stunning last paragraph until President Johnson made the announcement on television. Indeed, the relationship of Washington with the press serves as a reminder to those who speak of a contemporary "credibility gap" that officialdom and the press have always had their antagonisms. Washington had about as difficult a time with the journalists as any President in American history. Bache went so far as to say that the nation had been debauched by Washington. Despite Jefferson's plea for journalistic responsibility, the press was neither free nor responsible. Both Jefferson and Hamilton backed opposing papers. Jefferson was represented by the *National Intelligencer and Washington Advertiser*, edited by Samuel H. Smith, and Hamilton published the original *New York Evening Post* which has survived to this day, at least in title if not in form and substance, as the country's oldest published newspaper. Despite Jefferson's idealism, the press was poisonous, malicious and irresponsible. But Jefferson's oft-quoted statement still articulated the basic need and principle of a free and responsible press: "Were it left to me to decide whether we should have a government without newspapers, or newspapers without a government, I should not hesitate to prefer the latter."

The public—and eventually journalists—evidently agreed, for in the long run America developed one of the freest and most responsible systems of journalism in the world. At the close of the first quarter of the Nineteenth Century, there were about 500 papers in the United States. Most of them were still published on a weekly basis and most were in the East where the ups and downs of politics were reflected in a predominantly party press. But factionalism, as we have noted, was receding before a more colorful kind of journalism. Newspapers were beginning to crop up in the West as the country expanded its frontiers. Pittsburgh started a paper called the *Gazette* and newspapers were established in St. Louis and as far west as California. In general, however, the press continued to operate along political party lines, particularly in the period of Andrew Jackson. Indeed, Jackson was accused of setting up Francis P. Blair as editor of the *Washington Globe*, a newspaper which was considered the mouthpiece for Jackson's administration.

Dominant Figures: Great Newspapers

Sooner or later, dominant figures emerged in various professions, and journalism, as it became more news-oriented and circulation minded, began to bring out a series of great newsmen. In the "penny dreadful" period, in 1833, one Benjamin H. Day published *The New York Sun*, a newspaper which was to become one of the finest until its demise in the attrition period of the Twentieth Century. The first issues were of four pages and replete with local color, personality and human interest news. Day's determination to publish a penny newspaper marked the beginning of a period of colorful and flamboyant figures in American journalism—James Gordon Bennett, Horace Greeley, Joseph Pulitzer, William Randolph Hearst and the Scripps family. Journalism also developed distinguished and more sober figures such as Henry J. Raymond, Adolph S. Ochs and Charles A. Dana. In succession a series of great newspapers was founded. *The New York Sun* was established in 1833. The *New York*

Herald began publication in 1835. And *The New York Tribune* went into publication in 1841. The greatest of newspapers, *The New York Times*, came upon the journalistic scene in 1851.

These newspapers and others, some of which became the flagships of great publishing empires, established an age of mass communication for the American press. They became, in a sense, the first of the mass media—journalistic ventures whose goal was to reach the largest possible circulation. In order to do so, they were obliged to depend upon advertising, to engage in promotional and editorial gimmicks and exploitations and to expand their content from sheer information to more provocative areas of human interest and entertainment. Above all, however, the press as a mass medium needed galvanic and dynamic figures to provide the impetus that drove journalism forward as a tremendously powerful force in informing and reflecting public opinion, a mass communicator in every sense of the term.

The first of these larger-than-life figures was James Gordon Bennett, one of the most vigorous and colorful in American journalism. Bennett displayed a talent for news, a penchant for timely and human interest stories. He established coverage of finance and religion, of society and the theatre. Journalism became more sensational, but also more sophisticated. Bennett, above all, realized that competitive conditions necessitated beating the opposition to the news with what became known as "scoops." He utilized the new telegraph and cable, developed and trained foreign correspondents and, in general, opened new horizons for journalism as a mass medium. Although he exploited the news and sensationalized it, he was one of the first bona fide journalists, one of the truly forceful editorial personalities. The thrust was toward the mass audience, the new and growing public of immigrants that crowded the cities and were hungry for news. Bennett's *Herald* covered the teeming life of a growing city and, if his brand of journalism was frequently trenchant and distasteful, it displayed a pragmatism that resulted in success. He was succeeded by his son, James Gordon Bennett, Jr., in 1872, who, while able, was also unreliable. His claim to distinction was the adventure of one of his correspondents, Henry M. Stanley, who went to Africa to find the missing Dr. Livingstone.

The elder Bennett's chief competition came from Horace Greeley, one of America's distinguished journalistic figures. Greeley, who founded the *Tribune*, has been called "the father of American journalism." His distinction rests basically on the concept that the editorial was an important part of journalism as a communications medium, that the editor ought to take a stand and espouse causes with conviction. Greeley was what many of his peers were not—a journalist of integrity. He took a position in support of anti-slavery and his views were essentially liberal and humanitarian. Greeley gathered about him a corps of excellent journalists and published a first-rate newspaper. While the *Herald* was colorful and sensational, the *Tribune* had journalistic candor and an editorial point of view.

In 1851, Henry J. Raymond established *The New York Times*. The distinction of *The Times* from its inception was sobriety, balance and non-extremism. It presented contrasting points of view thoughtfully and soberly, without invective or partisanship. Misleading advertising was not accepted and scandal was rejected in the pages of *The Times*. After Raymond's passing, *The Times* failed to achieve the stature of a paper such as Godkin's *New York Post*, despite its excellent editorial direction. It lost circulation steadily until it was taken over by Adolph Ochs who had been successful as publisher of the *Chattanooga Times*. Ochs bought a solid enterprise and made it eminently successful. Circulation increased as *The New York Times* became the premiere newspaper of the country with its editorial criterion of "all the news that's fit to print."

What was to become the most important conservative newspaper in America was established by Edwin Lawrence Godkin as *The New York Evening Post*. Godkin had been editor of *The Nation*, founded in 1865 as a journal devoted to the discussion of public issues. After selling *The Nation* to Henry Villard, Godkin became editor of the *New York Post*. For many years, this newspaper, like *The New York Sun*, was a model of conservative journalism. Still published today, it has changed its format to a semi-tabloid and, as New York's only evening newspaper, includes a varied assortment of columnists and feature writers and an editorial policy which is utterly different in tone and substance from the original newspaper of the same name.

The press, in its newly developed pride in itself as a vigorous mass medium, covered the Civil War adequately. Bennett, in his zeal to get the news to his readers before the competition, established a corps of war correspondents, as did Raymond of *The New York Times*. But, as in colonial days, the tensions produced by the struggle once again developed a partisan press which frequently became vicious and slanderous. Joseph Medill, publisher of the *Chicago Tribune*, was even accused by President Lincoln of helping to foment the Civil War. The impact of the war on journalism was to increase newspaper circulation, develop the importance of the war correspondent and reveal the usefulness of the newly established wire services. In the aftermath of the war, Bennett, Greeley, Dana and Raymond survived as successful publishers with fairly strong and established newspapers.

The major newspaper in the midwest was Medill's *Chicago Tribune*, a paper which challenged the *New York Herald* in flamboyant, personal journalism. It was a vitriolic publication which, despite its overt emphasis on ideal values, did not hesitate to use its power as a mass medium to pour invective on those with whom it was in disagreement. But circulation soared and then, as now, the *Chicago Tribune* has been considered a newspaper with a strong conservative—its critics call it reactionary—

point of view. It was anti-labor and defended the status quo with vigor and stubbornness. But, despite criticism of its editorial viewpoint, it became one of America's most forceful newspapers.

There were papers of distinction in other areas outside of New York and the Eastern seaboard. William Rockhill Nelson established a superb publication in the *Kansas City Star* and showed what a medium of mass communication can accomplish when it determines to drive corruption out of a city by exposing it to public view through the instrumentality of the press. The *Kansas City Star* remains one of the great independent newspapers of the United States. In general, however, the newer papers which sprang up in the South and West after the war were not particularly distinguished. Chicago's papers, in addition to the *Tribune*, were the *Daily News* and the *Chicago Times*, the latter highly sensational in content. The *Denver Post*, a fine publication today, was launched on sensationalism and a series of wild exploitations and promotional gimmicks by Harry H. Tammen and Fred G. Bonfils. The *Denver Post* did not stand out as one of the proud examples of fine journalism. In San Francisco, the *Chronicle* was an enterprising and exemplary journalistic enterprise until challenged by the emergence of William Randolph Hearst who established the *San Francisco Examiner*, a sensational example of lurid journalism, replete with roaring headlines and other circulation-building devices. The third San Francisco paper was *The Bulletin* until it merged with Hearst as the *San Francisco Call Bulletin*.

In the South, too, journalism was undistinguished with the exception of Henry W. Grady's *Atlanta Constitution* which reflected the blunt and enterprising disposition of its publisher and became one of the great newspapers of the country. The University of Georgia School of Journalism, which offers the annual television Peabody Awards, is named after Grady. One other fine newspaper in a generally lackluster area was Henry Watterson's *Louisville Courier-Journal*, a paper which, like the *Atlanta Constitution*, looked forward toward the rehabilitation and development of a vigorous South.

The Associated Press which, like International News Service and the United Press (later to become United Press International) revolutionized journalism with the development of simultaneous wire service copy to hundreds of member newspapers, did not begin auspiciously. It was Victor Freemont Lawson, publisher of the *Chicago Daily News* and a journalist of uncommon integrity who accused the AP of short-changing midwestern newspapers in favor of the Eastern press. Actually, what Lawson uncovered was an anti-trust arrangement between AP and UP in which those who controlled the United Press also exercised authority over the Associated Press. Lawson's exposé of this illegal arrangement to many of the editors ultimately resulted in the establishment of two great independent news services in AP and UP until the latter became United Press International. It was the enterprise and decency of editors such as

Nelson, Lawson and Raymond which began to give journalism what was even more significant than the growth importance of mass media—the image of decency and integrity.

Journalism Becomes Institutionalized

After the Civil War, the momentous changes in American life were reflected in the media of communication, the newspaper and the magazine. The press changed from a political and factional organ to a vast institution, a medium of mass communication which distilled in its coverage the rise of urban America and the far-reaching consequences of the Industrial Revolution. Advertising became an essential ingredient of newspaper publishing, circulation became essential for success in attracting advertisers. The press not only became a national institution. It became institutionalized. Newspapers began to become part of large, business enterprises. But journalism also became more newsworthy and more informative, and editorials were written cogently, rather than out of fierce partisanship. The end of the Nineteenth and the beginning of the Twentieth Century witnessed the appearance of such titans of journalism as Pulitzer and Hearst and the development of powerful—some believed too powerful—communications empires.

Joseph Pulitzer published *The New York World* in 1883. The paper immediately established a reputation for combining sensationalism with crusading journalism. Indeed, a cynical appraisal might conclude that the Pulitzer technique of revealing abuses had no objective other than to provide a vantage point for the publication of sensationalized news. Pulitzer himself was one of the more interesting phenomena of American journalism. An immigrant from Hungary, Pulitzer originally acquired a foreign language paper, *The Staats-Zeitung*, which he promptly sold. He then turned to the law, but ultimately gravitated towards journalism. His combining of *The St. Louis Dispatch* with *The St. Louis Post* became an immediate success and was followed by the acquisition of *The New York World*. This publication began auspiciously. It was to be a people's paper, devoted to journalistic integrity, and it did not hesitate to take on authority and privilege in its editorial crusades. But, paradoxically, while the editorials were couched in a vein of journalistic idealism, the news emphasized sex and violence and the sensational exposé of corruption in high places. Pulitzer also instituted the editorial cartoon. As a result, circulation grew tremendously. By 1886, *The World* had the largest circulation in the country, about a quarter of a million.

At this juncture, the titanic battle between Hearst and Pulitzer began. Unfortunately, a nervous disorder kept Pulitzer from his business a great deal of the time and forced him to edit his paper in absentia. The battle was joined when Hearst's challenge was met by Pulitzer's decision not to attempt to beat Hearst in sensationalism, but to make *The World* a fine liberal newspaper. In this, Pulitzer succeeded for a number of years. In 1895, Hearst, who had taken over *The San Francisco Examiner* with signal success, bought the *Morning Journal* which became famous immediately for the so-called "yellow journalism" comics. Hearst's journalism was flamboyant, shocking and frequently lurid. The editorial page was the antithesis of sobriety and rationality. Hearst was a powerful advocate, so powerful that he was accused in some quarters of helping to foment the Spanish-American War. This was a journalism of color comics, editorials of a no-holds-barred nature and news pages of unadulterated "front page" variety. Like Pulitzer, Hearst's empire flourished and circulation bounded to unprecedented levels. But there were editors of more sober demeanor who considered both *The Journal* and *The World* the nadir of journalistic integrity. Yet, in their own flamboyant way, both Pulitzer and Hearst contributed importantly toward the growth of American journalism. Newspaper circulation soared. The demand for news was voracious. And, to the oblique credit of Pulitzer, he did endow The Columbia University School of Journalism in 1912.

Hearst's success ultimately forced the sale of *The New York Herald* to that most utilitarian of journalistic dealers, Frank Munsey, who sold it, in turn, to *The Tribune*, establishing the famous *New York Herald Tribune*. But not even this distinguished paper has survived, for in the retrenchment of the 1960's it became part of the *World Journal Tribune* which went out of business in 1968. At the time of its original sale, however, several fine papers were flourishing—Bennett's *Tribune*, Hearst and Pulitzer, Dana's *New York Sun*—an excellent and exemplary journalistic enterprise. The *Sun* ultimately became a highly conservative paper before succumbing to the attrition that attacked most New York newspapers until, by 1969, only three out of an original fourteen survived—*The New York Times, Daily News* and the *New York Post*.

In 1896, Adolph S. Ochs became publisher of *The New York Times*. The paper had gone into decline, but Ochs' enterprise turned *The Times* into what is probably the greatest journalistic publication in the world. With the credo "all the news that's fit to print," *The Times* covered the news—national and international, cultural, political and economic—with a thoroughness and integrity matched by no other newspaper in the country. This spirit of fairness, thoroughness and probity continued under the direction of great family publishers such as Arthur Hays Sulzberger. In the past few years, however, the administrative, as well as the journalistic, policies of *The New York Times* have come under criticism. Gay Talese, a former *"Times"* writer, and others have written pointedly of internal jockeying for control, of office politics, of a growing estrangement from what had once been an enviable relationship between management and employees. The *Times* has been experimenting with cultural news departments, with "split-page" features, with greater use of photographs.

The *"Times* style" has undergone subtle changes, too, in an apparent effort to liven up the paper. Several drama and movie critics have come and gone and there were periods when, except for reviews and Sunday pieces, television news was virtually ignored. The paper remains a great journalistic enterprise, but there are those who feel that some of its aura has dimmed, largely owing to the more impersonal "computerized" approach both to its employee relations and to its coverage of the news.

One of America's largest newspaper chains was developed by Edward W., George H. and James E. Scripps. The Scripps empire began in the middle West with such papers as the *St. Louis Chronicle,* the *Cleveland Press* and the *Cincinnati Post.* With these papers, Scripps went into competition with Hearst and Pulitzer. In 1920, Roy W. Howard and Robert Scripps (son of Edward) joined forces and the chain became known as Scripps-Howard. One can note only with nostalgia and regret that such Scripps-Howard papers as *The New York World* and *The New York Telegram* no longer exist after undergoing a series of tortuous mergers and combinations which finally brought about their passing. The final effort, *The World Journal Tribune,* went out of business of 1967 because of a combination of internal dissension, lack of circulation, union difficulties and general lack of strong management. Yet, such papers as *The World* have left a permanent legacy of fine journalism. The *World* at one time could boast of such brilliant editors as Frank Cobb, a crusading and fearless editor, Walter Lippmann, one of the greatest of contemporary journalists, and such literary luminaries as Heywood Broun and Franklin P. Adams.

Concentration and Consolidation

The Twentieth Century has been an era of concentration and consolidation for American journalism. Frank Munsey early made a business of buying and selling newspapers, but the trend toward mergers has been inevitable as newspapers were forced to merge in order to survive. Philadelphia, which once boasted thirteen papers, is down to two. Similar attrition has taken place in Boston, Chicago, San Francisco and Los Angeles. The once great empires have dwindled. In the earlier decades of this century, such enterprises as Hearst, Pulitzer, Scripps-Howard, McCormick-Patterson (*The Chicago Tribune* and *New York Daily News*) were formidable, powerful voices. While the editorial policies were conservative, the news was sensational and the use of pictures and comics helped to increase circulation. In New York State, Frank E. Gannett built a chain of fifteen major newspapers, while John S. Knight developed formidable papers in Miami, Chicago and other cities to which he contributed his own signed personal column.

Although most of these organizations still function successfully, there is no doubt that their enormous power has been somewhat eroded. Labor-management difficulties are only part of the reason. Automation has played a part. Economics has played a part. And the immediacy of television news has forced changes in newspaper journalism. Contemporary journalism is an impersonal corporate-type enterprise. Many papers depend on wire copy from AP and UPI. Printing of pictures by telephoto has speeded up both transmission and printing enormously. Newspapers are printed and circulated with dispatch, thanks particularly to Ottmar Mergenthaler's development of the linotype machine which replaced setting of type by hand.

Progress has also brought about stereotyping and standardization and consequent loss of independence and enterprise. While AP and UPI do tend to standardize news, however, there is no doubt that they have made an enormously successful contribution to communications by making national and international news events available quickly and, for the most part, accurately to their hundreds of member papers. But ruggedly independent journalism is still to be found in many large papers, along with the weekly and small-town newspapers, although even these now receive the wire services. At one time, there were almost 500 weekly papers in the United States. Most of the news came by plate from a service called Western Newspaper Union which supplied features, serials and other prefabricated material. Other syndicates, such as King Features and McClure, also distributed ready-made, prefabricated material. But the strength of the weekly paper was its independent coverage and its trenchant editorializing. The greatest rural editor was William Allen White who published America's finest weekly in *The Emporia Gazette* a publication which achieved world-wide distinction. In addition to White, such figures as Ed Howe and Harry Golden achieved national and international fame through their weekly publications. Howe, remembered for his novel, *The Story of a Country Town*, also published a rural daily, the *Atchison Globe*, in which his sardonic wit was displayed. Golden is best known for his *Carolina Israelite*. While country papers have declined, larger areas with extensive suburbs, such as Los Angeles, now boast of a number of suburban newspapers, most of which depend heavily on local advertising.

Journalism as a whole leans heavily on advertising and circulation today to keep it viable economically. For, if the press is an institution, it is also a business and must function with economic success if it is to remain in business. Costs of producing and distributing newspapers have risen exorbitantly over the past decade, and yet the owners of a journalistic enterprise—publishers and stockholders—are entitled to expect a fair return on their investment. Most mass media are corporately owned and most are financed by the sale of stock. The basic investment of a newspaper is in the printing plant. This investment cannot be operated at a profit on circulation alone, hence the heavy reliance on advertising. In terms of its economic wealth, the contemporary newspaper is an utter paradox. According to all reports and surveys it is flourishing. Yet, it is dwindling as more newspapers go out of business or merge with the competition. After New York was left with three newspapers out of an original number of fourteen, both *The New York Times* and the *Daily News* tried experimental editions of afternoon newspapers on an internal trial basis. But the experiment ended in the plant. Both papers decided it was too risky to add even one more organ of communication to the extant afternoon daily, the *New York Post*. Time, Inc. also decided to drop its announced intention of acquiring *The Newark Evening News*.

This caution is the trend in contemporary newspaper journalism. Papers that cannot function with economic success are frequently absorbed in mergers where success prevails. And the continuance of mergers, as well as multiple ownership of radio and television stations and newspapers by one management, raises the question of monopoly and the possibility of FCC intervention or Department of Justice investigation in terms of the anti-trust laws. There have been cases where the Supreme Court held that metropolitan newspapers must give up ownership of nearby suburban papers because such ownership violated the anti-trust provisions, but publishers have circumvented this ruling by publishing so-called "satellite" editions. There has been no restriction, however, against two newspapers using the same plant as an economy measure. Indeed, there is evidence to show that, even under the same ownership, morning and afternoon papers compete vigorously against each other for advertising as well as news.

The press today, as a medium of mass communication, is not a series of isolated colonial publications. It is a huge and powerful institution with an enormously delicate and complex involvement—on an international and national scale—in the whole complicated process of influencing and representing public opinion. The newspaper suffers not from a dearth, but from an overflow, of news. And, in the reporting and interpreting of the news, the newspaper becomes an immensely significant force for education and information. As private enterprise, the press is institutionalized, but it is also—and explicitly so—a public service. Newspapers do more than communicate sheer information. News is selected and handled on the basis of value judgments and, as technology increases the scope of newspapers and other media, these media must assume a greater degree of social responsibility in response to a system that permits them to function freely. As free enterprises, the media are accountable not only to the public, but also to other social institutions for their behavior as instruments of communication. The very "reach" of the press, in terms of readers, gives it an opportunity to manipulate as well as report and interpret. News can be slanted and truth distorted. Ethics can be subverted. The press, as do most other media, needs to maintain a delicate balance between the freedom it demands and the moral responsibility which this freedom imposes upon it. For print journalism, more so at this juncture than the electronic media, is unique in that it gives the public partly what the public wants and partly—by means of the editorial position it takes—what it thinks is good for the public. It is this delicate balance of juxtaposing and equating freedom with responsibility which sets American journalism apart from that of Red China or the Soviet Union. But it does more. It requires, particularly because so many cities have only one newspaper, greater fairness and balance in reporting and interpreting the news, as well as in editorializing.

The Press as Mass Medium

The primary function of the contemporary newspaper is to communicate news along with editorial opinion. As a medium of information, the press takes its place as an important adjunct to the school as an educational institution. Fortunately, there is a new breed of journalist who views the press in precisely these terms. Contemporary journalists, now trained in the social sciences and the humanities, practice journalism with professional regard for the press as a medium of education and mass communication.

A newspaper, despite its need to present "the facts," has a point of view which is reflected both in its news columns and on the editorial page and, to some extent, in the columns of its syndicated writers. While the fiercely partisan press of the Seventeenth and Eighteenth Centuries has happily disappeared, it is still difficult to discover a newspaper which is utterly neutral. Nor is it desirable. A newspaper, as a free medium, should have a point of view and should interpret the news in depth. But it must still maintain a balance and an integrity in which the news is not slanted and the editorial, while taking a position, is not false or misleading. Even a degree of partisanship should not be prohibited. But there is a point where espousal must stop in the interest of maintaining accuracy of information. A paper which becomes too involved in advocacy tends to lose its audience, because its essential function as an information and communications medium is compromised. The Canons of Journalism of the American Society of Newspaper Publishers, devised in 1922, established a mode of conduct or Code of Ethics for American journalism. In addition, such an organization as The American Newspaper Guild functions to help preserve the integrity and economic welfare of its members. Many papers which failed to survive blamed their troubles on union pressures and in some cases this was palpably true. At the same time, however, the Guild has done much to eliminate unfair practices, low pay and long hours and has given journalists a necessary bargaining position with management.

Journalism, in addition to its own canons, functions within the framework of American law. Under a democratic government and in a pluralistic society, a newspaper is not prohibited from printing any data it wants to print provided what it prints is not libelous, slanderous or obscene. Even in time of war, the media are quick to impose self-censorship. But a medium like the press is also responsible for what it prints and is susceptible to the laws of libel. As an institution, the press suffers the same limitations and restrictions as other media and other social institutions. The law of the press, as it is called, offers a framework within which a free press can operate. But freedom of the press—or of any other medium—is not something which has been established and then forgotten. It is subject to a continuing struggle, a continuing appraisal and a constant effort by pressure groups to erode it. The Congress spelled out press freedom in the First Amendment when it prohibited itself from passing any law to abridge freedom of speech or the press. This freedom applies to all media, although in the aftermath of the political campaign of 1968, television was attacked from many antagonistic quarters and was obliged to insist that the First Amendment was as applicable to electronic journalism as it was to print. As the difficulties which the television industry faced after the Chicago Convention of 1968 show, however, freedom of the press simply means that what the press does cannot be subject to censorship a priori, or before publication. It does not imply the license to print anything at all, and it is subject to legal review as well as to the pressure of public opinion. The issues involved, however, are seldom of a polarized nature. In most instances, the rule of reason prevails and media stop short of engaging in practices which are contrary both to the law and the public interest.

The fact of the matter is that it is not a democratic society alone which has made freedom possible for the media. It is the press, and other mass media, which are equally responsible for the successful functioning of a democratic and pluralistic society. Mass media such as the press and television are the most powerful forces in society for creating an informed public opinion. In terms of sheer technical facilities, the media are unsurpassed for the speedy gathering and transmission of news. And, in terms of content, there is little doubt that both print and electronic journalists are the best informed communicators to be found anywhere in the civilized world. In a society which is almost universally literate, almost everyone has access to print or electronic journalism. No other institution has the scope and authority of the press in informing, reflecting and influencing public opinion. Yet, the relationship of the press to the central government has always been, and is today, a delicate and troubled one. In the Johnson Administration, readers of newspapers were told of the existence of a "credibility gap." The administrations of Presidents Eisenhower and Kennedy came under fire, in varying degrees, for an alleged failure to give reporters open sesame to the news. Indeed, there have been few, if any, political administrations which have failed to irritate the press on the question of free access. And this in itself is a healthy sign. Newspapers, always on their mettle, have argued vigorously to preserve their right to receive and report the news. As recently as the 1968 political conventions, the electronic media were forced to insist that their equipment be permitted to be set up so that radio and television journalists could have adequate access to coverage of the convention events. And the press has the right to cover unless it can be demonstrated categorically that such coverage would be contrary to the national interest. The coverage of the Chicago riots was clearly in the public interest.

From time to time, newspapers and other media have been accused of corrupting the news. Certainly, particularly in the colonial period, there have been venal and biased editors. Reporters also have been accused of slanting their stories. Publishers have been scored for harassing liberal writers and for insisting on a conservative point of view. But these cases, while they occur, are rare. Few trained journalists would fail to resist editorial or owner pressure to slant the news. Few contemporary editors would exert such pressure. More important, however, are the pressures from without, particularly from government. For the attitude of each administration is critically important in maintaining a free press. The greater the difficulty in gaining access to news, the greater the credibility gap between government and the mass media. The press has an obligation to go beyond the press release or the "tip" or "leak" in an effort to get all of the news and to report it fairly and impartially. It is the maintaining of a healthy interaction between the press and society, between the newspaper and the reader, which is the basis for a truly democratic society. And, in this context, American journalism, despite its limitations and its problems, gives to its readers the most accurate information and the most unbiased coverage of the news of any other press system in the world.

BIBLIOGRAPHY

Armstrong, William M. *E. L. Godkin and American Foreign Policy, 1865–1900.* New York: Bookman Associates, 1957.

Barrett, James W. *Joseph Pulitzer and His World.* New York: Vanguard Press, Inc., 1941.

Berger, Meyer. *The Story of The New York Times, 1851–1951.* New York: Simon and Schuster, 1951.

Bird, George L. and Frederic E. Merwin. *The Press and Society.* New York: Prentice-Hall, Inc., 1952.

Brown, Francis. *Raymond of The Times.* New York: Norton, 1951.

Bryan, Clark W. *The Progress of American Journalism, as Illustrated by the Reminiscences of Horace Greeley.* Holyoke, Massachusetts: 1885.

Buranelli, Vincent, ed. *The Trial of Peter Zenger.* New York: New York University Press, 1957.

Carlson, Oliver. *Brisbane: A Candid Biography*. New York: Stackpole Sons, 1937.

Childs, Marquis and James B. Reston, eds. *Walter Lippmann and his Times*. New York: Harcourt, Brace and Company, 1959.

Clough, Frank L. *William Allen White of Emporia*. New York: McGraw Hill, Inc., 1941.

Cooper, Kent. *Kent Cooper and the Associated Press*. New York: Random House, 1959.

Daniels, Josephus. *Tar Heel Editor*. Chapel Hill: University of North Carolina Press, 1939.

Day, Benjamin H. *Day's Rapid Shading Medium for Artist's Use in Lithography and Photography*. New York: The Smith Publishing Co., 189?

DeArmond, Anna Janney. *Andrew Bradford, Colonial Journalist*. Newark: University of Delaware Press, 1949.

Dennis, Charles H. *Victor Lawson: His Time and His Work*. Chicago: University of Chicago Press, 1952.

Emery, Edwin. *History of the American Newspaper Publishers Association*. Minneapolis: University of Minnesota Press, 1950.

———. *The Press and America: An Interpretative History of Journalism*. New York: Prentice-Hall, Inc., 1954, 1962.

Ford, Edwin H. and Edwin Emery, eds. *Highlights in the History of the American Press*. Minneapolis: University of Minnesota Press, 1954.

Franklin, Benjamin. *The Autobiography of Benjamin Franklin*. New York: Century Company, 1901.

———. *The Papers of Benjamin Franklin*. Vol. I. New Haven: Yale University Press, 1959.

Garst, Robert E., ed. *The Newspaper—Its Making and Its Meaning*. New York: Charles Scribner's Sons, 1945.

Grambling, Oliver. *AP: The Story of News*. New York: Farrar and Rinehart, Inc., 1940.

Green, Bartholomew. *The Printer's Advertisement*. Boston, 1701.

Harper, Robert S. *Lincoln and the Press*. New York: McGraw-Hill Book Company, 1951.

Hart, Jim Allee. *A History of the St. Louis Globe-Democrat*. Columbia: University of Missouri Press, 1961.

Hecht, Ben and Charles Mac Arthur. *The Front Page* in Bennet Cerf, ed. *Sixteen Famous American Plans*. New York, 1941.

Hohenberg, John. *The News Media: A Journalist Looks at His Profession*. New York: Holt, Rinehart and Winston, 1968.

Johnson, Icie F. *William Rockhill Nelson and the Kansas City Star*. Kansas City: Burton Publishing Company, 1935.

Johnson, Walter. *William Allen White's America*. New York: Henry Holt and Company, 1947.

Lee, Alfred McClung. *The Daily Newspaper in America: The Evolution of Social Instrument*. New York: Macmillan, 1937.

Liebling, A. J. *The Press*. New York: Ballantine Books, 1961.

Lindstrom, Carl E. *The Fading American Newspaper*. New York: Doubleday and Company, 1960.

Milton, John. *Areo Pagitica*. Cambridge, England: Cambridge University Press, 1918.

Mott, Frank Luther. *American Journalism: A History of Newspapers*. New York: Macmillan, 1941.

———. ed., *The Case and Trial of John Peter Zenger*. Columbia, Missouri: Press of the Crippled Turtle, 1954.

Muddiman, J. G. "Benjamin Harris, The First American Journalist" in *Notes and Queries* (1932), Vol. 163, pp. 129–133; 147–150; 166–170.

Nixon, Raymond B. *Henry W. Grady: Spokesman of the New South*. New York: Alfred A. Knopf, Inc., 1943.

Ogden, Rollo. *Life and Letters of Edwin Lawrence Godkin*. New York: The Macmillan Company, 1907.

Perkin, Robert L. *The First Hundred Years: An Informal History of Denver and the Rocky Mountain News*. Garden City, New York: Doubleday and Company, 1959.

Pultizer Publishing Company. *The Story of the St. Louis Post-Dispatch*. St. Louis, 1954.

Rutherford, Livingston. *John Peter Zenger*. New York: Peter Smith, 1941.

Seitz, Don C. *The James Gordon Bennetts*. Indianapolis: Bobbs-Merrill Company, 1928.

Shipton, Clifford Kenyon. *Isiah Thomas, Printer, Patriot and Philanthropist 1749–1831*. Rochester. New York: Printing House of Leo Hart, 1948.

Stewart, Kenneth and John Tebbel. *Makers of Modern Journalism*. New York: Prentice-Hall, Inc., 1952.

Stoddard, Henry L. *Horace Greeley: Printer, Editor, Crusader*. New York: G. P. Putnam's Sons, 1946.

Stone, Candace. *Dana and The Sun*. New York: Dodd, Mead and Company, 1938.

Swanberg, W. A. *Citizen Hearst*. New York: Charles Scribner's Sons, 1961.

Talese, Gay. *The Kingdom and the Power*. New York: New American Library, 1969.

Tebbel, John. *The Compact History of the American Newspaper*. Hawthorne Books, Inc., 1963.

———. *An American Dynasty*. New York: Doubleday and Company, 1947.

Van Doren, Carl. *Benjamin Franklin*. New York: The Viking Press, 1938.

Villard, Oswald Garrison. *The Disappearing Daily*. New York: Alfred A. Knopf, Inc., 1944.

Wall, Joseph F. *Henry Watterson: Reconstructed Rebel*. New York: Oxford University Press, 1956.

Weingast, David E. *Walter Lippmann*. New Brunswick: Rutgers University Press, 1949.

White, William Allen. *The Autobiography of William Allen White*. New York: The Macmillan Company, 1946.

———. *Forty Years on Main Street*. New York: Farrar and Rinehart, Inc., 1937.

Wroth, Lawrence D. *The Colonial Printer*. Portland, Maine: Southworth-Anthonensen Press, 1938.

6

The Dilemma
of the American Magazine

IN A BUSINESS and financial page survey of the status of the American magazine industry, vintage Spring, 1969, *The New York Times* concluded that magazines were "thriving despite a few dramatic failures." The facts and figures extant, and the optimistic picture delineated by the Magazine Publishers Association, were impressive. The magazine industry was flourishing, at least in terms of revenues, although the business aspect had no relevance to the social impact of the magazine, when compared to media such as radio and television, as a medium of communication.

In 1968, 100 new magazines were started, and all but 21 survived. Over the past decade, in fact, 676 new magazines were published in the United States, and only 162 went out of business—an impressive statistic. Furthermore, circulation and advertising revenues were at an all time high during this period. This meant that advertisers were still, and despite television, buying considerable space in magazines. For the life blood of the commercial magazine flows from advertising revenues. Magazines, like television, sell advertising on the basis of what it will cost to reach each thousand readers, the so-called cost-per-thousand basis. This figure, it should be emphasized, is not a circulation estimate, but a readership parameter. A national magazine such as *Life*, for example, has a circulation of 8½ million and charges slightly under $65,000 for one page of non-color advertising space. But *The New York Times* quoted the president of Time, Inc. as informing the stockholders that *Life*'s audience, or its *readership*, had climbed "to forty-eight million viewers, bigger than any regular TV program." When compared to television over any period of time, this figure simply does not have much validity, but in terms of sophisticated public relations it obviously has impact. Taken literally, "viewers" may mean no more than the fact that *Life*'s constituents merely saw the cover without reading the magazine.

Significantly, the term "viewers" was used, because television, more than any other single factor, has been responsible for the dilemma of the contemporary magazine. For, despite optimistic reports, the magazine in America has faced the problem of how to achieve and maintain economic viability in the face of the continuing inroads of television, rising costs of printing and paper, increased postal rates and the difficulty of securing a flow of material from top-flight writers. The demise of *The Saturday Evening Post,* the most famous and successful of all American magazines climaxed a decade of declining fortunes for some of the greatest of popular publications. In succession, *Colliers, Liberty, The American Magazine, Woman's Home Companion* and *Coronet* went out of business. In most cases, the reason attributed was the phenomenal growth of television, along with the fact that the younger advertising agency executives were conditioned by a television-oriented environment.

The magazine world has attempted to resolve its problems through a number of efforts. In particular, there has been an enormous thrust toward research, designed to convince potential advertisers that, among the media of communication, magazines are still a worthwhile economic investment. Elaborate research on demographics and reader psychology is accompanied by the offer of attractive special regional issues, extra promotion and similar merchandising devices. The magazine industry also cites rising television costs, along with the fact that increased literacy and educational opportunity is creating a new reading audience for periodical publications of all kinds, to support its case for a share of the advertising dollar. But the fact remains that the face of the magazine medium is changing. The large, popular, mass circulation, "typically American" magazine like *The Saturday Evening Post* has disappeared from the mass communications world. The magazine field is becoming a highly specialized medium, exemplified by such publications as *Psychology Today,* which strives for a subscription audience of those interested in popular psychology; *TV Guide,* which combines regional weekly television listings with attractive art and features; or *Playboy,* which is designed primarily for the male reader. And those once popular general magazines, such as *Redbook,* have survived only after a long uphill battle to find a readership that would give them economic viability. *Redbook* has found this readership in the young, middle class housewife. In an age of mass communication, other magazines have had to relinquish the traditional goal of broad, general and popular middle class appeal and seek out large but specialized audiences, based in large measure on demographic and psychological criteria and buttressed by special promotional efforts.

From both an economic and social standpoint, however, the magazine in America has been a more perishable commodity than the other mass media. While there are upwards of 9,000 such publications, running the widest possible gamut of interests, no other medium has suffered the same kind of cataclysmic fallout as have magazines. The industry has seen publications grow to gigantic heights only to encounter difficulties and finally to give up the struggle to survive. This has not been equally true of book publishing, motion pictures or newspapers, and the television medium has grown at a pace unprecedented in the history of any of the media. From their very beginnings, however, the fortunes of great magazines—despite phenomenal growth—have tended to rise and fall. And, paradoxically, it has not been the gigantic, large circulation publications that have been able to ride out the storms, but publications that are relatively circumscribed in clientele such as *The Atlantic* or *Harper's* or the more erudite literary and critical publications such as *Partisan Review* and *Commentary*.

Origins of the Magazine

The magazine, like the book and the newspaper, was brought to America from Europe where magazine publishing had originated. The first tentative magazines, which may have been produced in France, were little more than pamphlets, and their function was to describe the contents of various books on sale at the booksellers. Indeed, the booksellers, many of whom were also printers, published these items as a kind of promotional literature for their line of books. *The Tatler* and *The Spectator*, to which Addison and Steele contributed their urbane and witty essays, were not magazines in the contemporary sense of the term, but a kind of literary newsletter. The essays themselves became landmarks in the history of English literature and prototypes of all that is considered great in the art of essay writing. Nor was Daniel DeFoe's pamphlet "The Shortest Way With Dissenters," a political-religious tract, strictly speaking a magazine. Thrown into prison because of the point of view he expressed, DeFoe eventually emerged from prison and brought out "The Review," a small publication containing diverse material.

In the sense that a magazine is a publication that is issued periodically and contains a variety of literary material, the first such publication was the *Gentleman's Magazine* which appeared in England in 1721. It did cover a variety of contemporary phenomena such as politics, songs, essays and even mundane news events, and it was distinguished by the 'byline' of Samuel Johnson who served as editor before embarking on his own ventures of *The Idler* and *The Rambler*. Publications such as *Gentleman's Magazine*, as well as several of the popular pamphlets, were brought to the colonies where there was a great hunger for information on the part of those who had left England and settled in America.

The earliest efforts at periodical publishing in the colonies were virtual facsimiles of original English publications. It is not surprising, then, that Benjamin Franklin should be identified with the first magazines, as he was with the first newspaper. It was Franklin who published the *Gen-*

eral Magazine in Philadelphia, a city which was to become famous for the many successful magazines issued under the imprimatur of the Curtis Publishing Company at Independence Square. Franklin's periodical, however, enjoyed a very brief span and became defunct within a year. But throughout the Eighteenth Century, a number and variety of magazines were issued. Some historians estimate that at least a hundred publications appeared between 1741 and 1800, most of them a kind of hybrid publication which took on the attributes of both newspaper and magazine in form and substance. Associated with these publications were many figures who became strongly identified with both politics and literature, such as Noah Webster and Tom Paine. But none of these periodicals survived longer than a year. They boasted little, if any, advertising and had no newsstand circulation.

The Nineteenth Century did not begin auspiciously for the magazine as a mass medium. One Joseph Dennie issued a literate and urbane essay-type publication called *The Port-Folio* to which John Quincy contributed. It was distinguished both for the literacy of its presentation, as well as for its categorical support of the British Crown in the growing tension between England and the Colonies. But *The Port-Folio* also enjoyed the unique distinction of surviving, for it remained a fairly popular magazine for the next quarter of a century. There were other random periodicals, but only one was to have an enduring influence on the history of magazine journalism in America. That publication was the world-famous *Saturday Evening Post* which first saw publication along about 1730 and which survived, despite years of tribulation, until 1968 when it finally ceased publication after a heroic struggle to remain in business.

Prior to the appearance of *The Saturday Evening Post,* no other magazine had become either a commercial or journalistic success. The longest survival period of any periodical was the twenty-five year span achieved by *The North American Review* which included among its contributors many of the literary giants of the period. Two magazines which were popular for a time, but which failed to survive, were *Godey's Lady's Book* and *The Knickerbocker. Godey's Lady's Book,* the forerunner of the popular women's magazines of the Twentieth Century, was edited by Sarah Josepha Hale, a stalwart supporter of women's rights. *The Knickerbocker,* to which Washington Irving contributed, was a humorous and sophisticated magazine. Still other popular magazines were *The Southern Literary Messenger* which included the work of Edgar Allen Poe, *Harper's Monthly, The Atlantic Monthly* and *Leslie's Magazine. Leslie's* managed to remain in print until after the First World War. Published by Frank Leslie, it became an enormously popular publication throughout the Civil War period, but it could survive neither the increasing costs nor the competition of the Twentieth Century.

The Magazine Comes of Age

It was *The Saturday Evening Post* which was to become the phenomenal success of all magazine journalism. Although popular legend credits Benjamin Franklin as the founder, Richard Wolseley and other magazine historians show that the *Post* actually was established by Samuel Atkinson and Charles Alexander in 1821. The magazine became an enormous success, the most influential weekly periodical in America and the journalistic niche of some of the most gifted and popular writers on the American scene. The history of the *Post*, however, shows that it was not without its periods of difficulty. Its large circulation diminished after the Civil War, until it was purchased by Cyrus Curtis for a modest sum at the turn of the century. Curtis revived the publication, and thereby established one of the greatest of publishing organizations, an empire which was to have a unique and profound—if not always the most salutory or intellectual—impact on American life, manners and mores. Curtis' choice of George H. Lorimer as a kind of interregnum editor may have been fortuitous, but it was a brilliant one, for Lorimer turned the *Post* into a great, but essentially conservative, business-oriented middle class magazine, the quintessence of what has currently become known as "Establishment." No event in American journalism better indicates the temper of a changing time than the passing of *The Saturday Evening Post* in 1968. It was published for an America that had finally outgrown it, and, despite heroic efforts to bring it up to date, it failed to regenerate, because it attracted neither advertisers nor readers in sufficient numbers to keep it economically viable.

On the other hand, two less phenomenally successful—and quite different—Nineteenth Century magazines managed to survive and are even flourishing at the present time. These are *The Atlantic Monthly* and *Harper's*. The former, published at the same address in Boston since its founding, is now known simply as *The Atlantic*. It began as a literate and literary magazine, and its direction was toward "high culture" rather than popular entertainment or homiletics. But it made a reputation for itself among a loyal group of readers interested in a serious, but not necessarily highbrow, treatment of literature, psychology, education, politics, economics, medicine and sociology. *The Atlantic*, like *Harper's*, is a quasi-scholarly magazine written for the reader who is interested in ideas. Associated with it were such figures as William Dean Howells, James Russell Lowell and its brilliant editor, Ellery Sedgwick.

Harper's, published today as an adjunct of the book house of Harper & Row, appeared originally under many titles: *Harper's Weekly, Harper's New Monthly*, and *Harper's Monthly*. Similar in style and content to *Scribner's Magazine* and *Putnam's Magazine*—both were the products of book publishers, but neither survived the competition—*Harper's*, like

The Atlantic, managed to survive primarily because of the editorial genius of its editors. Both *Harper's* and *The Atlantic* still publish excellent articles, stories and poems directed toward the educated, upper middle class reader. Both are essentially literary, as well as liberal, in outlook. Neither magazine is particularly esoteric, and both eschew the arcane intellectualism and the obscure semantics of the consciously "literary" publications or reviews. It is encouraging, as well as significant, that both *Harper's* and *The Atlantic* have increased both circulation and readership in recent years. Recently, *Harper's* has changed its format and is publishing fewer, but longer, articles of general interest.

Many of the once popular middle class periodicals, however, are not surviving the Twentieth Century. *Colliers, Woman's Home Companion* and *American Magazine* ceased publication a few years prior to the demise of *The Saturday Evening Post.* Those that remain in publication have altered their editorial format radically by selling to a large, but still circumscribed audience, and by a variety of promotional techniques designed to attract readers and advertisers. Popularization—and frequently vulgarization—of personal problems, largely relating to dating, sex and marriage, are featured in many of what were once dignified family periodicals. At the same time, a publication like *The Reader's Digest* continues to flourish on the popular and conservative basis established by De Witt Wallace, its publisher, although the *Digest* a few years ago succumbed to the lure of advertising. The *Digest,* along with *Time* and the Book-of-the-Month Club were the outstanding publishing phenomena of the first half of the Twentieth Century, and *The Reader's Digest* magazine achieved the unprecedented circulation of more than ten million. The news magazines, such as *Time, Newsweek* and *U.S. News and World Report* and the combined picture and text publications, such as *Life, Look* and *Ebony,* have also achieved a phenomenal success, but each has had to fend off the growing competition of television during the past decade. Time, Inc. showed a loss in its financial report of April 1969, and *Life's* circulation has consistently diminished in recent years. Significantly, *TV Guide,* a publication which grew with the development of the television medium boasts a circulation of more than twelve million.

Magazines as Mass Media

Clearly, the magazine, as a medium of mass communication, encompasses an area so broad as to include virtually every educational, social, political and economic interest of contemporary man. The field is literally all embracing and includes periodicals that cover every phase of man's social and cultural and economic life—consumer magazines, news magazines, business magazines, literary magazines, professional and scientific journals, picture and text publications, digest type periodicals, academic publications, men's magazines, women's magazines, children's magazines, trade magazines, house organs, government publications, political magazines—magazines, in short, covering virtually an infinity of subjects. Taken together, these magazines become an integral part of the world of mass media, more circumscribed in scope and reach than television, but nevertheless covering literally every subject under the sun. The largest circulation newspaper in America, *The New York Daily News,* does boast a circulation far greater than the average among the thousands of periodicals in existence, but such phenomena as the *Reader's Digest, Life* and *Look* far exceed the great newspapers in circulation, because they are truly national magazines, with consumer outlets throughout the country and even the world.

As a mass medium, the magazine is as much a journalistic enterprise as the newspaper. But its function differs from the newspaper in that its objective is not to offer hard news, but rather entertainment, analysis and interpretation. The large national magazines embrace a multitude of editorial activities. *Life,* for example, may combine a serious scientific picture essay along with a political editorial and a probe into the life and times of rock-and-roll. Other publications are more circumscribed and limited in scope, and may deal variously with such diverse subjects as popular science, homemaking, erotica, news interpretation and a variety of other matters. The more serious publications, such as *Harper's* or *Saturday Review* have a distinct editorial point of view, tend to print "in-depth" articles on the great issues of the day and strive not only to inform but to serve as a stimulus for reflective thinking on the part of their readers. It is perhaps significant that the once great national magazines like *The Saturday Evening Post* and *Colliers* were edited primarily to entertain. With the advent of television many of these magazines went out of business.

Despite various estimates from diverse sources, the total number of magazines published in the United States has been estimated as low as 9,000 and as high as 16,000. By comparison, it is known that there are approximately 1,700 daily newspapers, 7,500 weekly papers, 6,000 radio stations and 600 commercial television stations now in existence. The grist for these giant communications enterprises comes from wire services and syndicates, staff writers, special and general columnists and commentators, special writers and editors and free lance journalists in various fields. Despite the fact that many well-known magazines are economically successful, the magazine—far more so than the newspaper—continues to encounter difficulties. These difficulties are due to the inroads of television in part, but they are also due to editorial and business mismanagement, rising costs and the growth of paperback books. At one time, the magazine's ability to convey news in greater depth than the newspaper was a strong asset. With the growing popularity of news interpretation on television and in the newspaper, even the weekly news magazines find themselves with new and potent competition. Television itself has instituted programs, such as "60 Minutes," which function as self-styled magazines of the air.

Because magazines cover so broad a spectrum, it is difficult to find either a dictionary definition or a functional one which could conceivably distill the multiplicity of interests and subjects covered by the thousands of extant periodicals. Journals of opinion, far different from the popular national publications, are magazines. Reviews, like the *Antioch Review*, are also classified as magazines. The magazine is distinguished less by arbitrary definition than by function and scope. It is usually a paper covered periodical, published at regular intervals, with varied text (or text and pictures) and usually, although not invariably, with advertising material. But not even this description takes into consideration such publications as *The New York Times Sunday Magazine* or the weekly newspaper supplements such as *Parade* or the late *This Week*. And, of all the thousands of periodicals in print, only about fifty boast a circulation of one million or more.

The magazine industry, in all of its varied ramifications, considers itself an important and integral part of American journalism, a potent aspect of the mainstream of mass communication. Magazines, like newspapers, derive revenue from newsstand and subscription circulation, as well as from advertising. They cover an enormous range of topics and disciplines. In one way or another, they entertain, they inform, they contribute to economic growth and abundance, they analyze contemporary problems and they attempt—implicitly or explicitly—to influence and reflect public opinion. As a mass medium, a great number of magazines exercise a degree of social control. Magazines, too, are uniquely different from newspapers in that far more care is lavished on their design, typography, color printing and layout. They are sold more through subscription and the mails than are books or newspapers.

The Magazine and Social Issues

Yet this fascinating medium faces the dilemma of where to go next in an electronic age. Even publications like *Time* and *Newsweek*, which appear weekly, must find a new way to tackle the news in an age of instant communication and replay. Cultural lag is nowhere more in evidence than in this medium. Furthermore, as Roland E. Wolseley has pointed out, the advertising in many magazines is not only far more attractive than the articles or stories, but tends to interfere with and vitiate the impact of the regular text. Competition from electronic media, as well as from other magazines of the same kind, has endowed the magazine industry with a stimulating, but precarious, way of life.

The popular, consumer magazines which depend heavily on advertising for survival must operate at a profit in order to survive. Their objective is analogous with, but not identical to, other mass media such as radio and television, in that they strive to reach large masses of readers. Their audience is heterogeneous, but they aim primarily at the large, middle-class, middle-income reader. A large proportion of their public is women, and a good many of their audience tend to read selectively and to look primarily at the advertisements, which, unfortunately both for aesthetics and general readability, are so placed as to interfere with the flow and sequence of stories and articles. The notable exceptions are publications like *Harper's* and *The Atlantic* which take pains to preserve the integrity and comprehensibility of their editorial material by separating it completely from the advertisements. It is ironic that many of the very magazines which are most critical of television commercials violate, in their own way, the spirit of sound editorial presentation by tasteless and irritating placement of product advertisements.

Because the national consumer periodicals appeal to a wide common denominator, they are basically quasi-intellectual in thrust and outlook. Their appeal is popular, and the subjects covered are romantic fiction, sex, crime, mystery, homemaking, along with an occasional article of broad cultural interest. Most of the general magazines take pains to avoid offending the middle class reader, although a new sexual permissiveness has permeated many magazines which at one time would have rejected subject matter now considered acceptable and even necessary. What were once called the "slicks" such as *Life* or *Look*, have aimed traditionally at a slightly higher audience income and educational level.

It might conceivably be argued that the problems all of these middle income magazines have encountered over the past decade stem not only from the competition of other mass media, but also from their own reluctance to tackle issues which have become of critical importance to millions of young readers—the black revolution, the student rebellion and the urban crisis. These overriding social problems have become so all-pervasive that some national magazines have begun to recognize their importance and their interest to the reader over the past few years. But for most of this century, many of the national magazines behaved editorially as though social issues did not exist. This persistence in perpetuating the myth of an America that no longer existed is at least one sound reason for so many readers abandoning magazines. *The Reader's Digest*, for example, still appeals to millions of middle and upper income Americans. But many of the aggressive younger public, sensitive to the great social issues of the time, have criticized publications of this kind for alleged conservatism, for a tradition-directed point of view and for a naive optimism which is neither fashionable nor germane in a world in turmoil. In the main, the periodicals which manage to survive are those which continue to appeal to large, yet circumscribed, audiences.

The popular movie and television fan magazines which explore the loves and lives of glamorous stars; the publications dealing with romantic confession and pseudo-psychology; and the special publications for men and women, such as *Esquire* or *Town and Country*, remain popular and economically viable.

The weekly news and business magazines are a unique entity, aimed partly for the general public, and yet also directed in large measure to the upper stratum of reader, both economically and educationally. In 1923, Henry Luce produced a new kind of magazine destined, like the *Reader's Digest* and the Book-of-the-Month Club, to become a dynamic force in American journalism. The magazine was *Time*, and it set the tone for a novel and provocative direction in magazine journalism, exemplified also by *Newsweek* and, to some extent, by *U.S. News and World Report* and *Business Week*. The technique of the news magazine usually is not to originate or to innovate. *Time* and *Newsweek*, to a great extent, are a combination of originality and derivativeness. They strive to analyze news stories that have already appeared in other media and to interpret the news with an editorial and stylistic approach which is uniquely their own. With these objectives, *Time* and *Newsweek* have become a kind of hybrid journalistic creation between the conventional newspaper and the conventional magazine. *Time*, in particular, for many years developed a "journalese" of its own, concise, terse and elliptical which became known and, for a while imitated, as "*Time* style." It has largely abandoned this style for a more conventional approach. But *Time* also has been criticized by its detractors for what they believe is a narrow and slanted editorial viewpoint, along with a tendency to make unsubstantiated observations and occasional unwarranted conclusions. To the accusation that it lacks journalistic objectivity, supporters of *Time* have asserted, first, that a news magazine cannot be all things to all men and, secondly, that its editorial viewpoint is clear-cut, overt and, therefore, legitimate.

The Time, Inc. empire also publishes *Fortune*, a beautifully produced magazine for the American business man, as well as *Sports Illustrated* and *Life*, in addition to its growing book publishing interests and its television stations. *Life* achieved a remarkable success and, despite the tremendous impact of television and the erosion of advertising, both *Life* and the enormously successful *Look* continue to be bought by several million readers each week. Both magazines have shown a remarkable facility to juxtapose the most plebeian articles and the sensational exposé or essay along with popularly cultural presentations on subjects ranging from Medieval Art to the latest developments in the birth control pill, space science or religion. In the area of the rapidly growing black market, *Ebony*, a picture and text publication, has attracted a large reading public along with increased national advertising.

But the magazine market, in particular, is rough on competition. Such potential challengers to *Life* as *Pix* and *Click* were simply unable to overcome the brutally competitive struggle for survival in this mass medium, and their appearance was short-lived.

The Special Magazines

Certain magazines that appear to survive best, in fact, are those which tend to subordinate advertising to editorial content, and which depend upon subscriptions from a loyal and intellectually superior reading public. Greatly influential in this field are *The Nation, The New Republic, Harper's, The Atlantic, The Commonweal, the* conservative *National Review* and, more recently, the new magazine simply called *New York.* These are journals of opinion—literary, educational, cultural, social and political. Students of magazine journalism, and certainly devotees of *The Nation* and *The New Republic,* believe that both are superb examples of magazines of social comment. But these publications also have had their critical detractors and, indeed, *The Nation* was banned from some school libraries until it was reinstated after protest by civil liberties organizations. *The Nation* was founded by William Godkin as a magazine for "the thinking masses" and, from its inception, it has published articles by a long list of distinguished editors and contributors of the calibre of Joseph Wood Krutch and others.

Unique in the magazine field is *The New Yorker* which, despite its apparently limited sophistication and urbanity, has maintained a consistently loyal readership and which has published many outstanding stories, poems, essays and editorials. Harold Ross, for many years its eccentric and brilliant editor, revealed how, by establishing and adhering to specific standards, a magazine can achieve a signal success. Ross knew precisely the editorial touch he wanted to attain, the level of reader he wanted to reach. As a result, *The New Yorker* has been a consistent success, the only change in many years being the insertion of a table of contents in 1969. *The New Yorker,* in its viewpoint, has been more than smart or sophisticated. It has revealed, on more than one occasion, a keen awareness of social problems, an editorial conscience and a penchant for political commentary and satire which is both sharp and frequently devastatingly accurate. This unique publication, too, has managed to keep its editorial viewpoint astutely tuned to the temper of the times. Its profiles of personalities have been variously brilliant and caustic, compassionate and trenchant. While many have tried, no publication has been able to emulate successfully the singular quality of *The New Yorker—* or, for that matter, *The Reader's Digest.* They remain unique in a fiercely competitive arena.

Whether specialized in nature or not, it is clear that most magazines which aim at any large segment of the public, and particularly those which strive for the widest common denominator, must function in an economically viable way if they are to survive in the fiercely competitive world of mass communication. Magazines, unlike television stations, are not licensed by any agency of the government. Like newspapers, they are free and independent and subject only to the laws of libel and obscenity and to the postal regulations which apply to them.

Freedom and License

Like newspapers, magazines are subsumed under the protection of the First Amendment. They cannot, of course, encroach on copyright ownership or invade anyone's right to privacy. The whole question of what is libelous and when the right to privacy is invaded is, indeed, a difficult one. It is not easy to prove precise and definite intent to ridicule or demean an individual's reputation, just as it is not easy to prove intent to provoke violence. Obviously, in the use of photographs and text, magazines walk a thin line, but one criterion cited has been the degree of news interest and the right of the magazine to access in covering individuals and events which are clearly in the area of the public's right to know. The activities of some individuals are, by their very nature, not private, but utterly public in nature. On the whole, while some magazines have come under fire for obscenity, they have not suffered censorship except in a time of emergency and, even during periods of war, censorship by all the media has been voluntary. Only the post office, at least in theory, can censor the magazine by restricting second class mailing privileges, but in this event the authorities must prove that the publication is obscene, libelous or seditious. In 1969, President Nixon, stating that "American homes are being bombarded with the largest volume of sex-oriented mail in history," asked the Congress for specific laws to curb this abuse. Acknowledging that many publications do claim protection under the "broad umbrella" of the First Amendment, President Nixon urged three specific steps be taken. Primarily, he urged a law against the use of the mails or other facilities of commerce to deliver material which contained sexual references which might be inimical to the best interests of anyone under eighteen years of age. Secondly, he proposed a law to bar the mails for the "commercial exploitation of prurient interest in sex through advertising." And thirdly, the President urged an expansion of a 1967 law to enable the reader in his home to be protected from "the intrusion of sex-oriented advertising." It is significant, however, that the President's message also included what many social scientists—sociologists, psychologists and students of the effects of mass-media—have long believed, that in the long run only the public itself can reject what is shoddy and meretricious in mass media.

The growing sensationalism in many magazines is due, in part, to competition. The inroads of television and, perhaps surprisingly, newsstand competition from paperback books also has created a change in the character and outlook of magazine journalism. Paradoxically, even with greater technical facilities and newer printing and color reproduction technologies, fewer of the traditional magazines manage to survive. Nothing revealed the end of a substantial era in magazine publishing more than the passing of *The Saturday Evening Post*. Those publications which are surviving have done so by means of astute editorial judgment, along with aggressive efforts in the direction of advertising, promotion and research. The basic purpose of research, such as that done by the Magazine Advertising Bureau, is to convince the advertiser that magazines are his best and most inexpensive market. To gather sufficient impressive data together, magazines have engaged in an aggressive research campaign in the areas of readership, reader interest and orientation, editorial subject matter, and preferred layout and typography. Research is done geographically, in terms of the distribution of the media audience. Questions asked in magazine research attempt to discover which segments of the general population read the particular publication, the economic status of the readers and their educational and social background.

Magazine Research

Apart from promotion and advertising, magazine research is also interested in who reads what and why. The editorial departments have been more concerned, in recent years, with the reader's opinion of content, while the advertising department wants to determine how the reader reacts to specific copy and layout. Several research organizations send periodic questionnaires to segments of the public in order to find out why readers prefer one magazine over another. Various research techniques used by magazines—and indeed by all media—include the survey or questionnaire, returnable by mail; telephone calls to readers; analysis of letters from readers; and in-depth studies of what motivations are involved in consumer buying habits. From these research findings, magazine research departments frequently publish elaborate promotional brochures, designed to show the advertiser why a particular publication is his best "buy."

In addition to conventional research techniques, many periodicals have conducted special readability studies, such as those pioneered by Rudolf Flesch. Dr. Flesch devised special studies of readability for both newspapers and magazines, based on an analysis of style, grammar, length of sentences and other carefully structured parameters. While there are those who look with considerable dubiety on these and, indeed, on most research techniques, they do offer the only pragmatic and feasible means available for measuring various factors. While there is some justification for the criticism that a clever researcher can manipulate data to suit his ends, it is nevertheless true that a considerable body of research does have at least some validity if only because present techniques, however limited and open to manipulation, are still the best and, indeed, the only ones available.

Research in the effects of magazines has not as yet produced any more productive yield than studies in the effects of other of the mass media. Effects of magazines, in fact, should be studied in inter-media terms, for what little is known of effect appears to apply with equal weight to all of the media. Like television, magazines exert social influence and act to some extent as an agency of social control, but sensitivity to opinions and their changing content indicates that, like other media, they tend essentially to reflect the society they serve. Magazine journalism, too, bears social responsibility. A periodical, regardless of its purpose, is responsible for its editorial substance. It is equally responsible for the acceptance, or rejection, of advertising in terms of whether the advertiser's product and message meets the publication's standards of taste and acceptability and, ultimately, the public's standards.

The dilemma of the contemporary magazine is not only one of economics, but also one of ethics. Faced with increasingly fierce competition from the other mass media, particularly television and paperbacks, magazine journalism is tempted to lower its standards of taste and to sensationalize and over-popularize in order to attract readers and advertisers. At the same time, there is the temptation to play it safe, to accept the traditional or peer-group point of view and to avoid facing the great social and cultural issues that demand recognition by the mass media. The dilemma centers basically over the question of maintaining economic status against the need, indeed the obligation, to remain aware of economic, academic, racial and political issues and to tackle these issues with what has come to be termed "fairness and balance." Magazine journalism ponders the question of providing provocative material for its mass of readers while recognizing and fulfilling its social responsibility. This responsibility, of course, varies because of the different nature and purpose of the many kinds of magazines in print. But almost all periodicals have certain basic obligations, the first of which is a healthy respect for the opinions of mankind and a need to treat its readers like intelligent adults. The news magazines, in particular, while exerting a strong force in the area of public opinion certainly should not attempt to manipulate opinion by slanting of the news.

In general, critics of the popular consumer magazines find that they tend, as other media are accused of doing, to aim for the lowest common denominator and that they are timid about raising their editorial standards. With the exception of the self-styled and avowedly "liberal" publications, magazines have been scored as being too "conservative." Economists such as John K. Galbraith would say that magazines and other media create unnecessary wants and needs through advertising and thereby divert funds badly needed for social ends. But the Magazine Publishers Bureau would counter by asserting that, through advertising, magazines help to maintain a consistently and uniquely high standard of living by helping to move goods from producer to consumer and that, in addition, they provide both information and entertainment. At their best, they are an educational and enlightening force in American life.

Too little, unfortunately, is yet known of cause and effect in magazine journalism. Research has not defined in depth the effects of magazine reading, and such findings as are available are at best tentative. Like other media, there is no categorical evidence to show that magazines either elevate or lower taste, that they do or do not incite crime or that they are juvenile in content because they substitute popular culture or *kitsch* for serious art. It is probably true that all mass media, including magazine journalism, tend not to innovate but to reflect and to canalize pre-existing values, goals and needs. Over a period of years, most magazines have on more than one occasion revealed a sense of responsibility by refusing to accept shoddy and misleading advertising. It would be ideal, of course, if magazines and other mass media set their sights higher all the time, but there are those who question whether the public really wants the magazine to aspire to a higher level of culture simply because a minority of readers have set such heights for it. Because there is a fairly wide variety of choice in the area of magazine journalism, the public has a multiplicity of reading choices. In the American magazines, as in the newspapers, motion pictures, radio and television, there is no restriction as to the availability of multiple choice, nor is there any external control over content. What appears is a result of an interaction between the publication and the reader. In the magazine world, in particular, there is virtually something for every reader.

BIBLIOGRAPHY

Allen, Frederick Lewis. *Only Yesterday: An Informal History of the Twenties.* New York: Bantam Books, 1946.

Bainbridge, John. *Little Wonder, or the Readers Digest and How it Grew.* New York: Reynal and Hitchcock, 1946.

Bakeless, John. *Magazine Making.* New York: Viking Press, 1931.

Curtis Publishing Company. *The Life and Times of Cyrus H. K. Curtis, 1850–1933.* New York: Curtis Publishing Company, 1953.

De Foe, Daniel. *The Shortest Way with Dissenters.* London, 1702.

Dennie, Joseph. *The Lay Preacher, or Short Seminars for Idle Readers*. Walpole, Massachusetts, 1796.

Flesch, Rudolf. *The ABC of Style*. New York: Harper and Row, 1964.

Franklin, Benjamin. *The Papers of Benjamin Franklin*. Vol. I. New Haven: Yale University Press, 1959.

Galbraith, John K. *The Affluent Society*. New York: Houghton, Mifflin, 1958.

Gibbs, Wolcott. "Time . . . Fortune . . . Life . . . Luce," *in* E. B. White and Katharine White, eds. *A Subtreasury of American Humor*. New York: Coward-McCann, 1941.

Hobart, Donald M., ed. *Marketing Research Practice*. New York: Ronald Press, 1950.

Hotchkiss, George Burton. *Milestones of Marketing*. New York: Macmillan Company, 1938.

Kramer, Dale. *Ross and the New Yorker*. Garden City, New York: Doubleday and Company, 1951.

Lorimer, George H. *The False Gods*. New York: D. Appleton and Company, 1906.

McClure, S. S. *My Autobiography*. New York: Frederick A. Stokes Company, 1914.

Mott, Frank Luther. *History of American Magazines, 1741–1850*. Cambridge, Massachusetts: Harvard University Press, 1957.

Peterson, Theodore. *Magazines in the Twentieth Century*. Urbana, Illinois: University of Illinois Press, 1958.

Regier, C. C. *The Era of the Muckrakers*. Chapel Hill: University of North Carolina Press, 1932.

Sedgwick, Ellery. *The Happy Profession*. Boston: Little, Brown and Company, 1946.

Stewart, Kenneth and John Tebbel. *Makers of Modern Journalism*. New York: Doubleday and Company, Inc., 1948.

Tebbel, John. *George Horace Lorimer and The Saturday Evening Post*. Garden City, New York: Doubleday and Company, Inc., 1952.

Time, Inc. *Four Hours a Year*. New York: Time, Inc., 1936.

Van Doren, Carl. *Benjamin Franklin*. New York: The Viking Press, 1938.

Villard, Oswald Garrison. *Fighting Years*. New York: Harcourt, Brace and Company, 1939.

Wolseley, Roland E. *The Magazine World*. New York: Prentice-Hall, Inc., 1951.

Wood, James Playsted. *Magazines in the United States*. New York: The Ronald Press Company, 1956.

7

The Cartoon Narrative

CARTOONS, in one form or another, literally are as old as man's first efforts to communicate by non-verbal symbols. Although there is a world of difference between early cave drawings and pictographs and contemporary comics, there is nevertheless a common communicative root in this form of popular art. There is also a considerable difference, indeed some would say a disparity, between the drawings of many of the world's greatest artists and the popular cartoons of today. But here, too, there is an inevitable generic analogy. For the cartoon narrative was—and is today—not always intended as popular comic art, although its use is almost always popular in the sense that it is drawn for the many, rather than for the few. Early drawings were either purely ornamental, or intended to convey specific meanings, or a combination of both. In the Eighteenth Century, the drawings of Hogarth were brilliantly, scathingly satiric renderings of unsavory segments of life in the London of the period. The art of Daumier was equally caustic, although its social comment is more trenchant and more painful than that of Hogarth.

Contemporary cartoon art does not, for the most part, aspire to such aesthetic or social heights. It must be emphasized, however, that, despite the commonly accepted version of the comic strip as humor, the cartoon is not always simple and popular fun. There are superb editorial cartoonists, such as Herblock, who by drawings and text, provide an insightful and frequently unerringly accurate portrait of the social and political mores of the time. This type of cartoon is always meaningful and frequently satirical in thrust and intent, and invariably it strikes at the root of timely topics that are being hotly debated. It always has a point of view. It is also motivated by the convictions of the cartoonist or by the editorial posture of the medium—usually a newspaper—for which he draws. Many of these editorial cartoons are widely syndicated. In addition to those which appear in the newspaper, many popular magazines carry cartoons. *The New Yorker* usually carries sophisticated cartoon art, frequently commenting on popular foibles or puncturing the ego of characters whom the cartoonist considers pompous. Even *The Saturday Review* includes cartoons germane to the general literary and cultural orientation of the publication.

These examples, however, are not generally subsumed under the category of the cartoon, and for this reason they have been mentioned to indicate that the scope of cartoon art is wider than is generally believed. The editorial cartoon, in fact, is just about the best example of this form as sheer, mass communication, for it is a kind of nonverbal graphic art that conveys affective or directive meaning, and its purpose is frequently to influence opinion on one of the contemporary issues of the period. But for the most part, the cartoon narrative can be divided into two entities—a division which is most significant, because of the differences in quality and substance. There are the comic strips, or boxes, which appear in the daily press, and these are usually innocuous. In addition, however, there are the ubiquitous popular comic books, read by millions of young children and adolescents, and these are far from naive. They have been the center of periodic storms of controversy over both their form and content, and at least one distinguished psychiatrist believes that there should be a law banning them from publication as inherently indecent and dangerous to the youth who devour them so steadily.

Both of these forms, however widely they vary in structure and content, are examples of graphic communicative art, although students of the medium agree that their purpose and effect are quite different from one another. The newspaper comics are intended for family consumption. The pulp comics, whatever their effect may be, are certainly designed to titillate and are concerned mainly with sex, sadism, crime, horror and violence. There is an in-between, hybrid kind of cartoon narrative which has also aroused considerable controversy. This is the cartoon book designed to make palatable, by drawing and narrative text, the great classics. Those who publish these books, based on Shakespeare's "Julius Caesar" and other masterpieces, claim they have educational significance. Their critics believe them to be a desecration of great literature and a cultural catastrophe, with equally abominable text and cartoons. Finally, there are the non-print cartoons. These include the animated motion picture cartoon narratives, such as the Terrytoons, and the Saturday morning animated television cartoons for children, ranging from Superman to Bugs Bunny. During the past year, in response to growing criticism, the television cartoon has largely eliminated shooting and other incidents of violence for more temperate, but nonetheless, exciting adventure series.

In terms of communication, therefore, the cartoon narrative covers considerable territory and has enormous popular appeal. It is estimated, for example, that as many adults as children read the daily and Sunday funnies in the newspaper. In recognition of their appeal, many advertisers are using cartoon techniques in the marketing of products through television commercials and even in newspaper advertisements. "Little Orphan Annie" recently served as basis for a series of ads for Father's Day merchandise by a major chain of men's shops. Cereal boxes have been used for cartoon narrative techniques, in order to arrest the attention of young children. There are few areas of graphic communication not covered by the cartoon in one guise or another. And the popularity of the form is based, of course, on the fact that it combines verbal and non-verbal symbols in a simple, easy-to-read and comprehensible style.

Although the newspaper comic strip originated in the era of Pulitzer and Hearst, both of whom quickly realized the audience potential of this type of entertainment feature, some critics subsume the cartoon under the category of magazines or paperback books. But, as has been indicated, there are actually at least two basic kinds of cartoon narratives—the newspaper comics and the pulp-type adventure comic books. The circulation of these comics runs to the astounding figure of about 300 million on an annual basis, and it is this type of comic presentation which has been scored for its depiction of crime, sex and violence—so much so that the comic book industry was obliged to set up a code of self-regulation. It was also criticism of the comic book which resulted in studies in depth of the effect of these presentations by sociologists, professional educators and psychiatrists, such as Dr. Fredric Wertham. Early newpaper comics began in the middle of the Nineteenth Century, but the comic book's enormous popularity is distinctly a Twentieth Century phenomenon. Of current vintage, too, are not only the children's television comics, so popular on Saturday mornings, but also the animated special programs, based on the Charlie Brown series and the Grinch which have raised the level of animated comics to a fine art.

The funnies, which appear in the daily press, and even the pulp comics which have aroused such antagonism, are both media of mass communication, although obviously with widely different effects. Each reaches millions of readers, as do the other mass media of radio, magazine and television. But the newspaper funnies also serve a promotional function. They provide the necessary ingredient of entertainment which helps to stimulate and build circulation. It is the comics to which a large majority of newspaper readers turn even before reading the news columns. The daily and Sunday funnies are as absorbing to millions of adults, many of whom are college graduates, as they are to children. Some of the funnies, indeed, are characteristically adult in their intellectual appeal, but the basic thrust of the daily comic strip, or the cartoon box, is invariably built around recognizable and appealing characters who become a daily staple and whose activities are a reflection of the foibles and aspirations—and sometimes the frustrations—of the reader. Scholarly studies in the funnies have presented them as cartoon narratives, based on the use of the cartoon as a form of graphic communication. As a communicative art, the cartoon represents an excellent example of stereotyping. Because the line drawings and balloon-type copy are simplistic, the funnies minimize any effort to comprehend on the part of the audience. At the same time, however, certain kinds of cartoons, particularly those of an editorial nature, can be quite pithy and meaningful in terms of social or political comment.

The Startling Advent of Comics

The cartoon narratives—colloquially known as the funnies—were an integral part of the period of yellow journalism, the era when an intense rivalry over circulation and readership existed between the Hearst and Pulitzer papers, particularly *The New York American* and *The New York World*. Quite fortuitously, there appeared one day a page of drawings with a yellow tint overlay in *The World*. The time was just prior to the turn of the century, in 1896. The boy in the drawing became known as "The Yellow Kid." With this phenomenon began a new era in graphic communications, largely non-verbal and as intriguing to adults as to children. The Yellow Kid proved quite captivating, and a new form of newspaper feature—entertainment, not news—became a daily staple in hundreds of papers. It was Richard Outculd's "Yellow Kid" which may be designated as the beginning of the comic strip in America, although this kind of art had appeared as early as the Eighteenth Century in England, albeit in a quite different vein. Almost immediately, the comics were to play a key role in the battle for popularity and circulation supremacy between Joseph Pulitzer and William Randolph Hearst. Hearst quickly seized upon Pulitzer's use of color and, as he was able to do in the case of many great newsmen, he succeeded in persuading Outculd to leave *The World* in what was probably the greatest journalistic coup of the period.

These early comics, immensely popular, were like all communicative art, reflections of their milieu. The settings were ghettos, and therefore not particularly attractive. Stereotyping and racial prejudice were permitted to appear unchallenged, with little black boys the butt of a kind of humor that would be intolerable today. Cartoon narrative journalism was popular journalism, but subtly its character changed as its popularity increased. A bourgeois environment became the standard background, and it was not long before millions of middle class Americans were to take the comics to their collective hearts.

Many of the contemporary newspaper comics are fine exemplifications of whimsical and homely folk art. A syndicated strip such as "The

Ryatts," for example, represents family humor at its literal best. "Dennis The Menace," which also achieved television fame, appeals to adults more than to the protagonist's contemporaries by its portrayal of an endearing youngster who manages to upset the modus vivendi of the grown-up world. "Peanuts," perhaps the most famous of all contemporary cartoon narratives, presents brilliantly humorous commentary about small fry which manages to have a universal meaning in terms of what it says about the human condition. Implicit in all of these cartoons is a kind of social history of the times, because the comic strip has always tended to reflect an era. Earlier cartoons, such as "Foxy Grandpa" typified the relatively quiet temper of the early 1900's. The humor was to be found in the simple fact that Grandpa—a different and more revered figure than today—was more foxy than the children who tried to inveigle him into embarrassing moments. Similarly, the era reflected in the first Yellow Kid comics—a rough and tumble period—changed radically to a depiction of middle class white collar life.

Among the earlier strips, of which some still appear today, were the antics of "Mutt and Jeff," probably the first strip to attain national popularity. Bud Fisher, like many other comic artists, began drawing for the sports page and wound up an internationally famous cartoonist when "Mutt and Jeff" began appearing in the pages of Hearst's *New York Journal*. The weekly strip still maintains wide popularity through syndication. Other notable pioneering newspaper cartoon strips were "Polly and Her Pals," a teen-age vintage comic; Ken Kling's horseracing cartoon "Joe and Asbestos"; and the famed "Katzenjammer Kids." All of these were among the pre-World War I strips which made the cartoon an indispensable ingredient of almost every daily and Sunday paper, although the *New York Times* to this day has not relented even to the extent of printing an editorial cartoon.

Two of the most famous pioneering comic strip artists were Rube Goldberg and George McManus. The latter's "Bringing Up Father" first appeared in the *New York American* and, as millions of readers know, told the incredible story of Jiggs, unhappy in top hat and tails, and Maggie, climbing to reach high society. It is not a pleasant family cartoon, but the contest between the two protagonists lured millions of readers. It was in this first quarter of the century that the cartoon narrative found a permanent place for itself in the newspapers of the country. Readers turned expectantly each day to follow the comic adventures of the cartoon characters of Goldberg and McManus, of DeBeck's "Barney Google," of George Herriman's "Krazy Kat" and the Kat's unholy liaison with Ignatz Mouse.

Comics Provide Mass Entertainment

It cannot be emphasized too strongly that the funnies, read by adults as well as by children, are different in kind and degree from most of the popular comic books. Most of the latter are not humorous at all. They narrate adventure-action stories of the most violent nature. These books out-sell even the most popular of national magazines by many millions of copies. In the beginning, the comic books were relatively innocent in content, since they were offered as premiums for promotion purposes, and were based on newspaper funnies. Eventually, however, publishers who put quick profits above standards of taste and ethics, began printing less savory material, and the comic books became highly competitive in their efforts to reach more lurid and violent heights.

At the same time, there were more reputable publishers who began with comics and later branched into large-scale paperback operations. One of these, Dell Publishing Company, developed a publishing empire in comics, paperbacks and eventually hard-cover books. Through distribution by American News Company came such highly popular comic books as *Popular Funnies, Batman, Superman, Action Comics,* detective comics and many others of similar vintage. The basis of popularity was, of course, the extraordinarily simple presentation of picture and text. Indeed, it was the utter simplicity, along with the growing addition of violence which aroused bitter controversy over the effects of this kind of art. Although some rather formidable figures in medicine and education believed that comics gave the child an opportunity to act out aggressions through a vicarious world of fantasy, others disagreed violently and called the comic book industry purveyors of pornography, sadism and intellectual trash. The fact remains, however, that children read comics —in newspapers and in books—because they are easy to understand, and adults read newspaper cartoons because they are relaxing and frequently irreverent in their social commentary. But, in general, the cartoon narrative has been less social commentary than humor, less satire than simple entertainment for the masses.

The best of the cartoon narratives have been those which appeared in the mass circulation newspapers. Many of these are syndicated. Most of them are interesting in the way in which they reflect the mores of the time and the way in which they seize upon events in which the public is absorbed. The two world wars, for example, were reflected by comic strips about army and navy personnel. The Twenties saw the growth of comics which limned the flapper girls of the period. There were the girl cartoons, the he-man comics, the kid cartoons, animal adventure strips, action strips, science fiction sequences and detective or suspense comics.

The format of comic pages is based on the editor's conviction that they are popular art, communicating to a wide spectrum of readers. Hence, the average daily page of eight or ten comic strips, and the Sunday papers, which usually are expanded to a full-page for each cartoon, tend to be an amalgam of various cartoon characters and ideas. This is roughly analogous to the television concept of a balanced program schedule, albeit with the important difference that the comics are variations of one basic entertainment theme, while television balance implies a "mix" of entertainment (situation comedy, western, drama) and news and public affairs programs.

Each comic strip tends to develop a loyal following, as is witnessed by the protests from readers when a particular cartoon is eliminated from the newspaper page. Most of the cartoons are distributed by syndication, which means that hundreds of newspapers across the country will be carrying the same strip, although not necessarily on the same day. The purpose of regularity and syndication is a pragmatic one; to gain the loyalty and arrest the attention of the reader so that he will look regularly to the familiar cartoon, usually on the same page each day. This regularity of readership has an obviously important implication for advertising and circulation, hence each paper attempts to buy and print cartoons which best serve its readers' interests. The old *New York World*, a middle-class newspaper, utilized editorial cartoons, along with the daily strips, but also carried a box cartoon which became nationally famous and was continued after the paper merged with the *Telegram* to become the *New York World Telegram*. This was Dennis Wortman's "Metropolitan Movies" which ran alternately with J. R. Williams' "Out Our Way," an equally famous cartoon box which attained enormous syndication, because of the easily understandable humor in such recognizable and sympathetic characters as Worry Wart.

Similarly E. L. Ahearn's "Our Boarding House" presented characters with whom the reader was able to empathize and identify in Major Hoople and his stalwart wife, Martha. Hoople is the epitome of the harmless, bragging fraud so familiar to all readers. These, along with cartoons such as Crockett Johnson's "Barnaby" and O. Soglow's "Little King" are more than bland, meaningless graphic renditions. They have a point of view and, in a most literal sense, they exemplify the cartoon as a communications art. "Barnaby," for example, may not have been styled for the cognoscenti, but it drew a considerable following of intelligent readers by its delightful light humor and fantasy. Young Barnaby's insistence on the existence of his mythical friend, Mr. O'Malley, despite the skepticism of his more mundane-minded parents, touched a chord of fantasy in readers. For O'Malley is the archtype of all leprechauns right up to "Finian's Rainbow." Barnaby, Mr. O'Malley, the dog and the ghost stem from the wellsprings of the universality of humor. And O. Soglow's silent "Little King," which began in the sophisticated pages of the *New Yorker* magazine, became one of the funniest of cartoons in which the utter silence of the portly monarch, no matter what the provocation, was both appealing and delightful.

These, and several others of the plethora of cartoons which appeared after the first World War, are phenomena in that they are intelligent, rather than simplistic in viewpoint, have bite and thrust, offer wry comments on the human condition, communicate an idea and appeal more to adults than to children. Indeed, as publishers discovered that comics appealed to adults, the character and substance of many cartoon narratives changed to an expression of humor that was directed as much to older readers as to the young. Jiggs and Maggie and their quarrels over social position; Harry Hershfield's "Abie Kabibble" cartoon, popular in its day for its depiction of the immigrant, but quite possibly offensive to some in the climate of racial and religious sensitivity; and the boxes of H. T. Webster and Clare Briggs were essentially adult-oriented in theme and art. Webster and Briggs, in particular, depict "ordinary" Americans. And their problems, aspirations and conflicts reach out to the core of homely family humor. Briggs was uncanny in his ability to communicate the individual's embarrassing moments. His "Mr. and Mrs." which appeared in the literate *New York Tribune*, drew the loyalty of great numbers of intelligent and urbane readers with its remarkable insight into the ups and downs of marriage. Webster, working in much the same genre as Briggs, distilled the foibles of modern man in his cartoon boxes in *The New York World*. Webster's humor is gentle, but telling. His captions, which capture a world of meaning in one brief line, became so popular as to become part of everyday colloquial usage. They included such pithy text commentary as "They'll do it every time," "The thrill that comes once in a lifetime," and others that summarize how most folks feel under conditions of joy or frustration, but are unable to communicate that feeling. Webster's classic presentation was "The Timid Soul," a brilliant example of communicative art in its delineation of a mousy character who became a household word as Casper Milquetoast, the little man whose reach exceeds his grasp, because his essential timidity refuses to leave him free to accomplish his goals.

But the major portion of comic strips were styled for all—children and adults—and they comprised simple narrative techniques consisting of line drawings and easy-to-comprehend dialogue, usually in the form of the balloon. Characters changed from local to national in character as syndication grew and, as we have seen, cartoons tended to cluster around several easy-to-understand themes, more or less universal in nature. "Smitty" and "Orphan Annie" were about youngsters. The first cartoons, in fact, were based on the antics of children, although the very earliest, such as "The Yellow Kid"—so-called because the printed page was yellow in color—were hardly the typical American boys and girls which "Smitty" and "Orphan Annie" were to become. But, as the cartoon narrative developed, cartoons about children achieved equal popularity with the young as well as the old. These included "Reglar Fellars" and "Just Kids," both typical American boy types, bright and energetic middle-class Americans, attractive, funny, worthy of the reader's sympathy and eliciting his laughter. Fontaine Fox's box, "Toonerville Trolley," appealed equally to children and their parents with such characters as The Skipper, Mickey (himself) McGuire and The Terrible-Tempered Mr.

Bang. Percy Crosby's "Skippy," and "Merry Mixup" and "Little Orphan Annie," each regaled readers with the daily turmoil of the world of growing youngsters. Crosby's contained an element of social commentary that made more than one adult sit up and take notice. Blosser's "Freckles and His Friends" explored the best and most endearing qualities of the American boy, and Brinkerhoff's "Little Mary Mixup" epitomized the lovable moppet who gets herself into and out of scrapes in good, old traditional fashion.

Similar to the children strips were the family-type cartoon narratives, such as "The Ryatts," "Our Boarding House," "Mr. and Mrs." and others. A particularly attractive character was Edwina's "Kap Stubbs and Tippie," a family strip about Grandma Bailey, certainly one of the most lovable of grandmother figures, her little grandson, Kap, and his dog, Tippie. The people are plain, homely, simple and enormously sympathetic. Another family-type cartoon was H. T. Tuthill's "The Bungle Family," which appeared variously in the old *Evening Mail, The New York World, The American* and finally *The New York Post*. Like "Bringing Up Father" it depicted the popular and widely prevalent phenomenon of the family squabble between husband and wife.

The popular adventures of modern youth, different from, and yet similar to, today's more social-minded younger generation, attracted large audiences after both world wars. These comics depicted a simpler America, more complacent and self-satisfied than the present. What would draw disdain from a large segment of today's readers won a large following in a less complicated era in American social and political life. Many of these cartoons, such as "Blondie," were so popular as to achieve the fame of motion picture or television production. "Blondie," distributed by King Features Syndicate and originally drawn by Chuck Young, detailed sympathetically, although with absurdity, the uncannily successful relationship between the beautiful and wealthy daughter of the Bumstead family and her simple-minded but lovable swain, Dagwood. Other cartoons, such as "Polly and Her Pals," by Cliff Sterret, synthesized the outlook of an earlier teenage world. Polly and Ernie Bushmiller's Fritzi Ritz are attractive females, shapely, and exuding a respectable amount of sex appeal. Similarly, Boots of "Boots and Her Buddies" was one of the genuine blonde beauties of the cartoon world, as was Carol McKee, the young heiress of "Captain Easy" who marries the diminutive Wash Tubs, a dedicated friend of the indomitable Captain Easy.

For the men—but followed with equal dedication by women and children—there was no dearth of fare. These ranged from wry humor, such as Elsie Crisler Segar's "Thimble Theatre" which began innocuously enough, but exploded in popularity with the addition of the salty Popeye and his romantic Olyve Oyl. Popeye crystalized the ability of man to conquer all. Nothing frustrated this swashbuckler who took on all comers, vanquished them and made spinach synonymous with strength and glory. In another vein, Al Capp's "Little Abner," a cartoon which formed the basis for a Broadway musical comedy, was less brash in its presentation of the relationship between Abner and Daisy Mae. Capp became one of the most famous of all cartoonists and, with Popeye, Abner became something of an American folk hero.

Science fiction, suspense and detective comics and adventure also were popular narratives which detailed the peregrinations of masculine characters of various kinds. Suspense invariably has been a sure-fire attraction for audiences, and the comics were even more susceptible to this form of action and adventure. The basis, of course, is the breathtaking cliff-hanger; and the more wild and eerie in tone, the more these comics lure the reader. The early suspense comics, such as "Hair Breadth Harry," were more humorous than suspenseful and were comparable to the naivete of the first chase movies. Later, however, the suspense comic took on a more serious and, in some comics such as "Alley Oop," a more fanciful direction. "Tarzan" by Harold Foster, and Milton Caniff's "Dickie Dare" were both in the suspense genre, but the most popular comic in this vein was a detective story by Chester Gould entitled "Dick Tracy," which could well have been one of the major factors in building the enormous circulation of the New York *Daily News.* Some critics have considered Dick Tracy a rather unpalatable character and have scored the cartoon for excessive action, but it is basically a daily detective story in cartoon narrative form. It attracted readers who were interested in crime stories without the totally lurid and objectionable approach of the comic book treatment of this subject. Tracy is a marvelously efficient detective, and the moral is that crime most certainly does not pay. It is probable that Tracy was suggested by the interest in the gangster world that was such popular movie fare in the 1930's.

Action adventure of another variety abounded in the well-drawn and successful "Tarzan," based on the Edgar Rice Burrough's creation which appeared, variously, in cartoon narrative, book, motion picture and successful television series. V. T. Hamlin's "Alley Oop" also appealed to the adventure-minded reader with its story of the prehistoric characters in the land of Moo who, eventually, are brought to the Twentieth Century by the device of the time machine and are then sent back on various expeditions in time, there to encounter fantastic adventures. Caniff's "Dickie Dare" and the same artist's "Terry and the Pirates" are both adventure strips, the former involved with undersea and in-the-air warfare of planes and submarines, and the latter a melodrama in an Asiatic setting with such famous cartoon creations as Terry, the Dragon Lady and Burma. Action and suspense also played a major role in "Superman" and "Batman," both of which appeared on television and became part of the cult of the "high camp" art movement of the 1960's.

Sports and science fiction were both popular with readers. "Joe's

Car" was more of a family-type cartoon, but Ham Fisher's "Joe Palooka" typified the big, semi-literate, hulking prize fighter who had more brawn that brains but managed to attract readers because of his good nature. Science-fiction characters became immensely popular in the pre-space age period. Many of these were uncannily accurate adumbrations of the Apollo moon flights of the past few years. These comics were suggested by the science-fiction tales of Jules Verne and H. G. Wells, but it is doubtful whether readers were able to predict that the wildest cartoon adventures in space would one day become a reality. Even as early as 1940 there were mentions of atomic bombs and other scientific discoveries that were to occur some twenty years later. "Buck Rogers" and "Flash Gordon" are typical of the science-fiction cartoon. In "Flash Gordon" there are visits to strange planets, similar to the narrative technique of the television series "Star Trek." Alex Raymond, creator of "Flash Gordon" was one of the best graphic artists, and his cartoon became one of the most popular of the science-fiction variety. The most successful of them all, however, was probably Jerry Siegel and Joe Schuster's creation of the ubiquitous and unassailable "Superman," a human with sufficient non-human, out-of-this-world attributes to make him internationally famous. In actual life, he is Clark Kent, an ordinary newspaper reporter. But when the going gets rough, Superman comes to the fore and, literally, there is no situation which he cannot handle, no obstacle which he cannot hurdle in his quest for decency in a crime-ridden society.

The cartoon narrative also attained considerable popularity with its presentation of animals. Some of these appear as characters in family strips. Others have the field to themselves, and comprise the major thrust of the cartoon. There is a larger group of these animal funnies devoted to the relationship of animals to each other, or to human beings. These comics are variously humorous and sentimental, and are predicated on man's fascination, and frequently his overwhelming affection, for animals. Krazy Kat and Ignatz Mouse are probably the most famous, but there were also Swinnerton's "Little Bears and Tigers," Harrison Cady's "Peter Rabbit" and "Felix the Cat." Millions of comic page readers followed the adventures of Orphan Annie's Sandy, Uncle Elby's long-eared Napoleon and the whole, delightful variety of Walt Disney comic characters. Barney Google's nag Sparkplug and the horse-racing strip by Ken Kling, "Joe and Asbestos" combined sports themes with a sympathetic portrayal of the relationship between men and animals.

Social Applications: Criticism

With the exception of the editorial cartoon, it can be seen readily that the newspaper comic strips, dealing as they do with family humor, teen-agers, animals, adventure and science fiction, are intended primarily to add a fillip of daily entertainment for the newspaper reader. In this they have succeeded admirably and, for the most part, innocuously. The cartoon narrative in the daily press and the magazine cartoon box are, at worst, banal but harmless and, at best, satiric, humorous and frequently touching and delightful. But the popularity of the cartoon is such that it has also been used for other purposes. The editorial and sports page boxes are good examples. The pulp comic books are unsavory exhibits. Still another use, which has important bearing on the whole question of the effect of mass media, is the application of the cartoon for various purposes which may be called social in character. One series, in particular, indicated most vividly the semantic barriers that make communication difficult because of stereotyping, and because of the wide differences of cultural background and orientation among the reading public.

This series was the famous Mr. Biggott cartoons, designed—ironically it turned out—to free man from racial prejudice. The cartoons were shown to various groups, under actual testing and control conditions. In one, Mr. Biggott is a middle-aged, presumably middle-class American who looks at a billboard on which are posted the names of war heroes in his community. The names appear variously to be Jewish, Italian and Irish in origin. In another cartoon, Mr. Biggott is seen telling an American Indian that the company for which he (Mr. Biggott) works employs only one hundred per cent Americans! Each of these cartoons was shown to various selected groups who were asked to explain its meaning and to draw inferences from it. The researchers reported, unhappily but not surprisingly, that more than half of the respondents failed to grasp the objective which was to reveal that prejudice is both socially unacceptable and intellectually ridiculous, particularly in the case of the Indian. Some of the respondents reacted no differently to this series than to the comics in the daily press. Others failed to see any satire, criticism or direct or implied commentary. And still others used the cartoon to reinforce their already existent bias, thereby underscoring one of the most interesting aspects of mass communications—its ability to reflect and to reinforce values and convictions, rather than to change them. The Biggott cartoons indicated that man reacts in terms of pre-existing value judgments, in the way he has learned to react to certain stereotypes. They showed also that an affective reaction to words or pictures is far more significant than a cognitive one. Finally, they revealed the need for extensive education in communications, because most of the respondents were simply unable to realize that the cartoons were not meaningless representations, but were devised with serious intent.

There also have been some serious appraisals of the possible effect of comics on youth. These have centered almost exclusively on the fare produced by the comic book industry. One of the most articulate critics has been the noted psychiatrist, Dr. Fredric Wertham, whose study

Seduction of the Innocent is a trenchant attack on many of the comic book publishers as purveyors of poisonous trash. No amount of rationalization can convince Dr. Wertham that these comic books are not a dangerous, destructive and disruptive influence. The signal failure of most studies of comic books is the failure to recognize the basic principle that mental hygiene is preventive. But the sex and violence which appear in comic books, Dr. Wertham found, goes beyond anything ever described by De Sade, Freud or Krafft-Ebing in its unhealthy emotional stimulation. The basic ingredients, occurring again and again, are crime, violence, eroticism, sadism—all based to an extent on the Nietzsche philosophy of the will to power and the blind force of the superman.

The paradox of intent and fulfillment is to be found in the way comic books are promoted. The covers of the most lurid of such pamphlets proclaim that their purpose is to prevent crime. But the cover lines are, in effect, simply added to allay criticism and to camouflage the actual content. Dr. Wertham found that some comic books condone the use of drugs and, in fact, that all juvenile addicts tend to be readers of comic books. Comics purporting to be conventional westerns are actually crime and violence stories. Black people usually are depicted as essentially inferior, while the white heroes seem to be invariably blond and "Aryan." The kind of hate that characterized Fascist literature of the 1930's blends into the superhero type stories. Even adaptations of conventional classics, Dr. Wertham insists, drive young people away from the original, because they are perversions of the basic story.

Contrary to what the defenders of comic books have claimed—and they number educators and psychiatrists recruited to do special research by the comic book industry—the conclusion is that comic books do not satisfy any "deep psychological needs." They do not help to rid children of aggressive impulses by living these experiences vicariously. Wertham, furthermore, does not agree with those who believe that neither comic books nor violence in other mass media will affect so-called normal children. He is convinced that the assertion that only children who reveal psychopathology will be affected is sheer sophistry. Thus, the case for comic books made by various educators in such publications as *The Journal of Educational Sociology* is labeled false and misleading public relations, and the Kefauver investigation is scored for having failed to influence an industry which devised a negative code to which it does not adhere. The use of comic books by hospitals to calm troublesome patients is also scored as poor therapy, and the entire comic book industry is flayed for ruthless exploitation of the child.

The comic book industry has had support from some who, while agreeing that these books may be dangerous, nevertheless argue that freedom of expression must not be curtailed and that the power of public opinion must exert pressure for reform. But Wertham and his supporters argue that neither public opinion nor self-regulation has succeeded. What is needed belongs properly in the realm of mental hygiene which would involve a vast "public health approach to the comic book problem" and would result in the passing of specific laws representing the limits to what can be published. To those who say, as did *The New York Times*, that this might violate the First Amendment, the rebuttal is that comic books pose a "clear and present danger" which demands a drastic program of action and reform.

Newspaper funnies, on the other hand, have been enjoyed and advocated by many critics of American literature. Such serious observers of American letters as Leslie Fiedler inquire why comic strips are so universally popular, why people turn to them before any other data in the newspaper, why adults read them avidly although they are couched in the simplest of verbal symbols. The answer lies in part in the fact that the cartoon narrative is the most popular of art forms, a kind of pop culture or contemporary folk art. Furthermore, they are easily accessible, not only in the newspaper but through distribution in supermarkets, drugstores and transportation terminals. They are very much a part of the expertise in technology, packaging and promotion of a consumer-oriented society and, while many believe they foster illiteracy, they are the perfect example of contemporary mass-produced "culture."

But there is an important point. Fiedler believes that the "true intellectual" reads both comics and detective stories, as opposed to the spurious intelligentsia who spurn the popular for the recondite and the abstruse. Only the false intellectual would criticize television and popular funnies, for both are pop art in the most literal sense of the term.

The point is well taken. Because the funnies are simple and blunt does not mean that they are meaningless or that they should be rejected out of hand. What is exemplified and stressed by critics of the cartoon narrative is the artificial distinction between high and low culture, between "serious" and "popular" art. This distinction is one of conflict between elite and popular culture. But this, according to Fiedler, involves a basic question of class distinction. Comics represent more than an economic conspiracy against the law by an industry of profiteers, bent on extracting millions from a gullible market. What has occurred is an ironic situation in which many serious literary scholars have come to enjoy the funnies, while those who aspire to the appreciation of arts and letters but have not learned how to see, read, hear or understand high culture, reject comics as beneath contempt.

The popular newspaper funnies, however, are here to stay. They have earned a place for themselves in the world of mass media, not only by proving an economic asset to popular journalism, but also because they are truly enjoyed by millions of readers of all age groups. The comic books, on the other hand, represent an entirely different problem. Although they continue to be devoured avidly by young people, there is some reason to believe that, even in an age of unprecedented permissiveness, there will be sufficient public demand by educators and parents to force publishers to eliminate the blatant presentations of sex and violence which characterize this medium more than any other. At the least, there is a need for studies in depth of the effect of comic books on the young reader. While such studies may not be conclusive, they can yield important data to serve as a guide toward ameliorating a situation which is badly in need of corrective measures.

BIBLIOGRAPHY

Becker, Stephen. *Comic Art in America.* New York: Simon and Schuster, 1959.
Hogben, Lancelot. *From Cave Painting to Comic Strip: A Kaleidoscope of Human Communication.* London: Max Parrish and Company, Ltd., 1949.
Hoult, T. F. "Comic Books and Juvenile Delinquency" in *Sociology and Social Research,* Vol. XXXIII (1949), pp. 279–284.
Murrell, William. *A History of American Graphic Humor, 1939-1965.* New York: The Macmillan Company, 1938.
Spencer, Dick, III. *Pulitzer Prize Cartoons.* Ames, Iowa: Iowa State College Press, 1953.
Spiegelman, Marvin, Carl Terwillinger and Franklin Fearing. "The Content of Comic Strips: A Study of a Mass Medium of Communication" in *Journal of Social Psychology,* Vol. XXXV (1952), pp. 37–57.
Waugh, Coughton. *The Comics.* New York: The Macmillan Company, 1947.
Webster, H. T. *The Best of H. T. Webster.* New York: Simon and Schuster, 1953.
Wertham, Frederic. "The Comics . . . very funny!" *Saturday Review of Literature.* Vol. XXXI, No. 22 (1948), pp. 6–7, 27–29.
Seduction of the Innocent. New York: Rinehart and Company, 1954.
White, David M. and Robert H. Abel, eds. *The Funnies, an American Idiom.* New York: The Free Press of Glencoe, 1963.
Wolf, Katherine N. and Marjorie Fiske. "The Children Talk About Comics" in Lazarsfeld, P. F. and F. N. Stanton, eds. *Communications Research.* 1948–49, pp. 3–50. New York: Harper, 1949.

8

The Motion Picture in Transition

THE MOTION PICTURE remains unique among the mass media in that it has undergone a transformation which, while generated by competitive and economic circumstances, is essentially cultural in nature. While many great magazines have gone out of business and newspapers have contracted, the film has changed from the fabrications of the "dream merchants" to a medium that has been called variously existentialist, realistic, naturalistic and even surrealist. Certainly the popular mythology of Hollywood as a place of glamour and luminosity, of romance laced with decadence, of stars in white limousines and directors in characteristically movie-set accoutrements, of vulgarian moguls in front offices, has receded before a more pragmatic and mundane image. Hollywood no longer has stars in its eyes. The great studios bear little resemblance to the setting of the 1930's. The directors are either purely utilitarian or consciously artistic or simply pragmatists about the sudden, booming market in sex and violence on one hand and the expanding home television market on the other. Hollywood is in deep trouble.

The film industry revived briefly after the traumatic experience of the Consent Decree of 1946 which split off production from distribution and exhibition, followed by the equal trauma of the explosion of television as a medium with more mass exposure than the movies could ever hope to achieve. Audiences were returning to the movie theaters, but neither the audiences nor the theaters were the same. Only New York's Radio City Music Hall, still "the showplace of the nation," bears any physical resemblance to the movie palaces of the 1920's and the 1930's, the vast, cavernous emporia with twinkling stars in the ceilings and pictures devised for everyone from nine to ninety. The great palaces have been replaced by the "art houses," boasting single features, many of foreign vintage. The great mass public—the mythical twelve-year mentality—has abandoned the movies and, presumably, turned to the television set which is now the medium of all things to all men. The gregarious social art of the period is television, an art that is both popular and isolated at the same time.

The new motion picture public is demographically a young public. At least half of all movie goers are of college or secondary school vintage, aged twenty-five and younger. Most regular patrons are under fifty. Presumably those who are past forty or fifty either watch television or shy away from movies, because they recoil with shock and moral indignation at the licentiousness and pornography that are characteristic of so many contemporary films. The term motion picture itself has become an anachronism, a throwback to an earlier, simpler world. *Film* is the thing for the younger audience, and the more avant garde the better. And film-making is flourishing on the campus and in the "underground cinema movement." Yet, and paradoxically, there is a cult of revival of many of the motion pictures of thirty years ago which draw a receptive audience to college town theatres and to the special showings of the Marx Brothers and Harold Lloyd at The Museum of Modern Art in New York City. Attendance, which was once as high as three or more billion a year, has been reduced to about one-third. A small part of the new movie industry is, once again, financially viable. Some theatres and pictures are doing business, and both the sale of old movies *to* television and the production of half hour and hour-long situation comedies and westerns *for* television brought a temporary affluence to the old studios. The fear that haunts Hollywood and the business officials on Wall Street is the spectre of pay TV, a possibility so awesome and so real as to have instigated a national motion picture theater owner's campaign, urging the public to "stop pay TV." In the main, however, many of the major companies are still in deep trouble.

The transformation of motion pictures from a popular art for everyone to a form that now virtually ignores the individual under eighteen has created a singular dilemma for the movie-makers. Since popular art is to be found on television and in the old movies which are available on television, has Hollywood any other alternative but to become conscious of the cultural needs of the college-trained intellectual? In addition, changing public attitudes no longer create a receptive audience for the stereotyping and the glittering fantasy of the conventional Hollywood product—the boy meets girl, loses girl and finally gets girl movies; the gangster who comes to his just deserts; the western hero who, laconic and masculine, wins over the bad guys and rides off into the sunset with his hard-won gold and a lovely bride to boot. The contemporary motion picture strives at least to be realistic and its excursions into fantasy are not romantic, but psychological, sociological or biological. There is a principle of selectivity operating in a medium which is still immensely popular, but still not the mass, mass medium that television has become. Audiences seek out and select what they want to see. And what they want to see are movies which, in the colloquial language of the younger movie-goer, "tell it like it is." If telling it like it is involves a naturalistic and frequently shocking expression of sexuality or sadism, more power to the new freedom of the movie-makers!

Even in its earlier halcyon days, however, when film was essentially a popular art, there were those who raised their sights higher. The documentarians, in particular, made forceful, beautiful and socially and culturally significant films. And many of the Hollywood figures, when they could circumvent the demands of the bankers and the home office, were able to produce motion pictures that went a long way toward being genuine works of art. This was true even from the beginnings, as a film such as "The Birth of A Nation" amply revealed. But, from the beginning, the motion picture was an ambivalent medium, torn between the demands of the boxoffice and its obvious potential as genuine art form. And genuine works of art have come from Hollywood—comedies and dramas that make many of the new-movement films a pseudo-art by comparison. Is it possible, some critics ask, that the Marx Brothers and Harold Lloyd films, and such westerns as "Shane," such portraits as "Citizen Kane" are revived and attended by college-age audiences because the immediate product pales by comparison?

What is most significant about current cinema is that it has undergone a metamorphosis from the early products of the dream factories, the movies that arrested the weekly attendance of the immigrant, the teen agers and the vast, solid middle class American public. This is still a cinema of mass reach, but the audience looks to film not so much for escape as for titillation, artiness and sensuality. But the adherents and the detractors are no less polarized than in the 1920's or 30's. More than the magazine or the newspaper, the movies are still a conversation piece. They continue to evoke strong emotional support or rejection, because they are the most fanciful and yet the most human of mass media.

Even before the sociological dissection of television became fashionable, the motion picture industry was all things to everyone. It was too violent, or too escapist, failing to come to grips with the variegated and frequently bitter world of post-war experience. It was preoccupied with the glorification of sexuality, or it failed to make a direct confrontation with sex as a basic human drive. It was socially conscious to a fault, or it was derelict in portraying the morbid, but nevertheless very genuine, phenomenon of man's brutal inhumanity to man. To the conservative, Hollywood was a seething cauldron of left-wing revolt. To the liberal, Hollywood movies glorified reactionary and rich heroes at the expense of the common man. But two decades ago, as well as now, the film at its best provides a remarkable intensification of perception through the miracle of cinematography. With or without sound, film can communicate the delights and tensions and anxieties of living through its sheer, intrinsic power as a communicative art. For it has a language of its own which, even when non-verbal, is no less powerful—a non-spoken language which makes the foreign film understandable and empathetic in a way a foreign language novel or play could never achieve.

The film has changed radically since its beginnings. It is absorbed today with introspection and morbid states of mind. It is brutally, appallingly frank in its treatment of sexuality, and its portrait of contemporary society is frequently violent and distasteful. But it is still, as always, exploring and it is, as always, a fresh and a new art even though its "language" has remained basically the same since its inception in the laboratories of Edison at the turn of the century.

The Development of Motion Pictures

Perhaps the question whether movies are pop culture or genuine art will never be satisfactorily resolved. There will always be those who look upon any truly mass medium as an opiate for the people. Nevertheless, whether as opiate or as cultural stimulant, no medium has commanded the total loyalty of audiences as did the movies of the 1920's and 30's and early 40's. Indeed, from its beginnings the motion picture was destined to become a communications medium of power, reach and enormous appeal. And its beginnings were humble rather than explosive. They were also derivative, for the basis for the motion picture was photography. Edward Muybridge, who used twelve still cameras to show "moving" pictures of a horse in motion, defined movies as a technique "for synthetically demonstrating movements analytically photographed from life."

What the motion picture accomplishes is the creation of movement or action, by means of photography, from the frozen motion of the still camera to the dynamic motion of the moving picture. It is this sense of movement which gives the viewer a vicarious sense of involvement in action, a variant of Coleridge's "willing suspension of disbelief." Young people have felt this involvement with movies, because they offer the opportunity for vicarious experience more powerfully than any of the communicative arts. This is one reason why, in addition to original scripts, motion pictures are adapted so frequently from biographies, novels and stage plays.

Until the invention of motion pictures, reproductions of reality were accomplished through the filter of the still photograph, the painting and other graphic arts. Still pictures could suggest, but could not reproduce, the booming, buzzing kaleidoscope of reality. It was an inevitable consequence of man's technological skill that a means would be found to mirror the teeming confusion of life through moving pictures. And, as a painting is also an expression of the artist, so the motion picture must become more than a facsimile of life. At its best it must reflect the heart and soul of the human condition.

The idea, like most, was not new. As Leonardo's drawings foreshadowed a time when man would fly, so other artists and philosophers speculated and experimented with the notion of a way to project pictures that would simulate movement. During the Renaissance, and even before, the idea of moving pictures was an intriguing one. Projection techniques were developed ultimately in France, England and the United States. In the Nineteenth Century a device called the Zoetrope, actually no more than a child's toy, created the illusion of pictures that moved by whirling them at high speed. In principle and practice, motion picture film comprises still pictures printed on celluloid and projected on to a screen at a determined rate of speed. This process, interacting with human perception, gives the illusion of realistic moving pictures. The basis is photography, particularly the process developed by Louis Daguerre whose daguerrotypes formed the basic method of still photography.

Edison and His Successors

There were simultaneous efforts to produce motion pictures in France and England, but it was Edison's conception and development of the basic technique which proved to be the most formidable technological advance in the communicative arts prior to the invention of television. By 1900, Edison and his enormously gifted assistant, William Dickson, perfected the kinetoscope, a primitive motion picture film, with sprockets, which projected forty-eight individual frames, almost simultaneously. The first such film, the peep-show, was brief. It was exhibited at Edison's West Orange, New Jersey, laboratory. Unfortunately, Edison was disinterested and careless about copyright, and his invention was quickly adapted by rivals abroad as well as in the United States. Cameras and projection techniques were developed in England and Germany, and particularly through the work of the Lumiere brothers in France. Ultimately, Edison coordinated his work with Thomas Armat who developed the vitascope, and out of this venture resulted the first official kinetoscope projection at the Koster and Bial Music Hall in New York City. The first showing provided the needed incentive. It was not long before the early Biograph Company was established, and moving pictures became available throughout the country.

Motion pictures, if they were to succeed as entertainment and communicative art, had an enormous potential still to be achieved. The first tentative efforts to reproduce reality were truly literal in thrust. They concentrated on such phenomena as trains roaring down tracks. But these isolated instances of sheer realism needed to be transmuted into stories that would distill reality and combine it with fantasy in such a way as to appeal to the waiting masses. It was the work of craftsmen such as George Melies in France who, in such an effort as "A Trip To The Moon," revealed the potential of the film for telling a story through such now standard devices as the dissolve, the fade-in and other techniques which soon became conventional. Melies proved that motion pictures could do more than reveal scenery in review, for his early experimental films showed the drama of firemen answering an alarm, fighting flames and rescuing imploring figures.

In the United States, meanwhile, experimental work was to result in the first genuine motion picture, adapted from a stage play, produced by Edwin S. Porter and called "The Great Train Robbery." It has been called the first western, a one-reel film done on location and exhibited to the public in 1903. It proved immediately successful, and it was inevitable that the American businessman would seize the opportunity to venture into the promising new field. The early theatres were no more than stores. The admission price was five cents, hence the term "nickelodeon." The silent film was accompanied by the ever-present piano player who provided appropriate mood music for the action on the screen. By 1910, there were several thousand theaters extant to meet the now voracious demand for available one-reel motion picture entertainment. Avidly watched by the thousands of immigrants who could not speak the language, but could nevertheless react to the action on the silent screen, the early films dealt with subjects that were to become staples: the ever-present good guys versus bad guys, the chase, the hair-raising rescue of the heroine and the pseudo morality play involving the perils of too much alcohol. As the CBS News television documentary "Of Black America" revealed, prejudice was rampant and racial stereotypes were casual and accepted without flinching.

Edison's failure to maintain his patents proved disastrous for him and opened the door to the formation of the Motion Picture Patents Company which, even at the start, created the kind of monopoly that forced exhibitors to accept movies from this one outlet or do without product. But, the aggressive drive of businessmen was not to be denied for long. Pioneers in the motion picture industry such as Adolph Zukor, Carl Laemmele and William Fox succeeded in developing empires of their own, and broke the hold of the early trust, only to witness the growth of other trusts until the government's Consent Decree in 1946. The battle between the patents company against the attempts of independent entrepreneurs to establish production of their own joined, along with the inducement of a favorable climate, to bring the industry to California. There, Hollywood, in all its glory and glamour, became the film capital of the world after the First World War.

The Birth of Hollywood

This move to Hollywood witnessed a genuine revolutionary development in motion picture history. It was the beginning of an era of prefabricated popular art for the masses, fashioned by the merchants of dreams and images, and it marked the emergence of the great star system, those synthetic sirens and heroes whose names linked romantic appeal with boxoffice success. Through a combination of flamboyance and sheer press agentry, Laemmele was able to challenge the trust by publicizing his famous "Biograph Girl." The favorable reaction of the public was all that was needed to give the star system a tumultuous beginning. It was essentially the development of the Hollywood production studios, along with the struggle of Laemmele and William Fox against the trust, which led to the explosion of the star system. Once begun, the glamour of stardom became an American obsession until about 1950. The Hollywood star of today is relatively faceless when compared to the exploits and the fanfare that hung on every word and deed of the Mary Pickfords, the Gloria Swansons and the Humphrey Bogarts. The establishment of the United Artists independent company by Mary Pickford, Douglas Fairbanks and Charles Chaplin set up a conflagration of blazing glory for Hollywood stardom which endured for thirty years.

The star system developed out of economic necessity and the temper of the times. The first and most important thing was the film itself. Significantly, what was to develop into a multi-million dollar business, controlled by Eastern economic interests, also began as an art form. And the director who showed the way toward the first realization that movies were a communicative art was D. W. Griffith, America's first, and one of this country's truly creative cinema geniuses. Griffith established that the motion picture was more than a reproduction of reality, more than a static medium. After a career as an actor, he turned to directing at the Biograph studios in New York. He worked with the conviction that film had an artistic purpose and integrity of its own, a unique character which could be found in no medium other than motion pictures. If film art had a form and rule of its own, Griffith discovered and developed that art form. He struck out in fresh ways in the use of the camera, in the development of long shots, close ups, angle shots and other techniques. He developed a company of stars including Mary Pickford and Mack Sennett, and he directed with both discipline and a desire to explore new ways of film presentation. Griffith determined to move from the one reel film to a longer film, for he saw in the full-length feature the genuine creative potential of the motion picture as art form. From a novel entitled *The Clansman* he produced one of America's classic films, "The Birth of a Nation." The dramatic power, eloquence, vigor and beauty of this classic of 1915 remain unchallenged. Unfortunately its racist overtones and its social point of view would undoubtedly incite a riot in the world of today. Griffith's stereotype of the Negro as set against the Ku Klux Klan is tragically antithetical to every principle of contemporary civil rights philosophy, but the revolutionary techniques of the picture remain unquestioned. It remains a towering achievement and, above all, a motion picture from which innumerable directors have learned the art of film-making.

At work at about the time of Griffith was one Thomas Ince who, with Griffith and Mack Sennett, set up the Triangle Productions Company. In addition to the comedy of Sennett, Triangle could boast also of the histrionics of Douglas Fairbanks and the emoting of the first great granite-visaged western hero, William S. Hart. It was Mack Sennett's experience in burlesque which provided the necessary training for his marvelously comic screen improvisations, the mad, scrambling, hilarious and fast-moving antics of the classic Keystone Komedy Kops. Sennett was the true forerunner of America's greatest screen comedian, the immortal Charlie Chaplin. Chaplin is perhaps too well known over the past decade for his political alienation and his disenchantment with the values and virtues treasured by middle class America. His contribution, however, was not political, but artistic. In the realm of cinema art he had few peers. Chaplin exemplifies the Horatio Alger legend come alive on the screen. Literally, he rose from rags to riches through his extraordinary depiction of the inner tragedy, the comic and anguished and mute inglorious frustration of the little man, pathetically buffeted by fate but winning the hearts of millions in such classics as "The Tramp," "The Gold Rush," and even in his later films such as "The Great Dictator," a serio-comic representation of the Hitler mythology. Chaplin epitomized the poor soul of his day, the brow-beaten tramp who aroused a unique combination of sympathy and laughter. Ostracized for many years because of his political views, Chaplin's artistic genius is beyond dispute.

There were contemporaries of Chaplin whose success as stars was legendary, but whose charisma could not come across on the screen as it is constituted today. Mary Pickford, "America's Sweetheart," was the first great feminine star, the first to become rich on an acting career in Hollywood. An incredible mixture of Pollyana and sentimental romance, Mary Pickford was probably the best-known name in America during her reign as the industry's premier leading lady. And America's leading cinema idol was Douglas Fairbanks, famous for the Fairbanks smile, calisthenics and penchant for swashbuckling romance. His films were highly romanticized, intricate in plot and laced with dynamic action and glamour. At the same time, William S. Hart, who acted in, wrote and directed his own westerns, produced the forerunners of the serious television westerns of the last decade, such as "Gunsmoke" and "Have Gun Will Travel." His westerns were in the forthright tradition of "The Ox-Bow Incident" and Hart himself epitomized the grim-visaged star whose pictures set the pattern for the good-guys-versus-bad-guys kind of western.

Film Becomes a Mass Medium

The motion picture industry suffered during the years of World War I, but the post-war years, the frenzied and plush years of the 1920's, saw Hollywood established as the film center of the world. The star system soared in full orbit. Theatres mushroomed throughout the country, and producing companies engaged in the practice of so-called "block booking" which forced the exhibitor to take all of the films distributed by a given company in order to secure the few major box-office attractions. Although there were some strictures offered against the immorality of early films, the sexuality of Hollywood in the 20's centered more around the newspaper and magazine exposés of the private lives of the stars than on what happened on the screen. What happened on the screen was suggestive and mildly salacious by current standards. A sex goddess of the period such as Theda Bara, was basically the fabrication of Hollywood press agentry, for in the contemporary film her sultriness would not be so much erotic as a comic travesty on sexuality.

From 1920 until 1950, when independent production companies and stars began making more pictures abroad for tax purposes, and when it became evident that movies would have to join television, not fight it, Hollywood was the one major film center. Unfortunately most of the films produced during these years were vapid efforts, starring popular personalities but produced without genuine artistry, social context or moral value. Films were epics, and the price tags helped to sell the product to the public, the premise being that expense necessarily meant quality. The business side of the industry overshadowed the aesthetic, and motion pictures were budgeted to include vast campaigns of advertising, publicity and exploitation. The star system reached its apex with such box-office attractions as Gloria Swanson, Clara Bow, John Barrymore and Buster Keaton. Basic staple story forms predominated, particularly the western, the pseudo-sophisticated comedy and the slapstick and farce genre.

Curiously, the criticisms of Hollywood were not based only on the quality of film, but on the private lives of the stars. What would have been perverse and offensive on film in the 1920's would be considered harmless and insipid in the present climate of permissiveness. What the clergy and the parent and teacher groups were concerned about after World War I were the much publicized orgies and romantic alliances of the movie personalities, climaxed by the notorious Fatty Arbuckle case in which a young actress died after a wild party. This shabby affair, along with other complaints about sex and drugs, stirred up sufficient furor to result in the establishment of the Motion Picture Producers and Distributors of America, a trade association which set up its own production code under the aegis of movie "czar" Will H. Hays. The Code proved salutary in an academic sense and puerile in terms of practice, for abuses still prevailed but were glossed over by the hypocritical conclusion that all was well with the world as long as good triumphed over bad and the hero ultimately married the heroine. Producers responded to the

Code with a double standard of spurious morality, while the films reflected the frenzy of the Jazz Age, the "era of wonderful nonsense."

European Influences

Impetus toward an art of film came from abroad, not from Hollywood. In Germany, France and Russia economic considerations did not thwart the desire for genuine experimentation. The flowering of a postwar art in Germany, misanthropic and disillusioned but nevertheless striking and effective, was also evident in films where there was an effort to probe the emotions and tensions of the post-war generation. In a period which saw the production of a number of sordid, pathological and realistic films, Robert Wiene's "The Cabinet of Dr. Caligari," a brilliant and highly expressionistic treatment of madness and evil, is still exhibited today as one of the great achievements in foreign film-making. From post-war Germany came other memorable motion pictures such as Emil Jennings and Marlene Dietrich in Josef Von Sternberg's "The Blue Angel." Symbolism and expressionism were exemplified by G. W. Pabst's "The Joyless Street," a film typical of the dour temper of the period as revealed in the behavior of ordinary citizens brooding dispiritedly about their frustrations on the streets of German cities.

The post-war period in Europe was accompanied by an interest in the "art" film, but the foreign motion picture industry still suffered economically from the effects of the war. In France and Russia there were manifestations of authentic talent, particularly in France where film was influenced by the fashion of surrealism and impressionism and Dadaism in the ateliers of contemporary artists. René Clair, in France, used film to achieve a truly comic effect with a sophisticated and light gloss. Jean Renoir, son of the impressionist painter, produced motion pictures with the touch of a poet. Jean Cocteau experimented with surrealist and symbolist themes and Luis Bunuel, perhaps the most brilliant director of the period, turned toward a naturalistic approach that did not eschew the most sordid aspects of the human condition. All of these directors were, to an extent, experimentalists. And all set a pattern for growth and sophistication in the development of the motion picture as a communicative art, while in the United States the Hollywood factories turned out product designed to further the development of the movies as a medium for the masses.

One of the most controversial philosophers of the film art was the Russian director, Sergei Eisenstein, whose "Ten Days That Shook The World" and "Potemkin" are representative of the use of film to reveal the struggle of the Russian people in a period of revolutionary change. In Eisenstein's films the Russian people, the disenfranchised masses, are the true heroes, symbolically represented so that one significant event epitomizes an entire social movement through the crucible of the motion picture. Eisenstein theorized widely in books and articles, but his works are brilliant examples of the use of the camera to reveal the symbolic impact of time and space. Eisenstein's films combine expressionism, realism and symbolism, but his refusal to accept the restrictive tenets of the Soviet propagandists brought him into repeated conflicts with the political authorities. His work is primarily artistic, and only secondarily political. His juxtaposition of time and space, his handling of large crowd scenes, his ability to extract every symbolic significance of social contrast and his use of montage gave a new luster to movie-making and greatly influenced serious students of cinema in this country.

The Arrival of Sound

Meanwhile, the Hollywood studios distilled dream packages for the delectation of millions of weekly fans at the local palaces. The movie fan magazines became urgent reading for the teenager, and the stars bathed in an ambience of money, power, glamour and glory. The movie moguls, intent on achieving what the trade journal *Variety* called "boffo" at the box-office, thwarted any remote tendency that sensitive directors might have manifested toward sensitivity or artistry. Westerns, comedies, and sophisticated romance predominated. The stars of the era were typified by Rudolf Valentino, enormously popular Latin romanticist, and Gloria Swanson in what were then daring sex comedies. Ironically, it was Miss Swanson who years later distilled the curious mixture of tragi-comedy that characterized the period in a film like "Sunset Boulevard." Erich Von Stroheim, who appeared in "Sunset Boulevard" with Miss Swanson was one of the leading directors of the period, along with Cecil B. De-Mille. Von Stroheim's films, concerned with dramatic studies of moral values, were a cut above the bland comedies and the action westerns that predominated.

In 1926, the motion picture industry underwent a dramatic metamorphosis. Lee DeForest, one of the greatest of communication technologists, recorded sound on film, a technique that was to revolutionize the art of film making. Through the introduction of sound, motion pictures became the first true audio-visual medium of mass communication. The advent of sound was propitious, for the industry had been experiencing an economic recession of its own. Indeed, the Warner Brothers studio which first introduced sound with the historic line, "You ain't heard nothin' yet" in a film called "The Jazz Singer," had itself fallen upon lean days. But sound put Warner Brothers back in business, and ushered in a fantastically successful era for the Hollywood studio. Unfortunately, most of the great stars of the silent film could not make the transition, and talking pictures developed a new crop of players to star in the technicolor and sound dramas and musicals. Jeanette MacDonald and Maurice Chevalier played in sophisticated musicals directed by Ernst

Lubitsch. Warner Brothers brought out a plethora of vapid singing and dancing musical comedies, directed by Busby Berkeley, whose penchant for characteristic dance routines of lavishly gowned girls in long shots against sylvan fountains became a standard presentation and, ultimately, an object of satire. James Cagney and Edward G. Robinson teamed in a series of gangster films of the "Little Caesar" variety, films which were really caricatures of gangland, with none of the sordid naturalism of such pictures today. These were a far cry from the realism, for example, of Humphrey Bogart in "The Petrified Forest." The four Marx Brothers and the magnificent W. C. Fields elicited unrestrained laughter—genuine and not canned—from audiences, with the Marx Brothers satiric and absurd, and Fields uproariously and sardonically pathetic. Westerns and comedies, of course, continued their inevitable course, but there were occasional quality films such as Lewis Milestone's "All Quiet On The Western Front," adapted from the best-selling novel and King Vidor's "The Big Parade"—films which can be termed "The Bridge On The River Kwai" of that period.

Inevitably, the talking film transformed the motion picture industry, writing an end to the careers of famous stars and catapulting new personalities to fame. As the use of color was to change television, so sound changed the movies. Costs multiplied tremendously. Studios became more dependent on Eastern banking interests. But genuinely artistic progress was slow. The first talkies were primitive. Directors, writers, producers and players were groping for a way to use the new technology creatively. One of the finest Hollywood productions of the 1930's was John Ford's "The Informer," a film that still attracts appreciative audience on those rare occasions when it is exhibited. And a film which many critics consider one of the greatest in Hollywood's history was Orson Welles' "Citizen Kane," a brilliantly psychological and biographical study based on the career of one of America's most powerful and enigmatic publishing figures. There were other pictures of varying merit in the mystery dramas of Alfred Hitchcock and the biographical dramas, such as Paul Muni in "The Life of Émile Zola." By the 1940's, attendance at the motion picture theaters was at an all-time high. More than 600 million admissions were recorded. But the shadow of the Consent Decree of 1946 lengthened, along with the tumultuous arrival of television in 1948.

The Consent Decree and Television

After that era, the movies have never been the same. Attendance diminished to about one half of what it had been in the early 40's. The studios were forced to divest production from distribution and exhibition, and companies such as Warner Brothers sold their several hundred theatres in order to remain in the business of making pictures. Independent production companies sprang up. Foreign films began to draw audiences to the newer, smaller "art" houses. Hollywood, to its eternal shame, knuckled under shamelessly and needlessly to pressure groups in the fortunately short-lived era of the "blacklist." Where the average annual film production ranged at about 500 features, the 1950's saw these reduced to about half that number. Meanwhile, Hollywood struck back at television through such technological gimmickry as three-dimensional films and Cinemascope. It tried new kinds of spectaculars, but it was not until the new realism of the 60's that the motion picture once again began to attract a loyal public. It was, however, a very different kind of audience for a very different kind of feature. Theatre films became naturalistic and sexually permissive. Many were produced as sheer exploitation of nudity and pornography. The movie advertisements vied with one another in achieving the distinction of announcing the most immoral film ever made. And, meanwhile, Hollywood sought its way back to economic viability by selling its older pictures for two presentations on television at more than $500,000 for each showing, and by producing comedies and westerns for regular series presentation by the television networks.

The 1960's may have ushered in the end of the great star system. The new stars are low key. Their private lives may not be any more exemplary than those of the 1920's, but they are less publicized. There is also an intelligence and a political and social consciousness among contemporary players that is new to Hollywood. And there has finally come to an end the shameful practice of racial and religious stereotyping. The black revolution has eradicated from films the eternally adolescent Negro Pullman porter. Other stereotyped characters, too, have finally been eliminated. The best of foreign imports—and it is often forgotten that what is imported is only the best—proved to be films of high quality. DeSica's "The Bicycle Thief" and many of the pictures of Roberto Rossellini drew enormous art house audiences. Several of the French, British, Indian and Swedish motion pictures gave American audiences a glimpse of the film as fine art—films such as "Apu," Ingmar Bergman's "The Virgin Spring," British films such as "Odd Man Out" and many of the films starring Alec Guinness.

There was a new audience for the American films of the 1960's. It was a young audience, largely of high school and college age. It was an audience which could take in its stride the new permissiveness in which psychological "hang-ups," sexual license and homosexuality are accepted as staple film fare. Many of these films were shoddy and disgraceful, such as "The Fox." A few were, if not works of art, at least of passing merit such as "The Graduate." And there were films produced by the experimental group that, apart from the "far-out" efforts of Andy Warhol, attempted to come to grips with the social dilemmas of a trying period. The serious interest in film art on the campus, the seeking for new styles and forms bodes well for the future of the motion picture as art form.

One of the areas where the film made a striking contribution is that of the documentary. The documentary came into its own in the era of silent films, particularly in the brilliant work of Robert Flaherty, who used actual scenes and people to create film of great beauty and economy. Flaherty's "Nanook of the North" and "Man Of Aran" are classics of this genre, as are such documentaries as Pare Lorentz' "The River" and "The City" which were both realistic and socially significant. In England, the enormously able John Grierson contributed to the development of this unique form of motion picture making. These documentarians were artists who produced films with rare social and psychological insight. But there were also documentaries of a more pragmatic and journalistic nature such as Time, Inc.'s "March of Time," a kind of film journalism based on the singular style of *Time* Magazine. The "March of Time" was discontinued when the impact of television news coverage made the newsreel theater an anachronism. And there were the documentaries of a quasi-educational nature, produced for use by the armed forces during World War II, many fashioned by eminent Hollywood directors as part of the industry's contribution to the war effort. The Hollywood documentary has all but disappeared with the use of the television public affairs program such as the "CBS Reports" series, the NBC "White Papers" and the special television presentations such as "Hunger In America" or "Of Black America."

The advent of television, in fact, brought forth a number of Cassandras who believed that the world of Hollywood would soon come to a cataclysmic end. But the industry, through a combination of factors, proved more resilient than the prophets of doom had anticipated. In short, the motion picture industry survived, but it was mutated. Attendance dropped appreciably, and picture going became a highly selective process. What ultimately was to prove the industry's salvation were the sale of features to television, the use of studios for television production and the development of a new morality for younger, brasher audiences, intent on doing "their own thing." Audiences began to return to the movie theatres, despite the fact that television, in 1969, boasted a movie on the air seven nights of the week. Colleges instituted courses in film writing and editing, and many of the campus film centers have been experimenting with various techniques. Unfortunately, the emphasis has been heavily on technique, rather than on substance or story. In film, unfortunately, the medium became the message.

Cinema and Society

Like television, the motion picture has borne the brunt of considerable criticism. The advocates and the critics of contemporary film are no less polarized than they were in the 1920's, 30's and 40's. Film, it is claimed, evokes stronger reactions than the newspapers or magazines. It caters to the twelve-year-old mentality. It is violent. It glorifies sex. It avoids sex. It is not socially conscious. It is too conscious of society. It is communistic. It is reactionary. Stanley Kauffmann believes that there is more interest in the motion picture as an art form than in any other medium at the present time. Today, many young people speak seriously of the art of the motion picture, both from a scientific and an artistic point of view. As movies continue to develop, they rely more and more on new techniques. 3-D, for example, was supposed to bring the viewer into the picture. There is a closeness between the technology of the movie today and the growing scientific orientation of our society. The best definition of what a motion picture is and does was offered earlier by Edward Muybridge who, through twelve still cameras, made "moving pictures" of a horse in motion. He defined movies as a technique "for synthetically demonstrating movements analytically photographed from life." Sergi Eisenstein defined movies as the creation of "a series of images in such a way that it provokes an affective movement, which in turn awakens a series of ideas."

What the motion picture does is show movement by means of photography. It goes from frozen motion of the still camera to dynamic motion. In this way, it brings the viewer, as a participant, vicariously into the action. It is more than a sport spectacular, involving physics, psychology and engineering. Indeed, movies probably portray the active temper of our times better than any other medium of communication, which is why so many young people are fascinated with the motion picture as an art form. It gives a dimension, a new dimension to literature. Kauffmann feels that the motion picture has gone beyond the novel. In the work of Bergman, for example, it transmutes reality into metaphor and vice versa. Photography can intensify perception. It can exemplify certain anxieties and tensions. Even without sound, it tells stories in a language of its own, for it does not always need spoken language. It can universalize the world, and does so by means of foreign films imported to this country. For example, a Russian novel must be translated, but a Russian film speaks volumes even without dialogue.

The potential of film has not been reached. It is still a new art and it is exploring new paths every day. The ferment on the college campus, the elements of experimentation, are exciting and healthy. There are areas still to be explored—education and religion, and social tensions. Characterizations of the movie today include an absorption in states of mind, of introspection; a frankness in the treatment of sexuality; a realistic picture of contemporary society. But the language of film remains essentially the same, as it has from the beginning. The film, to flourish, must exist in a society which gives the artist freedom. That is why the Russian film is no longer artistically powerful, as it once was.

The motion picture studios in America have been accused of stereotyping. However, the film reflects the tastes, standards and values of the period. Contemporary film deals with pornography, perversion, lechery and social evil, because the time is one of racial disquiet, campus militancy and general disillusionment. The generation gap and the demand that dissident youth be heard is reflected in film, as it is in the theatre, novel and poem. All of the media—even a family medium such as television—have been affected by the new morality. And the new morality has resulted, finally, in the scrapping of the old Hays Office Code, which was largely a compendium of what could not be done, for a new rating system which stamps pictures as suitable for adults, general audiences, mature young people, or restricted to those under sixteen or eighteen years of age. Like any such rating system, the classification does not take into consideration psychological patterns or individual differences, and is based upon an arbitrary concept of chronological age. Even during the relatively short period since its establishment, the rating system does not appear destined to divide audiences into any successful stratification. For the question is not one of arbitrarily rating the picture, but of the artistry and maturity of the film itself.

As a mass medium, the motion picture is still a powerful communicative art form. The dilemma of film makers is that they are troubled by their conviction that pornography is the one sure-fire way to entice audiences into the theatres. Movie advertisements have gone about as far as copy and layout can go in terms of sexual suggestiveness. Overt and explicit sexuality leaves nothing to the imagination in the contemporary motion picture. What appears to be forgotton is that the film, as a communications art, need not be clinical to be aesthetically or socially significant. Film as it exists in the 1970's is permissive, rather than artistic. It prefers to be unmoral, rather than to come to grips with the themes that give communicative art stature—romantic and realistic themes, social themes, poetic themes that drive home to the heart and mind of man the agonies and yet the glowing potential of what it means to be human. The medium of film may survive economically. It remains for motion pictures to overcome the dull temptations of lechery and pseudo naturalism and to survive as a resilient and stimulating communications art.

As art and technology, the motion picture industry is still in the transition that began in 1948. It is still groping for new forms and new ways of attracting audiences. What new role the film will assume as a mass medium depends in the last analysis on the further development of television, and particularly on governmental decisions concerning community antenna television, pay television and public—or educational—television. Much depends on the motion picture industry's own ingenuity and creativity in finding new ways of communicating with audiences without becoming merely a tributary to the mainstream of commercial television.

As early as 1940, the film industry was aware that a revolution in communications technology would occur as an inevitable result of the introduction of commercial television. In fact, television would have become operative as early as 1940 had not World War II intervened to prevent the completion of final technical developments. But the industry, if aware, was also both apathetic and bewildered, and the reaction to television was groping and tentative. The first response was to demean the new medium, to assert that television would accomplish little more than radio and motion pictures, that it was a skillful amalgam of both, but with no discipline of its own. Furthermore, television was flawed by commercials, by overemphasis on the spoken word and with little originality in use of camera. This criticism may have been true, but it was also irrelevant. And, in recent years, the television medium itself has concentrated on live-on-tape productions and, to a very great extent, on film. Live television is now pretty much restricted to special news events, sports and political conventions. In the documentary area, television was always at its best, with such efforts as "Victory At Sea," "The Search," "Omnibus" and, more recently, "Hunger In America."

At the present time, the motion picture industry is again shaky economically, but it is still viable. Pictures sold to television have brought a new source of revenue. All of the studios have turned to producing films for television. But complex problems remain. Sooner or later, old films will be exhausted. Beyond that possibility, however, is the very real problem of the television companies now making their own feature length films which will be shown first in theatres, but will eventually appear on the television screen. Still, serious observers of film are optimistic. Arthur Knight, one such perceptive critic and historian, points out that "one turns on the television set for distraction or, perhaps, for information. One goes to the movies for refreshment and discovers there, on occasion, that heady sense of personal involvement and spiritual refreshment that only true art can give."

No one can predict with certainty how television will ultimately evolve, vis-a-vis film, for it is still a growing medium. It is also subject to incredible pressures, partly brought on by the need to be all things to all audiences, partly because the industry is reminded from innumerable special interest groups that the public owns the air waves. But it would seem clear that dependence on old movies is not the healthiest way for a medium to grow. And it would seem equally clear that the motion picture industry, if it is to flourish, cannot hope to revive by devoting half of its effort to TV film production and half to the production of sensational and far-out movies. Motion pictures and television, despite their similarities, are not the same mass medium. The theatre film has a discipline and aesthetic of its own which is in need of revival. The interest in cinema by younger artists is such that ultimately this may provide the regenerative force needed to establish film again as a legitimate and indigenously creative medium in the universe of mass communication.

BIBLIOGRAPHY

Bergman, Ingmar. "Why I Make Movies," in *Horizon*. New York: Vol. 3, No. 1 (Sept., 1960), pp. 5–9.

Crowther, Bosley. *The Lion's Share*. New York: Dutton, 1957.

Croy, Homer. *Star Maker: The Story of D. W. Griffith*. New York: Duell, Sloan and Pearce, 1959.

Eisenstein, Sergei. *Film Form—Essays in Film Theory*, ed. Jay Leyden. New York: Harcourt, Brace, 1949.

Gessner, Robert. *The Moving Image*. New York: E. P. Dutton and Company, Inc., 1968.

Inglis, Ruth. *Freedom of the Movies*. Chicago: University of Chicago Press, 1947.

Irwin, William Henry. *The House that Shadows Built*. Garden City, New York: Doubleday, Doran and Company, 1928.

Jacobs, Lewis. *The Rise of the American Film: A Critical History*. New York: Harcourt, Brace, 1939.

Kael, Pauline. *I Lost it at the Movies*. Boston: Little, Brown and Company, 1965.

Knight, Arthur. *The Liveliest Art*. New York: Mentor Books, 1959.

Kracauer, Sigfried. *Theory of Film*. New York: The Oxford Press, 1960.

Powdermaker, Hortense. *Hollwood: The Dream Factory*. Boston: Little, Brown and Company, 1950.

Ramsaye, Terry. *A Million and One Nights*. New York: Simon and Schuster, 1926.

Schickel, Richard. *Movies: The History of an Art and an Institution*. Basic Books, Inc., 1964.

Simonds, William Adams. *Edison: His Life, His Work, His Genius*. New York: Bobbs Merrill Company, 1934.

Sinclair, Upton. *Upton Sinclair Presents William Fox*. Los Angeles, 1933.

White, David Manning and Richard Averson, eds. *Sight, Sound and Society. Motion Pictures and Television in America*. Boston: Beacon Press, 1968.

9

Broadcasting:
Mass, Mass Medium

IN THE UNIVERSE OF mass communications, the broadcasting media—television and radio—have been characterized as being all things to all men. To its enthusiastic proponents from within and without the broadcasting industry, television burst upon the heretofore narrow world of communications like a powerful colossus. Its virtues were extolled as the greatest boon to mankind since the invention of printing. Its potential for education and for cultural improvement was deemed unlimited, given the proper economic circumstances and creative incentive. But to its critics—and they are legion among special interest groups and in academic institutions—television has been called a soporific, accused of pandering to the lowest common denominator in the quest for high ratings and scored for presenting situation comedies and banal westerns which emphasize both sex and violence to an unwarranted degree. Dr. Fredric Wertham's complaint that the comics comprised a "seduction of the innocent" was applied with equal causticity to a medium which, it is estimated, millions of people of all ages watch as many as six hours daily.

Simple informational statistics reveal more than any rhetorical utterance the unbelievable scope, reach and power of the broadcast media. There are 285 million radio receivers in the United States, in homes, cars and portable transistors. There are 6,647 radio stations currently in operation. Each of the three major television networks owns five stations and has affiliation agreements with about 600 stations. In all, there are 880 television stations now operating in the United States. There are approximately 83 million television sets in homes throughout the country. More people watch even the lowest rated program than could fill a Broadway theatre in twenty or more years—even if it played to capacity every night of the week. Programs which are popular are watched by as many as thirty, forty or even fifty million persons. It is small wonder that television can be called with prodigious accuracy a mass, mass medium. Its audience goes beyond what the newspaper, the magazine or the book could ever hope to have achieved.

Beyond the most ambitious dreams of the pioneers of radio, the introduction of television in 1948 completed the third great revolution in technology. This development, following the invention of printing and the Industrial Revolution, was the revolution in mass communications, a technological phenomenon of such dramatic impact that its ultimate effects and consequences can only be surmised. The new technologies of satellites and community antenna TV, for example, have only begun to make their presence felt. A mass, mass medium such as television can accomplish a goal unattainable by any other medium, even with the presence of wire services. It can convey a message with immediacy and simultaneity to enormous, heterogeneous masses of viewers. All of the viewers can receive news or entertainment programming speedily, and at the same time. In the conveying of information, this has proved a decided boon. In entertainment, however, because one program reaches an undifferentiated mass at the same time, television has been scored by its critics for failing to present sufficient programs of cultural challenge or distinction. The audiences, nevertheless, seem to like what they watch, for the medium continues to attract vast numbers of viewers who are better educated, have more leisure time and more money available to buy the products advertised than at any other period in this country's history.

Precursors of Television

The miracle of television, the first medium capable of transmitting sight and sound live from its point of origin, was the result of a long prelude of electronic and other technical achievements which made the whole concept of mass communication possible. These achievements— the transmission of television programs over the air waves and the accessibility of wire service copy to hundreds of newspapers—need only to be viewed against the background of the Middle Ages, when manuscripts were laboriously copied, to reveal the long road which communication has traveled over the past five centuries. The newspaper, even after the invention of print, did not become a mass medium until the fruits of the Industrial Revolution gave publishers and printers the tools of speedier type-setting, reproduction and distribution. The development of the film brought masses into theatres to watch pictures that simulated movement which eventually became synchronized with sound. But the basic technical developments that made the kind of mass communication that is a commonplace in the Twentieth Century were the telegraph, the telephone and the cable. Stemming from Samuel F. B. Morse's historic telegraph message in 1844, "what hath God wrought," came the whole concept of the transmission of communication content by means of electrical energy. And the laying of the Atlantic Cable, in 1868, brought the marvel of interconnection of foreign countries with the United States—a phenomenon which seems placid in the light of communication from outer space and from satellites.

The invention of the telephone by Alexander Graham Bell, in which sound was conveyed by wire, added another building block in the development of the hardware of mass communication. These achievements were the true precursors of radio. But, since the inventors were technical geniuses but poor businessmen, the economic beneficiaries were the industries that became immensely powerful as manufacturers and carriers—the American Telephone and Telegraph Company and others. Since many contributed to the development of the electronic media, the credits were never clearly defined and resulted in continuing struggles for patent controls and in the development of large-scale enterprises which ultimately led to government investigation and intervention.

The earliest radio transmissions were experimental. Following a broadcast from the Metropolitan Opera, station KDKA in Pittsburgh made communications history by broadcasting the election returns of the Harding-Cox campaign of 1920. This was the station's inaugural broadcast, and may be said to have marked the beginning of radio as a true medium of mass communication. De Forest perceived quickly that the radio medium had tremendous potential in bringing music into the home, a conclusion which is particularly relevant today when radio has become largely a music and news medium. In any event, the inaugural broadcast over KDKA was an enormous success. Radio quickly became a household staple. Applications for licenses came from hundreds who were eager to get into the business of broadcasting. Within a relatively short period, more than a million primitive earphone-type receivers were in use. The telephone company, a huge and successful enterprise, realized the potential of radio communications and established station WEAF in New York in 1922. It proved to be not only the most modern and enterprising station on the air, but also the first station to carry advertising and the first to become part of a radio network. These first efforts at radio advertising were tame affairs compared to today's sophisticated copy, for there was prudence as to both price and product.

But the business community was not to find the new communications industry an uncomplicated one. There were endless battles over contracts and cross-licensing. Manufacturers of radio equipment and receivers proliferated, and millions were invested in the new broadcasting business. RCA, for example, was primarily concerned with selling hardware while AT&T, as today, was interested in the huge revenues that accrued from the lease of telephone line services and facilities. Despite the mushrooming of radio stations and the constant violation of patented rights, AT&T continued to extend its facilities until, by 1924, a network of more than twenty stations was operating. Ultimately, AT&T had the lines very much to itself, while RCA concentrated on broadcasting. Through a subsidiary, the National Broadcasting Company, the Red and Blue networks were established in 1927. In the same year the United Independent Broadcasters founded another network which, in 1928, came under the direction of William S. Paley and which was to grow into the successful and prestigious Columbia Broadcasting System.

Government Regulation of Broadcasting

At an early date, it was inevitable that the growing broadcasting industry, using the public airways and with limited spectrum space, would come under some form of government scrutiny. Questions of allocation of air space, of government control versus self-regulation were paramount. An original Radio Act of 1912 proved incapable of coping with the enormous increase in stations and the need for an equitable allocation of frequencies and, in 1927, the Federal Radio Act was established. It prevailed until 1934 when the Communications Act set up the Federal Communications Commission, a body which has survived into the present era of satellites and CATV. The original radio act of 1927 was a result of the realization that the Department of Commerce was simply not equipped adequately to handle the growing confusion in allocations. Stations made unilateral changes in frequencies until some form of regulation became imperative. Ultimately, the Communications Act of 1934 set up certain criteria which, despite the fact that they have come under some rather captious criticism, became the prevailing standards under which the FCC was to operate. Broadcasting stations were to serve "the public interest, convenience and necessity," a statement that has survived an infinite number of interpretations. The spectrum space was not the sole property of any individual or company, but belonged to all of the people. A license was a privilege, not a God-given right, subject to renewal and to revocation. All stations must operate under licenses on frequencies assigned by the FCC. Stations were to keep logs of their operating and program schedules, and the FCC set up standards to improve transmission and reception. Finally, while it was admitted that broadcasting was different from the newspaper in requiring a Federal regulatory agency, it was also concluded that radio—and later television—were to have the same protection of the First Amendment that was given to such other media as the newspaper and the magazine.

It was under this system that broadcasting became a major industry, particularly when radio began to function as an advertising-supported medium. The pattern of television networking which prevails today was established by radio with the inauguration of a network of stations, each station carrying programs distributed by the network, along with their own local programming contributions. And it was the setting up of a system of networking which made feasible the growth of broadcasting as a unique mass medium of both entertainment and information. For only a network system could bring to the millions the talents of great stars and the simultaneous and immediate transmission of significant breaking news events from all over the world. The radio industry, prior to television, brought live and recorded entertainment into millions of homes. But when television added sight to sound, radio became secondary and, after many years of struggling to remain in the black, has once again achieved economic viability by becoming essentially a news and music medium. In its heyday, however, radio was the phenomenon of mass media with its daily strip of serials or "soap operas," its music and comedy and its prodigious growth in terms of a national network of stations. The growth of radio gave rise to industry and government problems and to copyright questions resulting in the establishment of a trade association, the National Association of Broadcasters, and of other organizations such as The American Society of Composers, Authors and Publishers (ASCAP), designed to see to it that its members whose music was played received a royalty.

Government interest in the broadcasting industry was inevitable. The difficulty experienced by the National Broadcasting Company in becoming established resulted in the FCC's so-called Chain Broadcasting Regulations of 1941 which were designed to give affiliated stations greater independence and to encourage competition. One result was the sale of the Blue Network by NBC to what was to become the American Broadcasting Company. As television came close to realization in the 1940's, there were developing two, and later three, major networks. The National Broadcasting Company operated as a subsidiary of Radio Corporation of America. At the same time the Columbia Broadcasting System was succeeding on its own and growing into a major force in communications. When NBC sold the Blue Network, the battle between NBC and CBS was joined. CBS forged ahead with the acquisition of such great stars as Amos 'n' Andy and Jack Benny. Its philosophy of operation was based on the assumption of network control and responsibility, the acquisition of first-rate talent and the building of a strong network affiliation.

Its success carried over into television where, for the past fifteen years, it has had the largest audience and been the world's greatest advertising medium. ABC, the third network, came under the control of United Paramount Theaters in 1953. Although it has been a competitive force, it has not achieved the dominant position of either CBS or NBC. Each of the major networks operates by contractual agreement with its affiliated stations, although each television network is permitted to own seven stations under the law, but only five in the VHF band. Networking offers obvious advantages to both network and stations. Apart from the prestige which local stations stand to achieve by a network affiliation, the station also receives first-rate programming, talent and production values, major news service and considerable revenue. In return, however, the station agrees to carry those network programs in which the public will be interested during certain hours of the day. So-called "option time" no longer prevails. Under option time, the networks had the right, on a certain number of days notice, to insist that a station carry a network program. In point of fact, however, the networks could never apply the option time rule against programs of other networks.

Electronic Journalism

A major problem faced by broadcasting as a mass medium was that of access to news. It is the unique function of radio and television to offer live coverage of events. This coverage is unprecedented and immediate. But it is also true that this ability of broadcasting presented a formidable problem for print journalism. At the beginning, the major wire services—The Associated Press, United Press and International News Service—restricted their services to newspapers and refused to sell it to radio stations or networks. Eventually, however, the wire services were forced to include the broadcast media which now receive AP and UPI wire copy as regularly as any newspaper. As a news medium, television functions in several related areas. It presents evaluative and interpretative documentaries on a multiplicity of social and cultural topics such as "The Generation Gap," "Hunger In America," the NBC White Papers or the CBS news specials. It services the viewer with interview and panel programs such as "Face The Nation" and "Issues and Answers" in which authorities and figures who are prominent in the news discuss timely and frequently controversial issues, such as the campus riots, the missile controversy or the black revolution. It presents cultural specials such as "The Louvre" or a program devoted to the life and work of the contemporary painter, Andrew Wyeth. It offers a nightly newscast, such as that of Huntley-Brinkley or Walter Cronkite, which covers the highlights of national and international news events. It covers, live, momentous news happenings such as the various space flights. And, in moments of national tragedy, it has covered itself with glory for its magnificently combined news and documentary coverage of the aftermath of the shootings of President John F. Kennedy, Robert Kennedy and Martin Luther King, as well as the memorial coverage following the death of President Eisenhower.

In all of these, television excels and even its most captious critics have admitted that the medium frequently does a superlative job. But, say its critics—many of them editors in the print media—television does not devote enough time and energy to these programs compared to its heavy entertainment schedule, nor does it schedule such programs, except under emergency circumstances, in the peak viewing hours known as prime evening time. Admittedly, no medium can cover the breaking news events with the timeliness, the immediacy and the impact of television. But, its critics insist, the newspaper adds a dimension that television, in its relatively hurried and ephemeral coverage, cannot achieve. This is the dimension of depth and unhurried news interpretation and analysis. The newspaper and magazine are printed to be read and, if necessary, to be reread and pondered over. Television and radio are evanescent. This argument, however, is specious, for the broadcast media never intended to compete with, or take the place of, print media. Television offers a service which is unique and unprecedented in its speed and immediacy of coverage. It is where the action is as no other medium could possibly be. And it does combine straight news with analysis from such excellent correspondents as Eric Sevareid and Howard K. Smith. But the broadcast media did not set out to denigrate the newspaper. At best, the media complement each other and inter-relate, each achieving its own goal in terms of its own structure and character.

Criticism and the Code

Criticism and evaluation of television as an entertainment medium stems from other bases. Most recently, the medium has been accused of purveying too much "sex and violence," although why its critics, mostly from government or special interest groups, should link these two qualities has never been satisfactorily explained. In any event, the charges and counter-charges of permissiveness, the hue and cry over "censorship" versus editorial judgment in the cancelling of various so-called "controversial" programs, calls attention to the code authority of the National Association of Broadcasters. Recognizing that a medium as ubiquitous as broadcasting must have some standard of self-regulation if it is to avoid official regulatory legislation, the NAB Code was designed as a set of criteria for the application of taste and editorial judgment. It will be recalled that the Motion Picture Code, set up in 1922 after the Fatty Arbuckle scandal, was the result of considerable pressure from religious and other organizations to clean up the low estate of Hollywood's moral behavior. The so-called Hays Office was supplemented by the vigorous efforts of the Legion of Decency of the Catholic Church. The courts have ruled, however, that no religious group can censor films for everyone. The Church, for example, can only restrict the viewing of certain movies to its own parishioners, as was done by the late Cardinal Spellman in the case of the motion picture, "Baby Doll." But the Codes, even though the television code is far more enlightened than the one set up by the original Motion Picture Association, are not constructive documents. They do not inspire to creative effort, nor are they constructed in terms of a positive program of social, moral, political or economic action.

The codes are essentially defensive. They are reactions to, and buffers against, criticism from government, religious and other special interest groups. As such, as has been pointed out, the Codes are negative documents. Their concern is not with ethical issues, in the classical sense, but with problems of popular morality. Unfortunately, the view of morality is not a rational one from a semantic point of view, for issues are seen only in terms of all good or all bad. The result is that, particularly in film, a program can be morally acceptable to the Code authorities if all questionable elements are artificially but satisfactorily resolved at the end, even though the means to that end are morally shoddy. In television, in particular, the network program practices departments frequently have gone beyond the Code to set up their own criteria of taste, and these are frequently sounder than the rather restrictive and ambiguous language of the Code. The television code was adopted originally in 1952 when the so-called "freeze" on television station assignments was lifted by the FCC. It differed from the motion picture code in that it was less negative in tone, less concerned with sex and the doctrine of original sin. It also was particularly concerned with commercial advertising and with news. While Hollywood concentrated on mitigating the wrath of the advocates of a severe public morality, television relies on the broadcaster —the station and the network—to recognize that it is essentially a unique family medium, that a proper "mix" of information and entertainment is necessary and that the needs of children must be taken into serious account. Television is literally a medium for all the people.

The thrust of the broadcasting code is self-regulation and network responsibility. How well the industry has lived up to these doctrines is a matter which has been hotly debated before innumerable Washington hearings, educational conferences and industry conventions. Former FCC Commissioner Newton Minow accused television of being a "vast wasteland" and Minow was particularly critical of the quality of children's programming. Senator John O. Pastore (Dem., Rhode Island) has been critical of television for alleged over-emphasis on violence. Industry statesmen, such as Dr. Frank Stanton, President of the Columbia Broadcasting System, have steadfastly insisted that broadcasting must take full responsibility rather than yield to an external authority, either in government or, as was suggested, in the NAB Code Authority.

Growth of the Industry

The problems of responsibility, freedom and control, however, came after television had proved to be a medium of unprecedented power and reach. Television's first objective was to become established in the universe of mass communication. It was the very unique nature of the medium that forced a delay in getting television off the ground. Unlike a newspaper, which can be privately printed and published, the broadcast media use spectrum space which must be allocated in order to avoid interference. Furthermore, the airwaves are not anyone's private preserve, but both practically and theoretically are agreed to belong to all the people. As a federal agency, then, the FCC represents the people. But, prior to allocation, came the problem of technology. Scientists had realized, at the height of radio, that television would ultimately become technically feasible. The transmission of moving pictures over wire was scientifically practical, but there were technical problems to be resolved before successful transmission could be achieved. In 1923, Vladimir Zworykin patented a television tube called the iconoscope. At the same time RCA was doing extensive research in electronics, and the Dumont Laboratories perfected the cathode-ray tube and made a successful demonstration of television in 1939, the same year that NBC transmitted a program from the World's Fair. At this point, the FCC was faced with the necessity of establishing some method of setting up and allocating channels. In 1941, the Commission authorized the activation of VHF (very high frequency) channels. But the crisis of World War II set back broadcasting until 1945 when the industry was finally able to move ahead with astonishingly realistic developments in transmission and reception. Even at this early date, CBS developed its own color proposals, but the FCC held color in abeyance and pressed ahead on black-and-white receivers.

By 1948, four television networks were in operation. Advertisers were beginning to see the enormous potential of the medium. Milton Berle was a household word. Television was a reality. There were still technical problems, however, which needed resolution. There were questions of interference in spectrum space to be settled. Because these technical matters became pressing, the FCC set up a "freeze" on allocation of channels in 1948, despite the fact that the industry was moving ahead toward a system of national networking. Finally, in 1952, after a hiatus of four years, the Commission issued its Sixth Report and Order. This provided for twelve VHF channels (2-13) and seventy-two in the UHF (ultra high frequency) band (channels 14-83).

Significantly, the FCC reserved 252 channels, most UHF, exclusively for educational use. In 1950, the FCC set up color standards, but was challenged by RCA. Through the efforts of a committee, a compatible color system was finally agreed upon and adopted by the FCC. Television had achieved at last the status of the great mass communications medium which its advocates were always convinced it would become. RCA and other companies began large-scale manufacturing of receivers. CBS forged ahead in the area of programming and talent, developed a strong network and quickly became the leader in both advertising revenues and popularity with the public. Dumont, however, went out of business, and ABC was established as the third national network. All of the commercial stations broadcast on VHF channels. UHF stations could not be received by the conventional set without a special apparatus, although all television receivers are now equipped to receive both VHF and UHF programs. In 1964, the law required all sets to have an all-channel receiver, so that viewers could tune in on both VHF and UHF programs.

The leap from Morse's "what hath God wrought" to the reality of television transmission is a scientific marvel, but equally astonishing is the growth of this mass medium over the twenty years since the first commercially successful broadcasts. In 1948, when television began, there were sixteen stations broadcasting. Between 1948 and 1952, the FCC imposed a "freeze" on construction permits, thereafter opening the spectrum to almost unlimited growth. In 1970, there were more than 800 stations, commercial and educational in operation, of which almost 650 are commercially owned and operated and about 150 are engaged in educational broadcasting. It is significant, in the light of questions raised about restricted services to the viewer, that 99% of all television homes can receive programs from two or more stations and that 97% have access to programs from three or more outlets. About two-thirds of those homes which have television receivers can receive five stations, and about one-third have seven or more channels from which to select their programs. In the span of only two decades, television homes have grown from about 200,000 to more than 50 million, of which about 16 million can boast of more than one set in the home. Color receivers, at present at about 25%, are expected to grow to well beyond 50% in less than five years. In short, 95% of American families own television sets—more than own automobiles or telephones. And the public spends more on buying sets each year than is spent on print media—newspapers and magazines—combined. Even more significantly, the average adult viewer spends four times as much time with the television set than with the newspaper, and eight times as much than with the magazine. The average family watches at least five hours of television each day.

Most television stations are affiliated with networks, because only through national networking can a station receive the unique entertainment, news and public affairs programming which, along with its local programming, give it its character and prestige. Furthermore, network affiliation is financially lucrative. Almost 60% of the affiliated station's schedule is supplied by a national network such as ABC, CBS or NBC. About 15% is produced by the station. The remainder of the schedule comes from suppliers which prepare and/or sell programs for local broadcast. The affiliated station receives approximately one-third of the network's gross advertising revenue in return for transmitting network programs over its facilities.

The World's Largest Advertising Medium

One of the most controversial issues in which the television industry frequently becomes embroiled is the matter of commercial advertising.

As an advertiser-supported medium, television has been accused of pandering to the lowest standards, of programming vapid shows for the vast majority, of neglecting minority needs and interests, of permitting intrusive commercials and, generally, of failing to live up to its potential. But there are also many who believe that some of the recent commercials are intelligent, artistic and literate. And it is clear that only by means of advertising support can television bring to millions the entertainment, news and special broadcasts which have found favor with millions of viewers. Despite the increase in costs, national advertisers spent a total $2½ billion in television over a period of one year; $1½ billion was devoted to network television. It is the revenues from advertising that allow networks to create brilliant news and public affairs programs, most at a considerable loss, and to carry special programs of distinction such as a memorable evening with such great pianists as Vladimir Horowitz or Artur Rubinstein. In one year, the networks programmed 150 entertainment, public affairs and cultural specials. Critics of the medium say, however, that it is not these programs which lower the standards of the medium; it is the inevitable sameness of the annual crop of westerns, crime programs and situation comedies which produce tedium.

In a competitive mercantile economy, most large businesses spend a considerable part of their budget on advertising, partly by choice and partly by necessity. And a great deal of the advertising budget of many companies, particularly those which merchandise products to the retail market, is allocated to television. At the beginning, radio did not accept advertising. When it was accepted, it was integrated refreshingly in the framework of the entertainment format. Today, advertising forms the basic support of the television economy. The current method of television advertising, invariably placed through the advertising agency, is to pay for time, facilities and talent. But the single or dual sponsor of a one-hour program has all but disappeared because of rising costs. Hour-long programs now boast of multiple sponsors in addition to so-called station-break announcements which produce important revenue for local stations. Local advertising, in fact, is variously priced in terms of its adjacency to major network entertainment programs. In addition to a few institutional sponsors for full programs, most programs are sponsored by a number of participating sponsors, with the network supplying the program. Although most newscasts are fully sponsored, there are sustaining public affairs programs and an occasional cultural special which, because it will not produce a large audience, remains unsponsored.

The average half-hour prime time program, between seven and eleven in the evening, carries three commercial minutes, excluding local spot announcements and station breaks. And the basic problem—and one which has resulted in continuing criticism—is that of placing the commercials so as not to disturb the continuity of the program structure. The NAB Code also calls for advertising that remains within the confines of "good taste"—a phrase that is troublesome because so many groups have their own arbitrary standard of what is meant by it.

The advertiser spends considerable money on mass media, because both research and results show that it is to his economic and public relations advantage to do so. Television receives an enormous quantity of advertising because, again, it produces tangible results. Agencies, of course, select advertising in terms of the sponsor's objectives. Some buy purely national network programs. Others ramify into local markets. Still others buy both national and local spots. The advantages of television to national advertisers of automobiles and cigarettes is, of course, obvious. Indeed, one of the thorniest problems which television has faced in its meteoric history was the increasing demand from both government and pressure groups to prohibit all cigarette commercials—a decision that involved many millions of dollars in advertising revenues. In 1970, the FCC decided that networks could not accept cigarette advertising after January, 1971.

Particular advertising needs are met through national spot advertising, accomplished by means of station representatives through the use of taped or recorded announcements which are sent to selected stations in advance. The station "rep" acts as agent for a number of stations, and is the catalyst between the national advertiser and the local market. An affiliate of CBS or NBC, for example, carries advertising for its own area, along with the national network ads and the non-network national spots. This method divides advertising on television into national, national-spot and local. Since local and national spot advertisements are extremely lucrative, it is not surprising that the five stations which each network may own by law are even more productive of revenue than the network itself. Most stations might be economically viable without network affiliation, but at the same time stations simply cannot afford the enormous costs of large-scale network entertainment or public affairs programming. Secondly, network audiences are truly mass audiences and national advertisers demand large audiences. Still a third significant reason for network affiliation is influence and prestige.

What stations receive from networks today is rarely pure live programming, except in the case of special news events or sports. Most programs are either on film or live-on-tape. Two hours of every night of the week are now devoted to motion pictures. Stations may, if they choose, have a dual affiliation with more than one network, but in either case the agreement stipulates that the station will give the network time for sale to advertisers. Affiliates may now accept, i.e. "clear" a program for broadcast, or they may reject it in favor of local programming. Unfortunately, some stations reject fine sustaining cultural programs because economic self-interest supersedes the public interest. But, since the courts have ruled out the old option time agreement, no network can any longer force stations to take particular programs, any more than movie producers can force block booking of motion pictures. Each of the three major television networks has affiliation agreements with approximately 200 stations.

Television Network Operations

Thanks in great part to its large audiences and to vast advertising allocation, television has been one of the fastest growing industries in the world. But in recent years, costs have increased enormously, and then continue to rise with each television season. Motion pictures which once were purchased for a quarter of a million dollars, now cost almost a million. Production costs have tripled. And, as costs rise, the industry finds itself in the posture of having to take a hard look at expensive "pilots" and at equally expensive specials and national sports broadcasts. The need for circulation increases, too, although sheer circulation has paled somewhat because advertisers want not only numbers but specific demographic characteristics as well. Still, even with ever-increasing expenses, broadcasting continues to operate profitably—a fact which its critics seldom fail to forget in their demand for improvements in the program "mix."

Despite its size, the television industry is a rather tight little island from a creative viewpoint. The program heads deplore the lack of creativity. Yet, infusion of genuine talent is hard to find, and many well-trained people have great difficulty in securing positions in the many departments of a network operation—operations and engineering, programming, information services, affiliate relations, sales, research, legal and general administrative. Talent usually comes from middlemen or talent agencies. And almost every phase of the multifarious network procedures and operations can only be promulgated through one of the forty-six powerful unions which include AFTRA, the Writers Guild, the Directors Guild and the various engineering unions.

The dilemma of commercial broadcasting stems from the basic fact that it *is* necessarily commercial—one of the greatest industries in the world. But broadcasting, both its critics and advocates agree, also must function as an entertainment, informational and educational instrument if it is to realize its enormous potential as a medium of mass communication. What the broadcaster has to sell to the advertiser, however, is programming which brings a large viewing audience to the medium. Unlike the newspaper, there is no Audit Bureau of Circulation available. The television research department, basing its sales information on research statistics of particular programs in a given time period, can only predict probable future ratings. Advertisers, however, buy specific time periods which, at one juncture, were variously classified according to audience availability. Class A time meant prime evening, from six to eleven. Class B, C and D were rated lower accordingly in terms of early and late evening, daytime and Saturday morning. The station, of course, owes its reputation and standing to its geographical location, its "reach" and the audience it can deliver. Advertisers take many factors into consideration in time buys—ratings, demographics, competitive programming and the "lead-in" program preceding the one in which they are investing. Each network and station prepares a rate card which specifically outlines its charges to the advertiser and which is subject to frequent change. But only a most highly successful network can adhere to the card rate at all times. In the case of certain programs, where audience ratings may be weak, various contingency arrangements may be made among agency, sponsor and network.

Since advertisers demand some relevant information with respect to what they are buying, the network must resort to reports from various rating services. Those data are filtered through the research department, so that an optimum presentation can be made to the advertising agency. The so-called "ratings game" is under constant criticism, not without some justification, but it must be admitted that research information, if properly interpreted and applied, does serve as a direction-finder or barometer. Ratings, as part of the framework of public opinion polling, do reveal how television audiences behave under certain circumstances. Whether research actually shows that people buy products which are advertised on television is still a debated point, but from a pragmatist's viewpoint, it would appear that they do. In any event, one goal of television research is to predict as many homes as possible, as indicated by such rating service reports as A. C. Nielsen, American Research Bureau, Trendex and others. Since these surveys cannot reach every viewer, the services uses various methods to get a "reading" on an audience in microcosm. Nielsen bases its averages on 1,200 homes through the use of an "audimeter." ARB asks the viewer to keep a log or diary. What each service seeks is information about which programs are most watched, by whom, and over how wide a geographical area.

Ratings, therefore, are indices of program popularity, as in the Nielsen "Top Ten," and frequently—critics say too frequently—they are an important factor in determining whether a program will stay on the air, regardless of quality, critical acclaim or minority viewer opinion. But rating services also give fairly accurate and reliable information about demographics, share of audience and other factors of value to the network and the advertiser. Total audience, in terms of ratings, includes those millions who viewed all or part of a given program, while the share of audience means that portion of the viewing public which was watching a network or station at a particular time.

One of the factors militating against the uncritical acceptance of ratings is the frequent discrepancy between the various services. Another is demographics versus large audiences. A third is the conflict between total audience and so-called average audience. But the gravest problem comes from the accusation of critics that network research frequently interprets rating information to suit its own ends. But these, while substantial complaints, could be made against all public opinion studies. The objective is not to arrive at absolutes, but to find relatively useful information which will serve as a guidepost or direction finder. Research, in addition, offers useful information about viewing habits and preferences, family patterns and other relevant data. Surveys about public attitudes also are taken periodically by the NAB, the TIO (Television Information Office) and individual network studies, such as the late Dr. Gary Steiner's study "The People Look at Television." In addition, the individual networks test so-called program "pilots" privately before audiences before they determine whether the program will be scheduled to go on the air.

A great deal of the negativism about television which prevails in educational and intellectual circles results from the conviction that the broadcasting industry is concerned primarily with ratings, revenues and profits and secondly with public service. But it should be obvious that television, no less than other media, operates in a competitive economy and that, without entertainment program revenues, the frequently brilliant documentaries simply could not find their way on the air. Despite criticism, the industry is not unaware of its obligation to program for minority groups, and it is acutely aware of the strictures applied against it. The problem faced by broadcasting is to find a modus operandi to fulfill its economic obligation to the stockholders and its service to viewers, while at the same time recognizing its need to live up to that ambiguously worded dictum of programming in "the public interest, convenience and necessity." That networks are not insensitive to criticism, particularly from Washington and from powerful special interest groups, would be a gross understatement.

Paradoxically, the demand that a network take full responsibility for its programming has now given way to a movement to vitiate network control. This, as a *TV Guide* editorial properly points out, would be a distinct step backward. Particularly since the quiz shows investigation of 1958, it has been increasingly vital that the networks assume and maintain full responsibility for what they put on the air. Senator Pastore's proposal that programs be previewed by an NAB Code Authority was rejected categorically by CBS when Dr. Frank Stanton pointed out that the network would not abrogate responsibility to any outside agency. And, particularly in the area of news, the networks must be as totally free from advertiser or other pressures as the print media. Only by taking this firm stand can network television achieve the same standing and prestige as the press. In newspapers, the advertising agency has no control over editorial content. At one time, the agency exercised considerable control over network programming, but networks now program directly or buy "packages" from outside sources, although there are those who remain convinced that implicit pressures on all media still stem from advertising agencies and sponsors.

Television and Other Mass Media

Advertisers choose television for a major portion of their public relations and marketing expenditures for a valid reason. Commercial television is the most powerful of all media in terms of its ability to reach audiences directly as well as in its impact and its social influence. Whether television's explosive entrance on the communications scene is responsible for putting many national magazines out of business is conjectural, but it has undoubtedly had a major effect on magazine journalism, on motion pictures and on the newspaper—in the case of the last, particularly in the way in which print journalism now covers the news. Yet, major magazines and newspapers, although the field has been eroded because of a number of factors, are actually in an economic upsurge. And motion pictures, which in 1948 were given up as a lost medium, have adapted to change and are striving to function successfully again. The major problems facing commercial television today are not competing media, but competition within the same medium. Community Antenna Television (CATV) poses serious copyright problems, as well as the potential competition of additional programming sources, but commercial television was slowly entering the CATV field until prevented from doing so by the FCC. Pay television has been widely debated, but its experimental efforts have thus far not proved very successful. The viewer remains unconvinced that he should pay to receive an unscrambled picture when, by investing in a receiver, he receives the many benefits of commercial television at no cost other than his original investment in the television set.

There are other curious paradoxes in the relationship between television and other competitive media. Motion pictures have joined television by selling old films to television, and also by making films for television presentation. Newspaper publishers now own television and radio stations, although the government has begun to take a close look at newspaper-television ownership. And the book and general culture area which, theoretically, should have been hit hardest by the advent of television, are booming as never before. Sales of hard cover and paperbacks are at an all-time high, while opera, theatre, concert and ballet draw unprecedentedly large audiences. Finally, radio, which was the first to feel the effects of television, has bounded back and is flourishing on a music and news format through the sale of car radios, home sets and transistors. The dilemma of television is not so much competing media as its own need to find new creative resources. With films on the schedule every night of the week, many critics believe there is a genuine need for the industry to emphasize indigenous programming formats, rather than rely on the warmed-over fare from another medium.

A Regulated Industry

The pressures on the television industry come from other sources besides competing or analogous media. Because television is a regulated industry it is different from the other media. Because it is a ubiquitous medium, it draws more attention from pressure groups than other media —official as well as unofficial in nature. Majority pressures are always present, but there are also fierce pressures from the so-called political right and left, from racial, religious and ethnic minorities, from educators, parents and certainly from newspaper critics, a few of whom appear intent, for competitive or aesthetic reasons, on revealing that television is culturally inferior to other media. Obviously a medium as sensitive as television to government and other public opinion pressures, and particularly because it is dependent upon advertising, is not always in an enviable position. For the advertiser wishes to avoid offending potential customers. And the industry finds itself under pressure to avoid offending potentially troublesome special interest groups. Just as newspapers are in a position to distort or omit news, so television stations can make it a point sedulously to avoid all controversy; or they can try to present only one side of a controversial story in violation of the so-called "fairness doctrine." All media, television included, are guaranteed freedom of expression in terms of the First Amendment, but the limits of freedom of expression differ between press and broadcast media. Television operates under Section 315, the equal time provision of the Communications Act and, in theory as well as in practice, must grant all political candidates equal air time regardless of party affiliation. Newspapers and magazines have no such official limitations imposed upon them. Nor are they covered by the fairness doctrine which, while democratic on the face of it, also acts as a restrictive influence in terms of the ability of television to present controversy on the air. Largely through the efforts of Dr. Frank Stanton, Congress suspended Section 315 for the 1960 Presidential campaign, thus permitting the networks to carry the historic Nixon-Kennedy debates. But, in 1968, despite pleas from industry leaders, there was no inclination to pave the way for on-air debates—a decision which, many felt, deprived the public of another unique opportunity to hear and see the candidates discuss vital issues in a direct confrontation.

The regulatory powers of the FCC, as set up by Congress, are limited. Primarily, the Communications Act does not permit interference with programming, although various commissioners such as Minow and Nicholas Johnson have not hesitated to be critical of network program schedules. Although the Commission must look over a station's programming record in the renewal of its license, it has not attempted overtly to control program content. Licenses are granted, every three years, on the basis of how well the station has met the "public interest" clause of the Communications Act. But, until 1968, it was a rare event indeed when the FCC refused license renewal, so rare that critics called license renewals an automatic rubber stamp procedure. Recently, however, the Commission has been taking a hard look at the record of many stations whose licenses are up for renewal. In some cases, such as WHDH-TV in Boston, the FCC, in an unprecedented decision, refused renewal and granted a license to a group of Boston citizens which challenged WHDH. In New York City renewal of the license of WIPX-TV is being challenged by a citizens' group, as is the license of WFAM-TV in Washington, D.C. At the same time, a decision of Judge Warren Burger, then of the U.S. Court of Appeals for the District of Columbia, rescinding the license of WLBT-TV in Jackson, Mississippi, was protested by the FCC, which claimed that the FCC, and not the court, had the authority to revoke licenses. It was these developments which prompted Laurence Laurent, television critic of the *Washington Post,* to comment that "broadcasters claim they're fighting for their corporate lives in hearings before the Senate Communications Sub-Committee."

The Commission, however, is not a court. It can refuse to grant renewals. It can decide that cigarette commercials be restricted or prohibited. It can permit or prohibit sale of stations. It can question multiple ownership of newspapers and stations. But each of these decisions can be tested in the courts, and most of them must be acted upon by the legislative bodies in order to become law. The basic responsibility of the FCC is to carry out the tenets of the 1934 Communications Act as constructed by Congress.

The industry, criticized by Senator John Pastore (D.-Rhode Island) for allegedly purveying excessive violence, found support from the Senator in its assertion that the proliferating challenges to licensees were patently unfair. Pastore called for a greater degree of orderly procedure in license renewals, and also introduced a bill which would not permit an outside group to apply for a station license unless the FCC had decided not to renew the existing license. This prompted Robert Lewis Shayon, of the *Saturday Review,* to comment that the proposal, in effect, prohibited challenge to licenses until after the license had already been taken away from the incumbent. The arguments in favor of the Pastore bill were, first, that a broadcaster could not move ahead with long term commitments if a sword of Damocles was to hang over him every three years; and, secondly, that challengers can present all kinds of "blue sky" promises which may never come to fruition, while the station can stand on the record. But the FCC changed its policy on this question, and the bill went into limbo.

It must be emphasized strongly, however, that the FCC itself does not have judicial authority. Cases which come before the Commission, particularly on matters of license renewal, can—and do—reach as high as the Supreme Court. Indeed, the law of mass communication stems as much from judicial decisions as from FCC rulings. The courts recently ruled in one specific, but atypical case, that payments on copyright material used in CATV transmission were not required, but the whole question of copyright is still unresolved with respect to community antenna television. The basic purpose of the Commission originally was to regulate wire and radio communications, so that stations could be allocated in a way that would insure clear channels with a minimum of spectrum space interference.

The Commission members are selected by the President which, of course, gives the administration implicit, if not explicit, influence and party control over appointments. Under no circumstances, however, can any individual or agency use radio or any other public communications instrument for broadcasting purposes without a license from the FCC. Applicants for stations must file for a construction permit and must show, in the application, how the station plans to operate in the public interest. As has been noted, until recently the FCC rarely refused to renew, and rarely revoked, a license. But, despite FCC inertia, the courts have made it abundantly clear that right of granting and renewing licenses inheres in the FCC. The legislature, however, has determined that broadcasting, unlike the railroads, is *not* a common carrier. It is an instrumentality of public mass communication. Broadcast frequencies theoretically belong to all of the people, and it is on this philosophy that franchises are granted.

The Federal Communications Commission, then, issues and renews licenses every three years. It is concerned with clear channels, with broadcast engineering developments, with international standards and with research. Currently it is deeply involved in questions of CATV, pay television, educational (or public) television and in satellite communications. Its work load is so heavy and so fraught with bureaucratic procedures that it is estimated to be years behind in its schedule— a burden which it claims it is trying valiantly to resolve. Under FCC regulations, all sponsors of programs must be identified, and all stations are required to keep logs of programs and technical operations. In the case of competing interests, the FCC will grant a license on a number of criteria, chief among which are considerations of local ownership, public service and evidence of financial responsibility. On the question of programming, the Commission treads lightly, asking only that program schedules be balanced, that commercials be in good taste and that the

station fulfill that perennially ambiguous concept of "the public interest, convenience and necessity." Unfortunately, neither broadcasters,
commissioners, legislators nor scholars have defined satisfactorily what is
implied by, or expected of, the "public interest" phrase. Through years
of hearings on various phases of broadcasting, there is yet to be a clear
cut, extensionally operative definition of the most beguiling and ambivalent of all broadcast standards.

It is certain that, over the next several years, the FCC will be deeply
involved in an enormous technical and cultural revolution that may well
change the basic fabric of mass communications in this country. Compounding the question of one-city newspapers, which has troubled many
observers, is the whole matter of dual ownership of newspaper publications along with broadcasting outlets. Within the broadcasting industry,
questions must be resolved regarding dual ownership of radio and television stations, of AM and FM radio stations under the same banner,
of ownership of broadcasting licenses by companies primarily not involved in broadcasting, and of ownership of CATV outlets by newspapers. Over the past two years, a great many challenges have been issued
which contest the renewal of licenses by the FCC of television stations
which, under the FCC regulations, belong basically to the public. Still to
be resolved is the FCC decision in 1968 which would not permit ownership of more than one broadcasting station in any given area. At the
present time, more than 250 of the commercial television stations extant
in the United States are owned by about 150 newspaper publishing
companies. All of these stations pose mettlesome problems for the FCC,
the industry, and probably the courts.

Government regulation has always presented a Sword of Damocles
over the broadcasting industry which has resisted official interference
and fought for its own responsibility with all the moral, legal and
logical persuasion it could muster. The always present question is the degree of restriction which might be imposed and whether any restrictive
measures, or any degree of control, would come into inevitable conflict
with the First Amendment's protection of free speech and the press
under the Constitution. The First Amendment has always been considered sacrosanct by the courts, the American Civil Liberties Union and
other organizations interested in the preservation of a free and responsible press. On the other hand, each mass medium, if it is to enjoy the freedom guaranteed by the First Amendment, must work to preserve freedom for all media. Freedom becomes license under certain circumstances, such as using the mails for pornographic literature, but the
courts are extremely careful in restricting freedom to print. And they are
equally concerned that free speech not become libelous or treasonable or
socially harmful or defamatory. The basic strength lies in the fact that
comment in the press or other media cannot be suppressed a priori.
Material to be considered libelous must be published or voiced on the air.

Television and Society

There has been no dearth of critiques of the American press and the motion picture, but neither medium has been anatomized as painstakingly as television. The reasons for this absorption in the structure, function, potential and shortcomings of commercial television reside in the very nature of the medium itself. Television has been cited as a medium with the potential energy of generating the greatest cultural explosion in the history of man. And it has been as roundly condemned as one of the causes of youthful unrest and rebellion, and accused of excessive preoccupation with glorification of violence. These widely disparate viewpoints of the effects of the medium are, as most polarized positions tend to be, extreme in both cases. The answer probably lies somewhere in between, but any basic consideration of television's effect on American mores and character raises the inevitable question of whether society influences the medium or is influenced by it. It can be asserted with some conviction that any mass medium—and perhaps even more so in the case of television—tends more to reflect the character of society than to influence it. If, as some critics claim, the media portray violence, it is because society is not without violence. For it is not the depiction of violence that poses the ethical problem but the circumstances of violence. The violence of "Hamlet" or "Macbeth" and the violence of pulp fiction are not the same, either in form or substance. The sex "Ulysses" and the pornography of tawdry novels are quite dissimilar.

Psychiatrists have pointed out that there is such a phenomenon as therapeutic communication, a discovery made by Freud in his theory of free association and verbalization. But it is not justifiable to conclude that because some psychotic patients are kept quiescent by watching television, television ameliorates abnormal behavior patterns or that it is a soporific for the "normal" viewer. Paradoxically, television is simultaneously accused of fostering aggressive attitudes and of helping to keep manic individuals nonaggressive. This is the kind of reasoning that has resulted from uncritically drawn conclusions about a medium that theoretically strives to be all things to all men. Unfortunately, research on the impact of television, whether by the psychologist or the sociologist, has not yielded empirically verifiable results as yet, and many questions remain in the area of conjecture. David Riesman's peer group oriented "lonely crowd" sums up the viewing experience—a social or group act which is, at the same time, an act of individual concentration. There are those who believe that television numbs the sensibilities of the viewer to the richness of human experience, while others believe with equal firmness that many programs serve to heighten sensibility and perception.

It is clear, however, that one of the hurdles which television and, indeed, all mass media must surmount is the inevitable tendency to stereotype character and experience. While conventional racial and ethnic stereotyping has finally disappeared, there is still a tendency to standardize experience. This is evident in the way situations tend to polarize into good versus bad guys in many westerns, in the daytime serial and in many situation comedies. It is less true of dramatic specials where originality has an opportunity to be applied. But stereotyping in television is nothing new, nor did it originate in the broadcast media. The dime novels, the movies, the popular adventure magazines applied stereotyping shamelessly. So does the newspaper. Actually, it is equally possible to show that television, in many ways, has broadened the horizons of experience. The fact that millions watch a medium does not, as intellectual snobbery would have it, make that medium socially or culturally inferior. Both in entertainment programming and particularly in news and public affairs, television has stimulated an interest in books and has brought information to the masses in a way achieved by no other mass medium. Television, if it is to be evaluated objectively, cannot be approached only from the standpoint of an intellectual elite. It is a popular art and it must be accepted as such before turning to questions of how well it does its job. Only in terms of what television actually does can an appraisal be made of what it might become.

Critical standards cannot be applied to television without a realistic acceptance of its impact on millions of viewers as the most mass-oriented of all the media of communication. Television, evaluated from an aesthetic or cultural perspective, must also be accepted as a unique advertising-supported medium. This, in turn, demands an understanding of the extraordinary impact of electric technology as information and entertainment, of the need for national networking if television is to operate in a viable way and, most significantly, of the inevitable social problems inherent in a medium which reaches millions of viewers—of different age, sex, political persuasion, race, religion and economic status—simultaneously. A medium which has been termed all things to all men cannot function in the same way as the book or even the motion picture. Unlike the movies, it is a family medium, available to all at virtually no cost except an original investment in the receiver. Drama on television cannot as readily be coded for mature audiences as can motion pictures. Writers and producers, working in the medium, must cut a swathe across an infinity of publics, against any number of implicit pressures and aesthetic considerations. Yet in ventures such as CBS Playhouse or the NBC Hallmark series the artist can work in a relatively unrestricted creative atmosphere. In regularly scheduled situation comedy series, perhaps aesthetically inferior but popular with millions, the end product is necessarily the result of many collaborative elements. The medium, for the most part, is popular art and must be used selectively by the viewer. In the final analysis it really cannot be everything to everyone, nor can it please everyone simultaneously. Selective use by the viewer is the only intelligent way to draw the best from what the television medium has to offer. It is abundantly clear that, despite the criticism that television lowers standards of taste, more people currently attend concerts, read books and visit museums than at any time in history. Indeed, there is some evidence that television frequently elevates standards.

The broad implications of television as a mass medium include a consideration of its ultimate function as a socially and aesthetically constructive force in American life. There are those who believe that the potential of the medium has been achieved with the establishment of a fourth network or a national public (educational) television service. Commercial broadcasters believe that more and more programming heretofore reserved for cultural minorities will be accepted by majority audiences as the education explosion continues and standards of taste improve. Certainly, in the news area television has accomplished a singularly effective job of bringing both information and public affairs to the viewer so that, even with the restrictions of time, the American public is the best informed of any people anywhere in the world. It is because both print and electronic media have tended to present the news with considerable clarity and fairness that they remain both free and responsible. And this growing social responsibility by all mass media has come about through better training for the communicator and an increasingly intelligent and inquiring attitude by the communicant. A discerning public is increasingly aware of subliminal advertising, increasingly responsive to quality in all media. Unfortunately, and to a considerable degree, much newspaper criticism of television is affective, rather than cognitive, and frequently stems more from a sense of competitiveness than from candid and unbiased appraisal.

Responsible criticism of television can only accrue from an empirical or extensional approach to the medium. It cannot come from the kind of intellectual snobbery which rejects the medium without a first-hand knowledge of what, in fact, is on the air. And a critical attitude must stem from orientation in the communication arts, in the principles of semantics and in a study of public opinion and attitudes. Through this kind of orientation it is possible, by empirical analysis, to set up standards of judgment, parameters of taste and methods of selectivity. The same values cannot be applied to television as are applied to literature or to the graphic arts. Even in the news area, the same critical standards do not apply to television news broadcasts as to print journalism. Each must be judged in terms of its own unique ability to inform, and each operates differently within the same general realm of discourse. Popular art is different from fine art, but it is not necessarily bad art. Improvement in television may come about through the healthy competition of public television, but it can also be achieved by a healthy addition in the area of ideas, in the spirit of inquiry which is so essential if mass media are to function in an atmosphere of freedom and responsibility.

BIBLIOGRAPHY

Barnouw, Erik. *A Tower in Babel: A History of Broadcasting in the United States*, Vol. I (to 1933). New York: Oxford University Press, 1966.

Bluem, A. William. *Documentary in American Television*. New York: Hastings House, 1965.

———. *Religious Television Programs*. New York: Hastings House, 1969.

Bluem, A. William and Roger Manvell, eds. *Television, the Creative Experience*. New York: Hastings House, 1967.

Bogart, Leo. *The Age of Television*, 2d ed. New York: Frederick Ungar, 1958.

DeForest, Lee. *Father of Radio: The Autobiography of Lee DeForest*. Chicago: Wilcox and Follett, 1950.

deVries, Leonard. *The Book of Telecommunication*. New York: The Macmillan Company, 1962.

Donner, Stanley T., ed. *The Future of Commercial Television, 1965–1975*. Stanford, California: Stanford University Department of Communications, 1965.

Emery, Walter B. *Broadcasting and Government*. East Lansing, Michigan: Michigan State University Press, 1961.

Fang, Irving E. *Television News*. New York: Hastings House, 1968.

Gross, Ben. *I Looked and I Listened*. New York: Random House, 1954.

Head, Sidney. *Broadcasting in America*. Boston: Houghton Mifflin Co., 1956.

Lazarsfeld, Paul F. and Frank Stanton, eds. *Radio Research, 1941*. New York: Duell, Sloan and Pearce, 1941.

Lazarsfeld, Paul F. and Frank Stanton, eds. *Radio Research, 1942–43*. New York: Duell, Sloan and Pearce, 1944.

MacKenzie, Catherine Dunlop. *Alexander Graham Bell: The Man Who Contracted Space*. Boston: Houghton, Mifflin, 1928.

Maybee, Carlton. *The American Leonardo*. New York: Alfred A. Knopf, 1943.

Quaal, Ward L. and Leo A. Martin. *Broadcast Management*. New York: Hastings House, 1968.

Roe, Yale, ed. *Television Station Management: The Business of Broadcasting*. New York: Hastings House, 1964.

Sarnoff, David. *Looking Ahead—The Papers of David Sarnoff*. New York: McGraw Hill, 1968.

Seipmann, Charles. *Radio, Television and Society*. New York: Oxford University Press, 1950.

Shayon, Robert Lewis, intro. *The Eighth Art: Twenty-Three Views of Television Today*. New York: Holt, Rinehart & Winston, 1962.

Small, William. *To Kill a Messenger: Television News and the Real World*. New York: Hastings House, 1970.

Steiner, Gary. *The People Look at Television*. New York: Alfred A. Knopf, 1963.

Television Information Office. *ABC's of Radio and Television.* New York: Television Information Office, 1965.

Weinberg, Meyer. *TV in America.* New York: Ballantine Books, 1962.

Zworykin, Vladimir and G. A. Morton. *Television.* New York: J. Wiley and Sons, 1940.

Supplementary Systems:
PTV and CATV

SINCE THE TIME when millions of Americans discovered the phenomenal capability of radio, educators have had a dream. It was to harness the tremendously powerful new communications medium of radio—and later television—to the service of education, not only in the class room, but for general cultural programming to the home, as well.

The unfortunate, but nevertheless categorical, truth of the matter is that neither educational radio nor educational television has been able to get off the ground thus far, either economically or creatively. Despite the many conferences about the potential of radio as a teaching tool, educators failed to secure and use stations for either limited or broad educational purposes. Efforts to set aside a special service for education by radio were largely fruitless. Non-commercial, educational radio did not materialize, despite the fact that there were innumerable college seminars devoted to the potential of radio as an educational tool.

Until the appearance of the Carnegie Report on Public Television, it appeared that educational television would fare little better than radio. Yet, the interest in television as a teaching tool was widespread, and educators again held numerous conferences at which the infinite cultural possibilities of television were explored and proclaimed. It will be recalled that, in 1948, the FCC instituted a "freeze" on channel allocations, so that the Commission could study the whole question of spectrum space. During the four-year hiatus that followed, from 1948 to 1952, a movement toward the establishment of educational stations gained considerable support from government, educators and particularly from the Ford Foundation. A Joint Committee on Educational Television was formed, and supplementary briefs in support of allocating channels exclusively for educational television broadcasting were offered in a series of hearings before the Federal Communications Commission. Numerous interested parties, in American political and educational circles, urged the Commission to set aside such channels exclusively for educational institutions. Some 800 colleges and other educational and cultural organizations submitted supplementary briefs, indicating how they would inaugurate educational programming if channels were reserved.

Finally, in 1952, when the "freeze" was lifted, an FCC Sixth Report and Order was issued, establishing 252 channels exclusively for ETV, as educational television came to be called. Most of these channels, however, were in the UHF band, which meant that they could not be activated in the home receiver without the addition of a special converter. In 1966, the FCC increased the ETV allocations to 329 channels, and somewhat revised the VHF assignment table. In the interim, in 1964, the Commission also had established a special educational service to public and private educational institutions, with special antenna designed to receive educational material in schools and colleges.

Under the FCC regulation, ETV stations were to be licensed only to bona fide, non-profit educational organizations and to be used "primarily to serve educational needs of the community." There were to be no commercials on these broadcasts. The station was to transmit cultural, instructional and entertainment programs on a purely non-commercial, non-profit basis. The first station to be licensed exclusively for educational broadcasting was in Houston, Texas, in 1953. Others followed, but so slowly that even fifteen years later relatively few educational stations, out of the total number of channels reserved, had actually been activated. The Ford Foundation offered to contribute a considerable part of the cost, provided that stations could raise the rest from community support. Even with this support the progress of ETV proved abortive. As of January 1967, there were only 124 educational stations on the air, and the year-by-year statistics reveal the difficulty which ETV encountered: 1954 (10), 1955 (17), 1956 (21), 1957 (27), 1958 (35), 1959 (44), 1960 (51), 1961 (62), 1962 (75), 1963 (83), 1964 (99), 1965 (113), 1966 (124).

The educational stations now operating represent a variety of cultural, academic and informational ventures. Some are operated by school systems or by colleges and universities. Some are operating as appendages of state education departments. Others are community stations, such as Channel 13 in New York and the stations affiliated with National Educational Television (NET). In addition, special instructional television, designed specifically for closed circuit use in schools and colleges, reaches about ten million students throughout the country.

Several factors slowed down the growth of ETV, until even its strongest and most ardent advocates had to admit reluctantly that it had not lived up to the great promises made in its behalf in the original testimony before the FCC in 1952. One crucial problem simply has been lack of funds, thus restricting the relatively few extant stations to drastically curtailed services. In addition, equipment has been largely substandard. Program resources and creativity—the major promise of ETV as a healthy supplement to commercial television—have been a sad disappointment. Networking has been sporadic, and program exchange, even through the National Association of Educational Broadcasters, has not been particularly successful. Out of a total of about 3,000 hours of programming annually, the average station receives almost 50% from NET (National Educational Television) and the remainder from local production, film, inter-station exchange, state networks and commercial broadcasters. Most of the program distribution is by "bicycling" of programs through video-tape distributors, since the cost of interconnection by cable or other electronic methods has proved to be prohibitive. Nor has the expected financial support been forthcoming. Even a station with the prestige of New York's Channel 13 has been hard pressed for community support, and has depended on contributions from the commercial networks and the Ford Foundation in order to continue its broadcast efforts.

Report on Public Television

It was on the basis of the disappointing record of educational television that a special Carnegie Commission Report on public, i.e. educational television concluded there was a genuine and urgent need for a public television service, different in form and substance from ETV, and different also in thrust and purpose from commercial television. The Commission grappled assiduously with the problems of semantics and nomenclature. A careful distinction was to be made between "public television" and "educational television," even though this distinction was, essentially, psychological. Questions of what could be accomplished with, as well as without, a network were considered. Other problems were concerned with the need for audiences, the goal of providing a service *not* provided by commercial television and the desire to avoid duplicating what the news and public affairs departments of commercial television do so superlatively. Finally, there was the fundamental and crucial question of how public television could receive government sponsorship and still remain free and independent of official control, censorship and political pressures and interference. Related to these problems was the need for trained personnel which meant, in turn, the need for special training courses in electronic journalism in the various colleges offering courses in the mass media and the communicative arts.

The Carnegie Commission Report on Educational Television is a most comprehensive and exhaustive study of the need for, and potential of, educational television. As distinct from the Joint Committee briefs of 1950 and 1951, the Carnegie Report described itself as "a program for action," a series of pragmatic recommendations by which non-commercial educational television could be "most useful" to American society. The Report was in preparation for a full year, was the result of eight major meetings and was based on information culled from more than 200 individual specialists and educational organizations. It was prepared under the direction of Dr. James R. Killian, Jr., of the Massachusetts Institute of Technology, who headed a distinguished committee of contributors.

The Carnegie Report made haste to distinguish between two kinds of special television services, and to separate non-commercial television into these two parts. Educational television was to be designed for specific instructional purposes in the classroom. Public television was to be specifically directed to the community at large. While it was stated that all televsion can be both instructional and entertaining, commercial television's objective is primarily to entertain large, heterogeneous audiences. Instructional television is based on theories of learning, and imposes a responsibility and an obligation on the viewer to participate. Public television, however, "includes all that is of human interest and importance" which is used neither for instructional purposes nor supported by advertising. This, by definition, omits non-sponsored educational or "public service" programs—so-called sustaining programs—on commercial television networks.

A summary of the Carnegie Report makes clear some of the objectives, as well as the obstacles, in the way of achieving an economically viable and creatively successful public television service. The Commission correctly concluded that the present ETV service was not sufficiently well-financed to serve the variegated needs of the American public. In public television, as distinguished from ETV or from commercial television, there is no specific audience necessary to make the broadcast a success. The audience range can be from a few thousand viewers to several million. The important factor is that there be devised "a system that in its totality will become a new and fundamental institution in American culture." Public television is devised, therefore, as a supplementary service to commercial television which is traditionally thought to be concerned primarily with ratings, advertising and delivering large audiences.

In a letter to the Commission an American man of letters, E. B. White, suggested that the cultural potential of non-commercial television was infinite. Public television must set out to improve on what has been accomplished thus far in non-commercial television, so that man may both perceive and understand more vividly and deeply. As has so often been pointed out by critics of commercial television, the purpose of public television, or PTV, should be to serve important minority audiences, as well as the majority. Yet, the Commission Report recognized that both ETV and commercial television can entertain and inform, each·according to its own lights. Public television, in essence, can draw on talent in the universities which has not been tapped by educational television stations. It can present performing talent better suited to the needs of public television than to commercial television's entertainment standards. And it can present the thoughts and contributions of distinguished scholars, heretofore utilized only rarely on the closed circuit or on a program such as "Sunrise Semester."

Corporation for PTV

Public television, as envisaged by the Commission, would be structured along a well-defined plan of procedure. Primarily, the Congress was urged to establish a federally chartered non-governmental, non-profit corporation to be called the Corporation for Public Television. Government and private sources would contribute necessary funds in order for the Corporation to become operative. Local stations would be served, but not controlled, by the Corporation which would make programs available and would also offer every opportunity for local programming services. This, in essence, is the basic plan as devised by the Report. In order to promulgate the plan, there would be two national production centers, one of which, NET, is now in operation. Insofar as technical requirements can be met, the Corporation would make available live-interconnection between stations, would distribute programs to individual stations and would support a program of research and development to improve both creative programming and production facilities. In order to train necessary personnel, research centers would be established in key centers around the country.

Funding would be available through the passage by Congress of a manufacturers excise tax on receivers, beginning at 2% and graduating to 5%, thus providing increasing amounts from $40 million to a maximum of $100 million annually, plus support from private sources. In two final recommendations, the Carnegie Report urged legislation to permit the Department of Health, Education and Welfare to provide facilities for station operation, while the Corporation for Public Broadcasting provided program service; and it urged that Federal, State and local agencies undertake studies to improve instructional uses of the television medium.

Several facets of the recommendations stand out as of particular significance in evaluating the significance of a developing system of public broadcasting. There is tremendous emphasis on the importance of the local station, although it is admitted that a central program source will be as necessary for public television as for the national commercial networks. But the major strength of a public television service is thought to inhere in the local station which should be able to broadcast a full week, instead of going out of business over weekends, as is sometimes the case. The station must identify with, and relate to the community, in every conceivable way. At the present time, most states which have ETV stations simply have been unable to implement such plans because of dearth of funds. Those stations which function as part of university complexes fail to use the many creative and scholarly talents which are available, but untapped.

It was basically to further local programming that the Commission urged the chartering of a Corporation for Public Broadcasting which would also make it possible to weld stations together into a nationally interconnected service. But the question of federal control looms large in this plan, despite the built-in safeguards against it. And it is for this reason that the Report insisted that the institution which disbursed funds be non-governmental in character, free of political interference and totally devoid of control over local programming. The national production centers would outline an annual schedule which would secure the approval and support of the Corporation. The schedule would call for theatre and musical production, children's programming and documentaries on national and local problems. Structured into the plan would be ten hours of national, and twenty hours of local, programming each week, with the stations serving as a major source of program material. In this way, television would cover events in the community, as well as in the studio, and would literally serve the whole community.

Interconnection would set up a network of stations, with a signal emanating from a central point. Stations could use the program immediately or tape it for future broadcast. Among the present methods of interconnection are: wire communication, linking stations by coaxial cable; linkage by electro-magnetic waves and relay towers (microwave relay); and satellite communication through the transmission of electro-magnetic waves into space from which they are "bounced" back to earth. Congress was urged to take action which would give public television special preferred rates on communications facilities.

Because there is no need or pressure for high ratings and mass audiences, it was stressed that public television can be experimental, creating new kinds of programming and encouraging university talent to become involved in this exciting venture. New technologies can be spurred by experimenting with data processing methods, information storage and retrieval, new developments in film and video-tape recording, experimentation in satellite engineering and community antenna television. Under the Corporation for Public Broadcasting, almost all of the country would receive television service through 380 stations, with sixty stations set up for specific instructional television. In this way, ETV, which has not realized its potential, would gain in stature and significance.

Limitations of the Carnegie Report

While the plan for a Corporation for Public Broadcasting is the most ambitious and clearly thought-out program to date, it raises a number of practical questions which are left unanswered. The Corporation report states that "its progress will constitute the test of the system," but it does not reveal specifically how the promise of public and instructional television would be fulfilled in practice. It discusses a creative environment, a sense of commitment to community life; a way of looking at the diversity of American life; a deeper understanding of other natures and cultures. But it does not show, in terms of actual programming, how the objectives are to be accomplished. The heart of any broadcast service is programming, but the programs mentioned—documentaries and children's programs—are broadcast by commercial networks which have certainly presented documentary and public affairs programs of great distinction. Indeed, the experimental Public Broadcast Laboratory, supported by the Ford Foundation, failed dismally in its programming efforts which were judged to be an inferior duplication of what the news departments of the networks frequently do brilliantly.

It is true that public television will be free of the need for regular scheduling, which is restrictive on commercial television, and thus theoretically it will be able to innovate. But the Report is disappointing in its heavy emphasis on hardware and its failure to suggest specific kinds of innovative creative programming so necessary if public television is to offer a genuine supplementary service to commercial broadcasting.

Despite the fact that many perceptive critics recognized that the basis of a successful public television service was programming, the Report received enthusiastic endorsement from many quarters, official and unofficial. But the expected financial support from Congress was not forthcoming, with less than half the anticipated amount allocated to get the project started. Approved in principle, the Corporation is yet to receive adequate funding, and the future did not appear promising as a new administration moved into Washington in January of 1969. While there was general agreement that public television was a desirable objective, there were differences as to technique of operation, financing and programming. Fortunately, however, the Public Broadcasting Act was approved by the Senate without the restrictiveness of the so-called Pickle Amendment which would have prevented any entertainment programming on public television—a move which, if passed, would have precluded a variety of cultural programming, including music and drama. But, in essence, the Act was never clearly defined, and such riders as the statement that every program must meet the test of "objectivity and balance" raise questions as to creativity and experimentation. This language is simply a repetition of such ambiguous phrases as that of "fairness and balance" and other fuzzy concepts that have plagued broadcasting since its inception.

The final passage of the Act did not insure smooth sailing for public television. The $9 million appropriated by the Congress was infinitesimal in terms of the amounts believed necessary—at least $20 million during the first year of operation. The distinction between ETV and PTV was not clearly defined nor, in the opinion of some, was it a logical or practical one. Public support was not galvanized by any strong public information effort, and the major impetus came from a small intellectual elite which had small need of public broadcasting, since it is basically a book-oriented public to begin with, and has displayed little genuine interest in television service. What was also distinctly discouraging was the failure of the Public Broadcast Laboratory, not only in terms of critical reception but, more importantly, in the paucity of viewers. Indeed, these experimental broadcasts by Public Broadcast Laboratory accomplished two negative results. Primarily, they alienated considerable official support. And, secondly, they established that commercial broadcasting can handle documentaries in far superior fashion.

The fact that public television has not made an auspicious beginning, however, should not militate against its development. Commercial broadcasters have encouraged the structuring of an educational television service, and CBS contributed $1 million when the Public Broadcasting Corporation was established. In a letter in June 1969 to the House Subcommittee on Communications, CBS President Dr. Frank Stanton stated the conviction that "public broadcasting serves a constructive and valuable purpose in our society" and welcomed public broadcasting "not only as supplementary to, but competitive with, commercial service."

The heart of the matter is not technology, but creative programming resources, and those involved in public broadcasting are discovering how enormously difficult it is to devise a truly innovative program service. What is needed, as former FCC Chairman Newton Minow pointed out, is a program launching of such spectacular importance that not only the minority, but a vast majority as well, will turn to it for pleasure and profit. The distinction between ETV and PTV is also a rather spurious and arbitrary one. It implies that educational television by its very name, is dull, and it confines all instructional television to a kind of academic limbo. Public television should also be able to draw on the accomplishments of commercial television, as commercial television might benefit from the innovation that would accrue from PTV.

Resources for PTV

Here and there one can find programming by educational institutions which is imaginative, creative and socially significant. The University of Denver, for example, effectively dramatized the crisis in urban communi-

cation in a project funded by the United States Office of Education. The
program, entitled "Operation Stop-Gap" explored the use of television
directed specifically at a target audience of the disadvantaged. Socio-
logically and psychologically this audience was disenfranchised and isolated from the mainstream of middle class society. But 90% owned television sets and used the medium supportively—to assuage loneliness, to
kill time, to forget pressing daily problems. In a program called "Our
Kind of World," an eight-part family serial, the content explored categories of health, social service, jobs, family budgeting and shopping. The
protagonists were two families in a housing project. The format was
similar to the commercial network's daytime serials, or soap operas, but
the people were real and not fictional, and they faced a realistic social
situation. Even from a ratings viewpoint, the series was successful, because the viewer was able to identify with the story and characters.

It is in areas such as this, social scientists suggest, that PTV can make
a notable contribution in terms of genuine social service. And, as commercial television produced a program such as "Hunger in America," so
public television should have the resources to explore the very critical
areas of economic deprivation, racial discrimination, family problems
and psychological, as well as physical, well-being. If, as has been claimed,
the picture of the world offered by commercial television leaves something to be desired, public and educational television can function to
delineate areas of society not depicted by the commercial networks or
stations. This function, however, raises fundamental problems for the
PTV effort. Should public television program primarily for the minority
elite or for the socially, economically and educationally disadvantaged?
Public broadcasting can come to grips with these normative considerations only by hammering out a basic philosophy and a specific set of ends
and means. To this point, at least, educational television has been discussed in terms of only one segment of the public and is, therefore, not
public television at all. It has been structured in terms of that intellectual
minority which needs it least. Realistically, however, it is the culturally
deprived who stand most to gain from a public television programming
service. While it is true that ETV has rendered some service to those
who have been unable to attend colleges, the audiences have been far too
small, the times of broadcast erratic and the UHF channels largely unavailable.

When serving as FCC Commissioner in 1961, Newton Minow was determined that the Commission support a strong program of educational
broadcasting. And only through unstinting effort by Minow and a few
other supporters was the National Educational Television network
launched and the Public Broadcasting Act passed. Progress, however, has
been slow and arduous. Technology has preempted creative programming
considerations. Funding has been extremely difficult. Form has taken

precedence over content. Neither public nor educational television has decided what audiences it wishes to reach, has not established a rationale in terms of its programming philosophy, and has not determined whether it wishes to become supplementary to, or competitive with, commercial broadcasting. It is certainly not important that PTV reach all of the people all of the time. It *is* important that it reach vital segments of the public some of the time with a kind of special programming indigenous to public television. Newton Minow recommended that public television "should concentrate on doing few things, doing them well and repeating them often." There is, indeed, every reason for successful programming to be repeated, even several nights in a row, so that audiences to which it is relevant will have ample opportunity to view it. It need not, and should not, be patterned in terms of commercial broadcasting's objectives, but ought to provide a distinctly unique program service.

One of the major accomplishments of the public television study is not in the program area, but in the realm of technology. The Report synthesized many of the significant changes in hardware that are taking place in electronic communications—improved facilities, excellent information storage and retrieval devices, better reception on better receivers through newer techniques.

Through satellite transmission, international television will become a reality. Satellites might allow for direct broadcasting to homes and schools, but this is far in the future, since it might obviate the need for local stations. But, in any event, there is no categorical need for PTV to use only existing facilities. Under television as presently constituted, viewer reaction must necessarily be indirect. Direct reaction could be feasible, however, for the viewer may be able to control what is being shown by selecting out a particular sequence such as a work of art. It will be possible, also, to stop a motion picture at a given frame for more careful study. In programmed instruction on educational television, separate frames can be highlighted by the use of a stylus or pointer, special programs can be reproduced by EVR (Electronic Video Recording) and newspapers can be reproduced by facsimile. These developments are predicated primarily on the directing of PTV to minority audiences where the interests of many discrete groups can be met. Such interests would include local news and sports, town meetings, and library and museum visits. The Carnegie Report envisions also that instructional television will be able to use Professor B. F. Skinner's techniques of learning reinforcement. Finally, the computer will come to play an important role in instruction and information.

The Congress has appropriated a miniscule sum of money for the activation of public television. But it would be naive to believe that money alone will solve the essential challenge that faces the whole area of educational television at its best. The failure of ETV has been partly the result of lack of funding. Even with an unlimited budget, however, there is no guarantee of creative success, as the Public Broadcast Laboratory clearly demonstrated. Nor will the goal of ETV or PTV be achieved through warmed-over techniques of commercial broadcasting. Public television might benefit from the experimentation now being done so actively in film on the college campuses, and it might learn a great deal from the little theatre movements around the country. And, apart from the program challenge, there is the acute need to ensure that public television be free of political pressure and other harassments, that it function with the same freedom and responsibility that should be accorded not only broadcasting, but also all media of mass communication.

Community Antenna Television

The most challenging development in communications, and one which has absorbed the broadcasting industry, the FCC and the legislature, is that of community antenna television, or CATV. The efficacy of CATV in bringing commercial programs over mountainous areas and to high-rise apartment buildings has long been established. At its optimum, it has been predicted that there could be as many as twenty or thirty CATV channels available to the viewer for regular broadcasts, live transmission from theatres and sports events, shopping services, facsimile and a multitude of other services not now available. But CATV also poses problems for the present system of broadcasting, and the FCC, in June of 1970, ordered the networks to disengage themselves from CATV activities. The proponents of public television—those who are convinced there must be a genuine supplementary service to commercial television— believe that CATV may well supply the ultimate solution. Cable television is envisaged as providing a multiplicity of channels, thereby increasing the choice for the viewer, and doing so at a nominal fee of about five dollars monthly. Thus, there is an immediate difference from commercial television. In the latter, the advertiser pays the freight and majority audiences are, for the most part, a necessity. In CATV, the consumer pays as he goes. CATV is also believed by its advocates to be capable of greatly expanding the coverage of news.

Cable television has been called "the wave of the future" by Richard K. Doan, writing in *TV Guide*. It promises exciting new vistas in transmission, reception and special program content. Technically, CATV is not received over the air waves by means of television antenna. It operates by means of wire or cable. Its first uses were simply for the purpose of achieving better reception in areas where the reception was difficult, owing to the interference from mountain ranges or tall buildings. At present, however, CATV is a rapidly growing industry with resultant problems to be resolved in the way of copyright, technology and allocation.

Advocates of CATV assert that its distinct advantage is that the viewer pays a fee each month, as against advertising-supported television. They believe, too, that cable television is essentially locally-oriented and therefore best suited to serve community needs. And, finally, they make the point that, while the present television system can program only through a given channel, CATV will have many channels available. Thus, it can serve many interests, including facsimile reproduction of news, as well as entertainment programming. The viewer will have a multiplicity of choices.

Leonard Chazen, a consultant to President Lyndon Johnson's task force on communications policy, estimates that if only three million television homes paid five dollars per month for a news channel, these viewers could support a news organization with a budget as large as the news division of the National Broadcasting Company. It is estimated, too, that CATV—like FM radio—could better fulfill special local programming needs. By presenting a "magazine approach" to programming, cable television would provide many channels and offer unprecedented opportunity for minority interest program services.

The pros and cons of CATV have been debated widely by industry, as well as government leaders. The networks claim that CATV copies programs without consent of the copyright owners but, in one Supreme Court action on the question of whether CATV infringes on the owner's rights, the Court held that, based on the facts of that case, it does not. Nor was the case definitive. But even at that the copyright problem is far from resolved. Motion picture producers will not accept revenue from use of film, but will demand payment for their copyright ownership. It is claimed, too, that CATV will be duplicating to some extent the extant network services. Complicating the question further is the corollary question of pay television. Its advocates believe that pay television will offer better programs than the networks and at a nominal cost. But the commercial networks remain convinced that commercial television offers a superior service and at no cost to the viewer beyond the investment in the receiver. Under a system of commercial television, quality programs are available to all, and usually by a choice of at least two channels and, in many areas, as many as five. It is pointed out, too, that there is no evidence that pay television would increase cultural and educational programming. Since commercial television is an advertising-supported medium, the entire economy benefits, because one of the positive contributions of advertising is that it helps to move goods from producer to consumer.

Meanwhile, community-antenna television continues to grow and expand into an ever-increasing number of markets. It is estimated that CATV now serves about three and one-half million homes, but it is expected ultimately to reach millions of viewers. Its reality as a major communications force was recognized in June 1969, when an agreement was reached between the National Association of Broadcasters and the CATV interests which opened the door for growth of cable television while protecting the interests of commercial broadcasting. The NAB and the National Cable Television Association gave CATV interests the right to carry their programs from great distances into major television markets. It permitted CATV to program commercially for the first time. But it guaranteed the networks that the 2,000 CATV systems would not link up a national system of closed circuit television, and it provided also for a limit of six commercials which could be carried on any cable system. Professor Leonard Chazen was prompted to point out that the agreement would prevent the development of responsiveness to minority interests and needs which is one of the most promising aspects of customer-supported cable television.

Described as a form of cartelization, with the implicit approval of the FCC, by *The New York Times'* Jack Gould, the "pact" was rejected out of hand by the networks, with CBS stating categorically that it had no prior knowledge of, and was not consulted about, any such agreement. The problem, therefore, remains as complicated as ever, with the FCC, the Congress and probably the Justice Department ultimately involved in its final disposition. The efforts by Congress to pass a new copyright law, beyond the one which has been in effect since 1909, have been held up by the problems inherent in CATV. There is no doubt, however, that CATV is a significant and promising development. Commercial broadcasting interests, as well as others, have entered the field, and there is little doubt that cable television has proved to be a boon to those who cannot otherwise receive clear reception. It is clear, too, that the next decade will see an enormous growth of community-antenna television as part of a major expansion in the whole spectrum of communications technology. President Johnson's Task Force on Telecommunications policy looked upon CATV as a supplement to, but not a replacement for, commercial broadcasting. But its ultimate usefulness cannot be minimized. It provides a special and unique broadcast service which can be addressed not only to large groups, but also to particular interests and segments of the whole communications audience.

In the late spring of 1970, the Federal Communications Commission, in a complete reversal of policy on CATV, proposed that CATV systems would be permitted in the nation's 100 largest markets. This meant that, despite the difficulty it would create for struggling UHF stations in communities, cable television operators could import programs from anywhere outside the city in order to attract subscribers. The decision provided that producers and writers would be paid for the use of their material. The proposal, on the heels of a decision giving CATV systems the right to originate programs and sell commercials, was greeted with enthusiasm by operators who felt that they were in business at last. The National Association of Broadcasters, however, stated that the FCC proposals on cable television would "convert the present over-the-air television system to a wired pay-TV system."

New Developments in Telecommunications

There are other technological developments of major importance in the world of telecommunications. Satellite communication which has already proved to be a scientific breakthrough of the first magnitude in the news area, will become even more significant with the further development of global communications over the next decade. In the United States, the satellite system was set up in 1962 for the purpose of establishing international telecommunications. The first satellite, SYNCOM, was experimental, designed to determine the proper height for satellite transmission—which turned out to be 22,000 miles above the earth. By 1969, through INTELSAT, global communications were fairly well established with the exception of a temporary breakdown during the investiture of the Prince of Wales. It was predicted that, by the 1970's there would be more than sixty satellite earth stations operating, with INTELSAT IV launched with greater power than ever before, in 1971. Approximately sixty-five nations are part of INTELSAT.

Economic, as well as technical problems, remain to be resolved. INTELSAT is the international communications nexus of the Communications Satellite Corporation (COMSAT). In 1962, when the Congress promulgated the Communications Satellite Act, COMSAT was a kind of semi-public enterprise, operated partly by the public through investment and partly through commercial enterprise. The ultimate disposition of COMSAT awaits a final decision by the FCC and the Congress. It is possible that COMSAT simply will operate a domestic satellite system. It was originally thought that COMSAT would carry the major brunt of international telecommunications, but this apparently drew objections from AT&T, IT&T and RCA. If the FCC should decide that COMSAT will operate domestically only, INTELSAT will be disengaged from COMSAT.

In a general classification of satellite systems by a United States Committee, 1984 was projected as the target date for direct satellite transmission to the home. Three kinds of satellite are described. In Relay satellite, now operating in INTELSAT (International Telecommunications Satellite Consortium), the program is relayed point-to-point between a few fixed locations. Distribution satellite sends program material to earth terminals, where it is delivered to local broadcast stations directly or through terrestrial circuits. Broadcasting satellites send program material for reception by individual or master receiving installations. The only application available in the United States at this time is the Relay satellite system.

Still another development now in the experimental phase is the transmission of pictures by telephone services. With the growth of computers, it was inevitable that thought, planning and research be given to the exciting prospect of combined audio and visual transmission and reception by telephone. In the United States, AT&T may have some television-telephone systems operating in the 1970's. Great Britain, Japan and Sweden are also experimenting with this new development. The basic problem is one of technology. Television and telephone, or voice and picture combined, require the use of 100 more circuits than telephone alone. This problem is expected to be resolved to a great extent with the development of underground cables. The basic merit of voice and picture phones, both technically and commercially, will be closely related to computers which are expected to provide data and answers to questions on a television screen, instead of on a typewriter. Western Electric also is currently developing new push-button phones which, apart from the direct dialing numbers, also contain additional buttons for other services—routing calls, allowing several people to talk at once, or signalling to get through to a busy phone. The new electronic call routing system will be computer-controlled.

These developments are considered only a minimum of what can ultimately be accomplished in both domestic and global communications, if technology can receive the necessary funds for development and, most significantly, if it can harness and utilize the creative resources of man.

BIBLIOGRAPHY

Boutwell, William D., ed. *Using Mass Media in the Schools*. New York: Appleton-Century-Crofts, 1962.

Bushnell, Donald D. and Dwight W. Allen. *The Computer in American Education*. New York: John Wiley and Sons, Inc., 1962.

Carnegie Commission On Education Television. *Public Television: A Program for Action*. New York: Bantam Books, 1967.

Costello, Lawrence and George N. Gordon. *Teach with Television: A Guide to Instructional TV*, 2d ed. New York: Hastings House, 1965.

Goodman, E., ed. *Automated Education Handbook*. Automated Education Center, 1965.

Gordon, George N. *Classroom Television: New Frontiers in ITV*. New York: Hastings House, 1970.

Educational Television. The Center for Applied Research in Education, Inc., 1965.

Maccoby, Eleanor E. "Television: Its Impact on School Children" in *Public Opinion Quarterly*, 15 (1951), pp. 421–444.

McDonagh, E. C., et al. "Television and the Family" in *Sociology and Social Research*, 1950, 35, pp. 113–133.

Postman, Neil. *Television and the Teaching of English*. New York: Appleton-Century-Crofts, 1961.

Schramm, Wilbur, Jack Lyle and Edwin B. Parker. *Television in the Lives of Our Children*. Stanford, California: Stanford University Press, 1961.

Schramm, Wilbur, Jack Lyle and Ithiel de Sola Pool. *The People Look at Educational Television*. Stanford, California: Stanford University Press, 1963.

Shayon, Robert Lewis. *Television and Our Children*. New York: Longmans, Green, 1951.

Stanford University, Institute for Communication Research. *Educational Television: The Next Ten Years*. Stanford, California: Stanford University Press, 1962.

Witty, Paul. *Studies of the Mass Media 1949–1965*. New York: Television Information Office, 1966.

The Information Industry

Few developments in communications have had the impact, and the potential for challenging educational theory, as the growth of the information industry. There are those so dedicated to the pursuit of computerized knowledge that they are convinced that automated technology will not only yield the secrets of the universe, but will supply the ultimate answers to all of the major problems besetting modern man. Others are convinced that the computer at its best gives limited service to man, that it can never replace the human equation or improve the human condition and, at its worst, that it may well prove to be the bane of man's existence. A recent computer error which resulted in hundreds of unqualified students receiving letters of admission to a major college is cited as one prime example that computers are not infallible and that, when they err, their errors are heinous and immoral. But, say the stalwarts of computer technology, man would never have gone into orbit in outer space were it not for the accuracy and dependability of the computer.

From the standpoint of sheer technical achievement, the computer is an unequivocal scientific miracle. It succeeds in doing what science fiction writers merely dreamed about a half century ago. And, whatever its capacity for mischief, it has revealed an infinite capacity for helping man to resolve some of the major informational and communications problems so crucial to the functioning of an urban society. It may well be that historians will equate the development of the computer, as an information machine, with a revolution in communications as far-reaching as the Industrial Revolution of a century ago. As steam once replaced other sources of power, so the information revolution may be as significant a breakthrough as the findings and applications of quantum physics. This is particularly true because media of information have become all-pervasive in the affairs of modern man. Paradoxically, as *Scientific American* magazine has speculated, the information explosion actually may act to reverse, rather than enhance, the trend toward uniformity and mass production. The computer, contrary to what its critics predict, may not drive man toward thought control, but may instead prove to be a liberating influence.

The information industry has become a major force in business, education and science. Few endeavors of any scope remain beyond its influence, and companies engaged in the manufacturing of computers have taken on the glow of a glamorous new industry. The growth pattern has been astonishing. The first efforts at computer storage and programs occurred in 1948 almost simultaneously in the United States and Great Britain. In 1950, the first commercially used computer, called Univac, was tested and found to be successful. In less than twenty years, high speed computers contribute to man's information in peaceful pursuits, in the military, in classrooms, in the science laboratory, the hospital and the business organization. Computers play an indispensable and critical role in the space program, in missile operations and in thermonuclear energy. What has developed is a startling new communications technology which involves the use of programmed machines. And these programmed mechanisms are called computers. Implicit in the title is the fact that the computer, by its very nature, involves mathematical concepts, although some scientists would prefer that the term computer be replaced by the more accurate designation of information machine.

Computer Technology

The first computers of 1950 vintage operated through the use of a vacuum tube. This was replaced by solid-state triodes and diodes which, in turn, were succeeded by so-called integrated circuits. The unusual feature of the integrated circuit is that it incorporates all of the essential elements into a tiny piece of microscopic semi-conductor material. The latest computers involve the use of micro-electronic networks where integrated circuits are fused. It is this constant refinement of the computer which has resulted in its advocates enthusiastically calling it a substitute for the human nervous system and proclaiming that the information machine is, indeed, a thinking machine, capable of doing virtually the same kind of work as the human mind. This ability to store and retrieve information, the capacity to teach and to "think" has become part of a whole new spectrum of use for the computer known as "information technology." Both colleges and private industry have developed vast recruiting and training programs where qualified individual can specialize in programming computers—a procedure which, in its simplest form, involves telling the computer how to accomplish what one wants it to accomplish. There are about 50,000 computers in use in the United States at the present time according to data from the American Federation of Information Processing Societies. This compares to only ten or fifteen in 1950, and the estimate is that there will be close to 100,000 operating by 1980. And computer operations have been accelerated from one hour to a few seconds.

Two basic elements enter into the construction and application of the computer—the hardware and the software. The hardware comprises the technical structure, and involves the in-put and out-put, the basic mathematics of use, the control circuits and the memory storage devices. The software is comprised of the "thought" material which is programmed into the hardware of the computer itself. Obviously, therefore, it is the software which is the heart or essence of the communications, or information, system. The in-put accepts what is literally put into the computer from the external environment. The informational data which is fed to the computer is combined, according to the regulations set down a priori by the program which is stored in the computer's memory devices. This information is combined with the informational material already stored in the memory, and new information is sent back to the external environment through the computer's out-put device. It is this unique operation which has led enthusiasts to compare the work of the computer to that of the human brain and nervous system. The analogy is intriguing, but will not stand up under careful psychological analysis. It is true, of course, that the brain takes in information through the sensoria, by means of man's capacity for sense perception. This information is combined with previous information stored in man's memory, and man then reacts to the environmental stimuli by means of response or, in computer language, out-put. But the analogy ends there. Man's mind is a unique instrument which simply cannot be duplicated by any machine, nor can human stimuli and responses be fabricated in computer technology. Above all, however, is not only man's quest for information and knowledge, but his infinite capacity for value judgments, for normative thinking and for metaphysical speculation.

Computers are, in fact, able to operate at a rate infinitely faster than the human brain can function, and they can work over and over again. It is this speed, repetitiveness and efficiency which has made computer programming so essential a functional component of the modern, large business organization and which is making the teaching machine and computer so helpful a tool in educational theory and practice and in scientific research. The efficiency of the computer has been established, and its efficiency is matched by its ability to produce information in terms of the way it is programmed. The computer is able to interact with its outside environment at tremendous speed, with its in-put and out-put devices working repeatedly. In this way, with a complete operation in work almost all of the time, the computer more than pays its way in terms of original investment, for the more it is in use, the less costly it is in the long run.

The technology of the computer is a highly complex and skilled procedure. What is stored in the computer is a basic unit of information, called a bit, which consists of a theroid core or a transistor. The most significant aspects of the computer, when evaluated as a communications or information tool, is the kind of information with which it can deal, how it carries out its task and what is actually accomplished by using the computer as a more accurate and faster mechanism than the human machine. In the use of computers, information can be built on layers of previous information so that, bit upon bit, the machine functions to take on questions or information, combine them with information previously stored in its memory and provide an answer with uncanny speed and precision through out-put.

The in-put and out-put system of the computer is comprised essentially of the programming elements which allow the machine to communicate with those who use it. For the basic function of the computer is to establish immediate and effective communication, in terms of information flow, with the world outside of the machine. In order to do so, the computer must receive data and programs which must be put into the machine in order for it to operate. The computer functions also to record, and store for future reference, a variety of information which it has been structured to process. Through the device of the computer, answers to specific questions put to it are immediate and accurate. Indeed, the computer which is used sporadically by one person hardly pays its way, for its speed and efficiency are such that it becomes economically feasible and viable only when several users put questions to it simultaneously. The in-put and out-put elements comprise the "software," or program, and the mechanical devices or circuits which perform the essential task of communication are the "hardware."

Despite the speculative science fiction writers, who depict the robot as replacing the human being, it must be remembered that computers are no better and no worse than the programs which are put into them by the humans who construct them. A computer, while an effective communicative device, is a man-made machine, programmed by man, used by man to serve man. Its function, as a so-called servo-mechanism, is to lighten and to fulfill certain human needs. The human equation cannot be relegated to limbo, for computers must be told what to do, must be constructed to process data and to yield information which is logical and useable by man.

Developments in Information Storage

The newer type computers have distinct advantages over the early, tentative models. They are structured to receive considerable data in the form of several in-puts, and they can oblige by doing several assignments simultaneously. The so-called "interrupt" systems reduce computing delays by permitting several in- and out-put operations to occur while the computer is in operation, thus increasing the computer's service to those who use it. Not all computers have the same in- and out-put systems. A typical model of computer installation would consist of a card reader, magnetic tape units, a typewriting unit and a high speed printer. The information, on punch cards, enters the computer through the card reader. The tape units provide storage. Modern computers operate several in-put and out-put devices at the same time, thus eliminating waiting time and, since in- and out-put facilities are separated, the computer can be put to work at its maximum capacity. The "interrupt" system, the key to efficient in-put and out-put, announces the arrival of information. The system itself can interrupt the computer operation, and it is set up to give speedy responses to questions put to the computer. All computers have a program interrupt of one kind or another, as well as a type system which can operate several in-puts and out-puts at the same time. The basic and all-important function of those who program the computer is to specify the precise need for information. As Ivan E. Sutherland pointed out in a discussion of the computer in *Scientific American*, it is not enough for the computer merely to calculate and print answers, for "the answer is useful only when it leads to new human understanding."

There are newer and more experimental computers which are using diagrams, rather than print or type, as the communicative medium between the computer and the user. This involves graphical in-put and out-put equipment, the basic hardware for which is the cathode ray tube. In order to function, electronic devices are used through which the computer controls the tube. Cathode ray tube displays are used also as an in-put device. Through the use of a stylus, which is used as an in-put device, the computer can receive diagrams, symbols and other graphic data for interpretation. The computer, through its memory devices, takes in stylus in-put in what is actually a new programming method which is based on pictures or graphics, rather than words.

In all computers is use today, information is coded in binary form, processed by binary switching elements and represented by binary symbols. The term computer "memory" is applied to those parts of the computer which make it possible to store information. This consists of the instructions that acompany a program, the information fed into the program and the results of the computations. One of the most formidable problems in computer construction is the appropriate design of the memory system. The rapidity of operations of the computer is restricted by the amount of time required to store and retrieve information. The most common method of addressing the computer memory is through the process called structure addressing. In this procedure, each word is given a number by which it is identified or addressed. The memory itself is comprised of magnetic materials in the form of millions of minute cores or rings, each of which stores one bit of information which is recorded on extremely thin magnetic tape. While there are other modes of storage, most computer information is stored on magnetic cores. Some circuits are made up of tiny resistors and transistors, and the memory storage of the computer consists of about a half-million transistors and resistors along with other electrical elements. Early computers had circuit elements made of vacuum tubes, but technical problems arose which made the vacuum tube impractical. At the present time, computers are structured with what is known as an integrated logic circuit which, it is estimated, can produce very complex circuits at low cost.

One of the most fascinating aspects of computer technology is the way in which a computer communicates so as to achieve what the programmer expects it to achieve. In the process known as systems analysis, an appraisal is made of what precisely must be accomplished, along with the concomitant adoption of a plan to carry out the projected idea. From this original analysis, the plan must be put together in such form as to be acceptable for use by the computer. This involves the development of techniques of preparing information for the computer, as well as techniques for storing and retrieving information. The computer itself, if properly constructed, can actually assist in getting a program running accurately. But the software, or programming, of the computer still involves the human equation, and the human being cannot operate with complete accuracy.

Limitations of the Computer

As in many other areas of communications technology, many management experts have come to the belated conclusion that computers will not provide the solution to all of the multifarious problems that a business institution encounters in its operations. Between $5 billion and $10 billion per annum was the average expenditure on computer technology in 1969-70, exclusive of the exorbitant cost of operation. Increasingly, however, it became clear that expensive computers were not being used to full capacity, nor were they being used effectively. Their essential contribution, owing to the quantitative and mechanical nature of the instruments, appears to have resolved into basic data and information service. The sophistication and intelligence which the advocates of computer technology predicted have not come to pass with any enormous degree of success as yet. The philosophy that management could make no decision of basic importance without consulting the computer is passing. But the computer *is* important in mathematical and statistical areas, in marketing and operational information, in production and distribution, and related areas. It has not lived up to what its advocates expected of it, at least to the present, in areas of value judgment, or in areas where decision making must follow careful evaluation and thought. In short, the computer has not challenged human intelligence or value judgment.

Programmed Instruction

One of the truly extraordinary accomplishments of Twentieth Century technology is the development of the process of programmed instruction by means of the computer. Educators and scientists who have worked in programmed instruction are convinced that this process will make an enormous contribution to the whole field of knowledge, and will result in radical changes in what are becoming anachronistic educational practices and theories of learning. Programmed instruction is an educational, i.e. learning, process in which the "program" assumes the role of human instructor and, by a kind of Socratic method, takes the subject, or student, through a set of procedures which comprise a learning process. Programmed instruction is popularly known as the "teaching machine" method which is being used experimentally in a number of school systems. The program is comprised of a series of questions to which the subject is asked to respond. The responses may be of various kinds— direct answers to questions, filling blank spaces, selecting one correct answer among various possibilities. Upon receiving the subject's reply, the teaching machine supplies the correct answer by corroborating the subject's answer, showing it is wrong or requesting that he try again. In those programs designated by Professor B. F. Skinner, of Harvard, questions are presented, the subject replies and the results are immediately available. The subject learns by proceeding from what is already known by him to the confrontation with new data. The Skinner method is essentially behavioristic and is based on the principles set forth in Pavlov's theory. Programmed instruction owes much to the original work by Skinner who first outlined its possibilities to psychologists and educators in the early 1950's. Each successive year has seen growth in the use of programmed instruction, and experiment continues as the computer becomes a more sophisticated device. Programmed instruction is based primarily on the behavioristic theories of psychology of Pavlov, Watson and Skinner, the basis of which is reinforcement. The Skinnerian method is predicated on the conviction that overt responses to stimuli, along with immediate knowledge of the results, tends to accelerate and reinforce the learning process. The work of Skinner and his associates in the construction of programmed teaching machines has gone a long way toward bringing the laboratory experiement in educational psychology into the crucible of actual testing and application in a classroom situation.

Advocates of programmed instruction declare that it has the great advantage of allowing the student to proceed to learn at his own pace and in keeping with each student's ability. The instruction becomes individualized, in a sense. It is not intended to replace the instructor, but rather to supplement the teacher as do television, films and other audio-visual aids. Thus far, the results of programmed instruction have been tentative, but promising. The technique needs further research and development, particularly in the area of training teachers to use programs and to adapt to individualized, rather than large classroom group, methodology. Still to be accomplished is a practical way of integrating programmed instruction into the fabric of the general teaching program. It is clear, however, that programmed instruction is healthy in its emphasis on the learning process, and the ultimate contribution of this new technology may be in revealing additional information about how human communication takes place, how people learn, how intelligence functions. It is not the panacea for the ills of education that its proponents believe it to be, but it may well be another significant tool of learning.

There have been a number of experiments in the use of programmed instruction in education. Computers themselves are research tools, and the so-called teaching machine has contributed significantly to the whole process of individualizing and pacing instruction so that slow learners and fast learners can each move at his own appropriate speed. Some educators question the basis for the Skinner program, particularly on the matter of reinforcement, but there is no doubt that the technique does reveal a great deal of information about the learning process which is resulting in new theories and techniques in the field of educational psychology. It is evident that programmed instruction can teach successfully. Techniques in the use of closed circuit television, film and tape have long proved their value in a number of training programs, both military and industrial. Furthermore, the teaching machine is individualized and, in some respects, superior to the large, heterogeneous classroom system. But the ultimate success of the teaching machine will depend, not upon the efficiency of the technology, but upon the sophistication of the software, or program. Many who have done research in programmed instruction feel that the market is expanding more rapidly than the development of appropriate programs. The result, in their opinion, is inadequate programming and a confused teaching situation.

The present, however, is a time of remarkable change and experiment in education in which old techniques and theories are challenged by newer discoveries in communications technology. The increase in scientific technology resulting from the space program has had important ramifications and repercussions in the world of education, with an increased emphasis on ways of learning and a closer juxtaposition of basic and applied research. The fruits of scientific experiment have been a change in emphasis from lockstep teaching to a consideration of semantics, meaning and the whole complicated process of human communication. This kind of teaching can be enhanced through the use of programmed instruction, because it acts as an incentive to scientific method. The Skinner method of programmed instruction differs from conventional teaching and learning in that it involves the basic application of reinforcement. Others, however, place equal emphasis upon "creative discovery" type of teaching as upon conditioning processes. There appears to be a place for both types in a well-integrated educational program.

Programmed instruction provides a challenge to what its advocates consider outmoded educational methodologies. It offers alternatives to teaching procedures, based on a consideration of the student as an over, or under, achiever. It questions the dogmatic dedication of those who believe in the sanctity of the intelligence quotient, and it provides new ways of looking at the concept of learning aptitude and readiness. The teaching machine endeavors, not to weed out and separate the good from the poor students, but rather to pace learning processes in terms of what is best suited to the individual's needs, ability and aptitudes. Thus is dissipated the time-honored pattern of educational evaluation based exclusively on the parameters of age, chronology and I.Q. Students can pace themselves and progress at their own pace, the brighter moving more rapidly than the slower. This method, of course, provides a change in direction for the classic educational situation where the class moved along at a pace set by the teacher and applied to all equally.

The background for this newer type of instruction was provided, before the use of the teaching machine, by such a mass medium as television which, despite its ubiquitousness, allowed for a kind of individualized and unique instruction. In particular, it provided classes with the best teaching talents available. But neither television nor programmed instruction, despite the foreboding of critics, attempts to replace the teacher. What these communications media do accomplish is the setting of individual progress, as a supplement to, not a substitute for, the classroom instructor. They provide the teacher and student with a new relationship, based on individualized instructional procedures.

The teaching machine assumes particular importance as an educational aid, because of the crowding of classrooms which has resulted from the population explosion of the last twenty years. On every level, from elementary school through college and university, more students seek educational opportunities. But many of these students are not equal to the task imposed by higher education. The introduction of programmed instruction not only provides a practical tool for individualized learning, but also offers an opportunity for new and fresh approaches to educational psychology and to teaching methods and techniques. There are, however, many questions still unanswered about the use, and abuse, of programmed instruction. There is still much to be learned about how this medium of instruction can contribute significantly to new theories as to how the individual learns. There are questions as to how the machine can be structured in order to provide the best method for the student to pace himself. And there are questions pertaining to possible uses of teaching machines beyond the school, in the home and in industry. Programmed instruction, to be successful, must be imaginative and explorative. Teachers must be trained to use the machine effectively. The machine must be juxtaposed with such media of communication as television, books and tape recordings. In the last analysis, programmed instruction will be an effective adjunct to learning if the programming is sophisticated and challenging, the student learns productively and the teacher realizes that the machine can provide a valuable supplement to his own effort.

Education has traditionally been a passive process. Student-teacher relationships have tended to be conventional and stereotyped, with little opportunity for the teacher to allow for individual differences. With the computer, the student can work with greater independence, can learn to have confidence in his own ideas, can determine directly whether his thinking is correct or wrong and can proceed at a pace commensurate with his ability and needs. Those who are convinced that programmed instruction is the wave of the future, foresee computer consoles in schools, homes, offices and factories. The console will consist of a typewriter keyboard and a television type screen which will carry both pictures and text. Subscribers to the use of the console will each have a kind of private "file space" in the computer and will be able to consult, add information and receive information at will. In such an ideal situation, the information in the great libraries will be as close as the use of the console. In an educational situation, one computer can handle requests from several hundred students, each working at a console and proceeding at his own rate of speed. The computer itself works most economically and efficiently when used constantly.

Social and Ethical Problems

Not all educators have embraced the computer with enthusiasm. Apart from reservations about the efficacy of its software, there are misgivings about the computer and the whole sensitive question of the right to privacy. For the computer is more than an educational tool. It can store and retrieve information in an uncannily accurate manner, and this function has provided cause for concern from several scholars and scientists who see in the computer a potential threat to the individual's right to privacy. Computer advocates claim that the machine does not, and need not, jeopardize individual freedom or integrity. But critics worry about official use and abuse of computers. There is concern about gathering every last datum of information in a central file where its use can be abused by those who have no legal or moral right to personal information. A centralized information file, without adequate safeguards and controls, raises many ethical problems, and particularly the question of political and social abuse of private information. But those who believe that the computer is an immensely valuable tool assert that abuses can be prevented by appropriate safeguards. Both the legislatures and the efforts of organizations such as The American Civil Liberties Union can assure that individual privacy is not violated. Individuals, furthermore, can have the right to see their own information files, can raise questions with respect to such data and can demand correction when necessary. Those who use such computer information should also provide valid reasons for so doing, and their use and purpose should be reported. Properly used, its advocates believe, the computer is not incompatible with democratic principles or the Bill of Rights.

A perceptive critic such as Lewis Mumford has pointed out that automated machines tend to standardize human endeavor and human society. Mumford and others question whether the computer will not increase the growing bureaucratization of society. They are concerned lest individual freedom and integrity become obsolete, and the individual become symbolized by a punched card. Their concern also is whether, in the long run, automation will not diminish man's worth and his pride in individual achievement and whether computer files might not, under social stress and tension, be used for ends other than democratic ones.

The problems raised are obviously very serious ones, but those who believe in the contribution the computer can make are convinced that, with proper use, the computer can make man more, rather than less, free. In any event, the programmed machine has provided a fascinating and provocative new instrument of communication whose potential is only beginning to be realized. This whole area of communications is closely linked with the techniques of mathematics and engineering and with their application to human thought and to the ways in which man communicates with man. Dr. Norbert Weiner has called this new field of science Cybernetics and has stated that it applies mathematics and engineering to thinking and to control in communication. Cybernetics, according to Weiner, functions to "find the common elements in the functioning of automatic machines and in the human nervous system and to develop a theory which will cover the entire field of control of communications in machine and in living organisms." This is obviously a large order.

Theories of Communication

The science of Cybernetics is based primarily on developing concepts of similarity between the function of the human brain and nervous system and the functioning of the automatic or thinking machine, such as a computer. As a science, its advocates believe that Cybernetics has complete and universal application to the needs of the Twentieth Century and is as significant a development as was the use of steam in the Industrial Revolution of the Nineteenth Century. As a scientific procedure, Cybernetics deals with the application of engineering to the *entire process* of communication. It is concerned with the reproduction and transmission of electronic signals from the sender, via channels of communication, to the receiver. But, according to Wiener and his associates, the implications are far greater than the simple linear communications from source to receiver, for the science also offers "new and valid approaches to psychopathology and even to psychiatry." The computer, for example, can offer insight into the difference between functional disorders, or neuroses, and various organic diseases of the human brain and nervous system. Freudian psychology, for example, believes that psychotherapy and psychoanalysis functions to dredge up repressed and forgotten material which is stored in the human mind. Wiener has compared the functioning of the machine to that of the human brain, and the development of neuroses and psychoses are analogous to the breakdown of a machine when it can no longer cope with a situation because too much in-put makes it difficult to store instructions with some degree of rational behavior.

Other scientists also have taken up the application of mathematics to communication, among them Colin Cherry and Anatole Rapoport. Cherry's view is that anything which links together or relates organisms is known as communication. In the broadest and most literal sense, therefore, this means conversation, use of the telephone or telegraph, as well as the means by which mass media reach the public. A breakdown or severing of communication links means the disintegration of the organisms involved. But Cherry concedes that the mathematical theory, while applicable in the field of technology, such as radio or television communication, is still tentative in terms of its implication and application in the broader areas of the social sciences. As has been indicated earlier, the one disturbing factor which limits the efficacy of communication is the element of noise.

Another concept was developed by Anatole Rapoport who studied methods by which mathematics could be applied to the quantitative measurement of information contained in any given message. The mathematic theory of communication is, therefore, a quantitative method of measuring information. But it must be re-emphasized that it is not a fact, but a theory, although its champions are convinced that it is as important as methods of measuring energy or matter. The information communicated by any given message is fundamentally deceptive. It contains only what is said, not the potential of what conceivably might have been said, and the information communicated in the message is measured by attempting to find all of the possible messages which are contained in the message source. In its simplest form, human communication is naive and direct. A talks to B. And B either understands or does not understand what A has said, or communicated. According to the mathematical theorists, full understanding can only occur—at least in theory—if the actual mechanism or process of human communication is analyzed and understood. Roadblocks which stand in the way are basically due to difficulty in transmission of the signal, because of noise or because the language used is foreign. Clear reproduction of signal is of vital importance, because noise gets in the way of clarity of transmission of the message, or information. One must question, however, whether it is true, as Rapoport believes, that technical problems involved in telecommunication can be studied totally independent of the semantic principles involved as a basis for all human communication. The mathematical theory cannot be divorced from the social environment.

John B. Newman puts forward still another viewpoint towards a definition of human communication. He feels that communication is so complicated a phenomenon that it virtually defies all attempts at definition, by dictionary or other source and he calls for a "pragmatic," rather than an epistemological, approach. In other words, an operational or functional approach in which communication is viewed in action, as an extensionally verifiable fact. As the semanticists have pointed out, the whole tedious process of definition involves using words to describe more words so that the whole procedure ultimately becomes tautologous. The only practical definition, then, is an operational one. One way of looking at communication is in terms of "the discriminatory response of an organism to a stimulus." The key word, of course, is "discriminatory." And, unless the message elicits a response—in human communication as well as in the use of computers—communication has not taken place in a completed form or circuit. But this definition, while apparently tenable, flies in the face of scientific evidence, for it is not the response alone that takes place, as Cherry points out, but "the relationship set up by the transmission of stimuli and the evocation of responses."

Another way of looking at communication, in the light of what is now known about the way programmed machines work, is that communication is not purely verbal. It is not merely concerned with the transmission of messages or information, but with the whole question of personal influence of one individual to another. The idea represented here is that all human action is communicated in nature if perception is at all involved. But this concept, Rapoport believes, limits communication only to human beings and there is, according to the mathematical theory, very definite communication between men and machines.

The development of the computer and the postulation of the various mathematical theories of communication indicate that communication is a very complicated process about which much is still to be revealed. Communication as a process can involve not only a stimulus-response among human beings, but an interaction between man and the machine. It is certain, of course, that human communication involves verbal exchange among individuals either face-to-face or by means of telephony, machine transmission, newspapers, magazines, lectures, seminars and other media. Communication is becoming a highly diversified concept, involving not only verbal symbols, but gestures as well. And it must not be forgotten that an important aspect of communication is not merely the sending of the message, but the receipt as well. The art of listening is as integral to the process of communication as that of speech. In the computer, the communication is not complete until in-put has elicited information in the form of out-put. In the human situation, unless there is an accurate transmission from the "semantic system" of the sender to what Wilbur Schramm calls the semantic system of the receiver, effective communication has not occurred.

BIBLIOGRAPHY

Bartee, Thomas C., Irwin L. Lebow and Irving S. Reed. *Theory and Design of Digital Machines*. New York: McGraw-Hill Book Company, Inc., 1962.

Becker, Joseph and Robert M. Hayes. *Information Storage and Retrieval: Tools, Elements, Theories*. New York: John Wiley and Sons, 1963.

Bourne, Charles P. *Methods of Information Handling*. New York: John Wiley and Sons, 1963.

Bushnell, Donald D. and Dwight W. Allen, eds. *The Computer in American Education*. New York: John Wiley and Sons, Inc., 1967.

Cherry, Colin. *On Human Education*. Cambridge, Massachusetts: Massachusetts Institute of Technology Press, 1957.

Coulson, John E. *Programmed Learning and Computer-Based Instruction*. New York: John Wiley and Sons, Inc., 1962.

Crowley, T. H., G. G. Harris, S. E. Miller, J. R. Pierce, and J. P. Runyon. *Modern Communications*. New York: Columbia University Press, 1962.

Feigenbaum, Edward A. and Julia Feldman, eds. *Computers and Thought*. New York: McGraw-Hill, Inc., 1963.

Goodman, E., ed. *Automated Education Handbook*. Automated Education Center, 1965.

Greenberger, Martin, ed. *Computers and the World of the Future*. Cambridge, Massachusetts: The Massachusetts Institute of Technology Press, 1962.

Miller, G. A., E. Galanter and K. H. Pribram. *Plans and the Structure of Behavior*. New York: Holt, Rinehart and Winston, 1960.

Mumford, Lewis. *The Myth of the Machine*. New York: Harcourt, Brace and World, 1967.

Pierce, J. R. *Symbols, Signals and Noise: The Nature and Process of Communication*. New York: Harper and Row, Publishers, 1961.

Sass, Margo A. and William D. Wilkinson. *Computer Augmentation of Human Reasoning*. Spartan Books, 1965.

Scientific American. "Information." W. H. Freeman and Company, 1966.

Shannon, Claude E. and Warren Weaver. *The Mathematical Theory of Communciations*. Urbana, Illinois: University of Illinois Press, 1949.

Simon, Herbert A. *The Shape of Automation for Men and Management*. New York: Harper and Row, Publishers, 1965.

Wiener, Norbert. *Cybernetics*. New York: John Wiley and Sons, Inc., 1948. *Cybernetics: Or Control and Communication in the Animal and the Machine*. Cambridge, Massachusetts: The Massachusetts Institute of Technology Press, 1961.

12

Foreign News
and Global Communications

In the rapidly changing world of mass communications, there is one major area that has been given short shrift from both a technological and cultural point of view. It is the entire field of foreign affairs and international news—a vast, complicated, vital and sensitive area which presents a striking example of the paradox of poverty amidst plenty. Communicators are prone to point with pride that, as a result of mass media, the world has grown smaller. Telephone, cable, satellite transmission, short wave radio, microwave relay—all the technical paraphernalia and trappings for bringing countries into closer communicative proximity are available. Yet, partly because of semantic and partly because of logistical difficulties, nations have not grown closer. Nor has the public's knowledge of foreign affairs and international news events approximated the success of sheer technology. This gap is understandable in countries where foreign news is censored and where the media serve the state. But it is difficult to comprehend in a country such as the United States which has the most sophisticated technology, the most unencumbered and free journalism and the largest number of newspapers, radio and television receivers, books, movies and magazines of any country anywhere in the world.

Yet, it is safe to say that the American people, and particularly the newspaper reader, have been short changed in terms of information concerning this country's deep and inevitable involvement in foreign affairs. There is no new isolation in the United States. Communication and transportation have made it impossible for this country ever again to insulate itself from the rest of the civilized world. The world is, indeed, too much with us. And our interests, economic, social and political, are deeply involved in what is happening in Eastern and Western Europe, in

Asia, Africa and the Near and Far East. Yet, the plain facts are that only a few of the 1,750 daily papers which are published in this country devote any appreciable space, or give any major attention, to America's inextricable involvement in the international community. The reasons for this are at least twofold. There is, in the first place, a paucity of good reporting on foreign affairs and a lack of reportorial expertise in foreign policy matters. And, secondly, newspaper publishers appear to believe that the public is simply not interested in reading about the intricate and complicated field of foreign relations, unless there is some specific traumatic incident that can provoke headlines, such as an account of fighting in Vietnam or in the Middle East. The sensitive and arduous daily business of diplomacy are beyond the ken of the average reader, and the average newspaper is neither equipped nor interested in covering foreign affairs beyond a cursory item buried somewhere in the run of the paper.

In addition, the number of adequately trained, working journalists who are expert in foreign affairs is woefully small. The number of newspapers which devote respectable space to international news probably amounts to considerably less than 50 out of a total of more than 1,700 dailies. Few papers, with the exception of *The New York Times* and *The Washington Post*, have any sizable staff of reporters who have had first-hand training and experience in foreign policy. Still fewer have news organizations in foreign countries. In this respect, the television network news bureaus have become far better equipped to handle breaking news around the world than the daily newspapers, although those papers which do have foreign correspondents usually boast of individuals of high calibre and integrity. Because the vast majority of newspapers do not have correspondents specifically assigned to foreign news, the average paper depends exclusively on wire service copy from the Associated Press, United Press International, Reuters and the few other news organizations which provide global service. This world news flows constantly over the teletype. There is no dearth of wire copy, but most of it is neglected and much of it is not worth printing. Furthermore, the very nature of wire copy press service is to provide the news speedily, to convey what is happening in terms of sheer information, but not to dwell upon analysis or interpretative reporting.

This kind of sophisticated writing, which provides the news-in-depth reporting so essential to adequate coverage of foreign affairs, comes from the national and international correspondents and from pundits such as James Reston, Walter Lippmann and the small group of writers whose copy is styled, not so much for the average reader, but for a knowledgeable, urbane, intellectual elite. Beyond the Eastern seaboard, foreign reporting of any consequence is hard to find, and the vast number of daily newspapers which do not syndicate the trained correspondents simply pick up and distill wire copy news in a casual and thoroughly unimaginative manner. Small wonder that the public is neither vitally interested in, nor cognizant of, the tremendously important events that are ocucrring all over the world and which have a significant effect on American politics and policy. Even the 500 odd Sunday papers, with several sections to fill, do not dwell on international news or foreign policy, unless the story is so sensational as to titillate the interest of the editor and, presumably, the reader.

Dearth of Foreign Policy News

There is both a knowledge gap and a credibility gap in the average citizen's exposure to foreign policy news in the American press. The knowledge gap is a result of the failure of the press to provide adequate coverage. And the credibility gap stems from a combination of both official and press reluctance to disseminate and print foreign policy news with the same degree of candor with which domestic news is covered. Washington does not want for newspaper reporters. It is in countries around the world, where American interests are vital, that only a handful of major newspapers have reporters or foreign bureaus. In addition, and despite the fact that television news of international events is accurate and immediate and is adequately covered, television public affairs programs could do even more in the way of foreign policy analysis. In the long run, the public is deprived of adequate journalistic coverage of foreign affairs because of inadequacy and dereliction both by government and by newspaper editors. When the press does cover foreign affairs, value judgments tend to be more intrusive than in the coverage of other national and local news. The editors and publishers appear to be convinced that the majority of readers have neither the background nor the interest to read complicated reports about the devaluation of the franc, the common market or the intricacies of diplomatic maneuvering. Frequently, vital news is omitted, and the more patently provocative item is included.

Of course, as Lippmann and others have asserted, it is fallacious to assume that the people base their judgments and decisions concerning foreign policy solely on what they are exposed to on mass media. The average individual in the United States, or anywhere else for that matter, has no direct say in decisions which may affect his way of life and even his chance of survival. Nor is the press always successful as the self-styled voice of the people. The controversy over the deployment of ABM saw a press which was largely antagonistic to the missile. But it was never put to a direct vote, nor were the polls of any value in the final decision which was based on a vote of 51 to 50 in the United States Senate, with one single senatorial vote swinging the decision in favor of deployment. The media, then, as has been emphasized, may reflect opinion, they may even influence it to some extent. But, unless the issue is one which is so close to the lives of the people that opinion and consensus are inevitable, the impact of both public and media is frequently not a final determinant in foreign policy.

The politicians, however they may vote, are acutely sensitive to the mass media. The press is read avidly in Washington, and there are officials in various government departments, even at the highest echelons, who have admitted that they learn more about what is going on from the press than from intramural communication. Even the top officials look to the wire service news from the foreign bureaus for an immediacy of information which is invariably ahead of the more sluggish diplomatic channels. A good many governmental officials are privy to foreign news which is frequently unavailable to the rest of the public. And, too often, what the public reads is news which is distilled through the crucible of the editor's opinions and value judgments. On this important, but tenuous, factor rests the base for what the public absorbs about this country's involvement with the rest of the civilized world. Even with these limitations, however, the flow of information is free and uncensored. True, there are the usual trial balloons and leaks to the press, the usual information by press hand-out and the usual efforts to control news by attempting to persuade editors that it is in the best interest of the country to omit it. At the same time, the press can be critical of foreign policy in this country. A columnist in Russia writing about foreign policy, as Reston and Lippmann have done when they tend to disagree with policy, would soon find himself in a position too precarious for personal or economic comfort.

The American press seems to understand that, in the area of foreign affairs, the public does not act, but rather reacts to information received from the mass media. There are many political and economic decisions of a domestic nature where the opinion poll and the weight of press and public pressure is important and is felt keenly on the governmental level. In foreign affairs, however, the conviction has prevailed that neither press nor public has the knowledge or the sophistication to make vital decisions. The feeling is that these decisions are best left to the State Department, the Chief Executive and Congress. At the same time, the small group of knowledgeable commentators who are privy to diplomatic maneuvers and channels, do exercise some power in that their opinions are sought, read, and sometimes even followed, by officialdom. A few key columnists enjoy the exalted position of being asked, on occasion, to become an unofficial part of the decision-making process. These writers, who operate with intelligence, as well as with high journalistic integrity, are of crucial importance. Because so few newspapers do have trained foreign correspondents, the major columnists have become an important, and even an essential, factor in breaking down credibility gaps, criticizing ambiguous releases and puncturing official pomposity and recalcitrance.

Foreign Policy and the Press

In times of outright hostilities, resulting from a declaration of war, the American press has worked closely with government information officials to preserve the free flow of information, while not revealing data which would be useful to the enemy. But in situations such as the involvement in Korea or Vietnam, foreign correspondents have not hesitated to be critical and even excoriating of government policy. Press and public opinion were partly responsible for President Johnson's decision that he would not seek re-election, despite the fact that his domestic program had been favorably received. There have been times when the press has even arrogated to itself the decision to temper or eliminate news, not because of pressure, but because the editor's value judgment was that printing the news would be contrary to the best interests of the country. A case in point is the decision of *The New York Times* not to run a story on the impending Bay of Pigs invasion, even though the paper had exclusive advance information. Subsequently, President Kennedy is reported to have said that it might have been healthier for all concerned if "The Times" had broken the story, for the disastrous project might never have occurred.

In general, newspapermen who cover foreign affairs look upon their assignment as an obligation to gather and disseminate news about international events from various capitals of the world, so that the public can receive a free and responsible flow of information. Even more so than domestic journalism, it is felt that foreign policy reporting must be interpretative as well as factual, provided that what is rendered is not editorial advocacy, but an informed judgment based on knowledge, training and experience. Facts alone, many journalists feel, are a seduction of the innocent, for the news that comes from official publicity agents is usually couched in such a way as to persuade the newsman toward accepting a desired point of view. The experienced foreign correspondent knows when, and how, to separate wheat from chaff, and he accomplishes this public service by combining a report of the facts as rendered, along with his contribution as an interpretative reporter. The press has a responsibility not only to keep the public informed, but also to take foreign policy makers to task when it is felt that policy clashes with the public interest. The best reporters are, then, both political critics and watchdogs of the public interest. In both the domestic and foreign areas there are examples of this kind of responsible reporting. James Reston's castigation of President Nixon's communications staff for refusing to confirm Reston's query about a Supreme Court appointment brilliantly exemplified this kind of reporting in a column entitled "Lower Your Voice."

The interaction between foreign correspondents and columnists and the Washington image-makers is a continuing one, and humorous examples of it are frequently to be found in the columns of *The New York Times*, *The Wall Street Journal* and the *Washington Post*, as well as in the pungent and thoughtful television commentary of correspondents such as Eric Sevareid, David Brinkley and Howard K. Smith. The tug of war between the journalist and the official is a never-ending one. When an official is the recipient of a favorable story, the correspondent is likely to enjoy favored access to news. But let the writer turn out an antagonistic piece and there ensues a closed door policy which, fortunately, is temporary in nature, for most politicians cannot afford to neglect the press for too long a period.

This curious relationship, however, is not always in the best interest of the public. Both writers and officials, if they are not careful, soon begin operating in a circumscribed area where the correspondent writes more for the Washington crowd than for the people, and the politican tends to operate more in the interest of securing a favorable press than in the interest of the public. Foreign policy news tends to stem from personalities rather than from events. Sometimes it is sparked, or fabricated out of whole cloth, by the official. At others, it is developed from a comment or "leak" picked up by an enterprising and imaginative writer. The main sources of news are the information divisions of various government agencies, although the experienced correspondents get their news at private luncheons or briefings.

At best, however, the coverage of foreign affairs is not extensive. Beyond the relatively few major columnists, the news is almost exclusively wire service copy. Most newspapers devote about 10% or 12% of their total news coverage to foreign affairs, with the preponderant space given over to local and national events, features, sports and comics. What is printed, however, is read with keen interest by government officials throughout the world. In many countries, including the Washington agencies, the press reports are considered accurate renditions of events in the fascinating arena of foreign affairs. More than one hearing or debate over foreign policy has been based more on what has appeared in the press, both foreign and domestic, than on any other source. No particular public is more interested in, or more sensitive to, what appears in print and on the air than that powerful, circumscribed segment of American society which makes up Washington officialdom.

Media Around the World

It is interesting to note that the very nature of colonial society created a demand for news from abroad far beyond that which exists today. The Colonists, recently separated from England, hungered for news from the original home. But the colonial press was a controlled and censored one. The contemporary newspaper account, and the television news programs, are both free and keenly aware of their reach and power as media of mass communication. Most writers who cover foreign affairs work out of a sense of conviction that their words have an important influence. This may or may not be true, depending upon the paper and the reader. But, in general, it is difficult to ascribe any major influence on the majority of readers, simply because most newspapers do not cover foreign affairs in depth, and most readers are not sufficiently informed on international relations to make significant judgments. A public better educated in foreign affairs ultimately will demand greater coverage of the area from the mass media. It is the minority intellectual elite who benefit most from foreign affairs coverage in the few great newspapers of the country—this group along with government officials on all levels in the nation's capital. From the latter, however, there is a genuine need for a new attitude toward the press corps. Phrases such as "credibility gap" would not be used by the press if the interaction between foreign affairs reporters and officials were what it should be—a relationship based on the philosophy that, in a democratic society, it is not the press which should be used by government, but rather that government should be accountable to the people through the press.

International Telecommunications

It is clear that the United States has a commanding quantitative lead in all media, but particularly in the number of daily newspapers and in radio and television sets. But progress in growth of mass communication in countries throughout the world is rapid, and the greatest impact is in the area of telecommunications. While some countries still do not have even adequate telephone facilities, others are deeply committed to the growth of both radio and television communications and to the potential of satellites. There is general agreement that there must be some feasible way of establishing a regulatory agency, not with respect to content, but in terms of growing technology. With spectrum space at a premium and resources limited, vital decisions must be made regarding the ultimate disposition of precious wave lengths throughout the world.

Curiously enough, foreign affairs are covered far more convincingly and completely (if from a biased viewpoint) by many countries abroad than by newspapers in the United States. Yet, this country has more of the mass media than any other, and twice or three times as many as most. A United Nations report of newspapers, radio, television and books, based on the most recent figures, indicates the disposition of these media in many countries around the world, including the United States. The figures reveal the sheer quantitative size of each medium in this country as compared to other countries. The figures, unless otherwise indicated, are 1967-68 for all media, except television which have been updated to 1969:

Country	1967–8 Newspapers	1967–8 Radio Sets	1969 Television Sets	1967–8 Books Published	1967–8 Motion Pictures
Argentina	176 (1966)	800,000	1,950,000	—	25
Australia	60 (1966)	2,538,000	2,341,532	2,151	1 (1966)
Belgium	54 (1965)	3,190,000	1,800,625	3,202	5
Brazil	242	—	5,000,000	—	21 (1963)
Canada	113 (1966)	12,050,000	7,271,000	2,724	6 (1966)
Central African Repub.	2	33	—	—	—
Chile	46 (1964)	—	150,000	1,479	—
China (Mainland)	392 (1955)	—	—	—	—
China (Taiwan)	32 (1963)	1,402,000	240,000	—	—
Columbia	25	2,200,000	450,000	706	—
Czechoslovakia	28	3,844,000	2,700,000	6,688	49
Denmark	59 (1966)	1,588,000	1,200,000	3,837	20 (1966)
Finland	68	1,663,000	939,277	3,523	3
France	117 (1966)	15,256,000	8,879,316	19,021	73
Germany, E.	no data	5,874,000	4,100,000	—	15 (1965)
Germany, W.	423	27,800,000	14,492,340	24,846	105
Greece	133 (1966)	944,000	60,000	1,123	105 (1966)
Hungary	25	2,479,000	1,282,667	4,170	22
India	588	7,579,000	6,500	10,186	333
Ireland	7	816,000 (1966)	382,589	223	1
Israel	25 (1966)	744,000	45,000	1,329 (1966)	2
Italy	88 (1966)	11,621,000	7,700,000	7,313 (1965)	258
Japan	174 (1966)	24,787,000 (1966)	20,610,000	14,988 (1966)	719 (1966)
Kenya	3 (1966)	—	14,000	162	—
Lebanon	37	—	175,000	410	16
Netherlands	91	3,154,000	2,630,000	6,249	5 (1966)

Country	1967–8 Newspapers	1967–8 Radio Sets	1969 Television Sets	1967–8 Books Published	1967–8 Motion Pictures
New Zealand	41 (1966)	646,000 (1966)	586,660	788	—
Nigeria	24 (1966)	—	52,526	—	—
Norway	24 (1966)	1,135,000	650,000	3,027 (1966)	5
Poland	43	5,539,000	3,000,000	7,848	28
Portugal	29 (1966)	1,345,000	280,280	5,227	5 (1966)
Rumania	33	3,019,000	577,000	5,925	14
S. Africa	21 (1961)	2,700	—	2,433	—
Spain	118	7,150,000	3,345,000	17,849	140
Sweden	116	2,928,000	2,325,834	5,345	4
Switzerland	126 (1966)	1,734,000	961,521	5,921	2
Syria	8 (1966)	1,745,000 (1965)	75,000	340 (1965)	—
Turkey	472 (1961)	2,789,000	6,000		60 (1959)
U.S.S.R.	616	80,700,000	19,000,000	66,894	175
United Arab Republic	14 (1965)	1,613 (1965)	450,000	1,710 (1966)	28
United Kingdom	106 (1966)	17,493,000	15,152,566	22,537	82 (1966)
United States	1,749 (1969)	303,400,000 (1969)	83,000,000	53,240	215
Venezuela	35	1,676,000	652,000	—	3
Yugoslavia	23	3,059,000	1,000,000	8,290	33

On a global basis, there are not sufficient frequencies available to permit uncontrolled proliferation of telecommunications. Competing against one another are telephone facilities, radio, television, satellites and still other electronic developments. With the prospect of direct broadcasting by satellites being discussed seriously, decisions will have to be made with respect to many problem areas in international communications.

The success of communication satellites, first employed successfully in 1962, has been pretty well established with the exception of a brief failure, in the summer of 1969, of satellite transmission of the Investiture of the Prince of Wales. By 1971 it is expected that as many as sixty satellite earth stations will be operating and INTELSAT IV should be launched with greater power and magnitude than any of its predecessors. At the present time, 65 nations are involved in INTELSAT, each member of the satellite group contributing toward its function and support. INTELSAT, an extension of the United States' establishment of the communications satellite corporation, COMSAT, is essentially an international commercial satellite network with the member countries paying for satellite service. At the same time, the International Telecommunication Union (ITU), a United Nations body established in Geneva and, unlike INTELSAT, selling no commercial service, is essentially concerned with international regulation of communications. INTELSAT's total membership consists of 65 countries; ITU boasts a membership of 133 nations. While INTELSAT is commercially oriented and ITU is concerned with allocation of space and other technological problems of international communications, the International Broadcasting Union, operating under a modest grant from the Ford Foundation and with headquarters in Rome, is concerned essentially with international communication law, educational television and in research in international systems of communication and information.

Unfortunately, most countries simply cannot muster sufficient funds to set up a viable and successful communications system. Other priorities get in the way, while ITU does not receive sufficient funding from the United Nations to realize its genuine potential. In general, however, even under less than optimum working conditions, ITU has managed to become a constructive force in underdeveloped areas where communications facilities are sorely lacking. As early as 1947, the International Telecommunications Union had set up an international frequency registration board under the auspices of the United Nations for the purpose of keeping a record of all frequencies in use. ITU also grants new frequencies and works toward eliminating interference in frequencies throughout the world.

The ultimate objective of ITU is to establish a successful system of permanent frequency allocations. Whether this can be done with scientific accuracy and success is still conjectural. Obviously, the most important area is the VHF band where most television now operates over a forty- or fifty-mile area. One solution to the crowded space problem is the use of the UHF band and, eventually, it may be necessary to go to the very highest limits of the spectrum, the extra high frequencies, to the use of microwaves and to millimeter waves which offer a wider spectrum. But there are still international problems to be discussed and resolved in these upper limit waves, and, in time, the answer may be the decision to convey signals under the earth, rather than above. There has been speculation, too, about experimenting with the use of light waves which are still higher than millimeter waves, and there has already been work done in the use of laser beams.

Mass Media in Great Britain

Meanwhile, mass communications facilities are increasing each year in many countries around the world, particularly in the television medium. The British always have been interested in the growth of mass media, and point with pride to the achievements of the British Broadcasting Corporation. Traditionally, communications have been subsumed under the authority of the British Post Office. Shortly after the development of wireless by Marconi, Great Britain developed a commercial system of radio, and the BBC was established in 1922 under the supervision of the Post Office. Fees were collected for radio broadcasting licenses. In 1926, the BBC received an official charter and a ten-year license, thus establishing broadcasting as a government operation, instead of a commercial enterprise. The BBC existed and operated exclusively until 1954 when the Independent Television Authority (ITA) was established. Until the advent of ITA, the BBC had exercised what amounted to a monopoly. Radio receivers were subject to fees, and the BBC functioned as a public corporation, similar to what has been proposed along the lines of a Public Broadcasting Corporation in the United States. Television in Great Britain did not develop until after World War II and, in 1949 after an exhaustive study of BBC operations, it was determined that it should continue to program without benefit of commercial advertising. However, a corollary commercial system would be set up in ITA, thus ending the BBC monopoly. Despite considerable misgiving, ITA began to program commercially in 1954. In 1964, Parliament issued the Television Act which renewed ITA's license until 1976, permitting it to derive revenue from advertising.

Thus, Great Britain now has more than fifteen million television receivers and two television systems. The BBC is a non-profit, government controlled organization and the ITA is a commercial network, comprised of fourteen companies, each of which operates independently of the other. Programs for ITA are provided by contractors and must comply with the standards set by the Television Act of 1954 which require balanced programming, presented in good taste. Programs are not sponsored in the same sense that they are in the United States, and the programs are not directly linked with the advertisements. Program originating areas are London, Yorkshire and Lancashire. The BBC, operating under the supervision of a Board of Governors, is responsible to the office of the Postmaster General. It provides two separate television services, BBC I and BBC II. Its programs are essentially news, public affairs, educational and cultural in nature.

In Great Britain, the Post Office is operated as a public corporation, instead of a department of government. While the British Post Office Corporation has stated that it believes in competition and free enterprise, it is operating as a virtual monopoly. Brenda Maddox, writing in *The*

Economist, of August 1969, is concerned that the British broadcasting system actually tends to thwart enterprise and initiative. In effect, however, ITA was established for the express purpose of offering an alternative, commercial system to the heretofore exclusive BBC.

Mass Media in France, Italy, Germany

Television receivers in most other countries lag behind Great Britain, although Japan has more than twenty million receivers and Russia has nineteen million sets in operation. In France, although communications are under commercial aegis, they are still linked strongly to government. After World War I, radio became a private enterprise, but government broadcasting facilities also existed. This side-by-side arrangement of a National Radio Network on both private and government stations continued until World War II. At that time, the government assumed control over all broadcasting communications with the establishment of Radio-Diffusion Television Française, responsible for all radio and television broadcasting under government supervision. France developed four separate radio networks and, during the 1950's, television became operative. At the present time, France boasts about nine or ten million television receivers which carry a varied program schedule of news, entertainment, documentaries and children's fare. Radio-Diffusion Television Française, with three radio and two television networks currently operating, provides a service throughout Europe. There is considerable pressure at the present time for the development of a full-scale commercial system, with advertising, in France.

Italian broadcasting suffered the misfortune of developing during the Fascist regime of Benito Mussolini. As in Japan and Germany, throughout World War I, party control of all media of communication—the newspaper, magazine, book publishing and radio—was absolute, and the media were used exclusively for the dissemination of propaganda. The one broadcasting company, Unione Radiofonica Italiana (URI) was the controlled system until the fall of the dictatorship when Radio Audizioni Italia was established. Shortly after the development of American television, Italy set up a commission to study the potential of broadcasting. In 1953, there began some experimental programming in a few major cities under the auspices of the newly established Radio-Televisione Italiana (RAI) with authority over radio and television. By 1960, there were three radio networks and one television network in operation. In 1969, Italy had two television networks in service, with basic programming originating in Rome. The RAI is under the jurisdiction of the Italian government and is regulated by the Minister of Posts and Telecommunications. At present, Italy has about eight million television receivers.

The major contribution of Italy has been in the area of educational broadcasting. Tescuola, as the educational venture is called, has been so successful as to command the attention of educators in other countries, and Italy has become widely known for its innovations in school broadcasting and in adult education. The Italian broadcasting system has made an enormous contribution to education by utilizing television in areas where there has been considerable illiteracy.

In Germany, the problems besetting broadcasting and other mass media stem from the fact that the country is divided. Both East and West Germany have their own press, radio and television—one basically free and the other Communist controlled. Since Germany has been traditionally a country of marked scientific achievement, an interest in radio communications developed early. In the 1920's, there were more than one million radio receivers in operation, with broadcasting facilities controlled partly by government and partly by private, commercial interests. With the rise of Hitler, all media were placed under the control of Goebbels, the Minister of Propaganda, who was keenly aware of the enormous impact of mass media in the area of public opinion and propaganda. As in Italy and Japan, mass communications were taken over by the state, and the media functioned to indoctrinate the public toward Fascism, while at the same time directing propaganda about the scope of German military prowess to other European countries. As German conquests rolled on, the first agencies seized were the press and radio. This situation prevailed until the Allied victories, after which there was a genuine effort to establish a spirit of freedom both in Germany and in the liberated countries.

After the war, German broadcasting developed under the license of a government-chartered corporation which functioned as a public broadcasting corporation similar to that of Great Britain. Two radio networks developed, each attempting to provide balanced and varied programming. Television developed along similar lines, with two separate program services on national networks operating approximately seventy hours per week. The costs of broadcasting in West Germany are paid for by license fees on both radio and television receivers. Unlike the Hitler regime, the control of government over mass media is restricted, with the association of broadcasting companies functioning with considerable autonomy. The proposal to set up a national television system has aroused considerable controversy, particularly over the demand of newspaper publishers that they become an integral part of such a broadcast service. Ironically this has occurred when, in the United States, the FCC is taking a hard look at newspaper-television enterprises under a single ownership. West Germany has about fifteen million, and East Germany about five million, television receivers in operation.

Mass Media in Scandinavia

Both radio and television in the Scandinavian countries, while functioning on a limited scale when compared to other European nations, have been both popular and democratic media. They have also been viable economically and quite enterprising in the area of cultural, religious and educational broadcasting. Linked by common cultural ties, these countries also function in similar fashion in the operation of mass media. The essentially democratic spirit that prevails in Scandinavia has assured considerable freedom of press, radio and television. Educational broadcasting has been most successful and there is considerable exchanging of programs because of similarity of language. Television was begun in the 1950's and, while there is government supervision in each country, state control is held at a minimum. Through Eurovision, as well as through their own Scandinavian television system, Norway, Sweden, Denmark and Finland enjoy a varied program "mix." Educational broadcasting is employed both in schools and at home where it is widely accepted as an instrument for adult education. Financial support for broadcasting comes from fees on receivers, rather than from commercial sponsorship.

Each of the countries has granted what amounts to a virtual monopoly to the national radio and television organization. Although under government aegis, the media operate freely and, indeed, the government encourages the development of educational broadcasting. The programs, in addition to religion and education, include considerable music and drama. In Sweden, as in Norway, the media are under the supervision of a Minister of Communications. One of the major problems in all of the Scandinavian countries is the difficulty of reception because of the rugged nature of much of the terrain. At the present time, Norway has almost one million television receivers and Sweden has about two and one-half million sets in operation.

Telecommunications in Canada

On this side of the Atlantic, the major neighbor of the United States is Canada, a large and growing country, but with a relatively small population for its size. Its population is varied, and the mass media face the difficulty of a country with two distinct languages—French and English. Because of this separation into English and French Canada, it has been difficult for the newspapers, radio and television to publish and program in two languages. Under the Canadian Broadcasting Commission, established in 1932, program content and supervision were under the government auspices. The broadcast facilities were to be owned by the public, represented by CRBC. A few years later, in 1936, a public corporation known as the Canadian Broadcasting Corporation was inaugurated, and expansion in the development and use of radio was rapid and extensive. A study undertaken in 1949, one year after television began in the United States, concluded that the CBC should continue to exercise control over broadcasting, working toward the development of what, in the United States, would be called a "balanced schedule" of entertainment and educational programming. Early in the 1950's, a coast-to-coast television system was proposed, to be composed partly of CBC stations and partly of privately operated enterprises. By 1955, television was in operation in several major cities. Because of the disparity between public and private stations, however, a Board of Broadcast Governors was set up to supervise all broadcasting. Unlike the FCC, the Board regulated both advertising *and* programs content, and decreed that at least 50% of all content was to be Canadian originated.

At present, the CBC operates two radio and two television networks, in English and in French. There are a variety of CBC stations, private affiliates, independent stations broadcasting on separate English and French networks. In addition, Canadian Television (CTV) is a privately operated network which provides coast-to-coast service in English. This network is an advertising sponsored operation, similar to commercial broadcasting in the United States. Various studies of broadcasting in a nation with two distinct languages have indicated the need for closer cultural exchange between English and French Canada. While there has been some discussion of placing the public and private broadcast services under one roof, the CBC has persisted in maintaining a dual system in Canada. In 1970, Canada reduced the amount of programming which could be brought into Canadian television from the United States.

While telecommunications is growing more slowly in other countries and there are still areas where all communications, including the newspaper, are both primitive and controlled, there is no doubt that two phenomena are developing throughout the world. There is, first, a growing literacy and a concomitant demand for information and for a free flow of communication by peoples everywhere. Secondly, there is imminent a vast expansion of technology and communication services throughout the world. Within the next decade, communications on a global basis will develop through the activation of a variety of technologies. Telecommunications on an international level will attain a high degree of perfection. The result, despite ideological and semantic differences, can only be to give the peoples of the world an opportunity to communicate on a scale heretofore unparalleled in the history of civilization. The successful activation of global telecommunications cannot come about without both money and manpower, but above all it can only be achieved through the cooperative efforts of people who genuinely seek a dialogue with other people throughout the civilized world.

BIBLIOGRAPHY

Barghoorn, Frederick. *The Soviet Culture Offensive.* Princeton, New Jersey: Princeton University Press, 1960.

Bauer, Raymond A., Alex Inkeles and Clyde Kluckhohn. *How the Soviet System Works.* Cambridge, Massachusetts: Harvard University Press, 1957.

Briggs, Asa. *The Birth of Broadcasting—The History of Broadcasting in the United Kingdom,* Vol. I. London: Oxford University Press, 1961.

British Broadcasting Corporation. *1967 Handbook.* London: 1967.

Brown, Cecil B. *Suez to Singapore.* New York: Random House, 1942.

Buzek, Antony. *How the Communist Press Works.* New York: Frederick A. Praeger, 1964.

Canadian Broadcasting Corporation. *Broadcasting in Canada: History and Development of the National System.* Ottawa: Canadian Broadcasting Corporation, 1960.

Coase, R. H. *British Broadcasting: A Study in Monopoly.* Cambridge, Massachusetts: Harvard University Press, 1950.

Cohen, Bernard C. *The Press and Foreign Policy.* Princeton, New Jersey: Princeton University Press, 1963.

Desmond, Robert W. *The Press and World Affairs.* New York: Appleton-Century, 1937.

Durham, F. Gayle. *News Broadcasting on Soviet Radio and Television.* Cambridge, Massachusetts: Center for International Studies, Massachusetts Institute of Technology, 1965.

Fischer, Heinz-Dietrich and John C. Merrill, eds. *International Communication: Media—Channels—Functions.* New York: Hastings House, 1970.

Harris, Robert D. G. *A Report from Spain—The Press in an Authoritarian State.* Los Angeles: University of California Press, 1964.

Independent Television Authority—ITV 1967. *A Guide to Independent Television.* London, 1967.

India, Ministry of Information and Broadcasting. *Aspects of Broadcasting in India.* New Delhi: Ministry of Information, 1959.

Inkeles, A. *Public Opinion in Soviet Russia.* Cambridge, Massachusetts: Harvard University Press, 1950.

King, Vincent S. *A General Study of the Channels of Communication Between Communist China and the Western World.* Cambridge: Center for International Studies, Massachusetts Institute of Technology, 1964.

Kruglak, Theodore. *The Foreign Correspondents.* Geneva: E. Droz, 1955.

Lippmann, Walter. *Public Opinion and Foreign Policy in the United States.* London: Allen and Unwin, 1932.

Markel, Lester, ed. *Public Opinion and Foreign Policy.* New York: Harper, 1949.

Meyerhoff, Arthur E. *The Strategy of Persuasion.* New York: Coward-McCann, 1965.

NHK. *The History of Broadcasting in Japan.* Tokyo: NHK Press, 1967.

Paulu, Burton. *British Broadcasting in Transition.* Minneapolis: University of Minnesota Press, 1961.

Reston, James. *The Press and World Affairs.* Minneapolis, 1949.

Schramm, Wilbur. *Mass Media and National Development.* Stanford, California: Stanford University Press and Paris: UNESCO, 1964.

UNESCO. *Developing Mass Media in Asia.* New York: UNESCO Publications Center, 1960.

Mass Media in the Developing Countries. Paris: UNESCO Publication Center, 1961.

Social Education Through Television: An All India—Radio UNESCO Pilot Project. New York: UNESCO Publications Center, 1963.

White, Llewelyn and Robert D. Leigh. *Peoples Speaking to Peoples.* Chicago: University of Chicago Press, 1946.

Yu, Frederick T. C. *Mass Persuasion in Communist China.* New York and London: Frederick A. Praeger, 1964.

Zeman, Z. A. B. *Nazi Propaganda.* London: Oxford University Press, 1964.

13

Public Opinion and Propaganda

THERE ARE few major decisions involving industry or education, as well as social or political change, which social scientists do not ascribe to a nebulous phenomenon called public opinion. It is common practice for the semi-informed to characterize many published statements on foreign affairs, on racial and religious conflict and on political action as the result of a treacherous force entitled "propaganda." In effect, public opinion and propaganda interact, but it is possible for public opinion to function independently of propaganda, although it might be said that propaganda is always motivated toward directing or re-orienting opinion.

Both public opinion and propaganda are two of the most carelessly used terms in the entire vocabulary of communications. Dictionary definitions are futile, for a definition which characterizes public opinion as the expression of the opinion of the public is neither extensional nor intensional and adds up to a frustrating tautology. A similar semantic impasse confronts those who would define the term propaganda by using more words, for the meaning of propaganda has various shades and emphases, and even a functional definition has become obscured by meaningless differentiations between destructive versus constructive propaganda. As a starting point toward a meaningful operational description, both public opinion and propaganda should be viewed as part of the whole, vast complicated nexus of communication—a procedure involving the affective and directive use of language through the instrumentality of one or more of the mass media and with an end in view, or an objective, which has been established a priori.

There is a growing demand in the social sciences to apply the techniques of empirical research so germane to the natural sciences. And this is precisely what studies in the function of public opinion and propaganda attempt to do: to apply quantitative measurement techniques to the volatile and unpredictable phenomenon of human behavior under given sets of circumstances. There are social scientists who doubt that such techniques are very accurate or very helpful under any circumstances, and there are those who do not believe that public opinion is a meaningful concept at all. If public opinion exists, it is not amenable to dictionary definition, it is difficult to observe because of its mercurial nature and it is almost impossible to study scientifically because of the variables involved and the lack of appropriate control mechanisms. To define public opinion as the opinions of the public results in a semantic roadblock. How bring this high level abstraction down to an extensionally verifiable and definable level? If there is an operative public whose opinions are involved? Is there one homogeneous entity called the "public," or are there many discrete, but related publics? If a man's political decisions come about through "the power of public opinion" is this result to be ascribed to a "power elite," to an articulate minority, or to the whole, vast amorphous mass of people which comprises the basic public?

A Functional Concept

Clearly, these questions cannot be answered by any established set of semantic rules. Public opinion can only be described functionally, and then with specific reference to a given problem or topic. Propaganda, in terms of its efficiency, also can only be described functionally in terms of its ultimate effect on public opinion. Gauging public opinion is also a hazardous business, for it is as easy to decide on the basis of a subjective analysis that public opinion has done thus and so as it is to conclude, on the basis of objective measurement techniques, that courses of action are the result of the pressure of public opinion. The parameters for a scientific analysis of public opinion depend upon how one constructs the original concept of public—one public or many publics, how many in each public, how broken down and defined in terms of additional parameters of age, sex, economic status, and other criteria. The public opinion poll poses a fundamental problem: to what areas beyond the political can it be applied and how successfully? For it is simply absurd to claim, as some researchers do, that there is no problem which is not amenable to public opinion studies and which does not yield a direction-finder through the use of polling or survey techniques.

At the same time, it is pertinent to inquire as to the precise role—if it has a precise role—of propaganda in public opinion formation and change, and to determine whether propaganda techniques can be used to galvanize opinion toward a desired goal or point of view. If public opinion and propaganda are power phenomena, it is also relevant to inquire how they operate against such variables as individual attitudes, the prevailing values of the group, the nature of the issue and the alternative actions which might be taken in a given concrete situation.

It would appear to be a valid assumption, on the basis of the limitations of dictionary definitions, that public opinion can best be defined empirically or operationally. As a power phenomenon, public opinion and propaganda eventually must move from thought, planning and research to action. If it is assumed that public opinion, by the very nature of the phrase, involves an aggregate of individual opinions, in order for opinion to become "public," then opinion may reasonably be expected to include the attitude of the group (or public) toward a particular problem or subject which is implicitly, or explicitly, controversial and which occurs at a specific time and against a particular social or political background. Public opinion is always implicitly controversial, for the very expression of opinion implies that there may be differing viewpoints on the question under consideration. And, where propaganda efforts are involved in order to influence opinion, the two phenomena tend to interact. Opinion may be expressed both because of, and despite of, the effort of the propagandist. These efforts need not, as is popularly believed, be the result of hidden motivation, they need not be malicious or negative or destructive. And they should be distinguished from the process of education. While all educational effort may be considered, in a sense, propaganda, not all propaganda is educational in the conventional psychological sense of that term.

Both public opinion and propaganda are galvanic communicative phenomena of power and social control. At one time or another every social, political, religious and even scientific institution becomes involved in an exercise of power and social control through the instrumentality of persuasion. This is particularly true in a democratic, pluralistic society where the very nature of the social structure makes public opinion possible. The only area where propaganda is frustrated is in powerful religious dogma where opinion change is almost impossible. But in the major gray areas where mass media operate, public opinion and progapanda are always at work, although those are the areas where the study of public opinion is tenacious and does not readily yield to analysis.

Public Opinion and Political Action

Political action is such an area. Obviously, an expression of public opinion is considered vital if democratic government is to function in a successful manner. At the same time, the question frequently raised is to what extent political decision should conform to prevailing public opinion. The United States involvement in Vietnam is a clear example of public opinion in juxtaposition to political decision making. Despite an overwhelming rejection of Vietnam policy by large segments of the press and public, neither the Johnson nor the Nixon administrations found it easy to conform with any alacrity to the clamor of students, intellectuals and many other publics who demanded total withdrawal. For involved in such a situation is the always difficult question of the validity of opinion against the judgment of the leaders—in this case the military and the administration. Unfortunately, the information on which public opinion is based in a situation such as Vietnam is ambiguous and clouded by security and diplomatic considerations, and the winds of propaganda tend to blow from a number of conflicting directions. Very much in evidence are social and political questions regarding freedom, responsibility and authority which form the matrix of our social institutions.

All forms of democratic government, however, are based ultimately on political democracy—a structure where the government is responsible to the individual. This differs from authoritarian forms of government where the expression of public opinion is not only responsible to, but functions as a propagandistic extension of, the government. In a state-dominated society, public opinion and political action inevitably are one and the same. In a pluralistic society, public opinion can be expressed on many subjects and in a variety of ways. This effort to insure expression of opinion from all possible quarters which may demand to be heard troubled even so thoughtful a writer as Walter Lippmann, for it raised questions of the relative merits of majority versus minority opinion. It demanded that consideration be given to the question of how much people really know about the subject at hand, whether the majority was, indeed, better qualified or informed than the minority. And these questions, in turn, suggest others, such as the role of the newspaper in opinion formation, the amount of exposure to news and public affairs on television, and the place of education in opinion formation. There appears to be little evidence in the 1960's that exposure to a college education increases the individual's commitment to democracy. Some researchers in public opinion believe, on the contrary, that a great part of student activism and militancy is actually non-democratic and authoritarian in thrust, although presented in the guise of a democratic social revolution.

Public opinion, paradoxically, is atavistic. It is not so much the vanguard of change as a reflection of change, for it tends to lag behind scientific and social developments. For a number of reasons, opinions do not coalesce until after the fact, as the reaction to Vietnam so clearly demonstrates. And, despite the omnipresence of mass media, public opinion has actually become decentralized. The closeness and spirit of exchange which characterized the New England town meeting of a century ago has given way to indirect expression through the media of communication. The presence of mass media has resulted in an inundation of information and propaganda which makes perception and rational thought superficially direct and sharp but, in reality, quite difficult and indirect. Ideas which were once discussed on the basis of direct experience now yield to the seemingly direct, but actually prismatic, lenses of mass media. Despite the presence of media and the plethora of information, the public rarely, if ever, has sufficient information on which to form opinions which will influence the establishment of political policy. In the last analysis, the power elites set policies, not the public. It is possible, of course, for many publics acting with some unanimity of purpose to influence governmenal decision. But, even with free access to information, purveyed by a free and responsible press, it is a difficult accomplishment—which may be why Walter Lippmann placed greater emphasis and credence in a minority elite, similar to Plato's philosopher-kings, than in the masses of the common man.

Public opinion can be studied only by empirical or extensional means. When the head of the teachers' federation uses the medium of television to bring his case against community control of schools to "the public," he is exemplifying public opinion in action, as an operational procedure. The position of the American Medical Association which purportedly was against the appointment of Dr. John H. Knowles as Assistant Secretary of Health, Education and Welfare was scored by supporters of Dr. Knowles as an example of power politics and propaganda tactics. A group of dissident clergy, failing to agree with the Papal position on birth control, carry their case to "the people." Each of these is an example of public opinion and propaganda as power phenomena. A classic example of effort to enlist public opinion in support, or rejection of, an overtly controversial issue was the Congressional debate over the ABM system in 1968. In every case, however different the circumstances may be, what is involved is the nebulous, amorphous and mercurial power phenomenon of public opinion. In the AMA-Knowles case, however, public opinion appears to have been cynically disregarded in favor of power politics and propaganda.

Public Opinion and Issues

Public opinion has become so much a part of the process and effects of mass communication, and it is so closely linked with the functions of the press and the other mass media, that it has developed its own corps of experts. Particularly in national election years, but in other areas as well, various public opinion and research organizations such as Lou Harris, Samuel Lubell, the George Gallup organization and the Elmo Roper company take soundings of opinion on a wide spectrum of political, economic and social issues. Their results, widely quoted in the press and in promotional literature, can only be comprehended if public opinion is defined functionally. The opinion survey is invariably related to a controversial topic which has some extensional referant in the external world. It is possible to arrive at some tentative findings and to gauge opinion when reference is made to an attitude by a particular group, or groups, with respect to a particular issue under consideration. For public opinion tends ultimately to coalesce around a concrete issue which is implicitly controversial. The student intransigence at Columbia University and at the University of California, aroused widespread controversy both on and off the campus, but it became almost impossible to reach a point of rational discussion internally, because opinion became polarized into black and white, either/or alternatives. The large gray area, where the bulk of students and faculty remained uncommitted did not become operative, which is why the situation deteriorated to a point of no return.

Yet, those involved at Columbia were many groups, each with a well-defined, but adamant position—the Students for a Democratic Society, the administration, the police and the residents of the Harlem community. The opinions of each of these "publics" was highly articulate, because each had an opportunity to express a position through one or more of the mass media. But no consensus was reached, because affective and directive thinking dominated, and a rational and empirical approach became impossible. Only the vast, gray uncommitted area—which comprised the majority of students and faculty—could have broken the stalemate of debate, but failed to do so. In a sense, "true" expression of public opinion in this situation was inarticulate and inchoate, although the polarized segments were most articulate in expressing their demands through the mass media. To postulate, therefore, that every issue truly represents the "voice of the people" is to say little about public opinion, unless there is clear definition of what groups are meant by the public. Rarely do the people speak with one authoritative voice in a unanimity of expression of public opinion, except in moments of great national trauma such as the Cuban missile crisis or the assassination of President Kennedy.

Public opinion invariably centers around an issue which is implicitly, or explicitly, controversial. The attitudes may not be expressed overtly, except under direct questioning, for public opinion may be latent, rather than manifest. But it is nevertheless present and potential. When the issue becomes active, when some trigger mechanism calls it to the direct attention of groups, public opinion may become overt and articulate, expressed through pressure group meetings and through media of communication. There is always implicit dissent, which is not consciously expressed through overt activity until the latent issue becomes manifest. At that point, public opinion becomes articulate through many avenues, not the least of which are the mass media which both reflect and influence the expression of opinion. Even propaganda, which is aimed at changing prevailing opinion, tends, to a larger degree, to reflect the very attitudes it is attempting to change or direct.

Measuring Public Opinion

Social scientists, and behavioral scientists in particular, have tried for many years to study with some degree of statistical accuracy the efficiency of the public opinion survey or poll. Because of the variables and imponderables involved, their success necessarily has been limited. In the first place, it is difficult to apply the precise techniques of the natural sciences to problems in behavioral science. Conditions tend to change. People's psychological set and their attitudes change. Opinion does not stand still. Even beyond these capricious factors is the undeniable evidence of a margin for error in the survey situation which may involve, variously, the interviewer-interviewee relationship, or defects in the structure of the questionnaire itself. The only categorical way to determine the accuracy and success of a public opinion sounding is by precise, quantitative measurement techniques—a procedure which is extremely difficult to structure. But quantitative methods, whatever their limitations in polling, yield significant results which are born out under pragmatic testing. What must be determined is whether attitudes express themselves in positive action, whether behavior is empirically observed and whether this behavior can be evaluated against a given set of conditions or criteria. People not only fail to behave in a way which coheres with their *expressed* opinions, but their action frequently bears no relationship to what the interviewer has discerned from their attitudes. The problem of scientific investigation of human behavior is an extraordinarily complex one.

In the last analysis, then, polls and surveys are scientific only in a limited way, for the material under investigation involves psychology and sociology and is not amenable to pure mathematics or to accurate, scientifically *controlled* experiment. When public opinion tends to coalesce actively around a particular controversial issue, such as a presidential election, it is easier to study than when the problems are less circumscribed. Despite the admitted limitations, however, studies in public opinion are useful. In the area of media research and advertising, where the efficiency of various media are evaluated, public opinion research is considered vital. In politics, too, the poll has become an accepted device of testing the popularity, or lack of public support, of national figures and official policy. The late President Kennedy was highly sensitive to research information and to mass media, and the newspapers made it a point to report that President Lyndon Johnson usually carried the latest polling information in his coat pocket.

Unfortunately, the government poll all too often is taken after decisions are made, rather than before, so that the sounding of public opinion tends to be concerned with policies which already have been put into effect. Furthermore, since interpretation of the poll is not an exact procedure, astute politicians and pressure groups tend to evaluate information and apply it to buttress a preconceived bias. A reading, for example, of full-page "let's look at the facts" advertisements by union and industry in a labor controversy shows with amusing and tragic clarity how propaganda and public opinion can be used to shore up a parochial, self-interest objective. At times, political officials will deliberately "leak" information to the press as a trial balloon to see how the public will react. This is, of course, highly unscientific public opinion research, but it is both pragmatically useful and enlightening. Indeed, it is the very tenacious and unscientific quality of such investigation which makes it easier to give it an authority which, in reality, it does not possess. There is a wide chasm between what exists and opinions about what the public may think exists. For example, Daniel Katz has declared that assumptions are frequently drawn from some public opinion polls which are completely unwarranted. This was particularly true in the case where some political figures and newspaper columnists declared that the majority of Americans backed involvement in Vietnam when the overwhelming evidence, from mass media and many other sources, was precisely the opposite. As Katz pointed out, fact must be treated as fact and not in terms of "what people think are facts."

A major problem which has never been satisfactorily settled is the determination of whether polling itself—the very process of investigation—influences public opinion. In presidential election years, for example, the question has been raised whether the constant publication and reiteration of public opinion polls does not act as a force in influencing the voter toward one direction or another. There is some evidence to indicate that this may be the case, and the very possibility that the poll itself can influence opinion has aroused criticism and made the study of public attitudes a suspect procedure. The public opinion research experts deny such an influence. What the poll does may be limited, but is nevertheless highly significant. It serves to extrapolate the opinions of the group, or groups, sampled toward conclusions which may be considered representative of the opinions of the total population. Several methods have been devised to accomplish this study of the macrocosm through the microcosm. In one, there is a direct verbal exchange between interviewer and interviewee where specific questions are asked. In another, a questionnaire may be submitted for the respondent's replies. Various attitude scales may be used in which the respondent either writes the answer to specific questions and gives them directly to the interviewer, or is asked to mail them. In all cases, the research organization does not place the questions before the public until the questionnaire has been pre-tested and the questions carefully screened for bias or ambiguity.

In order to evaluate the results and to determine how public opinion operates in a given set of circumstances, the researcher obviously must have some specific parameter or measuring devices. These, as we have indicated, are quantitative, but still not exact, because of the volatile nature of the material studied and because of the human interaction involved. But every effort is made to select the group to be studied as objectively as possible. The situation in which the analyst will work must also be studied carefully. Even with the most scientific of motivation, however, critics of public opinion surveys still believe that certain essential elements simply cannot be purely objective or quantitative. The interviewer himself can be at fault. The psychological "set" of the respondent is not invariably the same. The questions, however carefully tested, may not be completely without bias. Above all, the analysis—even by computer—may not be objective.

It is patently impossible to be completely, scientifically objective in any sampling of public opinion. What the researcher does assert is that he can *predict,* on the basis of a poll, how the entire population would respond, for the results of a sample are essentially equivalent to a study of the entire population. This, in essence, is the major thrust of public opinion research and its significance to the field of mass communication. The researcher does take into consideration, of course, the so-called margin for error that is to be found in an statistical analysis. What is of importance is that the sample to be used be selected without prejudice. The number of persons studied must be an accurate representation of a larger universe, although it is still not possible to tell whether the sample, based on age, sex, color and similar parameters, is a true representation of the entire public. At best, the most perfect mode of sampling has its imperfections. At best, however, it is an important signpost or direction-finder.

Validity of Public Opinion Research

Obviously, problems that can be studied by quantitative measurement yield more accurate and more easily verifiable information than the kind of qualitative and relative issues which abound in the area of public opinion. Yet, the researchers claim, even though opinion and attitude studies are not studied with the same precision as those in the physical sciences, the information yielded by public opinion research is nevertheless valid and valuable. Opinion, according to the statistician, is measureable by the laws of statistics. With proper allowance for variables and margin for error, and with a carefully and accurately selected sample, it is possible to measure public opinion and arrive at tenable conclusions.

At one time, the newspaper columnist was an accepted source of sounding on public opinion and there are readers who still place great credence in this kind of subjective analysis. Frequently, the columns of James Reston, Walter Lippmann and other national columnists are both accurate and challenging in their analysis of political and social trends. But the columnist himself is an opinion-maker, not a researcher, and even the Restons and the Lippmanns rely to some extent on the findings of Harris, Roper and Gallup. It is possible, too, to glean a subjective sounding of public opinion by interviewing bystanders and other parties at a teachers' strike or a campus rebellion, but this is not a scientific sampling of public opinion. Scientifically researched public opinion is developed on the basis of a selected segment which purports to be representative of the total population and the sample is claimed to be an accurate microcosm of the larger universe whose opinions are being studied. There is, of course, not only the margin for error to be considered;

frequently egregious blunders have been made. The most notorious is the classic failure of the *Literary Digest* poll of 1936 which predicted categorically that Alfred M. Landon would defeat Franklin Delano Roosevelt for the Presidency of the United States. Badly conceived and structured as a basic sample, the *Literary Digest* error was so monumental that the publication was forced to go out of business.

The heart of a successful public opinion poll is, therefore, the sample which must represent accurately a cross-section of the entire public under consideration. Anything which deviates from this parameter invalidates the poll. The sample in an election year poll, for example, must be an accurate representation of the entire *voting* population, insofar as this is possible and within a minimum margin for error. Of course, problems remain, even with the most accurate sample. The microcosm simply cannot be quantitatively accurate down to the last integer. There are questions regarding the framing and phrasing of the questions used in the survey. There is dubiety about interviewer set and attitude. There are considerations of individual differences among respondents. And all of these problems have been taken into consideration by the polling and research organizations, both in the structure of the sample, the poll and the analysis. With great care, the researcher must decide how many possible respondents will be interviewed. He must decide on the kind of survey, and he must structure the survey as objectively as possible within the framework of human limitations. Despite the fact that public opinion cannot be quantitatively measured, in the manner of the physical sciences, there is general agreement that it exists. Most people have a healthy respect for this power phenomenon, and many place great reliance upon it at one time or another.

In clear-cut controversial issues, particularly in the political area, public opinion has considerable value. What makes the study and analysis of opinion difficult under any circumstances is the human tendency to polarize, to think in terms of black or white alternatives and to accept abstractions and stereotypes in place of extensionally verifiable data. These semantic difficulties are compounded by other communicative roadblocks. Questions are frequently put to individuals on problems and issues about which little is known by the respondent, since one's universe of discourse is necessarily circumscribed. As a result, many respondents, rather than admit they do not have any opinion, tend to reply glibly about such issues as inflation, the devaluation of currency and other more arcane problems. In fact, they know little about the issue. As a result, public opinion findings, which may be the wisest course to follow in the long run, are not without limitations. Many variables operate to color opinion in cases where the respondent does know something about the issue—value judgments, the opinion of the peer group, the individual's educational, economic, social and political orientation. All of these, illustrating the constant interaction between individual and environment, make the study of public opinion a challenging, and frequently valuable, process.

One of the findings of repeated research is that the same individual does not tend to adhere to the same opinions over a period of time. The public is a capricious body, selecting one course on a given day and rejecting it on another. Constancy is not a public virtue. This phenomenon is clearly illustrated by the attitude of those who fought with utter dedication for a civil rights bill, but who soon felt that civil rights legislation had opened a Pandora's box of trouble which threatened to undermine law and order. Although democratic and liberal in their espousal of the civil rights movement, they were conservative and even reactionary when faced with some of the pragmatic aspects of civil rights in action. Similarly, the public, if polled, would claim that war is anathema, yet many individuals have opted for a total effort in Vietnam, and wars have been fought on the basis that they were "preventive" in nature. The phrase, "war to end war," is not easily forgotten. Another example of the capriciousness of public opinion was the research which indicated some doubt about Senator Robert Kennedy's chances of winning the nomination for the presidency. But the very public which was so wary of Kennedy changed after his assassination, and an overwhelming number of people indicated they would have voted for him had he become a presidential candidate.

Factors Influencing Public Opinion

Many factors influence public opinion and attitudes. People are beset by anxieties. They face the daily decision of accepting, or rejecting, certain social norms in order to live in a society. Goals and aspirations frequently suffer frustration. The worst, by rationalization, is frequently made to appear as the better reason. Attitudes are justified and rationalized by the way in which people react to certain controversial issues. This is made particularly clear by the Black reaction to the civil rights legislation. The Black man, for the first time, simply refused to rationalize the social treatment meted out to him. Many anti-civil rights militants, however, did rationalize their basic prejudice against the Negro by a demand for "law and order" to curb the excesses of black power. And these attitudes, unfortunately, are learned in the school and accepted uncritically. Black anti-semitism, obviously the result of need for a scapegoat for social and economic frustration and deprivation, could well become a learned attitude if the paradoxical and ironic demand for black separation is applied to the educational system. In extensional terms, the Negro actually has been equated with the Jew because of similar frustrations faced by both groups. And both aggression and anti-semitism as public opinion phenomena are examples of the venting of social frustrations by an expression of attitudes through mass media.

In both positive and negative situations, the leader plays a significant

role in the opinion-forming process. Publics, particularly in an age
where communication is available to all, tend to identify with the charismatic approach of leaders, and they tend to take on and reflect the attitudes and opinions of the leader of the group of which they are a part.
If there were not this tendency to cohere with prevailing group opinion,
set largely by the peer group leaders, public opinion expression would
be chaotic and formless. It is the leader who gives it direction and co-
herence. In some cases, however, the follow-the-leader tendency is more
apparent than real. Some individuals appear to follow the leaders and the
peer group, but in reality have divergent opinions of their own. As the
late Dr. Gary Steiner's studies in television viewing patterns reveal, people do not always behave extensionally as they have indicated to the researcher. Many college graduates, for example, declared, in answer to a
questionnaire, that they watch only news programs and documentaries.
Additional empirical studies revealed subsequently, however, that many
of these individuals did not admit that they also watched action-adven-
ture and comedy programs. A society which moves by "other direction"
finds it convenient to conform to the standards expected of it by the peer
group. And this fact is particularly significant, for it demonstrates that a
carefully structured, applied and analyzed survey can contribute importantly to revealing people's "real" attitudes, rather than those which
they believe are expected of them.

The public also tends to reduce its opinions to the lowest common
denominator and to react in terms of abstractions and stereotypes. A
"let's find out" attitude is denigrated in favor of the easiest and most
palatable solution. It is much easier to accept uncritically the leader's
claim that the opposition in a controversial issue is "radical" or "reactionary" than to try and discover precisely what is involved in the issue
at hand. Here, again, the temptation to succumb to either/or conclusions
is less painful—albeit less meaningful. The difficult road is in thinking
extensionally and in weighing the merits of various alternatives. Much
simpler is the release of anxiety or frustration by identification or conformity with the leader and the peer group. It is particularly easy if the
media, willing or unwittingly, cooperate in the process.

Propaganda Analysis

These limitations on the expression and study of public opinion
often offer a superb opportunity for the dissemination of propaganda.
For propaganda is essentially a learning process in which old habits
are discarded and new patterns are learned and absorbed through stimuli conveyed by means of the various media of communication. Propaganda analysis is one of the more fascinating aspects of the behavioral
sciences. In many cases, fortunately, propaganda is not successful, for
while the message may reach the communicatee, the response is not al-

ways positive. And, unless positive action results, the propaganda cannot be deemed successful. The group does not always react to propaganda as the purveyor hopes it will. There may be no overt response, or the response may not take the anticipated direction. Other stimuli may intervene to crowd out the stimulus, for public opinion is formed by many channels and agencies. Furthermore, it is not an easy assignment to modify behavior, nor is it easy to alter the learning processes that enter into the formation of behavior patterns. When old habits must be relegated to limbo and new ones learned, propaganda frequently is most successful when it is direct and revelatory rather than hidden or subliminal.

In order for propaganda to function successfully, the respondent must react affirmatively to the communications content, or the stimulus involved. There must be not only an awareness, but also a dynamic interaction between the source of propaganda and the individual or group involved. Even this is not easy to achieve, for the group is bombarded by many propaganda stimuli, each competing with the other for attention. In the process, some tend to cancel others out. Not all survive and achieve recognition. This is why those who desire to reach large numbers of people with a significant message rely so heavily on the use of mass media which are both simultaneous and ubiquitous in terms of audience size and impact. There was no more effective mass communication than the color television presentation of the President of the United States offering his Cabinet choices to the nation.

As in the case of public opinion, there are no quantitative methods of measuring the effect of propaganda. Its use and abuse cannot be studied with total scientific objectivity, and the parameters of judgment and evaluation are at best tentative. Analysis of any communication content is at best hypothetical and at worst misleading. Nevertheless, the social and the behavioral scientist does produce illuminating data, despite the fact that his techniques might be challenged by the physical scientist. In the social sciences a great deal depends upon who analyzes the content and from what point of view. The psychologist, the journalist, the sociologist and the political scientist each approaches propaganda analysis from a different, if analagous, point of view. Yet, propaganda analysis—despite its limitations—is not a new and untried technique. Some thirty years ago, the Institute for Propaganda Analysis produced several significant studies of the content of American foreign policy, intended primarily for study in schools and colleges. The Institute studies broke down and divided various aspects of propaganda analysis which were presented in a pamphlet entitled "The Fine Art of Propaganda." It is highly significant that little more is known today than was revealed by these studies which were done three decades ago.

What was revealed in the early studies is still a perplexing problem in this age of mass media. There is, unfortunately, no direct and overt way of measuring and analyzing propaganda. Each method is open to criticism and each has limitations. Efforts have been made to develop statistical surveys and tables and to analyze according to various categories. But these methods are, at best, indications or signposts with a relative value. The chief difficulty is the setting up of criteria. How valuable is it, for example, to predicate propaganda analysis by determining how many times a subject or name has been mentioned in the daily press? How significant is this finding without also including the circumstances of the mention and the whole context of involvement? As criteria of the reliability of propaganda analysis, researchers have cited the use of more than one set of data to measure against other sets of data. Efforts also have been made to eliminate, so far as this is possible, the intervention of value judgments in the study and in the final analysis of data. With respect to the validity of the conclusions which may be reached, the researcher attempts to determine whether the conclusions do, indeed, provide specific data about what the survey set out to discover. If the conclusions provide any reasonable measure of the substance of the analysis, they may be considered valid, although it must not be forgotten that the ultimate test is not quantitative but, at best, qualitative.

The verbal uses and abuses of the term "propaganda" provide a ready exercise in semantic ambiguity. Essentially, the affective reaction to any communicative effort that is designated as propaganda is negative —a subtle and nefarious effort to subvert public opinion toward ends that are socially harmful. This, of course, leaves out all of the positive and beneficial uses to which propaganda, as a communicative device, can be directed. But the purpose and application of propagandistic efforts are curiously ironic, for the meaning of propaganda changes like a chameleon, depending upon toward what purpose it is employed and how the media are approached with communications content. In the most literal and classic sense—from its very Latin derivations—propaganda is the art of persuasion and its thrust is toward the propagation or dissemination of educational or religious messages. Propaganda originally stemmed from the fervent efforts of the Catholic Church to gather converts to the Christian faith. If, however, evangelists and teachers are propagandists, surely advertising, promotion and public relations men are no less so. The communications campaign which attempts to convince the public that cigarettes may cause cancer is as much a propaganda effort as is the advertising of popular cigarettes as a way toward romantic fulfillment. The difference, of course, is not in the technique as much as in the substance, the ethics involved and the end in view. The public relations specialist is obviously sensitive about the intensional meaning attached to propaganda. Hence the euphemism of "information specialist," or Office of War Information. The United States has never designated any communications agency with the term propaganda, although many foreign countries realistically have a Ministry of Propaganda.

Propaganda, Education and Social Control

Nevertheless, the student of communicative techniques must necessarily make some distinction between the ends of education, which are positive and which seek learning for its own sake or for the good of society, and propaganda which, as used and understood in today's world of mass media, generally takes on the affective meaning of pressing for a point of view designed to benefit a special interest—and one which may *not* redound to the good of society. In an informal and intuitive way, propaganda envelopes contemporary man simply because he is inundated with the messages from a multiplicity of mass media. And propaganda appears in other areas beyond media—in the history textbook, and the way history is taught in the school; in the learning of language; in religious education; and in courses in economics and political science. Even the physical sciences, in this nuclear age, are not immune to its influence. But, above all, it is present in the area of mass communication where norms and evaluative judgments operate, despite the efforts of the media purveyors to remain impartial. The purpose of education, in the classroom or through the media, is generally agreed to be the acquisition of knowledge and information which will be absorbed and imparted to future generations. Even the acquiring of esthetic, scientific or cultural knowledge, however, is not quantitative, for value judgments color the meaning for both teacher and student. It remains to be seen whether programmed instruction can be so structured as to eliminate traces of propaganda.

Since propaganda can be studied only from the limited perspective of the behavioral sciences, it is difficult to define in any extensional or denotative sense. As differentiated from conventional educational philosophy, which is concerned with theories of knowledge, propaganda is a much more powerful agency of social control. More often than not it has been correctly criticized for attempting to influence attitudes and behavior toward ends which may have little, or no, social, cultural or educational value to the individual or the group. There are differences, then, in the dissemination of sheer fact, (the informational use of language) in the process of education and in the practice of propaganda which may purport to be cognitive but is, in reality, directive and affective in purpose. While, from the standpoint of the social scientist, there is education involved in the exercise of propaganda, and propaganda involved in the practice of education, the propagandist tends to rely upon, and frequently distort, information. His purpose is to achieve a goal which is not empirical, but which has been established a priori. The propagandist rejects the spirit of empiricism and of inquiry in favor of preconceived ends. The "facts" are then made to conform to the achievement of those ends. This may be salutory if the ends are socially or morally good. But much depends upon who benefits from the achievement of those ends, and to what extent.

For these reasons, a democratic and pluralistic society tends to reject the use of propaganda or to invest it, perhaps unrealistically, with a connotation which is derogatory and demeaning. The American public has been conditioned by a curious form of propaganda to "look at the record," even though looking at that record may yield not fact, but unadulterated fiction. Practitioners of public relations are very much aware of the great store the public sets by the ability of people to arrive at judgments and conclusions on the basis of "the facts." Unfortunately, the facts too often are proffered with a strong overlay of opinion, and the reasoning is essentially affective and directive. Even if the facts were utterly correct, the inevitable tendency to color them through the prism of one's value judgments would make propaganda an implicit part of a great deal of communication that is intended to pass for information. Indeed, one of the goals of the propagandist, particularly in a democracy, is to draw upon converts to "the facts" to pass along the message by means of a communicative chain reaction. This does not mean that the respondent is asked to propagate rumor, for rumor is both indirect and sometimes unwitting, and propaganda—political propaganda in particular—is seemingly overt. But what does occur, in the passing of the content from communicators to communicatees, is that the content mutates and changes. This is a phenomenon that is difficult for the propagandist to control, and it is one reason why progapanda gets out of hand and backfires.

In the 1968 teachers' strike in New York City (and other large urban cities) there was not only polarization but considerable "backlash" against Mayor John Lindsay, despite his stated efforts to seek a solution which would benefit all parties concerned. In the racially tense situation, Lindsay found himself equally damned by the blacks and the whites, by the teachers and the local governing board. And accusations of propaganda were thrust at the Mayor from all committed quarters. Even with the most honorable of objectives, the success or failure of the propaganda message depends not only on the intent of the propagandist, but on the nature of the media, the "set" of the public and the degree to which the public understands what the issue is all about.

Propaganda usually cannot operate in a unilateral or circumscribed area. Many factors must be taken into consideration in the study of the use of propaganda messages through the mass media. Most important is the recognition that propaganda is not always intentional. The black power movement claims, for example, that no matter how earnestly white teachers attempt to reach black students, an element of propaganda must seep into the content. Equally significant is the question of "positive" versus "negative" propaganda, the assumption being that propaganda for socially beneficial ends is morally good, while propaganda for special interest purposes is ethically bad. But these distinctions, again, are polarized and leave out the large gray area which may be neither all good or all bad—or good to some and bad to others, depending upon their orientation and values. Of importance, too, is the stance of the managers of the media of communication who may, or may not, be aware that the content they carry may be propaganda. More than one newspaper has been accused of deliberate bias in favor of, or in opposition to, areas which concern special interests such as segregation, socialized medicine, interracial housing or legal rights of the accused.

Propaganda and Communication Content

Finally, the question may be raised about the legitimacy of propaganda as communications content. Does it make any fundamental difference to the public if it is aware of the fact that the message which is directed to it has overtones of propaganda as communications content? From the standpoint of the communicator, is there any genuine significance in distinguishing between overt and hidden propaganda? A newspaper editorial, for example, might be termed overt propaganda, unless by definition it is agreed that propaganda content is that which attempts to influence public opinion through methods that are *not* revealed to the public. If, by agreement, progapanda is a method which can be applied to all kinds of ends—charitable as well as nefarious—then propaganda can be considered either moral or immoral, depending upon the ends and means involved. In this sense, then, all depends upon how propaganda is applied in the extensional world of concrete and tangible issues. Whatever the ends, however, the application of propaganda as a communicative device invariably consists of a source (or special interest group), the substance (or content), the media through which the substance is communicated and, finally, the effect. Since mass media are institutionalized and serve as agencies of social control, the media obviously can be used for persuasive communication. What is more difficult to determine is the question whether *any* attempt to influence public opinion through media may be called propaganda.

The fact is that it is extremely difficult to establish a cause-and-effect relationship between public opinion and propaganda and the functioning of the mass media of communication. The need for research and content analysis in this ambiguous area is acute, and one of the striking criticisms of propaganda analysis is that it detours the questions of values and ethics, or truth and falsity, and is concerned only with "facts." The propagandist, to be sure, is not concerned with norms, but solely with the goal of converting the communicatee. But this does not excuse the propaganda analyst from recognizing the inevitable role of value judgments in this most sensitive area of communication. It is possible to examine propaganda content, for example, by attempting to determine precisely who is trying to influence whom, on what issue and toward what end. The fact that attitudes are difficult to measure in depth does not excuse the propaganda analyst from trying to pin down ends and means in extensional or empirical terms.

Propaganda and public opinion analysis are difficult to study and evaluate with complete scientific objectivity, but the techniques available are better than none. Through interviewing and other empirical studies of individual and group attitudes, and through studies of newspaper content, voting patterns, buying habits, television viewing patterns and other criteria it is possible to arrive at conclusions which may be fairly tenable and reliable. It is possible through research, for example, to determine attitude change, even though controls and "before and after" studies cannot be accomplished with scientific precision. It is also possible to study public opinion and propaganda in action by determining who or what source is involved, what the objectives are and how the media of communication are being employed to carry the message.

There is no ultimate or scientifically verifiable truth about public opinion and propaganda, for the area is too volatile for controlled analysis. But there are recognizable signposts, one of which is that propaganda of one kind or another is almost always present in communication and it can be analyzed by a healthy semantic (extensional) attitude. The ends toward which propaganda is put can be evaluated in terms of their social usefulness, or harm, in the extensional world of individuals and concrete issues. The revelation of propaganda, particularly in such delicate area as race relations or international relations, is a healthy finding which gives the public—society—an opportunity to perceive and to act. For propaganda analysis and public opinion studies can, and do, frequently lead to the abandonment of worn concepts and policies for new and healthier directions. Propaganda indeed can be "good" or "bad" depending on the ends sought and the means employed to achieve those ends. In this determination, research and analysis can be both revelatory and salutary.

Media research covers a wide spectrum. Advertising agencies engage in research to determine which of the media is the best "buy," in terms of delivery to the largest audiences, or audiences which are demographically relevant to the product which is being marketed. The media themselves employ large research departments to convince the agency that the particular medium is best suited to the advertiser's needs and sales objectives. But there are other kinds of research which are not related specifically to marketing or merchandising. Some organizations do independent studies, frequently underwritten by foundations, in the social or economic impact of the mass media. Other research efforts attempt to relate the function of the mass media in terms of their effect on public opinion, and this analysis may involve questions of ethics and propaganda analysis. Unfortunately, while much of the research data is parochial in nature, it is nevertheless relevant. On occasion, specific efforts have been undertaken by reputable authorities such as Ruth Inglis' study of the social effect of motion pictures, or the late Gary Steiner's survey of the attitudes of television viewers. It is difficult, of course, to apply empirical methods of propaganda analysis to the mass media. While propaganda was classically described as early as Machiavelli's *The Prince*, the techniques used today are in part explicit in the mass media—as in the newspaper editorial—or are the result of the efforts of public relations men and pressure groups on the media. The skillful propagandist learns how to gauge the potential and the limitations of each of the media, using each in terms of the maximum result it is likely to achieve.

Mass Media and Propaganda

In the Colonies the press was essentially an instrument of opinion, and propaganda was overt and flagrant. The contemporary newspaper is an amalgam of both information and opinion (fact with an overlay of opinion)—a result, in part, of the need for large circulation, the demands of the advertiser and the size of the public. Paradoxically, while the number of newspapers has dwindled and mergers are a common occurrence, students of modern journalism believe that the American press, as an institution, is essentially free, democratic, largely independent and highly responsible. And this, despite the growth of chains, conglomerates, wire service copy and national syndication—all designed to perpetuate stereotyping and to make the newspaper vulnerable to special pleading. Even in the area of advertising, which most newspapers separate scrupulously from the editorial and news function, the newspaper remains basically independent and resistant to advertiser control —as television is essentially resistant to sponsor or agency control. Indirectly, it is claimed, the advertiser does exert an implicit influence, because the media are not encouraged to break out of the status quo and to experiment. But, even in cities which boast strongly partisan newspapers, as in the New York *Daily News* or the *Chicago Tribune*, it would be difficult to conclude that propaganda subverts news. Even in one newspaper cities, where there is no competitive element—indeed, in spite of the fact that the town boasts one paper—there is a genuine effort made to present a catholicity of viewpoint in the coverage of the news.

The press came under considerable criticism, as did television, as a result of its coverage of the Chicago political convention in 1968, as well as for its reporting of the campus riots and its coverage of the racial upheavals in major cities. Media were accused of deliberately portraying violence, and television, in particular, was scored for allegedly seeking out violent scenes. In the case of the school decentralization crisis in New York City, there were critics who believed that reporters, if not explicitly, at least implicitly tried to write their copy in terms of what they believed would be the editorial position of their newspaper. The media stoutly defended their coverage, claiming with considerable justification that neither the newspaper nor television can turn away from violent events if these events take place and if they are legitimate news. The public, in short, was entitled to the truth, even though it was ugly. The fact is that no medium, however arduous an effort it makes, can bring the news to the public as immaculate truth. All news has an implicit overlay of opinion by virtue of the fact that it must pass through many hands—the reporter, the writer, the editor and the management. Each of these comes to the issue with value judgments which simply cannot be eliminated. In addition, much of the news which is purveyed to, and by, mass media is the result of the efforts of publicists. It may be directive and affective in overtones, but it frequently is newsworthy as well and therefore "fit to print." Certainly, the judgment of the editor of what is worth printing may unconsciously be propagandistic in the broadest meaning of the term. Each paper, for example, reveals a bias by the way stories are handled in terms of headlines, where they appear in the paper and how the news is emphasized.

Yet, despite all of the extraneous factors which tend to water down the impact of news or information, despite the presence of conscious or unconscious value judgments, the public often behaves in a manner dramatically opposite to what might be supposed from what one sees in print. It is a startling political phenomenon that the candidate most frequently given a favorable press does not always win a national election, as was revealed so clearly in the case of Dewey versus Truman, Nixon versus Humphrey and Landon versus Roosevelt. Perhaps this is because most newspaper readers look to the press for general information plus peripheral entertainment, such as comics and sports, rather than to editorials. It is a fact—and a regrettable one—that the syndicated political columnist has all but overshadowed the once provocative and stimulating effort of the committed editorial writer. Newspapers are read because they are quite inexpensive and offer a great deal for what they cost. They are read, too, for the advertisements, the cartoons and the popular features. In terms of impact on the public, the newspaper need not try too hard to serve as a propaganda funnel. Since many readers do not read much beyond the headlines, it is relatively easy for editors to slant leads and first paragraphs. Even those who try mightily to be objective may unwittingly reveal bias in the way headlines are presented. And this is quite significant, because most readers tend to be influenced by heads and sub-heads, rather than by absorbing the entire text of a story. It is possible to slant a story by highlighting certain aspects, leaving out others or positioning it in a special box. Photographs can be slanted even more adroitly than copy, while editorial cartoons are, of course, clearly partisan in point of view.

The press, in its own defense, insists that is ultimately responsible for what it prints and that it must be permitted to function according to its canons of good journalism and under the protection of the First Amendment. More and more, the newspaper editor and the television news correspondent insist that interpretation and news analysis are far removed from propaganda, and that they have a rightful and necessary place in contemporary journalism. *The New York Times* is said to insist that its reporters combine factual news reporting with interpretation, and many critics of the press also believe that the best reporting is interpretative reporting.

Television news and public affairs programming presents a more complex problem. The critics of broadcasting are plentiful and trenchant. Particularly because television is so powerful a medium of mass communication, it is beset with pressures from a variety of sources. Unfortunately, many of those who have attacked the medium do so more out of irritation or trepidation than from a desire to improve electronic journalism. From politics, from the academic world and even from a competitive medium such as the press, television is reminded that it must be all things to all men, must please an infinite variety of special interests and must never forget that the air belongs to the people, not to the stations or the networks. The viewing public, however, obviously places credence in television news, because it watches it consistently and with ever-increasing interest. A 1968 study of public attitudes toward television and other media by the Roper Research Associates yielded rather interesting data on the way the viewer felt about this popular medium. In general, television viewing is on the increase, and the people still prefer television to other media, as they have over the past decade. As a source of news, television continues to have rather high credibility.

Public Attitudes Toward Media

Queried as to where they got most of their news, 59% cited television news, 49% of the respondents selected newspapers, 25% radio, and 7% magazines. Even after the criticism of the 1968 convention coverage by numerous political figures, the public did not lose faith in the credibility of newspapers or television as sources of news. In cases of conflicting stories, 44% selected television as the first medium to believe (probably because they are eyewitness to events on the screen), 21% placed faith in newspapers, 11% in magazines and 10% in radio. Of those media which appeared least believeable, the public selected magazines first, newspapers next, radio third and television last.

If faced with a choice of only one out of four mass media, 50 of the respondents selected television, 24% named newspapers, 17% radio, and 5% magazines. Among the college educated, the figures were respectively 37% for television and 36% for newspapers. With respect to elections, newspapers were selected as the best source to become acquainted with candidates for local office, but television had a commanding lead as the medium best suited to offering information on figures engaged in a national election. When asked whether television stations should broadcast editorials (which have increased 17% from 1964 to 1968) in the style of the newspaper, 63% of the respondents replied positively, 26% said they should not and 11% were not certain. It is significant that 45% of the respondents did not want the station to recommend specific candidates, even though the recommendation was specifically labeled as an editorial.

Finally, it is significant in an age of social changes and upheaval that the public appears to be convinced that all indicated agencies—television and newspapers, school and government—had declined in terms of their respective service to the people. Television stations, which were chosen as the agency doing the best job in 1966, dropped 7% and fell behind the schools, but other agencies declined in the public's evaluation as well.

Although studies in the effects of mass media are still tentative and largely unrevealing, there is little doubt that so powerful and widely enjoyed a medium as television does reflect public opinion, both in the news and entertainment areas. Those who predicted that the advent of television would turn America into a nation of passive illiterates are confronted with an astonishing increase in reading and book publishing, and in increased attendance at museums and concerts. Although some entertainment programs have been criticized for blandness and repetitiveness, it is in the news and public affairs area about which considerable controversy has swirled. Confrontations on the campus and in the ghetto, criticism of the political convention coverage, questions of balanced programming pose a tremendous challenge to an industry which is beset by the demands of an infinite variety of special interest groups.

Those who would prefer to see harsh events glossed over euphemistically claim that television's coverage of violence serves to trigger more violence. The medium is scored by some for avoiding controversial issues and by others for over-emphasizing polemics. News analysis is labeled propaganda by those who do not agree with it. From individuals and organizations such as NAFBRAT (National Association For Better Radio and Television), from academicians, from FCC commissioners, from legislators, from educational, religious, economic and political groups television is under unrelenting pressure because it covers, or fails to cover, certain events in the news. Some consider this healthy, but it must also be recognized as a negative reaction from those whose ox may have been gored by the basic desire for integrity in television news and documentaries. If for no other reason than pragmatism, a medium as carefully scrutinized could not afford to be less than scrupulous in its coverage of events. In the last analysis, public opinion itself places enormous faith in the credibility of television news coverage, a faith which the increasing competence of electronic journalism shows is not misplaced.

Still, there are unresolved problems involving the "fairness doctrine" and other areas of social and political responsibility which may have portentous consequences for the future of television journalism and which will be discussed in a consideration of freedom and responsibility in the mass media. In the context of the effect of the media on public opinion, research continues to reveal that all media, television included, tend to reinforce values already in existence, rather than to instigate the development of a new set of value judgments. Some social scientists also believe that, while television has greater audience reach than print media, the newspaper may have a more enduring influence. But the most recent Roper analysis indicates a trend in which television's impact grows stronger each year.

Books, Magazines and Film

Books, magazines and motion pictures each tends characteristically to reflect society more than to influence social mores and behavior. The novel has always been a source of information about the social milieu which is depicted and, therefore, a reflection of society at a particular period in history. As Scott Fitzgerald caught the spirit of his own age in *The Great Gatsby*, so novelists have distilled the temper of a nation in the throes of war, in crises of racial strife, in periods of turbulence and quietude. Some fiction, such as Upton Sinclair's *The Jungle*, has been overt propaganda. A considerable number of non-fiction books also have been written to influence public opinion, notably books written by political figures who one day aspire to become candidates for the presidency. But the power of the written word, even though it does not reach the vast audiences of television, is thorough and deep and its influence has frequently been formidable and far-reaching. If it were not, books would not be banned by school systems as "propaganda," and authors would not be forced to the courts in order to be free to write and publish. Indeed, some of the most effective persuasive writing has come from the authors who wrote *Uncle Tom's Cabin, Common Sense,* and other documents whose importance has been more social and moral than aesthetic.

Unfortunately, the hard cover book is an expensive venture, and most publishers refuse to promote or advertise a book until it has been favorably reviewed or has somehow attracted a fairly wide circle of readers. New volumes by new authors are an expensive gamble for any publisher, which is why books were a relatively circumscribed medium until the advent of the paperback book. Thanks to this development, the book has become truly a mass medium. Volumes which may reach only a few thousand in hard cover may run into hundreds of thousands in paperbound stock. This additional circulation gives such books as reprints of self-help volumes, the popular psychology treatises and the expose type of literature a considerable influence on public opinion. Although the paperbacks are readily available on newsstands and drug counters, many fine books still suffer the disadvantage of inadequate and old fashioned modes of distribution. Cultural lag is nowhere more apparent than in the appearance of the paperbound volume in a society where the number of bookstores and public libraries are appallingly few and far between, and certainly inadequate to meet the needs of a growing and increasingly literate public.

At one time, the national magazine was a potent communicative force in American society. Millions looked forward eagerly to their magazine's arrival each week, and such periodicals as the *Saturday Evening Post* or *Collier's* were considered indispensible in households where television had not yet become a reality. At the period when the social influence of the large-circulation magazines was greatest—from 1900 to about 1950—although there were few studies in depth of their effect on public opinion or their propaganda overtones, there is little doubt that millions were influenced by magazine content. The *Saturday Evening Post* symbolized conservative America, and was far more concerned with perpetuating the status quo than in change or innovation. The so-called more "radical" or "liberal" publications, such as *The Nation* and *The New Republic*, attracted a small audience of intellectuals and were suspect, and even temporarily banned, in certain educational systems and public libraries, because they were alleged to be carriers of propaganda and inimical to the accepted way of life of middle class America. And many magazines did espouse a point of view toward politics and economics, toward capital and labor, toward liberalism and conservatism. *The Readers' Digest*, which has survived, albeit with the addition of paid advertising, consistently extolled the basic virtues of American life, even in the face of racial and religious prejudice, segregation and other ills which cried out for social reform.

It is probably true that, of all the mass media, the magazine labored under fewest restrictions in arriving at, and disseminating, a point of view. It could be chosen and read selectively, and it had none of the pressures which were applied to the newspaper, motion pictures or television. Certainly there was no need for any consideration of "fairness doctrine" and, unless libel or slander was involved, the magazine was seldom taken to task for presenting a point of view.

Magazine editors, of course, had to predicate their contents on three essential factors—what the reader, in fact, demanded, what the editor thought the reader ought to have, and what would attract and hold advertisers. The successful periodicals successfully juxtaposed these factors. More than the other media, too, the magazine, as an organ of public opinion, represents a good example of how values which the reader holds dear tend to be reinforced. Any radical change in editorial content may result in a loss of readership, and so editors become loathe to experiment. But, as the demise of several great magazines has shown, holding fast to outmoded values and refusing to change with the tides of public opinion, can prove disastrous. Like television, magazines tend more to reflect society than to innovate. Editors watch public opinion trends and interests carefully, and will tackle certain subjects only when they believe the public is adequately prepared—which is why the magazine is so late in catching up with changing times and represents a good example of cultural lag. Only the news magazines present a weekly analysis and comment on contemporary events and problems, and more than one critic has asserted that these interpretative analyses are frequently not an informative discussion of all aspects of the subject, but a subtle presentation of an editorial viewpoint.

The motion picture's effect on public opinion differs radically from that of the magazine, for movies are essentially "dream merchants" and their popular purpose has been romance, escapism and entertainment. Yet, a medium of mass communication that was embraced quickly and enthusiastically by millions of immigrants—a medium which was exported to foreign countries—could not fail to contain public opinion and propaganda overtones. During the silent film days, the motion picture attracted a great audience of lower middle class Americans. Today, it has assumed a new sophistication, and is the selected medium for experimentation on the college campus. The very group which looked upon motion pictures with intellectual snobbism twenty and thirty years ago, now embrace film as the medium of the future. In an earlier period, the motion picture was the dominant mass medium, involving millions of movie goers once or twice weekly. It became a powerful social and aesthetic force, both in America and abroad. But critics of film declared, and with considerable justification, that the motion picture gave a false representation of values both in America and foreign countries. Although the United States did not produce film for expressly propagandistic purposes, as did Russia, Italy and Germany, its effect on public opinion was nevertheless implicit. Films conveyed and reinforced social stereotypes which were false and deleterious. The impression given abroad was that America was a nation where lawlessness and gangsterism, sex, violence and spurious economic values prevailed. The negative precepts of the motion picture code were easily circumvented by having justice and romance triumph in the end, no matter what the means to that end may have been.

Furthermore, the motion picture, as an agency of control, was monopolized by five major companies—MGM, Warner Brothers, RKO, Paramount and Twentieth Century Fox—before the government Consent Decree of 1946 forced a divorce of production from exhibition and distribution of films. These five firms produced, distributed and exhibited pictures. They were able to demand selected showing through the device of "block-booking." It was the rise of independent companies, the appearance of television and the changing taste on the college campus which finally gave the motion picture a new and more realistic direction. But there is no doubt but that the film played a tremendous role in fashioning taste and setting moral standards for many years. Hollywood stereotypes were rampant during the 20's, 30's and 40's—the Italian gangster, the black Pullman porters, the Irish cop—but these have finally, and fortunately, disappeared from the contemporary screen. At its worst, however, Hollywood has never been the overt instrument of propaganda which film has been for the government of Red China and the Soviet Union. Its purpose has been to entertain, rather than to propagandise, but its impact on public opinion has nonetheless been significant.

The film industry has been subjected to unrelenting pressure from church groups and other pressure organizations, each particularly sensitive to its own sphere of interest. Indeed, had the industry listened to the various voices of dissent and pressure, it would have been impossible to make even the most innocuous and bland product. The Code was not much help. Although motion pictures were recognized as entertainment, their "moral" influence on public opinion was underscored. Until the new freedom which pervades film today appeared, movies were contrived to offend no one. Indeed, there are critics who believe that the movies, produced under the old Code, were far more hypocritical than the more honest, if more shocking, pictures that are exhibited today. Certainly, from a public opinion viewpoint, the conventional Hollywood film did not accurately represent either the American scene or character. Few persons behaved or lived in the style of the screen idols of the 30's. Basic human motivations were clearly distorted in films where love invariably conquered all, the good guys always won over the bad guys, and affluence was the common lot of all screen heroes and heroins. Nowhere was the Horatio Alger legend better perpetuated than in Hollywood dream world. All of these concepts were examples of a kind of subliminal or latent propaganda, for the movie goer did indulge in a "willing suspension of disbelief" and was therefore in a position to be rather easily influenced. What was true of Hollywood product, however, was not true of some of the great documentaries of Grierson and Lorentz. Nor was it true of the training and propaganda films producing brilliantly during both World Wars, nor of the many excellent films done for teaching and orientation purposes in business, industry and education. Far more than the Hollywood product, these efforts represented film at its best as a significant and powerful medium of communication.

All of the mass media, in substance, both reflect and influence public opinion. And each medium, overtly or implicitly, can serve, under certain circumstances, as an instrument of propaganda. All communication, insofar as it attempts to convey meaning or ideas, can be employed toward propagandistic ends, but it is the responsibility of the communicator to insure that what is conveyed as information does not subvert truth.

BIBLIOGRAPHY

Albig, William. *Modern Public Opinion.* New York: McGraw-Hill Company, Inc., 1956.
Public Opinion. New York: McGraw-Hill Company, Inc., 1939.
Bettinghaus, Erwin P. *Persuasive Communication.* New York: Holt, Rinehart and Winston, 1968.
Cartwright, D. "Some Principles of Mass Persuasion" *in Human Relations,* (1949)pp. 253–67.
Choukas, Michael. *Propaganda Comes of Age.* Washington, D.C.: Public Affairs Press, 1965.
Christenson, Reo M. and Robert D. McWilliams. *Voice of the People: Reading in Public Opinion and Propaganda.* New York: McGraw-Hill, 1962.
Dobb, Leonard W. *Propaganda: Its Psychology and Technique.* New York: Holt, 1935.
Public Opinion and Propaganda. New York: Holt, Rinehart and Winston, 1966.
Gallup, George. *A Guide to Public Opinion Polls.* Princeton, New Jersey: Princeton University Press, 1948.
The Story Behind the Gallup Poll. Princeton, New Jersey: Princeton University Press, 1957.
George, Alexander L. *Propaganda Analysis.* Evanston, Illinois: Row, Peterson and Company, 1959.
Hovland, Carl I, Irving L. Janis and Harold H. Kelley. *Communication and Persuasion.* New Haven: Yale University Press, 1953.
Katz, Daniel, et al., eds. *Public Opinion and Propaganda.* New York: The Dryden Press, 1954.
Kelley, Stanley, Jr. *Professional Public Relations and Political Power.* Baltimore: The Johns Hopkins Press, 1956.
Lippmann, Walter. *Public Opinion.* New York: Penguin Books, 1946.
Merton, R. K. *Mass Persuasion.* New York, Harper, 1946.
Paine, Thomas. *Common Sense.* New York: Remington and Hooper, 1928.
Powell, John Norman. *Anatomy of Public Opinion.* New York: Prentice-Hall, 1951.
Roper, Elmo. *You and Your Leader, Their Actions and Your Reactions.* 1936–1956. New York: Morrow, 1957.
Rossiter, Clinton and James Lare. *The Essential Lippmann.* New York: Random House, 1963.
Smith, B. L., H. D. Lasswell and R. D. Casey. *Propaganda Communication and Public Opinion.* Princeton: Princeton University Press, 1946.

14

Communication as Persuasion: Advertising and Public Relations

IT IS A difficult task to envision life in America without benefit of advertising. This mode of persuasion, commonly identified with marketing and merchandising, is omnipresent in America and, indeed, in most countries of the Western world. In no country, is it as extravagantly applied to the mass media as in the United States, although even the Soviet Union has not managed to escape some form of advertising. In the United States advertising is the main support of virtually all of the commercially-oriented media except the motion picture. It is, therefore, considered an indispensable aspect of the economy. Commercial television readily asserts that it is the revenue from advertising which permits the networks and stations to offer not only entertainment, but enormously expensive news, public affairs and documentary programs at no cost to the viewer except the original investment in, and amortization of, the television receiver. The American economy is, in a word, geared to advertising.

John Kenneth Gailbraith has argued that it is false to assume that the more man's needs are supplied, the more urgent those needs become. He asserts that these needs and wants are contrived by the very process of advertising and promotion. If production creates wants by means of advertising, it can hardly be defensible to believe that production also satisfies those wants. Such misleading thinking is typical of a value system which aggrandizes production above all other endeavors. The modus operandi for the creation of wants and the "direct link between production and wants" is the institution of advertising. Even more important, says Galbraith, than the manufacturing of the product is the manufacturing of demand for the product. Why, if products are so avidly desired by consumers, must so much be spent on advertising to create wants? For the fact is that "wants can be synthesized by advertising . . . and shaped by the discreet manipulations of the persuaders. . . ." The demand for goods is not spontaneous with the consumer. It is fabricated by advertising.

Despite the fact that advertising exists in various forms—newspaper, billboard, radio, television, magazine—it elicits a decidedly negative reaction from its critics because, to them, its connotations and effect are either of dubious ethics or altogether immoral. Both advertising and the techniques of public relations have been accused of being essentially dishonest in purpose, subliminal in method, appealing to man's affective or emotive reactions, taking advantage of human anxiety and altogether a deleterious influence on the American character. Nevertheless, the "hard sell" and the old pitchman type of advertising, as well as the flamboyant, or devious, approach to public relations, have changed considerably as the public became better educated, as the media set higher standards of acceptability and as special interest citizens and consumer groups prevailed upon government agencies, such as the FTC, to apply more rigid supervision over false or misleading practices. Advertising content, both as a medium of communication in itself, as well as in terms of its use by the mass media, has become more sophisticated. The aesthetics have changed for the better, and more artistic layouts, better photography and far more subtle and intelligent copy now prevails. There are viewers and critics alike who have pointed out sardonically that they sometimes prefer the commercials in the media to some of the program fare.

Advertising has developed, in effect, a unique and indigenous kind of literature, a form of prose altogether different, but nevertheless meriting attention. The best advertising writers, who looked upon their work as a mere prelude to accumulating sufficient money to write a novel, now write with greater conviction and respect for their craft. Many will not undertake assignments on behalf of clients or products which are of dubious virtue. The gifted advertising writer can write with romanticism, warmth, intelligence and sophistication. He can relate to the reader and show the reader how to identify with the content. Contemporary advertising uses all forms of literary endeavor. There are ads which combine poetry with illustration; which use the comic strip technique; which tell a straight narrative story; which are purely expository.

The literature of advertising and selling, whatever criticism may be made of it on psychological, sociological or economic grounds is an important form of communication, a combination of verbal and pictorial symbols, equally as significant in terms of numbers of readers or viewers, as poetry, plays and novels. Its symbols are those employed in other literary forms—happiness, need, goal-orientation, sex, youth, glamour. Commercials, however, have not only taken over symbols which have been traditional to American life but, critics believe, have demeaned these very symbols and have cheapened their aesthetic and ethical significance. The good life of today is what the advertiser tells America it is through language which is basically emotive and directive in nature. To its critics advertising portrays a hedonism far beyond that suggested by ancient Greece, it is full of Pollyanna, it holds out a potential cornucopia of riches to those who will buy its products. Its blandishments range from sex appeal to sheer ego gratification by the process of keeping up with the Joneses. But criticism has not deterred the rise of advertising as one of the major business endeavors in America. Those who are committed to the advertising world are convinced that the economy would collapse without it. The reason is that advertising moves products, involving billions of dollars of money and effort, and it has become an integral and utterly necessary facet of the economy.

The growth of advertising, as of other media, was a logical outcome —indeed, an inevitable result—of the Industrial Revolution, of the enormous commercial expansion that took place in the United States at the end of the Nineteenth Century. As media of mass communication became important institutions in American life, advertising became a vital part of the whole matrix of modern communication arts. Particularly since World War I, when it was found that newspaper advertising could accelerate the sale of government bonds, the impetus toward wider use of advertising and public relations techniques has been steadily increasing, resulting in the universal use of various modes of commercial advertising as popular communication. In a sense, mass media and commercial advertising acted as common spurs. The newspaper and magazine provided the media for advertising communication, and advertising was largely responsible for the growth and economic success of the newspaper and magazine and, eventually, of radio and television. The time is approaching when CATV transmission will provide a steady stream of informational communications concerning any number of items, from super-market specials to department store sales.

Origin of the Advertisement

Curiously enough, it is odd to look back and discover that, despite the shrewdness of the early American communicators, the first newspapers and magazines, such as *The Pennsylvania Gazette* and others, did not attach any particular commercial or literary importance to advertising. With the establishing of second class mailing privileges by the Post Office Department at the close of the Nineteenth Century, newspapers and magazines became ideal media for national advertising, and opened the door for the development for that much maligned institution, the advertising agency. The idea of advertising, however, was not dormant in the second half of the Nineteenth Century, for there were stirrings of interest in this powerful communications form. At the beginning, advertisers dealt directly with the medium (the newspapers) and transactions were effected between the two parties—and editor-printer and the advertising client. There was no middleman. As commerce expanded and the economy grew, it became both necessary and economically worthwhile for the advertiser to seek wider markets for products. Clients found advertising a necessary adjunct to sales, and newspapers found that they could achieve circulation and viable economy only by securing paid advertising.

Advertising eventually became a sufficiently complex procedure to require a catalytic agent between the media and the client, a so-called "specialist" in determining what space to buy and where and how to buy it. The advertising agent became a unique kind of specialist, although precisely how the agency evolved is not too well documented. At first, editors dealt directly with advertisers, and occasionally the Postmaster, who, under the licensing system served as printer, also acted as the catalyst. But the newspaper publishers who found advertising imperative for growth, also set up their own middleman who acted, in effect, as a kind of embryonic advertising agency. These middlemen could secure commissions from several newspapers while serving both the media and the advertiser who found it convenient to deal with one central source of placement.

Historically, the first advertising agency was probably that of Volney B. Palmer who set up his business in mid-Nineteenth Century Philadelphia. At about the same period, John Hooper was said to have opened an agency in New York. These first agencies represented newspapers, secured orders for advertising, placed the copy with the medium and handled details of billing the client or advertiser. They did not represent the client, however, but were agents of the newspapers and magazines. As advertising communications evolved, the agent ceased to represent the media and went into business for himself. His procedure consisted of selling a given amount of space to the advertiser, accepting his commission and then buying space in the newspaper. This method put the client in a favorable position, for he could now bargain with several agents until he found the deal best suited to his economic needs. It also put the agent in the position of representing both client and media, and thereby securing the best deal for himself.

After the Civil War, one George Rowell went into business in Boston, adding a third city where the advertising agency was established, in addition to New York and Philadelphia. Rowell added still another facet to the growth of advertising. He bought space in the media and parcelled it out to the advertisers in terms of the amount of specific space each client demanded to meet his advertising needs. Rowell was thus able to effect wholesale arrangements, and sell the space at retail prices over a period of time and at a regular fee. It was to the mutual advantage of the newspaper and the client to have Rowell buy an amount of space for a given amount of money and then sell the space to the respective advertisers. Subsequently, some agents paid the media a set sum for the right to take over the sale to clients of all available advertising space. The newspaper publisher found this a convenient procedure, for he was able to sell his space, was fully paid for it and had no further problem of offering it for sale to the advertiser. The agent, on the other hand, could buy up space in a number of newspapers and magazines, set a price of sale and market to the respective advertisers.

The first advertising agents, then, served a multiplicity of purposes, none of them clearly defined. But it was clear that the agent did serve as a kind of broker or middleman. What he received, in effect, was a percentage, or commission, similar to the procedure that prevails today. The difference was that the Nineteenth Century agent sold space *for* the newspaper to the client and advised the client where and what to buy. Consequently, the media of newspaper and magazine quickly discovered that they could not exist without advertising revenue. As the media grew, advertising kept pace with that growth. This was particularly true when clients decided to reach readers beyond merely local markets. As the advertiser extended his reach to wider areas, the agency became increasingly essential. The agency showed, too, that advertising on an increasingly wider scale gave an excellent return for the cost of the original investment.

A Period of Spectacular Growth

By 1875, F. Wayland Ayer, predecessor for the famous N. W. Ayer agency, was serving as a full-fledged agent for advertisers. In 1893, the American Association of Newspaper Publishers decided that it was proper procedure for agencies to receive a commission. In 1901, the flourishing Curtis Publishing Company agreed with the AANP position. Advertising became, like all mass communications, a singularly spectacular and lucrative Twentieth Century phenomenon. As of 1968, there were almost 4,000 bona fide advertising agencies functioning in the United States. Their functions, however, had by that date steadily increased beyond that of acting simply a middleman or broker. The contemporary advertising agency, an enormously complicated and solvent business in its own right, performs myriad functions for its numerous clients. It provides careful, sustained research data, with each client served by a special account executive who maintains liaison between agency and advertiser. It researches, prepares and places copy and layout for extensive multi-media advertising campaigns. Its media department determines whether to use newspaper, radio, television or magazines alone or in combination for a given campaign. At the same time, the agency's peripheral departments serve vital functions of production, billing, placement and so forth. Some agencies carry public relations departments as a special additional service to clients, but this practice has diminished, becasue the large clients prefer to select their own public relations firms to work in cooperation with the company public relations department.

The contemporary advertising agency provides more than a service to business. It has developed into a major industry in its own right with an annual outlay of billions of dollars. Although advertising continues to suffer from the critiques of its detractors—even the government has complained of monopolistic practices and has forced the American Association of Advertising agencies (the 4A's) to agree not to violate the anti-trust laws—advertising agencies continue to grow and expand. More than fifty major agencies are billing $10 to $12 million annually, and are spending more than a billion dollars on the world's largest advertising medium, television. Nor is national advertising the only aspect to benefit from the growth of industry. Local advertising media also have grown in the Twentieth Century, and local radio and television spots, as well as ads in local papers, have become a lucrative business. Despite the spate of books and articles which, quite properly in many instances, deplore the vulgarization of the countryside by outdoor billboards, national outdoor advertising continues to grow.

The reasons for this enormous expansion of advertising communications are twofold. Primarily, the highly competitive nature of business tends to force industry into advertising campaigns. Secondly, the reach of mass media, such as television, offer a tempting market for sales or institutionally oriented messages to many publics. Although complaints are common about the economic costs involved in advertising and public relations endeavors, few companies would do without either, and most tend to expand rather than contract these efforts. Meanwhile, rates have risen with increased demand and with the greater reach of the media. The so-called cost per thousand (the cost of reaching one thousand readers or viewers) has gone up. Advertising reaches more people with greater affluence than at any other period in history. It was inevitable that so powerful a communicative and persuasive force would attract the attention of the research psychologist and sociologist. Advertising reached a point where its influence as a social and educational institution were worthy of serious study.

Yet, advertising, unlike other industries, has no hardware or inventory. It functions, successfully or not, on the basis of human ability—creative efforts to communicate persuasively through layout and copy. It continues to be thought of by its critics as an exciting, frenetic and altogether superfluous business, but nevertheless a business which bills billions of dollars a year and employs a group of uniquely talented and creative people. And with the steady growth of television, agencies have undertaken new obligations and goals, both in research and creative techniques. Some agencies, in fact, depend almost exclusively upon television sponsors for their major share of billings; and the result for a long time was a recurring tug of war between agency and network on the question of program control and placement. A television network with a highly successful program in prime evening time (between seven and eleven in the evening) usually can develop a fairly good position with agencies and with clients who want to buy part of this prime, but limited, time.

Advertising and Mass Media

The consumer groups, in the last analysis, comprise the goal toward which advertising is directed. And the consumer, therefore, is in a position to exercise ultimate control over the media. But the consumers are fragmented and heterogeneous, rather than one homogeneous mass, and advertisers know that the publics they must reach are many and varied and based on a number of relevant factors such as age, sex, geographical distribution, religion, economic status and education. It is these groups which advertising reaches through the instrumentality of media of mass communication—more than 1,700 newspapers, some 600 television stations, several thousand radio stations, hundreds of magazines and innumerable outdoor billboards. These media are omnipresent. No advertiser, however affluent he may be, can use all media to reach all publics in all places. In each medium, and among the media, choice and selectivity are necessary. It is in this area of choice that the advertising agency and the sales departments of the various media are essential, although each operates from a vested interest viewpoint.

Advertising is based primarily on its "reach" or circulation. The rate card of a television station or newspaper offers the advertiser a cost-per-thousand figure, along with elaborate research statistics aimed to reveal why the particular medium will function successfully. Yet, despite all of the scientific contrivance which goes into choice, advertising campaigns are not always successful and advertising agencies and sponsors are never quite certain whether a newspaper "buy" might not have been better than a radio-television campaign, or vice versa. Each of the media, of course, offer persuasive reasons for buying that particular communication channel. Newspaper and magazine ABC figures (Audit Bureau of Circulation) are almost always uniformly accurate, although there are inevitable variables involved. No one knows precisely how many persons look at a magazine or a newspaper, although it is known that newspapers are discarded more quickly than magazines. Television research also falls short of absolute accuracy. The Neilsen surveys, which are based on 1,200 homes, are not presented as utter perfection, but merely as an accurate and practical measuring device and a guideline to the prospective advertiser. The ultimate accuracy or efficiency of any statistical research cannot be vouched for, but agencies and sponsors tend to look to the available research data as the most feasible information available and to act upon it.

Each medium offers possibilities and limitations which are built into the medium itself. Despite the fact that a newspaper like *The New York Times* offers truly national advertising, most of the daily press relies on local, retail ads—or national ads based on local franchise, such as automobile dealers and other nationally distributed commodities. The newspaper is the oldest and the most conventional medium. It likes to think of itself as the most prestigious of the mass media. Its importance for advertising communications is that it provides—or provided, before the competition from local spot on radio and television—a unique outlet for local advertising. The newspaper sells its ads by the line or column. Most advertisers will accept a "run of paper" position, but those who insist on a particular page are willing to pay a premium. Local advertisers receive a preferred rate over the national advertiser, primarily because the newspaper is assured of a steady and regular flow of insertions. Most of this local newspaper advertising is sold by media representatives which, like television station representatives, handle a group of newspapers throughout the country. Media representatives sell to many advertisers by representing a number of papers.

In the magazine field, particularly, advertising has declined since the growth of television. As a result, magazine advertising and promotion departments have developed elaborate promotional devices, designed to act as an incentive to potential buyers. These include special mailings and brochures and posters for window display with such legends as "advertised in *Life*." The basic idea behind this promotion is to indicate to the public the prestige which accrues from advertising in a major national magazine. Whether these so-called "gimmicks" are successful in a pragmatic sense simply cannot be determined, but they do have a psychological value in offering the advertiser extra communicative devices designed to spur the marketing of the product. In a less competitive period, magazines were one of the most popular of media for nationally advertised companies and products, and some periodicals still receive a respectable share of the advertising budget. There are a few old-time advertisers who, despite the power of television and newspapers, still prefer magazines, but the number is dwindling in the face of television's incontestable authority as an advertising medium. To specialized advertisers, in particular, magazines offer publications suited uniquely to meet a given need and directed specifically to a circumscribed group of consumers. In this sense, the magazine is the best buy for reaching specialized publics with specialized messages.

The magazine market is curiously heterogeneous, and yet it is uniform. In actuality, there is not one magazine market, but many overlapping areas which, in a national campaign, coalesce into one. For more specialized requirements, there are magazines extant which are suited to meet a multiplicity of needs—the home owner, the garden fan, the sports lover, the fishing enthusiast, the parent. These offer particular publics and are used frequently in conjunction with national advertising campaigns. Some of the special periodicals have achieved sufficient circulation and readership to qualify as general national outlets, among them the news magazines, the women's books and a sophisticated publication like *The New Yorker*. Each of these, however, tends to attract products in which its particular group of publics would be interested. And each magazine, specialized or general, offers much the same kind of space as the newspaper. Unless the advertiser requests one of the four available covers, the advertisement may run anywhere in the book. At one time, the television industry thought seriously of instituting a so-called "magazine concept."

The media and space buyers use a report prepared by the Starch organization, known as The Consumer Magazine Report, as a guide to the purchase and placement of advertising. This report breaks down statistically the potential consumer market which can be reached. It is put together on the basis of several thousand interviews, and generally has been considered a good barometer of the magazine market in terms of what it can discover about the orientation of the consumer, the products he buys and other relevant research data and criteria.

Unquestionably, the mass media which have become the most significant and potent for both local and national advertising are radio and television. Each delivers sheer numbers beyond any figure ever envisioned by newspapers or magazines. Each has proven to be a sales medium of unparalleled success, whether the advertiser buys nationally, on a network, or local spots on local stations. There are, of course, specific differences between the newspapers and the broadcast media. In the newspaper field, there are morning, evening and Sunday papers. Newspapers, too, can expand or contract their editorial space in terms of the advertising demand. But television stations, despite their enormous reach, necessarily are restricted in terms of space and time. They can offer only so many commercial messages in each hour format, and they also have set different rate card schedules for morning, afternoon and evening (prime) time. There are also differences between ABC circulation figures and surveys for newspapers and the various rating services for the broadcast media. Still another basic difference between the newspaper and television inheres in the viewer's prerogative of switching channels or tuning out programs at will, whereas most readers tend to read the same newspaper at about the same time each day.

Most television stations are affiliated with one or more of three national networks and this affiliation offers a tremendous advantage to the local station. Despite the rescinding of the option time arrangements and the great latitude and choice which stations have, the stations find it important from a program, prestige and economic point of view to take a large number of network programs, and most of the stations throughout the country have network affiliation. Only a network is able to provide coast-to-coast major entertainment and news programming to the stations and their viewing audiences. Yet, despite network affiliation, it is important to note that millions of dollars are spent on spot announcements on local programs, including so-called "participating spots" on local late night movies. These spots are the ones which are sold by station representatives who represent, and buy time, on several local and regional stations for national advertisers. In addition, the networks have their own spot sales departments, since each network owns and operates the legal number of five company-owned stations. Since motion pictures are now on the air every night of the week on a network basis, as well as on local stations, many advertisers buy national campaigns through local spots. The result is a continuing debate between local spot sales and national sales in terms of which works best for the ultimate benefit of the advertiser.

The continued growth of television has affected radio dramatically, but has not put it out of business. Radio has had to adjust to the overriding importance of television by changing its programming and advertising objectives. There are still national and local radio campaigns which take advantage of the fact that radio is an important medium in the car and the home. Studies show that millions listen to radio as a basic source of frequent news programs. Studies by Alfred Politz in radio listening habits show that the most feasible time to buy radio is the period during which the public drives home from business or to work in the morning. Early morning hours are considered particularly significant for local radio advertising.

National advertising does not stop with television, radio, newspapers or magazines. Through outdoor ads and through premium devices and other promotional endeavors, millions of potential consumers are reached by local and national campaigns. As advertising becomes increasingly significant and competition more intense, the major companies put greater emphasis on the use of brand names and trademarks. Product identification is considered essential in a successful advertising campaign and copyright ownership has been guarded zealously by companies which will not hesitate to bring lawsuits against competitors who may have infringed on copyright. Whether, in addition to the brand name, the premium offer is an important promotional device is a question widely debated by advertising agencies. There is no doubt that, at one time, premiums sold products, beginning with popular brands of soap. The idea of the premium began when B. T. Babbitt offered free lithographs to those buyers who would mail coupons from cakes of Babbitt soap. The device spurred sales so successfully that the Babbitt product became a popular demand item. Once it was discovered that premium offers could sell products, the idea caught on with both sponsor and public. If the premium was worthwhile, the public was motivated to buy the product.

In recent years, a variation of the premium offer is the offer of trading stamps which can be turned in eventually for a selection of various products selected from an extensive catalogue. Premiums play a particularly significant part in both the introduction of new products and in efforts to increase lagging sales of old ones. During the years when attendance at motion picture theatres was at an all-time low, the exhibitors offered dishes to lucky number holders on given nights of the week. In the earlier days of radio, the premium was a particularly successful promotional device, when the listener was urged to mail evidence of purchase, frequently with a token sum of money, in order to receive the coveted item.

Finally, the importance of outdoor advertising must not be overlooked. In recent years, criticism of billboards has become more savage, and at least one First Lady lent her efforts toward minimizing the use of outdoor boards in a "Keep America Beautiful" campaign. But the outdoor advertising fraternity comprises a strong special interest group, and a strong case has been made to underscore the need for billboards. Prior to the invention of printing, and the resulting rapid distribution of materials to the masses, the poster was the only convenient way of reaching the public on a "mass communication" basis. Printed posters were used in the Seventeenth and Eighteenth Centuries, and the landscape of Eighteenth Century London was cluttered as flagrantly as the outdoor billboard has defaced Twentieth Century America. Critics of outdoor advertising claim that it needlessly and ruthlessly makes the landscape of an otherwise beautiful country hideous. The motorist cannot escape the glaring presence of billboards, and the monotony of them, it is claimed, not only defaces the environment, but also is dangerous to the driver.

The late Senator Richard L. Newberger (Dem., Oregon) stated flatly that the billboard could not be defended by those who claimed that to prevent its use was to foster Socialism. On the other hand, the vocal defenders of outdoor advertising insist that it keeps motorists interested and alert, that it conveys important information and that it provides an outlet for the efforts of many highly creative people. The ultimate and still unresolved question is basically whether the goal is to keep America beautiful and totally undefiled, to yield to the implacable demands of advertisers or to find a way to place restrictions on the placement of outdoor advertising which would maintain a fair balance between the apparently irreconcilable ends of beauty and economic utility.

Controversy Over Motivational Research

Advertising has been criticized and scrutinized on other bases beyond the claim that outdoor advertisements spoil the country's beauty. It has come in for its share of discussion on psychological grounds, as well as aesthetic ones. Undoubtedly the most controversial aspect of contemporary advertising techniques is the area of motivation research, a complicated aspect of the behavioral sciences which involves a combined psychological-sociological approach to consumer habits, needs and wants. The whole area of marketing and sales is no longer a one-directional street, but rather a complicated, competitive arena in which various psychological techniques play a seminal role. Many of the techniques draw upon both behavioristic and Freudian psychology and are concerned with information gleaned from Freud's concept of subconscious motivation. At first blush, the idea behind motivational research is quite guileless. It is predicated on the assumption that the consumer's habits have become complicated, that they are based on a stimulus-response mechanism and that the sophisticated consumer must be given something beyond a hard sales "pitch." In short, he must be motivated. And the way to motivate is to discover those stimuli to which he will evince a positive response—to find out what the incentives are which will call forth a desired reaction.

Needless to say, these psychological techniques have aroused considerable controversy in psychological and philosophical circles. Those who subscribe to the findings and techniques of psychoanalysis swear by the efficiency of motivational research. Others believe it is utterly useless and may even be quite harmful. Clearly, the implications of deep motivational research, as a communications technique, are provocative. If advertising has found a communicative device which will reveal the basic and hidden motives which spur buying habits, then this psychological technique has struck an economic vein of pure gold. But the putative bonanza is not without severe ethical problems. As it is, advertising has been accused of exploiting human frailty. How much greater an inroad will it make when it begins to explore the deep recesses of the conscious and unconscious mind?

Motivational research is essentially based on the principles of applying classical psychoanalytic techniques to the area of human communication. Its purpose is to discover why individuals respond to, or resist, certain behavioral acts, such as buying or rejecting products. It may find, for example, that certain symbols used in advertising have unpleasant *unconscious* associations for many people and are therefore consciously rejected. The process of motivation research is, therefore, quite complicated. It goes far beyond the relatively simple techniques of the survey or the interview-in-depth. It is deeply involved in sociological and psychological dynamics of human behavior. To be sure, the research techniques employed call for interviews and questionnaires. But these are structured to probe and reveal obscure or repressed motivation. Such tests as the Rorschach or the Thematic Apperception Test may give valuable information about unconscious drives, so that motivation research is basically an application of the discipline of clinical psychology in the area of communication.

The two high priests of the field are Alfred Politz and Ernest Dichter, who is head of the Institute for Motivational Research. Politz believes in the straight statistically devised poll and thinks that Dichter's techniques are nonsense. Dichter, on the other hand, believes that his techniques reveal motivations which can never be explained through the more conventional procedures. Of course, research in human motivation is never direct. It does attempt to discover the "true" or "real" motives by asking seemingly simple and uncomplicated questions of the respondent. It is based on the hypothesis that, beyond and beneath the surface of human behavior, there exist unconscious patterns and drives. Dichter's modus operandi are clearly psychoanalytic in substance. Other teachings rely upon a study of group, rather than individual consumer behavior, and believe in the influence of the total environment on the consumer. A procedure developed by Dr. Herta Herzog and Dr. Paul Lazarsfeld, who directed the Columbia University Bureau of Social Research, uses a combination of conventional polling techniques along with motivation research, such as in-depth interviews and various projective tests. Why, for example, does an individual continue to change cigarette brands? The reason may be that he fears cancer and wants to find that brand which is least carcinogenic.

Motivation research claims to reveal areas of anxiety, guilt and other psychosomatic symptoms. Once these findings are brought to the agency, positive techniques, based on them, can be developed. One such technique, in the light of findings on cigarettes and cancer, might be to develop an advertising campaign which would describe a particular cigarette as "safest" to use. The term "safest," of course, is intended to allay overt or latent fears about the carcinogenic effects of cigarette smoking. But the trouble with motivation research, and with the way in which it is extrapolated, is, like most psychoanalytic theory, its lack of a scientific or empirical basis. Psychoanalysts, Freudian or otherwise, rarely agree on interpretation of motives. And motivational research, conducted for two respective agancies, is very likely to reveal highly conflicting data. In addition, because it instigates techniques of subliminal perception in advertising, motivation research has been scored for taking advantage of human frailty and anxieties. It takes advantage of the most vulnerable aspects of human perception and behavior. Unfortunately, however, it would vitiate the effect if subliminal messages on television were to be announced in advance of their appearance on the air. The message must be flashed on the screen so quickly that the viewer is not consciously aware of it. Yet, according to the motivation research analysts, this ephemeral message carries believeability, it does penetrate the unconscious mind and it does influence conscious behavior. It is to its credit that the television industry, through the efforts of the networks, has been aware of the dangers inherent in subliminal advertising and has agreed to reject it.

Motivation research, of late, appears to be going out of fashion in advertising circles in favor of more direct and overt investigative methods. But the advertising business, as a whole, has been the target of considerable criticism and has been forced into a defensive posture which has now become almost traditional. The agency man resents being known as a "gray flannel suit," Madison Avenue "type." The industry resents being labelled by such stereotypes as the "let's run the idea up the flagpole and see how it flies" syndrome. There is indignation over the depiction of advertising copywriters and account executives in novels and in non-fiction critiques of American society. The advertising industry deplores the image of a bacchanalian life between Madison Avenue and the affluent suburbs. All of these descriptions are rejected because, the industry insists, they offer a portrait which is false and not extensionally varifiable by what, in fact, advertising people do. And what they do contributes importantly to a better standard of living and to an improved economy.

Critics, however, base their evaluation of advertising not only on the lives of the personnel who populate the field, but also on the conviction that advertising aggrandizes false values and sets up spurious and self-defeating goals. Even the most sophisticated copy and the most clever layouts cannot erase, in the eyes of its critics, the basic fact that most advertising is essentially an exploitation of that which tends to be cheap, vulgar and banal. False standards of excellence are established, based on equally false criteria of values. Advertising, by offering goals that many cannot achieve, develops neurotic anxieties and also overemphasizes the exploitative side of sex and feminine attractiveness. According to Galbraith, it creates demands for products which people do not neeed and triggers expenditures that were better invested for urgent social ends. The semanticist and the social scientist question the meaning of a great deal of apparently meaningful advertising copy. They ask, not without reason, "less tar and less noicotine than *what?*" As Gilbert Seldes points out, this kind of advertising does have an enormous and far-reaching effect on American culture and values. Critics feel that there is considerable merit in asking that advertising agencies recognize that they have an obligation and a responsibility to the public. Only if subjected to critical scrutiny can advertising function responsibly and yet freely. An industry which employs thousands of people, and bills millions of dollars, has an obligation to function in the public interest.

A major consideration arises, however. Can advertising function in the public interest when, by its very nature, its objectives may be diametrically opposed to the interest of the public. According to Galbraith, for example, advertising is inimical and antagonistic to the public interest. It creates spurious and unnecessary needs, and stimulates unwholesome wants. Yet, advertising has become so large and institutionalized an industry that even so captious a critic as Dr. Galbraith would probably agree that a peremptory interdiction of advertising would throw the economy into a tailspin from which recovery would be extremely difficult and painful. Certainly, without advertising it would be difficult to operate a free, mercantile, competitive economy. Advertising is, for better or worse, closely identified with the "conventional wisdom," an integral part of a highly regarded free enterprise system. And, as advertising has come more and more to police itself and improve its standards, even its most articulate of critics have admitted that it has acquired respectability as a profession and even admiration for its contribution to the field of graphic art communications.

Positive Contributions

If it is an evil influence, as some of its more obdurate and trenchant critics insist, there are those who believe that advertising has become an essential evil. It cannot be denied that it makes a contribution to a competitive, mercantile economy. At the same time, it is questionable whether the industry actually does siphon off funds which might be put to better use in the building of schools, roads and urban renewal projects, for these areas concern the prudent spending of public, rather than private monies. The effects of advertising, as the semanticist would point out, are neither all good nor all bad. It is not without serious flaws, yet it contributes significantly to the economic growth. If it has created what is sometimes a false need for consumer goods, the public in the long run has benefited by an increased standard of living. Its purpose may not have been to make a better car or build a better mouse trap, but a competitive economy has frequently resulted in superior products, with the public as ultimate beneficiary.

Advertising has had its share of medicine men, pitchmen and fakirs, its hawkers and its charlatans. It has also boasted some extremely gifted individuals, particularly in the area of graphic arts. Over a period of time, the patent medicine men have moved on. The kind of expose in which such muckrakers as Ida Tarbell, S. S. McClure and Lincoln Steffens were engaged, would not be relevant under today's more stringent controls. The mass media themselves, in fact, helped to rid advertising of the patent medicine men by such acts as the Pure Food and Drug Act, the Code of Ethics ("Truth In Advertising") of the Advertising Federation, the establishment of Consumers Union, Better Business Bureau and other public interest organizations which help to clean up questionable practices. Nor has all advertising been restricted to hard sell of brands and products. Through the Advertising Bureau, public service advertising reaches millions with significant messages on forest fires, smoking and cancer and other information which is in the public interest. In no area has advertising been more successful than in fostering the sale of bonds during both World Wars.

It is true that advertising began inauspiciously from a social and ethical point of view. In 1929, however, it took on a semblance of respectability with the establishment of the Consumer Research Organization. Even though not all practices are exemplary today, there would be no relevance for a book such as 100,000,000 *Guinea Pigs*, for the advertising industry has assumed a responsibility which it did not possess in its days of mushrooming growth. Politically, advertising tends to be a conservative institution, and critics of liberal persuasion assert that candidates for high public office have been packaged to the public like any other brand-name product. There is some evidence of truth in this criticism, but it does not apply equally to all agencies and it demands further research by the political and social scientist.

As an institution, advertising—perhaps more indirectly—exercises as potent an influence on society as the home, school and religious institution. It is, in the broadest sense, an educational force of considerable power and magnitude, although its greatest influence is in the area of what might be termed popular culture. But, if it is not a purveyor of high culture and if its intellectual sights are not high, advertising exercises enormous influence as an instrument of social control. It is certainly responsible for the economic well-being of the mass media of communication. Neither commercial radio nor television—nor the newspaper or magazine—would have flourished so expansively without advertising. It is significant, too, that the press in America was considerably more captious, parochial and venal in the days before the advertising message than it is today when, presumably, the advertiser can exert pressure on editorial policy. The fact is that a press which depends on advertising in order to remain economically viable is more free and responsible than at any other period in its history. Pressures have come more from government and special interests than from the advertiser.

The dependence of mass media on advertising is amply illustrated by their phenomenal growth. The economic effects of advertising on mass media have been such that the figures have risen steadily from about $100 million annually at the turn of the century, $500 million in 1929, $1 billion in 1930 to more than $10 billion a year by 1969-70. With economic growth has come a change in style from a basically straight, hand-sell, factual medium to a sense of both form and substance. The best efforts of contemporary advertising are not only aesthetic, but they comprise a kind of popular literature, or mass culture. If, on the one hand, advertising has resulted in efforts to standardize national brands, it has also forced manufacturers to take a greater pride in improving brands as a result of standardization. If, as Galbraith believes, advertising creates a demand for unnecessary goods, advocates claim that advertising has been necessary, in an age of mass culture, to bring together efficiently the resources of production, distribution and consumption. As Professor Neil Borden has stated, the growth of the economy made funds available for large advertising campaigns, particularly when the manufacturer was able to produce beyond existing demand.

Economic competition is the basis for the continued growth of advertising. It is the competitive economy which makes it important for the advertiser not only to develop a distinct name and personality, but also to find ingenious ways and means of making the consumer aware that the product is not the same as others of the same species. This is equally true of all mass-marketed products. It is even applicable to the utilities, such as American Telephone and Consolidated Edison, of which the latter has embarked on a vast advertising and public relations campaign in New York City designed to convince the public that it cares about the needs of the consumer and is trying to ameliorate existing problems of air-pollution, rates and service. In every way, then—by hard sell or by the institutional approach—advertising operates in a consumer-oriented society with the buyer at the receiving end of a multiplicity of sales stimuli. Advertising is one catalytic agent which operates to make a change in attitude possible, and which does help to move goods from producer to distributor to consumer.

To those critics who question whether advertising contributes to the "good life" or to "the greatest good for the greatest number," the answer must be in terms of general evaluation. Much depends upon what values are placed on the good life in an affluent society. Advertising, its proponents insist, has increased economic abundance, has created employment and has been a social and economic asset. Its influence on the public through media of communication has been enormous. It is literally present everywhere, reaching man with a consistency of which he is not even fully aware. Its influence on media and consumer alike has been unprecedented. It has changed the newspaper and magazine media from dependence on consumer sales to media which are completely advertising oriented. The income from such media and radio and television accrues from advertising. Since advertising, in turn, depends upon circulation or "reach," mass communication through mass media is necessary in the present-day economy. In addition, however, newspaper and magazine content, at least implicitly, inevitably tend to cohere to some extent with advertising-circulation needs. With advertising, however, television is able to spend millions on public affairs programming.

Influence on Media Content

But there is a controversial issue to be considered: how much influence has advertising on media content? The reply from the management of the mass media is a flat denial that it has any influence. To a large extent, the evidence from newspaper content, and the substance of many television documentaries, indicates that this statement is true. Whether there is indirect or implicit influence, and to what extent such influence exists, is a question which is difficult to determine, for there is no empiric test of such a hypothesis. Few would deny that almost all of the press is remarkably free of advertiser influence. The reason may be that there are more advertisers than the media can accept, but there is little doubt that mass media are sensitive to criticism about advertising influence and take pains to avoid it.

The influence of the advertising-circulation complex perhaps may be seen indirectly. A newspaper is basically intended as a purveyor of news, yet the press carries cartoons, sports and special features which have little to do with sheer information. Magazines seek out articles which will titillate and build circulation. And critics of television claim that programs are banal and vapid because the medium must achieve large circulation in order to provide a low cost per thousand. It may be that media do seek a lowest common denominator, but there is incontestable evidence that public taste itself is subtly changing. Ten years ago, there was far less interest in foreign affairs. A decade ago, too, a television drama such as "Death of a Salesman" probably would not have arrested the viewing attention of some thirty million viewers. Unfortunately, such a program demands a special kind of advertiser of which there are all too few available. As a result, the networks stand to lose by investing in serious drama, whatever gains they may achieve culturally. As a rule only institutional advertisers are interested in investing in programs that do not deliver large audiences. The very structure of mass media makes it both attractive and necessary that the advertising message be directed toward the greatest number of readers or viewers. In turn, this places obvious restrictions on both medium and message. Critics of advertising and of the media believe that the desire to reach a lowest common denominator means that controversy must be avoided; that the message must be affective in order to be effective; that "facts" must be presented with an overlay of emotion. The content, to reach the multitude, must be popular, rather than intellectually challenging, emotive rather than cognitive, simple rather than involved, placid rather than provocative. Subjects must be of the broadest popular appeal, and topics with which the masses are not familiar should be avoided, except when special publics are the target. Nevertheless, even if these restrictions are true, the matter is not simplistic or all black and white. Advertising has improved enormously in both copy and art work, and media content has also raised its sights as educational opportunity has increased.

Old stereotypes, too, have been discarded. The conventional methods of treating race, creed and color have changed for a more realistic and more ethical approach. Questions of social importance are being discussed, particularly in public affairs programs, but in television drama as well, as a presentation such as "The People Next Door" has shown. The black man is no longer typed as a shuffling Pullman porter. More black people appear in national advertising. Religious and ethnic stereotypes of the Jewish merchant, the Italian waiter and the Irish cop have been expunged from media content. It is unfortunately true, however, that much advertising tends to avoid any subject which is remotely controversial. The impact and effect of content, however, is not merely based on economic criteria, but on normative and ethical ones as well. If advertising has contributed to economic growth, it has also set spurious standards of keeping up with the Joneses, of exploiting basic anxieties, of reaching for hidden motivations and of exploring the recesses of the unconscious which should be allowed to remain the individual's private domain. Values should not be construed in terms of the ability to buy what one's neighbor can afford to own. Social and psychological factors should not be exploited in order to sell goods. Status symbols should not become criteria of excellence and acceptability.

Yet, advertising's contribution cannot be minimized. It has proved an enormous service to producer, distributor and consumer. Costs and prices have been lowered, jobs created and the standard of living elevated. There has been an increase in scientific research and technology. Paid advertising on television has contributed to the entertainment and information of millions. In the international sphere, advertising, on the whole, has brought a positive image of America to the rest of the world community. As for the creation of superfluous needs, the advertiser asserts that, without the existence of advertising, there would be a chaotic dislocation of the entire producer-consumer oriented economic structure.

Responsibility in Advertising

Still there are nagging doubts about some of the practices that underlie advertising. If the advertising agency should become involved in motivation research and psychoanalytic techniques, how far should this kind of probing be allowed to proceed? How much of an inroad can research make into an individual's private life, and where should the line be drawn? In short, is not advertising still a pitchman's business, more refined and subtle in technique, but psychologically and socially immoral? There is reason to inquire why advertising techniques need to be based on psychological drives rather than on direct and overt methods of selling. There is a basis for demanding that advertising content give *all* relevant information instead of limited data with affective overtones. In this context, the consumer organizations can help by being alert to the failure of advertising content to tell the whole truth. Drugs which are identical despite different trade names should be sold as identical. Drug companies, for example, have come under fire for charging exorbitant sums for trade-name products which can be purchased cheaply from any pharmacist by their generic names. The responsibility rests ultimately not with the consumer, but with the advertiser and the media. Ethical advertising can develop consumer respect and confidence, as well as media support, under conditions of ethics and trust. The public has a right to be free from exploitation.

The achievement of these desirable goals raises further relevant questions. In particular, there is the prime problem of a strong regulatory agency for all advertising, stronger and legally more powerful than the Federal Trade Commission. Such a unit would be in a position to demand and enforce regulations concerning truth in advertising, backed by safety of product. But enforcing such criteria raises the inevitable questions of whether advertising communications is to be subsumed under the concept of freedom of the press as guaranteed by the First Amendment. If, on the other hand, regulation is considered to be against democratic principles, there is still the serious problem of protecting the consumer from dishonest and unscrupulous campaigns which emphasize the charismatic rather than the truthful, however prosaic the truth may be. The consumer's ego deserves protection from dubious psychoanalytic techniques of motivation. Particularly because advertising has access to mass communicative media which reach millions of people it must not seduce the innocent by setting false standards, goals and values, by extolling only the material and by aggrandizing the status symbol as the ultimate good. Persuasion, honestly developed, is not in itself immoral if it does not conceal, act upon hidden motives and thwart freedom of choice or action.

Because advertising communications do make a seminal contribution to American life, enormous responsibilities are faced by the advertiser and by the mass media. The advertiser is charged with creating truthful content, and the media with setting high standards of ethics and acceptability which will reject out of hand that which is cheap, tawdry or dishonest. At its best, advertising has set a high standard of living in a successful economy. At its worst, it has failed to contribute significantly to the growing problems of the ghetto, of discrimination, of hostility and fear. But, if the social effects of advertising have not been as important as the economic ones, they have nevertheless been significant. The consumer is offered a choice among many competing products. This choice tends generally to drive prices down, to increase quality and to make goods widely available. If the billions spent on advertising do influence the price of the product, the consumer still benefits from the results of mass production and consumption.

While not all advertising is scrupulous, the truthfulness of advertising has improved greatly and to the ultimate benefit of the public. If advertising tends to use emotive and directive means, both copy and layout have improved to the point where there now exists a rather respectable literature and art of advertising communications. In radio and television, in particular, it is the revenue from advertising which make free entertainment, news and public affairs available to almost all of the population. The cost of mass media to the public is minimal because of the existence of advertising. Even in a land which has a long way to go to ameliorate the problems of the cities and of the disadvantaged, the consumer undoubtedly enjoys a higher standard of living than any other consumer anywhere in the world.

Public Relations and Mass Media

Like advertising, public relations is a singularly American phenomenon. While advertising messages of a kind were used even as early as ancient Greece and Rome, and the fine art of propaganda was chrystalized in Machiavelli's *The Prince*, the practice of public relations is an old profession which has adapted to the mass communications oriented society of the Twentieth Century. Publicity and public relations enterprises are so widely employed that they include virtually every activity which impinges even remotely on public opinion and which looks in any way for public support, approbation or consent. With the omnipresence of mass media, techniques of public information and persuasion embrace such diverse areas as the professions, business, education and sports. Even the mass media themselves are inevitably involved in gigantic public relations campaigns, not only with the general public, but with Washington and with a variety of assorted pressure and special interest groups.

Public relations is an integral part of the processes of mass communication. It is not itself a communications medium. It functions more directly by utilizing the media, without which no campaign to influence or inform public opinion could be promulgated successfully in a society where institutions grow more and more remote from their constituencies. As a result of the growth and influence of the mass media, public relations and publicity have grown into full-fledged professional activities, employing thousands of people and servicing the press not only with propaganda, but also with considerable legitimate news and information. Some have called public relations, stemming, as do mass media, from the growth of a competitive economy, a fifth estate. But if public relations is frequently equated only with classic propaganda, the juxtaposition is generally false. Pure, unadulterated, purposeful propaganda exists only in an authoritarian state. The best public relations, as practiced in this country, is not inherently propagandistic because its incentives are competitive, not totalitarian. Good public relations, while aiming to create consent, is also involved in the free flow of information to the mass media that is part of the democratic system.

A great deal of the content that flows into and out of the mass media is public relations motivated, but that does not necessarily make it unethical or socially deleterious. It forms a considerable part of the news content of such mass media as the press and, at the same time, it utilizes the instrumentality of mass communications to convey cognitive, affective and directive meanings to one or more publics. In the competitive arena of public opinion and in the engineering of consent, public relations plays a powerful role. The public relations counselor or practitioner is very much a facet of mass culture and of the social and economic environment. As early as the days of Ivy Lee, almost five decades ago, business came to the conclusion that news, however tragic or unfavorable, could not be concealed from the people. The philosophy of "the public be damned" retreated before a new and healthy concept, that a business simply must recognize the public interest in order to survive and grow. A new philosophy based on the conviction that the public is entitled to a free flow of information replaced old and worn out creeds. The best public relations men have succeeded in convincing management that a policy of integrity is both morally and economically healthy. There is no doubt that some public relations is still practiced with sophistry, and that there are practitioners who function to make the worse appear the better reason. But if only for reasons of expediency or necessity, most public relations activities are predicated on the conviction that the best image is earned, rather than fabricated, and that the most favorable press is created by news and information rather than by press agentry.

What triggered the rapid proliferation of public relations into a profession with more than 100,000 practitioners was the growth of the newspaper and television—both media capable of reaching enormously large audiences. Public opinion and persuasion became important concepts in corporate and institutional thinking and planning. Public relations began to assume a central role as an adjunct to the daily news flow that shaped the character and content of the press as a social institution. Professional organizations such as the Public Relations Society of America and the American College Public Relations Association were established, and set up rigid standards of practice. The motivating forces, then, for the development of public relations were the presence of powerful mass media, the demands of a competitive economy and the rapid growth of the population to a point where the public and the institution became remote from one another. Public relations came to serve as a catalyst between institution and public through the mass media. Its purpose, however, was not basically merchandising, but the earning of good will and public confidence. Thus, public relations came to be described as simply the development of good relations with the public.

Inevitably, questions of ethics and value judgments arise in any consideration of public relations, public opinion and the mass media. The term itself implies a manipulation of public opinion, and it is not uncommon to read of the actions of corporate executives and politicians in terms of a cynical use of "public relations." There is the question, too, of whether publicity techniques might not come into conflict with the canons of journalism of the newspaper publishers. These critiques, however, might easily apply to other professions—law or medicine—if these are practiced unethically and without a regard for public opinion. On the other hand, if public relations is recognized for precisely what it is—a process of both information and persuasion designed not to subvert, but to earn the good will of the public, then it becomes a useful part of the whole complex of journalism and mass communications. Much depends upon the training and standards of the public relations man, and the evaluation of a public which has come increasingly to understand the purpose and role of public relations in the whole process of opinion formation.

Walter Lippmann pointed out as early as 1923 that the publicist could be an honest and pragmatic source of news to the journalist, a catalytic agent among the institution which he represented, the mass media and the public. In time, most public relations men developed a fairly tenable and defensible concept of service to press and public. Public relations has made positive contributions to innumerable socially useful causes and, most recently, has been instrumental in pointing out the need to absorb greater numbers of disadvantaged and minority groups into industry. While this may have been, in part, a result of the pressure from special interest groups, it has been also a result of the public relations creed of "good deeds in the public interest."

One of the main reasons for the need for public relations was the growing remoteness between institutions and the public they serve. The New England town meeting is virtually impossible in an era of urban development and mass communication, and it is this sheer distance between the consumers and institutions which serve them which created a useful function for the public relations man. The revealing and hard-hitting criticisms of the muckrakers also contributed toward the need for a catalyst between press and public which would function not merely to whitewash, but rather to clean house internally by demanding an end to the public be damned philosophy. If public relations has succeeded at all, it has succeeded in the direction of convincing many institutions that their best interests lie in a recognition that the public interest is best served by more forthright methods than manipulation. Today's public relations man is more than a former newspaperman. He is usually trained in journalism and the social sciences. He understands the uses of language and the importance of public opinion and propaganda. The best practitioners are part of the whole nexus of mass commnuications, and are a valuable source of news to the media.

Practical public relations involves four major stages, each identified to some extent with the process of mass communication. The best trained P.R. men do not function merely as publicists or press agents. They function primarily as social scientists and secondly as journalists. In a given situation, the skilled practitioner will confront the problem by a careful analysis of the public opinion aspects involved. These include an evaluation of the nature of the problem, the reasons behind it, the publics and the media involved, and the social, political and economic implications. The results of this research are then presented to the management of the institution or company, along with the public relations man's interpretation and evaluation of what is involved and why. The third step involves implementation, a process in which the recommendations of the public relations man are crystalized into specific internal procedures designed to resolve the issue at hand. Finally, having decided upon what must be done—and having accomplished internal changes in viewpoint and procedure—the public relations man is ready to enter the arena of positive action. This involves the journalistic procedures designed to reach public opinion through the media of mass communication—a publicity release, a press conference, a direct mail campaign, a series of speeches or a statement of policy.

In each of these procedures, the best public relations men function both as sociologists and journalists. And they function responsibly and with a respect and a regard for the ultimate power of public opinion, along with the kind of comprehension of the communicative process which makes an avoidance of stereotyping and affective language not only ethically sound, but functionally successful. Public relations at its best informs public opinion and thereby contributes significantly toward making it articulate. As such it is a valuable, if peripheral, aspect of the process and effects of mass communication.

BIBLIOGRAPHY

Agnew, Clark M. and Neil O'Brien. *Television Advertising.* New York: McGraw-Hill, 1958.

Bordon, Neil H. *Advertising in Our Economy.* Chicago: Richard D. Irvin, Inc., 1945.

The Economic effects of Advertising. Chicago: Richard D. Irwin, 1942.

Brembeck, W. L. and W. S. Howell. *Persuasion*. New York: Prentice Hall, 1952.

Brown, J. A. C. *Techniques of Persuasion*. Baltimore, Maryland: Penguin Books, 1963.

Dichter, Ernest. *The Strategy of Desire*. Garden City, New York: Doubleday, 1960.

Galbraith, John K. *The Affluent Society*. New York: Houghton Mifflin, 1958.

Hower, Ralph M. *The History of an Advertising Agency*, rev. ed. Cambridge, Massachusetts: Harvard University Press, 1949.

Kleppner, Otto. *Advertising Procedure*, 4th ed. New York: Prenctice-Hall, Inc., 1950.

Lesly, Philip, ed. *Public Relations Handbook*, 2d ed. New York: Prenctice-Hall, 1962.

Lucas, D. B. and S. H. Britt. *Advertising Psychology and Research*. New York: McGraw-Hill, 1950.

Machiavelli, Nicolo. *The Prince*. W. K. Marriott, trans. New York: E. P. Dutton, 1958.

Mayer, Martin. *Madison Avenue, U.S.A.* New York: Harper and Brothers, 1958.

Politz, Alfred. *A Study of Four Media*. New York: Time, Inc., 1953.

Presbrey, Frank. *The History and Development of Advertising*. Garden City, New York: Doubleday, Doran and Company, 1929.

Steinberg, Charles. *The Mass Communicators*. New York: Harpers, 1958.

Turner, E. S. *The Shocking History of Advertising*. New York: Ballantine Books, 1953.

Wood, James Playsted. *The Story of Advertising*. New York: Ronald Press, 1958.

15

The Impact of Mass Media

ALL MEDIA OF mass communications are social institutions. All are implicitly—and frequently explicitly—agencies of social control. Although extant studies in the effects of mass media are tentative and inconclusive and there is considerable research still to be done, there is little doubt from all available evidence that the media tend to reflect the mores, needs and aspirations of a society more than they influence them. Various hypotheses and assumptions, for example, have been raised with respect to the relationship between mass media and violence in society. None of these as yet has been substantiated by empirical evidence that there is any causual effect.

From this, however, it should not be concluded that the media are free to portray violence for its own sake. But, from the point of view of social pathology, the etiology appears to be found in many areas beyond any direct causal relationship with mass media—slums and urban ghettos, the underprivileged and the disadvantaged, stereotyps of racial and religious bias, economic deprivation and the wide chasm between groups in lower and higher economic strata. Indeed, the media on occasion have done much to explore these pathologies and social needs in the press, the magazine and on television. The motion picture industry, too, is capable of occasional films of genuine social, as well as aesthetic, significance.

Some social scientists have speculated whether the campus riots are not, in part, the result of a generation raised on passive exposure to mass media. It is an observation still to be verified by empirical evidence. Certainly, there is an interaction between media and society, and this very relationship imposes an enormous obligation on the media to function with awareness and responsibility. But many factors influence behavior prior to, and in conjunction with, the media of communication—the home environment, the social, the religious institution among them. In recent years, the secondary school and college generations have been more keenly aware of, and involved in, social and political action. If this is a result, in any way, of media exposure, the arousal of interest can only be to the good. It is the violent direction it has taken which is to be deplored. And there is no empirical evidence to show that mass media have been an instigatory factor.

Historical Background

Any consideration of the relationship between mass media and society, along with the analogous question of freedom and control in mass communication, must be viewed as much in terms of its historical context as of its relevance to contemporary society. Mass communication's impact on society was a direct result of the revolution that began in the Fifteenth Century with the invention of printing by means of movable type. The machine brought a new direction to society, and the results were to have an enduring effect on man's way of living. In terms of communication, it meant a radical change from the circumscribed world of the beautiful, but limited, medieval manuscript to a technique which would eventually bring literacy to virtually all of the civilized world.

The Gutenberg Bible marked a turning point in the intellectual history of man. At first, however, printing was accomplished only under religious restriction, but it was inevitable that this new device could not be held long from reaching the masses. The linear revolution brought with it social, political and economic change. As more people became literate, the opportunity for communication increased. And, with the increase in communication, came a greater individual sense of freedom and a greater involvement in government. Public opinion became articulate through print. The ultimate result was the growth of a large middle class along with the concomitant development of the philosophy of liberalism to replace the older sacred and secular authoritarianism.

As the printing press became technically perfected, mass distribution, larger readership and the appearance of paid advertising resulted. In time, print journalism—the newspaper and magazine—was followed by electric technologies which would result im the development of the audion tube and the development of the audio and visual marvel of telecommunications. Communication became a mass phenomenon as the wireless provided the means of serving newspapers, radio and television with immediate information. What Riesman termed the "tradition directed" and "inner directed" societies became "other directed" as man looked to the peer group for leadership and approbation and as communication became widespread, but indirect. Inevitably, entertainment began to assume a major part of the content of mass media. But the media also were acknowledged to be enormously useful sources of information and learning. With the invention of the computer and the teaching machine, man found a marvelous technical tool for revolutionizing the whole psychology of education, but has yet to find a solution to the proposition that automation is only as good as the programming which man can develop for it.

The effects of the development of mass media, beginning with print and pushing forward to the present age of information storage and retrieval, are only beginning to be appraised. Little is known, as the result of controlled scientific research, of how the media interact with society. Certain results of the revolution in mass communications are apparent. Vast economic changes were wrought by such sheer technical developments as print, wireless and telephony. Political involvement became greater as public opinion found a voice. Information became available speedily and accurately to the masses. Education became a universal accomplishment. Cultural changes are still under way with the development of new modes of entertainment on television and with the wider use of community antenna and satellite communications. Mass media are ubiquitous, and their influence is obviously profound. Virtually every family in the United States has one or more media available to it. This broad dissemination of information and education has raised inevitable questions of minority as opposed to majority interests, of the needs of special interest publics, of how best to meet the interests of all while, at the same time, recognizing the interests of some.

Concentration and the Public Interest

There are questions, too, of the reconciliation of concentration of control with the need to serve the public interest. Obviously mass media must be economically viable—and this viability is possible by means of advertising—but media must also serve all of the people. Their obligation is, paradoxically, both public and private at the same time. The first and most significant contribution of print and electronic media is their magnificent power to inform. They have replaced the circumscribed world of the town meeting, have made the educational experience almost universal and have provided new techniques of preserving and transmitting culture. They move goods and they are a unique source of entertainment. To McLuhan, the media are an integral part of man, operating as extensions of the human nervous system. But, they still operate from the external environment. The flow of information is still one-directional, and what feedback there may be is implicit. The time is close, however, when genuine two-way interaction between man and medium will become a reality. Even when this does occur, however, it is probable that, in the last analysis, interpersonal communication will still operate as the most powerful source of public opinion formation.

It will be recalled that the very first newspaper publishers could not print without permission of the government. This, in essence, meant censorship and authoritarian control. The first publishers and printers were not independent entrepreneurs. They were postmasters, licensed by, and beholden to, the government. But the growth of media, despite control, was inevitable, because there was a hunger for news, a public demand for information. This was particularly true of the seaport towns where trading took place. It is probable, however, that the kind of free press which took such firm root in America would not have developed if this country had not become involved in a struggle against the crown. The United States, once established, functioned as a political democracy with a strong middle class which greatly influenced the growth of mass media. The waves of immigration and the extension of voting rights also contributed significantly to the development of the press and, at its beginning, to the popularity of the early motion pictures.

Other phenomena were instrumental in the way the media developed. The role of the Industrial Revolution and the rapid technological growth that resulted from it, as well as the development of a large, heterogeneous urban society, have been indicated. Another critically important factor was not only population growth, but the establishment of a free compulsory system of universal education which made possible a rapid extention of literacy to the masses. Education, along with the development of the telephone, the telegraph and related electric technologies, enormously influenced cultural life and made possible the development of mass media. As early as 1865, it was evident that technology would have a far-reaching effect on American society—an effect which resulted in extensive changes in ways of thinking and living as mass production gave rise to large enterprises which, in turn, led to mass consumption and, inevitably, to mass communication.

Obviously, these technological achievements were not without limitations. The tremendous contribution of mass production and consumption led to standardization of product, to stereotyping and to vast and impressive techniques of mass persuasion. Public opinion and the consumer became vital targets in moving products. Standardization resulted in advertising, and paid advertising revolutionized the economic structure of the media. Despite the great pockets of indigence in this country, the middle class was a powerful factor in the economy. The masses earned more, spent more and ultimately developed more leisure time as the result of technology. A further result was the rapid proliferation of mass media capable of reaching millions of people with entertainment and news *and* advertising messages.

What, in essence, occurred were a number of social and political developments in which the media of communications and society interacted. The development of radio and television delivered millions of consumers

—simultaneously—to the advertiser. The increase in literacy, the influx of immigrants and the growth of urban society created enormously large audiences for the nation's press. And the press and other media became the chief sources, not only of entertainment, but also of information, for the American people.

Limitations of Media Research

Unfortunately for those who would seek a truly scientific method of measuring the impact of media on society, the techniques of the social sciences are not as quantitatively accurate as those of the physical sciences, nor are the media themselves as amenable to empirical research. The media are volatile and changing. Society itself is in a state of becoming. Despite the contributions of the semanticists and the mathematical theoreticians, the language of mass media is elusive. Writing and print resulted ultimately in man's discovery that words and things are not the same, that words represented or symbolized things. Ideas demanded equal testing in the crucible of experience. Print enabled man to learn more and absorb more and become more involved. Television and radio offered still further opportunity to be both informed and entertained, although some social scientists believe they are less participatory than print. Each of the media, however they may overlap and interrelate, uses verbal and visual symbols in terms of its own creative discipline. But it is important to note, in terms of effect, that the only *direct* method of communication at the present juncture is face-to-face. Direct feedback is possible, but still not feasible. The reader and the viewer, of course, have many ways of reacting, but none of them is as yet direct and immediate. Lippmann stated that the newspaper, when it is delivered to the reader, is "the result of a whole series of selections as to what items shall be printed, in what position they shall be printed, how much space each shall occupy, what emphasis each shall have." Although the reader participates in the content of the press, the participation is remote and indirect, a result of the editor's combined evaluation of what the reader wants and what the reader ought to have.

The response of each communicant, despite the enormous reach of mass media, is ultimately personal. The classic description of communication, "who says what to whom through what channel and with what effect" is deceptively simple. Each stimulus elicits a response—frequently many responses. The determination of effect in media reaching very large audiences simultaneously is neither easy nor practical, for there are no means of overt, direct response. Harold Lasswell has defined various ways of studying response in terms of such criteria as attention, environment, evaluation and action. But each action and reaction yields with difficulty to measurement, because other stimuli intervene. There is no direct communication-response link, and there is also a time lapse between the origination of the communique and the response to it. People respond to communications content in terms of many factors. These include the personality of communicator and communicant, the nature of the communications content, the particular medium through which the message flows and the reaction of the group to it. In an interaction between media and environment, each communicant will respond in terms of his own value system, his orientation and his status in the peer group.

Investigation has revealed that, despite the thrust and reach of mass media, interpersonal communication still tends to play an ultimate and powerful role in influencing opinion and behavior. Even nationwide debates on television, seen by millions simultaneously, go through the crucible of personal discussion before decisions are made and courses of action taken. Media influence behavior but are not the sole, or the strongest, determinant. Man still resorts to direct communication, and the impact of media is also buttressed by the influence of home, school, church and the peer group. What mass media do accomplish, as Wilbur Schramm has pointed out, is to help guide or "canalize" drives which already exist. The media entertain and inform and sell products and even ideas. But each of these messages must filter through the human nervous system. Media are not the ultimate determining factor in opinion and behavior. Indeed, it must be emphasized strongly that all the evidence reveals that they reflect social and other phenomena, rather than influence these phenomena. Within this framework, the impact of media is formidable, but it is tempered by psychological set, previous experience and conditioned behavior and by group customs and value judgments. This is why some sociologists and psychologists believe that children who react pathologically to the depiction of violence do so because the drive was present in the first place. Opinion change, too, is difficult through the media, because man confronts the media as a previously conditioned individual. Media can effect change only after the message has been interacted upon between individual and individual and from group to group. The content, in other words, goes through the crucible of experience, discussion and interaction.

Reach of Mass Media

The mass media, however, offer a continuum of communications content. The flow never ends and, indeed, the public has become conditioned to expect instant information. The newspaper's appearance in the morning is as inevitable as the rising sun. Even in the most disadvantaged of areas, radio and television are available most of the twenty-four hours in the day. Contemporary man, if he were not selective, could be inundated with the flow of information. Because the media press constantly on one's consciousness, because they are always present and familiar, there is a tendency to accept them uncritically. The social impact they have is, itself, a part of the osmosis that takes place between society and the media, each influencing and reflecting the other in a steady interaction. It is true that all societies, however primitive, have some form of non-verbal or verbal communication, but the mass media are qualitatively and quantitatively different from anything that has appeared before. One broadcast of one single event can be carried live, and with miraculous immediacy, to forty or fifty million viewers. Any system of communications, as Harold Lasswell pointed out, functions in terms of surveillance of the environment, correlation of the components of society in responding to the environment and transmission of the social heritage. Mass media, and particularly print and television, are particularly germane to these functions. A communications system is more than an instrument of social control; it can also provide, under optimum conditions, a forum for non-violent social change. Media reflect values, and provide the information that may precede change. The press has been accused of tending to preserve the status quo, but the press has also functioned as a dynamic instrument of political, social and economic change.

If media, paradoxically, tend to preserve traditional concepts and to change old patterns, they also function as agencies of social control. The implicit power of the media for influencing opinion is great, but it is still implicit. The power of the media works against countervailing influences from other social institutions. Mass communication has its own healthy system of checks and balances, stemming primarily from the demands and the philosophy of a pluralistic and democratic society. Whatever maneuverability the media may have, in terms of influencing public opinion, there are limits to their uses for social control. In the Soviet Union and Red China (and in the German state of the 1930's) press and radio are subservient to the demands of the state which uses media, variously, as a source of power, as an instrument of control or as a device to maintain the authority of the governing group.

In a democratic society, the media not only reflect social phenomena, but they also affect cultural dynamics. The very presence of magazines, newspapers, radio, motion pictures and television exert a profound effect upon a civilization, not only in terms of content but also by their technology. The medium is, indeed, the message but, contrary to McLuhan's assertion, the medium also becomes operational by purveying communication content. Communications are a conveyor belt for the transmission of knowledge. Their very appearance served to wrest control from authoritarian influences in church and state, and to democratize society by making a linear culture available to all of the people. It was the invention of printing, more than any other single factor, which had the direct social effect of developing a democratically inclined middle class. It was unfortunate that, as print provided a means beyond the oral tradition for transmitting man's cultural achievements, it also resulted in stereotyping, abstracting and standardization.

Man's dependence on media is almost total. Newspapers and television are expected to inform and entertain, and they perform both functions in exemplary fashion. It is what man does with the information supplied to him, however, which makes the difference between a society which accepts content uncritically and one which has learned to absorb and distill information as a guide to thought and action. Critics of the performance of mass media deplore the fact that they are accepted without evaluation. The public tends to repeat what it has read and heard from the columnists, the pundits and the commentators without critical judgment of its own. According to Walter Lippmann stereotyping—a common indulgence in mass communication—provides a shorthanded way of minimizing human thought and effort. The media can easily do man's thinking for him, except for the fact that a pluralistic society does provide for many viewpoints to be printed and aired, and this offers the communicant alternatives from which to choose. How well the choice is made depends clearly on the whole experiential nexus of the individual—his psychological "set," educational training, the background of concepts and percepts that form a frame of reference. The better educated individual tends to be more critical of the media than does the less educated.

The Media and the Public

Man's concept of the world—the so-called pictures in his head—is greatly influenced by the juxtaposition of communications content with his backlog of previous experience. Social scientists differ, however, as to how this content affects man and his behavior. Some insist that the media are powerful agencies of control, others that they are less coercive than persuasive through the techniques of public relations and propaganda. While it has been claimed that there is a communications-industrial complex, it is difficult to accept the idea that media are merely a cultural appendage of industry and they serve only to preserve antiquated institutions. There is ample evidence to the contrary, many examples of the press, radio and television as free and responsible media functioning capably, and frequently powerfully, as sources of information for all of the people. If media reinforce prevailing mores, if they reflect these mores, they also provide grist for change.

The whole area of the effect and impact of the mass media is a hotly debated one. To some the media are all pervasive. To others the media are slight and superficial. Probably both judgments are correct in terms of a specific situation as defined. Some will respond uncritically and lazily to popular art on television and in motion pictures, and some will not. Some individuals may respond pathologically to violence in mass media, but most will not. Abortion may be permissible for discussion on a documentary, but interdicted on an entertainment program in family viewing hours. Audiences may react quite differently to a sexual symbol on a public affairs program than on an entertainment show. Each situation is quite different from others, and the only rule is the rather ambiguous, but still efficacious, rule of reason. The original motion picture code, for example, was not helpful because its thrust was not positive, but negative. It did not suggest how the medium could deal constructively with certain social taboos, but simply closed the door on subjects such as narcotics, venereal disease and prostitution, thereby failing to confront realistic and pressing social problems. Each of the mass media insists that violence is permissible if it is an integral part of the story, but the film codes have insisted unrealistically that the villain simply must get his come-uppance in the end. Thus, a two-hour motion picture, replete with sex and violence of the most flagrant variety, was condoned, provided that romantic love triumphed or retribution was included. Today's film, in a total reversal, does not even bother to recognize the original code.

In their attitude toward the codes, the media—particularly the motion picture—are curiously ambivalent. Movie advertising has always been flagrant in its violation of the code, by its suggestiveness and its overt manifestation of sexuality. Yet, the production code, up to the time the new rating system was introduced in 1968, insisted that the denouement of the films be "moral." This, of course, is a consummate exercise in social and moral hypocrisy. The film advertisements displayed every possible physical enticement, but the language of the advertisement was couched in euphemistic terms. Current advertisements, like the films themselves, have pulled out all stops in permissiveness, which may be deplorable in one respect but at least avoids the manipulative techniques that characterized film under the original code.

In other directions, the demands of minority groups for a voice in public affairs, along with the contribution of the semanticists, have done much to discard simplistic and stereotyped representation of racial and religious minorities. The Negro is no longer a shuffling old faithful. The Jew is no longer a sharp-tongued merchant. All Italians are not volatile in temper. Beyond this clear-cut achievement, however, polarization of alternatives still remains to plague media content. Good is pitted against bad, honesty against evil, virginity against sexual license. All loose endings must be resolved at the conclusion. The criminal is always punished. The murder is always solved. Only recently have motion pictures begun to display a semblance of greater realism. Unfortunately, this more credible depiction of reality is somehow inextricably linked with a greater—and often needless—display of sensuality, not because it is integral to the content, but merely to titillate the public. But progress toward a greater realism and honesty in film is being made. It is now realized that endings, like life itself, can be tragic, that sadism is brutal, that crime is not always punished, that cops are not always good. Mass media, while they may still have a long road to travel in their recognition of the public's basic intelligence, have begun to ask a greater involvement from their audiences, a greater literacy and a depth of understanding of psychological and social issues.

There may be, in fact, a curious cultural lag between the taste-makers and their audiences. For, one of the difficulties besetting mass media in their quest for a greater honesty and realism may simply stem from a lack of confidence in the intelligence of the public. Too many producers have small confidence in man's ability to distinguish between alternatives of good and evil, right or wrong. The view of the world to many writers and producers is an either/or perspective where the viewer's alternatives are clear-cut and little thought is demanded of him. This reveals a basic distrust and cynicism about the public's ability to withstand exposure to the very problems which beset people in the course of their lives—triumphs and tragedies, composure and anxiety, impulses that are socially unacceptable as well as those that are affirmations of life. As educational opportunity increases, and as the public becomes more aware of semantic pitfalls, a black or white picture of the world can no longer be acceptable. In the motion picture, efforts to insert a tone of greater realism have resulted in a shift of the pendulum toward total permissiveness. But television, a family medium, faces even greater dilemmas. Even when television tries to eschew simplistic representation in entertainment, there is still the demand—brought about by both the nature of the medium and the public—to become all things to all men. There is a need to find themes which are popular and to use these themes repetitively. In the past year or so, however, television has shown a greater awareness of the need to present problem areas with greater realism. Unfortunately, when it does so, the accolades from critics are often offset by criticism and pressure from powerful special interest groups. None of the other media has evoked the pro and con discussion that centers around television, for no medium has created such awareness of its potential.

The media are still seeking a way out of the dilemma of minority versus majority interests, of the need to purvey to the many while recognizing the legitimate demands of smaller audiences. The British broadcasting system operates on a two network basis, for example. In the United States, the possibility of public television and CATV offer feasible supplementary services. The new motion picture code, while deplorable in its arbitrary selectiveness, is a step ahead of the spurious morality of the older code. But arbitrarily defined codes of conduct are not the answer toward a greater realism and honesty in the mass media. These rule books came about, not as voluntary and positive steps, but as a negative reaction, based on the demands of small special interest groups, intent on controlling media content. The result was not a positive set of values, but a series of maneuvers designed to falsify reality. In this way, too, the media reflected the mores of the society of which they are an integral part.

The Question of Violence

The codes have not, in the long run, resolved the ever-recurring criticism of the media for their portrayal of sex and violence. Yet, Senator Pastore's peremptory suggestion that the National Association of Broadcasters Code Review Board preview television programs was accepted very tentatively by ABC and NBC and rejected out of hand by CBS which, on the premise that a mass medium must itself take full responsibility in order to function independently, offered television critics the opportunity of reviewing programs in advance of their presentation on the air. In this way, the public is best served through the instrumentality of a free and responsible press. Similarly, various surveys and suggestons with regard to mitigating sex and violence have not been helpful, because the basis on which they are predicated is not substantial. There are those who would insist in the face of the violence which is so pervasive in American society, that the media ignore this phenomenon in favor of a romantic view of the world. But eschewing violence on mass media will not diminish violence in society. Nor, on the other hand, is there any evidence to show that an honest, although devastating, report on violence at home and in Vietnam in the mass media will foment greater violence, as some tend to believe. The problem is not resolved by avoiding coverage of violent events, but in covering these events with journalistic integrity and by the application of the rule of reason. Television can yield to many examples in the daily press when it comes to lurid headlines and photographic coverage of rape, murder and other crimes. *The New York Times* sees fit to carry a factual and sober account of these events on the back page of the paper, but other newspapers emblazon them on the front page, replete with gory pictures.

In the aftermath of the assassinations of Robert F. Kennedy and Martin Luther King, Jr., President Johnson established a National Commission on the Causes and Prevention of Violence, to which the media pledged their total support and cooperation. Other similar research efforts have been established, including an adjunct study under the direction of Dr. George Gerbner, of the University of Pennsylvania's Annenberg School of Communication. As Jack Gould, the television critic of the *New York Times*, pointed out, even the preliminary report of the Annenberg study was not particularly useful or germane. For, like most studies, it appeared to rest its case on a head count of the number of violent acts over a given period of time and over certain selected hours of the evening. On this quantitative basis alone, Shakespeare's "Hamlet" or "Macbeth" would be driven off the air or the stage.

The heart of the matter is not, contrary to what research to date has revealed, how often violence occurs, but under what circumstance it occurs. There is, as yet, no demonstrable cause-and-effect relationship between violence on media and violence in society, nor is there ever likely to be until much more sophisticated parameters of judgment are established than now exist. This fact, however, does not—and should not—absolve the press, motion pictures and television from their respective obligations to see to it that violence, when portrayed, is not only integral to the content, but that it is also portrayed with literary taste and moral decency. Popular art need not aspire to high culture in order to conform to the Aristotelian concept of tragedy as a catharsis that purges the emotions of fear and pity.

The tendency to quantify acts of violence by a head count of the number of violent episodes in a given number of motion pictures or television programs is, however, becoming endemic. In addition to the studies of the National Commission on the Causes and Prevention of Violence, a number of other official and unofficial studies have been undertaken, chief among which was a year-long study by the United States Surgeon General's office, authorized by the President at the instigation of the Senate Commerce Committee. None of these studies can hope to contribute any positive or useful information regarding the impact of violence in the media if they do not go beyond a quantitative recital of the number of violent deeds committed, without reference to the context in which they are committed or the moral consequences of the act. To eliminate violence from mass media would simply perpetuate and intensify the very blandness with which critics quarrel so vehemently. In essence, much depends upon how each study defines violence, what statistical evidence is used to document the head count and under what circumstances, and with what consequences, violence is committed. Even under the most carefully structured and promulgated research conditions, it is extremely difficult to show by empirical evidence that there is a direct correlation between media violence and violence in society. It can only be assumed, if not proved, that violence in the media may trigger violence in individuals psychologically predisposed to commit violence; or that depictions of violence may inure the public to the many violent acts which occur in society. It is true, of course, that violence in the novel is qualitatively different from motion pictures or television, because the novel reaches a more mature, adult and smaller audience, while the other media—and television in particular—are viewed by millions and are inevitably family media where children are exposed to the communications content.

The solution to violence, as one of the possible effects of mass media, is surely not by extrapolating sheer numbers in a wholesale condemnation of the media. There are differences in *both* kind and degree of violence in each medium. Violence which does affect and involve the viewer both morally and emotionally, violence which is integral to the portrayal of the tragedy of character and events, which is drawn from aesthetic and creative resources may, indeed, have a salutary effect, as critics believe it has in the Greek or Shakespearian tragedies. While the purveyors of mass communication are not expected to emulate Sophocles or Shakespeare, they are expected to set high standards for the depiction of violence. In any intelligent application of the rule of reason, there is little to be gained in interdicting all crime and western movies or television programs from being presented to the public. But violence which is presented creatively, as Dr. Otto Larsen, consultant to the National Commission, has suggested may have both moral and aesthetic significance. Violence, in short, should be germane to the necessities of plot. It should stem from character in such a way as to involve the cognition and emotion of the viewer. It should indicate a sense of responsibility for what transpires, and a recognition of the consequences of the act.

These criteria convey at least a sense of difference between violence in mass media which exploits the audience and those acts which involve the audience creatively and emotionally. Producers who condone violence because it intrigues large audiences are less moral than those who would legislate all violence from the screen, but neither approach is realistic. Violence, as well as sex, must be recognized as very much a part of the human condition. In terms of this recognition, its presentation on the media can be condemned only when it is presented for its own sake, when it exploits the audiences and when its consequences are morally and socially indefensible. In the last analysis, the media cannot pretend that sex and violence do not exist.

Mass Media as Entertainment

What is too frequently overlooked by critics of the media is that, in addition to their importance as conveyors of news and information, they function primarily to bring entertainment to millions of viewers and readers. The newspaper, once exclusively an organ of foreign news and propaganda, now combines its informational function with a number of adjunct services which are purely of an entertainment nature. These include the funnies primarily, but also various light and humorous columns, advice to the lovelorn, advice on the playing of bridge, as well as feature stories of a quasi-informational variety. This growing preoccupation with entertainment, a result in part of greater leisure time, has led to what has been termed a new hedonism in which the pleasure-principle assumes a magnified importance in American life. It has resulted also in speculation whether "pop" culture is not replacing both serious cultural presentations and true folk art. If Dwight MacDonald's concept of folk art as something spontaneous and shared by all of the people is accepted, then popular entertainment does not fit, because it is not spontaneous and it is largely machine-made and prefabricated, rather than truly "folk" in origin. On the other hand, despite the popularity of run-of-the-mill entertainment, there is paradoxically a greater audience for so-called "high" culture than at any time in this country's history. Folk art flourishes along with "pop," and never have audiences for opera, symphony or dance been as large, as involved or as critically perceptive.

The popular arts, such as television, radio and motion pictures, are close to the communicant in a physical sense, but psychologically they are also remote. An irate audience in the theatre or opera house can express its reaction by cheers, applause, boos or the throwing of eggs on the stage. The option available to the television viewer is the alternative of tuning in to another channel, turning off the dial, writing a letter or making a phone call of complaint. The movie audiences cannot even get their money back for a film which they consider offensive or absurd. The rule of thumb in determining the effect of a program or movie is not by an aesthetic poll, but by the numbers who are watching. Size of movie attendance and rating and share of television audience are partial determinants of success, even though the critical reaction may be negative. The dilemma of the mass, mass media is to reach the greatest number of people and give pleasure to *all* of them. It is a formidable and frequently an impossible task. The media can claim with some truth that what is presented does conform to what the public wants, for the public can express its opinions by turning to other activities such as reading or listening to music on the record player. The dilemma of mass media is one which is still to be resolved: that of achieving a balanced effort whereby the public gets not only what it appears to want, but also what the intellectual elite believes it ought to have; by programming for majority interests and needs and, at the same time, considering the legitimate needs of minority publics. In many ways, television has accomplished this admirably.

On the assumption that minority interests would be met by a public broadcasting network, efforts were made in 1968 to create a series of special broadcasts. The result was, unfortunately, merely a rather inferior repetition of what the national networks were doing so well. Even if, however, it were to be decreed that the public *must* be served by a programming "mix" different from, and supplementary to, the standard fare, the question still to be answered is who is to determine what the public ought to have? Plato's answer was a divided nation with philosopher-kings the arbiters of taste. Walter Lipmann, who respects the majority but does not believe it is capable of decision-making in politics or aesthetics, envisions an intellectual elite. There is no reason to conclude, however, that the public will accept the taste standards of an elite. Nor is there evidence that superimposition of aesthetic standards by any special group will result in superior media service. There is, furthermore, the inevitable factor of cultural lag between determining what the people want and the time necessary to prepare the actual presentation of the product on the air or on the screen. Public taste is ephemeral and evanescent. More than once, a form has become popular with the few, only to find that tastes have changed by the time it reaches the masses.

The major difficulty with taste-making which is superimposed from without is the very nature of American society, which is pluralistic. A pluralism of viewpoint, the result of more than a century of democracy, does not accept authoritarianism in the arts any more than it has accepted authoritarianism in any other area of life. Public opinion is never monolithic. There are many publics, many viewpoints out of which consensus is finally made. Even an audience of thirty million for "Death of a Salesman" is but a small part of the total population of two hundred million. Moreover, it is not true that minority audiences have become smaller with the growth of popular entertainment. Folk artists do get a hearing, not only in concert halls and theatres, but even on television, and folk art exists side by side with "pop" art. It may be true as Dwight MacDonald suggests, that Gresham's law also operates in the arts, the bad tending to degrade the good, but the media inevitably reflect public taste. And the evidence is too often not based on critical reception or standards of taste. It is based, necessarily, on the need to reach a large circulation. The significant issue is to find a feasible method of combining superior art *with* large circulation. A popular national magazine tries to resolve that problem by juxtaposing an expose of the private life of a movie idol or a public figure with a serious essay on life at the bottom of the sea. Television tries to resolve it by striving for a "balanced schedule" of news, drama, entertainment, discussion, documentary and special programs. The "specials" which are growing in quality and quantity have contributed importantly toward the maturity of the medium and toward serving special audiences not ordinarily interested in the regular schedules.

Unfortunately, the media—particularly a medium like television which is constantly reminded that the public owns the air—cannot literally be all things to all men at all times. Stereotyping must result in an effort to please all and offend none. Abstractions thwart the need toward extensional verification in the "real" world. A program or a motion picture that tried to please the AMA, the plumbers union, the bar associations and all of the diverse educational and social groups must wind up pleasing no one and irritating all. It is a difficult tightrope to walk, made necessary in part by the fact that the media *are* confronted by political and economic pressure groups and by the implicit and long arm of censorship.

It is a curious paradox that the very officials who condemn mass media for their blandness are frequently the first to react with indignation when the media speak out or tackle themes which may be inimical to special interests. Certain areas of programming are, of course, unpopular by common consent. Movies or television which obviously are antagonistic to the prevailing values or norms of the group invariably fail to create consent. Content which is overtly anti-religious or patently incites to crime is rejected. But these are black-or-white cases, and the issue is far more subtle. Great art has been written around themes of crime and pathology, and the courts have declared that obcenity depends upon many factors, particularly on the purpose and the ultimate moral and aesthetic value of the work under consideration. It was such considera-tion which prompted the courts to refuse to prevent the showing of a motion picture like "The Miracle" or the distribution of James Joyce's *Ulysses*. At the same time, a book which is not questioned when it appears in a limited or expensive hard-bound edition may arouse a furor of indignation and controversy when it is distributed on drug counters in a paperback edition. Nothing more significantly highlights the difference between majority and minority audiences, and the attitude of guardians of the public morals toward each, than the application of two such standards.

Media Limited in Effect

Yet, at the base of judgments on the impact of the media is the central fact that communication is the fundamental crucible through which knowledge is acquired and opinions formed. There is a quantita-tive as well as a qualitative difference between mass communication and personal influence and, in the controversial area of opinion formation and the engineering of consent, personal influence appears to have a more powerful effect than the mass media. The media are limited in effect for several reasons. The respondent is not a *tabula rasa*. He brings his training, orientation and judgment to communication content, but the flow is still one-directional. Interpersonal communication offers an oppor-tunity for hammering out a position through the dialogue of direct con-frontation. In addition, much is still to be learned about the tri-partite relationship which embraces the content of mass media, the respondent's reaction and the medium itself. In some instances it may have greater influence than in others, but the ultimate influence of the media would seem to take a place secondary to the home, school and church. What the media do accomplish, social scientists agree, is the "canalization" of *existing* drives. But the tendency to smoke, for example, must be present implicitly if the communicant is to respond positively to cigarette com-mercials. As John Dewey stated, there is a constant interaction between organism and environment—a principle which can be extended logically to an interaction between the media and their environment.

It is difficult to appraise the impact of mass media in terms of weighing their assets and liabilities. They do not balance out one against the other. Nor does mass communication remain frozen or static. Mass media are part of a dynamic functional process, reflecting society and, at the same time, influencing that society. Within this operational framework, the mass media have been called the most significant instruments of mass education and culture. The impact, however, is "potential," for the mass media are always in a state of becoming. When television began, educators saw in it a great potential for teaching. Yet, despite the enormous cultural accomplishments of the medium, it is generally believed that its potential has yet to be realized. Public broadcasting may provide the ultimate in achievement, but thus far the PTV movement has frittered considerable time on technical problems, and has yet to address itself to the heart of the matter, which is program content.

In a related area, society demands information from the media as much as it does entertainment. It is in the area of news and the documentary that a medium such as television has lived up to its promise most significantly. There are, of course, limits to instant information. A Cronkite news broadcast would fill only six columns of space in the *New York Times*. Television news, however, is a different medium from the newspaper with an indigenous and unique discipline and function. What television can do cannot be accomplished by the printed press, and what the newspaper accomplishes is different from the purpose of television news which is a medium of unparalleled immediacy. To immediacy, however, television has begun to add news-in-depth and an interpretation and analysis of events which have proved to be informative and educational. The news special on television and the interpretative column in the newspaper offer the public a unique opportunity to get all of the news with speed, accuracy and a high degree of responsibility. The television news and special report documentary program, exemplified brilliantly in the networks' coverage of the Apollo 11 moon flight, was an illustration of the heights to which this much discussed and analysed medium can reach. An account in the newspaper, assuming there were no television, might have been both accurate and superb pictorially and verbally, but the print medium simply cannot achieve the visual immediacy and the educational power of television. Both print and electronic journalism, however, cover themselves with glory on such occasions of national importance, television with the ability to reach the millions of viewers with live and immediate coverage; and print with the kind of in-depth analytical writing which American journalists do so well.

Granted the access of the public to information with unprecedented immediacy and accuracy, the question which remains to be weighed is how valuable this "instant information" is in the long run and what is its ultimate effect on society? The answer is yet to be forthcoming, and it must come from other agencies, such as professional communications and journalism studies in the field of higher education. Commercially sponsored research may provide one-half the answer—the commercial, or the numbers, half. In the field of academic social research, there remains the challenge of evaluating the assets and liabilities of the mass media. There are a number of important disciplines for example, which have been unable as yet to keep pace with the information explosion. The field of medicine has been cited as a paramount example. True, there are closed-circuit facilities available in many medical schools and teaching hospitals. But the growth of scientific knowledge far outpaces the means of *communicating* this continuous information explosion to the practicing physician. This, again, is an example of the way in which mass communication illuminates the cultural lag between scientific breakthrough and communication about it.

The average reader or viewer—the communicant—is assumed to be better informed than ever before, owing to the sophistication of the media. This *may* be true, but no research has established that it is categorically true. There is a growing accretion of sheer information available, and there are new methods of presenting it and even new techniques of hastening its absorption. But it is not known, at this juncture, whether rapid reading increases knowledge of and *meaning* along with rapid comprehension. Nor is it known whether inundating the public with the stimuli from many media increases the ability to grasp *meanings*, make distinctions and, above all, arrive at intelligent and useful decisions on the major problems of politics, economics or sociology. Mass media have accomplished a great deal if they have aided in the respondent's ability to make value judgments, predicated not only on informational data, but also in terms of intelligence and moral integrity. Within the next few years, the steady flow of information will not only increase, but the means of storage and re-use will be more easily available through the distribution of Electronic Video Recording, tape and microfilm and through information storage and retrieval in the newer computer models. As early as 1955 it was predicted that, by 1970, the individual at home would be able to utilize the computer's central storage memory system for a multiplicity of information and guidance. This revolution has arrived, but the social questions that go with it must be confronted —questions of whether rapid information increases comprehension and clarifies meanings. The still to be determined and central problem of the information explosion is primarily one of impact—how have instant information and entertainment affected, if they have, value judgments?

Students of the mass media differ in their evaluation of the effect of the media on society. Television's limitations, they assert, stem primarily from the need to reach and please the largest audience at the lowest cost per thousand. The new motion picture code which designates programs as G (general audiences), GP (all ages, parental guidance suggested), R (under 17 restricted, unless with adult) and X (no one under 17 admitted) applies a distinction to all, without regard to individual differences, and may also be compounding the basic hypocrisy of the original code. The number of national magazines in publication has dwindled through a slow process of erosion over the last decade. There are, however, several thousand fine publications designed for limited circulation to minority audience. Some of the prestige business and news magazines show an unfortunate inclination to reflect, and to strive to maintain, the status quo, rather than the keen spirit of inquiry which should be the goal of all good journalism. Finally, the newspaper field has also grown smaller, but editorial excellence is still to be found in a number of major newspapers. Competition for circulation, however, has forced many papers to fight the competitive battle, not on journalistic grounds, but through the device of added comics and popular syndicated features, with an unfortunate paucity of reportorial coverage in such areas as international news and foreign affairs, science and medicine, art or book reviews.

The medium which offers the consumer the greatest choice is the book, paradoxically the form with the least mass circulation. Particularly since the inexpensive paperback became available, the public does not lack a wide choice of titles—in both fiction and non-fiction. Even though the distribution through newsstands and drug counters has, in the opinion of some critics, cheapened the book business because of the plethora of lurid titles on display, there is still a variety of good literature to be found and purchased cheaply. The paperback revolution has made literature available to greater numbers of readers than ever before, but the increase in readers has not been paralleled by a necessary increase in fine bookstores or public libraries. In an age of literacy, it is a profoundly discouraging sign that some of America's large urban library systems may have to curtail services and hours because of a shortage of funds for necessary maintenance.

Public Interest in Media

In every area, however, the public is making use of the media of mass communication on an unprecedented scale. This is due in part to the population explosion, as well as to the easy availability of the media. Prices have generally been modest, despite increased production costs, and in the case of newspapers, magazines, radio and television, the advertiser pays the greatest part of the freight. It is only because of advertising expenditures, in fact, that news, information and entertainment can be brought to the public at relatively inexpensive rates. It has been said that television programming would be far superior if the advertiser did not pay the piper and call the tune—which is why there has been such absorbing interest in the establishment of a non-commercial, public broadcasting system as a supplementary electronic service. Certainly, with the possible exception of the British system, free competitive television infinitely is to be preferred to foreign systems where, under government subsidy, media are also under government control. And it is a striking and rather significant phenomenon that the media in this country, which are both competitive and largely advertiser-supported, offer what is undoubtedly the most free flow of information to be found anywhere in the world.

The communications media in this country present a paradox. Advertiser supported, with all the limitations which such a system imposes, they have remained largely free from pressure and censorship by either government or private sources. At the same time, in an era where the public is inundated with the symbols of mass communication, there is little known of the effect of the media, nor have the media been adaquately harnessed for the education and cultural benefit of modern man. Of quantity there is no dearth. Virtually every city has at least one newspaper. Most people can watch three or more television channels. Movies are available on television and at the theatre. National magazines appear regularly on the newsstands. Homes and cars are equipped with one or more radios. Paperbacks are plentiful, even though libraries are not. Yet, thoughtful students of the media are troubled by a dearth of quality in this cornucopia of plenty. An intellectual poverty threatens, they believe, because matters that should be of concern to all citizens are not covered adequately. What passes for in-depth analyses of racial violence, urban crises and other social and economic and health problems is fundamentally superficial because its direction is not cognitive, but emotive and directive. The proliferation of communications has reached a point where it is almost impossible for the communicant to be without information. Yet, some sectors of the country remain without information, or even proper educational facilities, and much of the information, it is claimed, is simply inadequate and non-meaningful. It is not enough to present straight fact, or even fact with an overlay of opinion. The pressing need is for a dynamic spirit of inquiry, a cultural explosion which will stimulate the imagination and prod the intelligence of all those who will read or listen.

These critiques, however well-meaning, are, at least to a degree, simplistic and without foundation. If it is true that there is intellectual poverty amid a plethora of communicative arts stimuli, one of the causes is that knowledge of content analysis and effects is still tentative. The behavioral sciences are inexact disciplines and mass media, above all, are volatile and in a state of cultural lag. Teaching has had to undergo a radical reorientation in order to keep pace with the new technologies, and the humanities and liberal arts have suffered. Although the public is better informed about political and economic issues than ever before, owing to mass media, it does not follow that the public has developed greater *comprehension* or that it understands the *meaning* of social and political phenomena any better than it did in the period of the circumscribed town meeting.

Mass media, like other aspects of a mass society, may generate and transmit simplistic, either/or thinking. Only through greater awareness of the implications of language, and the surmounting of the sematic roadblocks that make communication difficult, can the communicative arts function with genuine freedom and responsibility. The needs of a pluralistic society must somehow be met by the mass media in terms of broadening the range of experience and the alternatives available to the communicant. In the opinion of some, these needs will be met by the supplementary services of public television, but educational television has not shown, thus far, that it is superior to commercial television in its programming effort, nor is there any warranty that public television will function free of interference or control by special interests. Of all the media, television appears to offer the greatest potential, not only through the efforts of the commercial networks and stations, but also through CATV, public television and the eventual activation of UHF channels. In the final analysis, the service offered by all of the media will be precisely in proportion to the demand the public makes upon them. An intellectually alert, literate and informed public will, by its own felt and expressed needs, set the standard of performance for the mass media.

BIBLIOGRAPHY

Berelson, Bernard. *Content Analysis in Communications Research.* Glencoe, Illinois: The Free Press, 1952.

Bird, George L. and Frederic E. Merwin. *The Press and Society.* New York: Prentice-Hall, Inc., 1952.

Cantril, H. *The Invasion from Mars.* Princeton, New Jersey: Princeton University Press, 1940.

Hovland, Carl I. *Effects of the Mass Media of Communication*

Jacobs, Norman, ed. *Culture for the Millions.* Princeton, New Jersey: D. Van Nostrand Company, Inc., 1959.

Klapper, Joseph T. *The Effects of Mass Communication.* New York: Free Press, 1960.

The Effects of Mass Media. New York. Columbia University Bureau of Applied Social Research, 1949.

Krutch, Joseph Wood. *Human Nature and the Human Condition.* New York: Random House, 1959.

Larsen, Otto N., ed. *Violence and the Mass Media.* New York: Harper and Row, 1968.

Lazarsfeld, Paul F. and Frank Stanton, eds. *Communications Research: 1948–49.* New York: Harper, 1949.

Lazarsfeld, P. F. and R. K. Merton. "Mass Communication, Popular Taste and Organized Social Action" *in* Bryson, L., ed. *The Communication of Ideas,* pp. 95–118. New York: Harper, 1948.

Lindsey, Gardner. *Handbook of Social Psychology*, Vol. II. Addison-Wesley Publishing Company, Inc., 1954.

Nafziger, Ralph O. and David M. White. *Introduction to Mass Communications Research*. Baton Rouge, Louisiana: Louisiana State University Press, 1963.

Peterson, Theodore, J. W. Jensen and William L. Rivers. *The Communications Media and Modern Society*. New York: Holt, Rinehart and Winston, 1966.

Schramm, Wilbur. *The Process and effects of Mass Communication*. Urbana, Illinois: University of Illinois Press, 1954.

Seldes, Gilbert. *The Great Audience*. New York: The Viking Press, 1950.

Stephenson, William. *The Play Theory of Mass Communication*. Chicago: The University of Chicago Press, 1967.

Wright, Charles. *Mass Communication: A Sociological Perspective*. New York: Random House, 1959.

Yu, Frederick T. C. *Behavioral Sciences and the Mass Media*. Russell Sage Foundation, 1968.

16

Freedom and Control
in Mass Communication

THE CRUCIAL AND perplexing problem of freedom, control and responsibility in the mass media looms ever larger in the context of a radically changing society. At the heart of the matter is not only the question of responsibility which, in turn, involves a weighing of ends and means, but also the fundamental problem of the degree to which media reflect society and are affected by social change. All of the media have become institutionalized and function as instruments of social control. They also are subject to controls which may be implicit but are nevertheless potent and far-reaching. These controls threaten, in times of social tension, to become overt through pressure groups and legislative action, thereby raising over and over again the thorny question of freedom of communication under the umbrella of the First Amendment. This states specifically that "Congress shall make no law respecting an establishment of religion, or prohibiting the free exercise thereof; or abridging the freedom of speech, or of the press; or the right of the people peaceably to assemble, and to petition the Government for a redress of grievances."

Basic to any consideration of the effect of mass media, and central to the question of freedom for mass communications, particularly in a medium such as television, is the determination of how and to what extent the mass media reflect the society in which they function and which they serve. It is clear that mass communication is influenced by its social environment and, in turn, absorbs and delineates the goals, tensions and aspirations of that environment. If social, political and economic ideas influence media, certainly the cultural standards and goals —the parameters of public taste—which prevail at a given time are also enormously influential. The media do not foist content on an unsuspecting public, but tend to react to implicit criteria of taste by meeting the needs of the majority while, at the same time, attempting to print and program for minority publics. The mass media perform, to a great extent, as the public expects and wants them to perform. Their influence seems, at least, to be secondary to the significant way in which they reflect their social milieu. Pertinent to an evaluation of the problem of freedom and responsibility are the achievements which thoughtful students expect of the media, as well as the external and internal forces which enhance or limit the accomplishment of desirable goals. Are there, for example, clear-cut distinctions between the so-called majority and the various minority publics? At what point do minority interests join with, or become distinct from, the majority? Do the media have a primary obligation to purvey to the greatest number, or should the preferences of an intellectual elite be paramount?

These are normative questions, involving the broader question of precsiely what responsibilities the media are expected to undertake to fulfill, what obligations they are expected to perform and, most significantly, whether any group is to determine to what extent, and how well, the media have assumed and promulgated their obligations. At the core of the matter is the concept of the fundamental role of mass communication in a democratic, pluralistic society, the delicate balance between freedom to communicate and responsibility for what is communicated.

Communication and Political Philosophy: Libertarianism

One concept of what media of communication ought to be, particularly with respect to the press, was evolved from such libertarian philosophies of the Seventeenth Century as those of Locke, Berkeley and Hume. These philosophers were among the first to postulate an idea of freedom and responsibility, enlarged upon in Rousseau's conviction that men were born free and with certain inalienable rights. This was the concept which took root in colonial America, that men are governed by consent. It was a concept which has been espoused by political and journalistic figures from Thomas Jefferson to Walter Lippmann, and it has been defended against repeated efforts to erode the right to communicate freely and without restrictive legislation or pressure. The press was licensed originally in the colonies by royal decree and, until the Zenger case, there was indeed stringent censorship of newspaper content *prior* to publication. There was a ban, too, on reporting the deliberations of government. But the basic thrust of the Eighteenth Century, in England as well as in the colonies, was toward freedom to communicate. The philosophy of libertarianism, the notion of freedom with responsibility, stemmed basically from the Eighteenth Century philosophers who believed that, in a democratic society, man could enjoy the benefits of liberty. It was the growing spirit of intellectual inquiry that sparked the need for a free press in a society where the individual demanded that government function by means of the consent of the governed. This kind of democratic society can evolve only if mass media are permitted to function freely and responsibly and to achieve free access to information and ideas. Censorship, in such a climate, is heinous. In the colonies, it not only violated the fundamental rights of man, but it enabled those in power to perpetuate authoritarianism by placing restrictions on the function of the press as a medium of information and communication.

Although John Milton would cavil with contemporary theories of free inquiry, undoubtedly his "Areopagetica," published in Seventeenth Century England, became a milestone in the long and arduous road toward the achievement of a press that could function without the restrictive measures of a tyrannical government. Milton's basic contribution is to be found in his argument that the licensing of the press is an affront to free inquiry and to man's right to search for truth. But Milton's notion of freedom fell far short of the libertarian concept. It was John Locke who expressed the view that man, as a rational being, must not be denied freedom of expression as his natural right. In a laissez faire economy, in a society where the government that governed least is best, nature's laws could operate without restraint. Government had no business, in this society, either operating the press or controlling it. Newspapers were to function freely in securing larger circulation, reaching the greatest number of readers in a free, mercantile economy. The press is, of course, accountable to its readers—the public—but to no one else.

In America, Thomas Jefferson envisioned the role of the press as a free institution and set up specific criteria for the attainment of this freedom. Following the Seventeenth Century philosophers, Jefferson believed that man was a rational creature and that society could manage to function harmoniously and successfully through the exercise of reason. The press, in Jefferson's view, was the prime instrument of enlightenment. It functioned to further the improvement of man as a moral and social being. The opinions of the people are all-important, for it is the peeople who must determine the kind of government they wish to have. And the instrumentality for the achievement of political freedom is a responsible press, for "where the press is free, and every man able to read, all is safe." Jefferson pointed out that, were there a choice between newspapers without a government or a government without newspapers, he would choose the former: "Were it left to me to decide whether we should have a government without newspapers or newspapers without a government, I should not hesitate to prefer the latter." Newspapers were to be made available without restriction to all men who were capable of reading them. Beyond the libertarianism of Jefferson, it was Cato—the joint pseudonym of two Whig journalists, John Trenchard and Thomas Gordon—who asserted vigorously the need for a free press.

The libertarian philosophy, of course, has not survived intact into the differently oriented world of the Twentieth Century. But much of the basic laissez faire philosophy still prevails in many quarters. The complexities of modern life and a rapidly changing technology made libertarianism an anachronistic concept when applied to the contemporary mass media. The Twentieth Century, even with the phenomenon of instant technology for international information and communication, has seen two World Wars, a Korean conflict and the devastating consequences of Vietnam on American mores. Freedom of communication means something quite different in these circumstances from what it meant in the Eighteenth Century. While censorship in times of crises was voluntary on the part of the press, the tendency to control media has grown rather than receded, and the whole question of freedom versus control has been exacerbated by the ubiquitous reach of mass communication. Secretary Rusk, at Senate hearings on the Vietnam conflict, proposed, with some apparent exasperation, that it simply was impossible for him to discuss certain privileged matters before a press gallery and in full view of millions of television viewers, because these matters were delicate and involved the whole nexus of American diplomacy.

The potency of mass media has also instigated the temptation to withhold news—or to "leak" news to the press—thereby giving rise, in the Johnson administration, to accusations by the press of a "credibility gap." Studies of restrictions on a free press, such as that of the Commission on Freedom of the Press, reveal how various individuals, from the lofty position of President of the United States right on down the chain of command have managed to restrict access to the news, despite the clamor that a free press is entitled to information if the national interest is not thereby endangered. What is involved is man's basic right to express his opinions freely, subject only to what Oliver Wendell Holmes called the contingent circumstances of "a clear and present danger" to the national interest.

Concepts of Mass Media

Just what constitutes a "clear and present danger," however, is a thorny proposition, despite the fact that Justice Holmes was quite precise in his meaning. His intent was not to offer an excuse to censor communication content, but rather to delimit the inroads of pressure and censorship on the freedom to communicate. Relevant to a consideration of freedom and control is the broader concept of what is expected of the mass media in terms of the way they reflect society and are influenced by their social environment. And this involves fundamental considerations of a philosophy of mass communication. Four theories of mass communication have been postulated by scholars of the media, and have been considered in depth, particularly by Wilbur Schramm and Theodore B. Peterson. The libertarian position is one of those theories. Its origin, as has been noted, was in the philosophy of the Enlightenment of the Eighteenth Century. It resulted from the new vistas of experience which were opened to man, the increase in educational opportunity, the rise of secularization, the growth of industry, the economic theory of competition and the concomitant rise of a middle class in England and America. It presented the concept that man was finally master of his world, that in the hard-work ethic on an "inner-directed" society, man could achieve success by dint of his own effort and will.

In this society, the press was to be completely free of control from government and was to be subjected only to the searching scrutiny of the people. Freedom in mass communication meant a press free from the tyranny of official power and the censorship of government. It meant a world of private enterprise in which the press could express any or all political viewpoints. Were the libertarian theory to prevail today, however, it would pose hard questions for such media as motion pictures— questions of freedom and license, of bald truths versus the restrictive and negative doctrines of the motion picture code. If the public interest is truly to be served, for example, should not some of the current licentiousness in motion pictures be restricted? The libertarian theory, even at best, relies rather heavily and naively on the belief that a "self-righting" process will somehow prevail.

Diametrically opposed to libertarianism is the theory of authoritarianism. Print began under authoritarian conditions. Control was exercised by the government which licensed and censored the press. Concepts of liberty were not tolerated. Man and media survived only through the sufferance of the state. In a sense, this was a rather distorted application of the Platonic concept that an intellectual, ruling elite knew what was best for the rest of society. But an elite, even Walter Lippmann's enlightened democratic elite, tends to be self-perpetuating, because it is in its own self-interest to in-breed power. Thus, authoritarianism in society and in communication prevailed throughout the Middle Ages and the Renaissance, until the rise of a liberal philosophy in England, France and America. In such a society, where the media serve only the state, it was inevitable that the authorities would move quickly to control printing and publishing. And that is what happened. Printers published only by license and decree, and manuscripts were censored. This kind of medievalism has not yielded to liberalism universally, for the press operates under some censorship in almost every part of the civilized world except in England, the United States, and the Scandinavian countries.

Schramm and Peterson believe that the Soviet system differs somewhat from authoritarianism. For in this environment, all media serve the Communist Party and are an integral and indigenous part of the Party. The English and American systems of mass communication are incomprehensible to the Soviet mind, for the media must serve a monolithic society and must have one master—not the public, but the state. In the Soviet Union, therefore, and in Red China, the state and the media are one. The press, therefore, serves exclusively as an instrument of propaganda and its basic purpose is to further the goals of the Communist regime. The Communist Party speaks through the media of press and radio. Internally, the media voice the philosophy and goals of the state, and externally they purvey propaganda from the state. Obviously, in this system, any genuine consensus through the crucible of public opinion is patently impossible. What is "true" is what is disseminated by the media. Truth, paradoxically, must be what the state decrees it to be, not what the public decides on the basis of free flow of information.

Finally, there is the social responsibility theory under which the mass media are believed to operate in a democratic society. It does not claim to be a doctrine without flaws, but merely the most pragmatic and successful method in a pluralistic society, and clearly more relevant to the Twentieth Century than that of authoritarianism and more responsive to democratic values than state control. Its advantage for a democratic philosophy is that it places responsibility not in the state, but squarely in the hands of the communicators and the public. The government does not censor or control, but rather exists to perpetuate and guarantee freedom of communication. It is a theory believed to be singularly germane to the cataclysmic changes in technology which have taken place in the Twentieth Century, a theory which is tenable and adaptable to contemporary developments in psychiatry, sociology, government and economics. It *assumes* that the press and other media must operate freely under the First Amendment, and it seeks ways to guard that freedom from erosion, while at the time stressing the need to operate responsibly and in the public interest.

But the theory of social responsibility did not exist unchallenged by the muckrakers of the 1930's who inveighed against what they believed was a venal and corrupt press, just as some contemporary critics of mass media would like to see the press and television programming regulated. The critics of the social responsibility concept point to controls by monopoly, advertiser domination of the media, political pressure, self-perpetuating dynasties and license in the handling of sex and violence. Their proposal, then, is not responsibility and freedom, but some form of regulation and control. The media, on the other hand, also have been stoutly defended as making a genuine effort to give a fair presentation of diverse points of view, and as separating editorial opinion from information and news. Significantly, such media as radio and television insist that the responsibility for what goes on the air must be theirs, and theirs alone, and that they alone must be accountable to public opinion for what they present.

The Ethic of Media Responsibility

This assumption of responsibility implies that the media must be prepared to live up to their obligations or face the consequences of implicit or overt control. It is a unique ethic and one peculiarly relevant to a pluralistic society, for it puts the issue of truth and fairness in communication squarely up to the media. It assumes a healthy interaction between the media and their social environment. Conditions under which communication functions are never absolute and always relative to time, place and circumstances. Absolute truth comes not from a Platonic ideal, but from empirical inquiry, accomplished in a spirit of freedom to communicate. It assumes that sex is a part of life, that violence is a phenomenon of modern society. But it also undertakes to present these biological and social phenomena with judgment, discretion and responsibility. Finally, it operates on the conviction that the assumption of clear-cut obligation and responsibility for what is communicated is a fundamental and basic obligation of the media. Newton Minow, when chairman of the FCC, accused television of being a "vast wasteland," but he did not imply that the Commission should control communication content.

Other critical observers—official and unofficial—have been more peremptory in a growing demand that some form of control be exercised over the mass media, and this is particularly true of the broadcast media. The result, so far as television is concerned, has been threats of non-renewal of licenses by recent FCC commissioners, along with the pledge from Senator Pastore that, while the media should submit to some form of program review on questions of violence, the sword of Damocles will never be held over the heads of licensees—a statement that found a receptive audience in the broadcasting industry. At the same time, broadcasters on the network and station levels have insisted that ultimate responsibility for what is on the air must be theirs alone, without the imposition of prior restraint in the form of censorship of program content or, indeed, of regulation of content in any form.

The dialogue over what responsibility the mass media should arrogate to themselves and what regulations, if any, should be imposed is far from settled. Nor is the issue an easy one to resolve. It provides a climate in which the assets and liabilities of the media can be weighed and evaluated against a background of the rapid growth of mass communication, the growing sophistication in technology and the enormous power of modern communication as an instrument of persuasion and social control. Modern culture is a technologically oriented one, a result of the fact that the communication arts are the most significant cultural development of the Twentieth Century. The media permeate every aspect of modern living and are instrumental in illuminating the drives, goals and mores of contemporary civilization. But, curiously enough, power is in inverse ratio to size. The scope of mass communication is widespread, and yet it is circumscribed by the fact that there are three commercial networks, a contracting number of newspapers and a diminution in the number of magazines and motion pictures. The chances of a successful venture in mass communication in the 1970's are economically small and growing smaller, with the exception of some phases of broadcasting communications. It is certain that the newspaper, magazine and motion picture industries will never again achieve the sheer quantitative magnitude which they attained in the 1930's and 1940's.

This paradox of increasing power and influence with a decrease in numbers raises serious questions of freedom versus control, regulation versus individual responsibility. How, for example, can the democratic concept of individual freedom be perpetuated in a society where the public is subjected to a plethora of stimuli from the media, from pressure groups and from various merchants of persuasion and manipulators of public opinion. In terms of the classic concept of ethics, there must be considered the basic responsibility of the mass media to the individual and to the society which they serve, the problem of freedom of information as against the right to personal privacy and the requirements of national security and interest. Closely involved in the function of the media are those pressure and special interest groups, many of them enormously influential and powerful, whose goals are propagandistic and whose views are purely parochial. Special interest groups must bear responsibility for their acts, as the media must weigh their responsibility toward minority interests. And one source or another ultimately must set acceptable standards and criteria.

Who Sets the Standards?

Widely debated is the question whether that source should be government regulation or the media themselves. If, as media critics are convinced, the communicators cannot self-regulate because of commercial and other pressures, is the government—with equal pressures and an inevitable tendency toward self-perpetuation of power—a feasible alternative? Even if regulation in one form or another were philosophically justifiable, the matter of individual differences would remain, for no regulatory agency or law could cover all of the mass media adequately. If the editorial policies and the news coverage of newspapers and television are totally free of advertiser influence, there would still remain the question of whether, indeed, there is sponsor influence in entertainment programs and, if so, to what degree? If television programming on the commercial networks does not meet the need of cultural minorities, as the critics believe, is the answer regulation of scheduling and content or the development of supplementary services such as an educational or public broadcasting network? In opposition to those who believe that television is a superb instrument of cultural diversity, there are those critics who remain convinced that all of the media—broadcasting, motion pictures and print—tend to increase conformity, to perpetuate the status quo and to obscure rather than inform. Critics of the media believe, further, that no segment of the public can be served adequately if mass communication is geared to please everyone, that quality and taste must be abandoned in the inevitable and insatiable need for circulation and numbers.

Some peripheral results of the technological revolution also raise problems of freedom and control. According to Lewis Mumford, for example, man stands a very good chance of becoming enslaved by the very fruits of his own technology, a servo-mechanism of the computer, rather than the computer functioning as a servo-mechanism of man. Individual initiative and responsibility are difficult to maintain in a peer group oriented civilization where standardization and automation permeate virtually all of society. If man is not to become a victim of his own technology, ways must be found to maintain freedom of choice and will as against the inroads of a machine-made determinism. A genuinely democratic philosophy of communication, allowing for the exericse of both freedom and responsibility, is the alternative to control and to technological determinism. The central problem for communicator and communicant is to find ways of mastering and harnessing technology to democratic ends, of using mass media to expand the cultural and spiritual horizons of man rather than to vulgarize them. At issue is the need for a philosophy of mass communication which will encompass the ethical ideal of how the media can serve society as instruments of enlightenment and a pragmatism that will permit the media to function successfully in a free, mercantile economy.

These issues can be resolved only if the media operate in an atmosphere of individual responsibility, accountable to the public and free of political and social pressures. Mass media may not as yet be the ideal instruments of entertainment or enlightenment, but it is doubtful if political regulation will ameliorate them by legislative action and administrative fiat. The obligation faced by mass media is an overwhelmingly challenging one, and it has not been made easier by cataclysmic social and technological change. Newspapers have become fewer, but bigger. Television has changed the character and thrust of information and news. The public is heterogeneous and its needs are various. The task of programming for almost an entire nation defies the imagination. Yet, the broadcast media are asked to become, in a very literal sense, a kind of national town meeting of the nation and even the world, to provide all things to all publics.

What is at basic issue, then, is the categorical imperative to operate freely and yet to fulfill responsibilities to all of the people. There are those who remain convinced that this can only be assured through intervention by government. But many believe that the government already exercises too much regulatory control over the electronic media, and too much functional control over all media through management of information. Others assert that the public must be the ultimate arbiter. Still others are convinced that only through the effort on an intellectual elite can the mass media achieve a cultural integrity. Each viewpoint, however variant from others, involves the way in which mass communication functions in a democratic society.

The basic obligations of mass media are to inform and to entertain. Some would add the obligation to increase man's knowledge through the academic use of mass media as instruments of education. The media as commercial enterprises also have an obligation to stockholders and, for the most part, they are dependent for their economic viability on advertiser-support. These obligations, despite captious criticism to the contrary, need not be either/or alternatives to cultural or informational excellence. It is largely the revenues from advertiser supported entertainment programs, for example, which allows the commercial networks to present an excellent news and public affairs service. The libertarian philosophy asserts that the press exists to seek and print the "truth," and to give the people enough light so that they can see their way to a democratically arrived at consensus. This is one of the goals described by Walter Lippmann, to help create a consensus, because the public simply cannot do the research and the digging essential to ferreting out the kernels of news amid the welter of national and international events. The press, therefore, must accomplish this end in the interest of the public. The press, furthermore, must do more than help the public to find the news. It must serve as a genuine voice of the people, a guardian of individual liberty.

But the responsibilities of the press in a democracy are not clear-cut. Are there occasions, for example, when the press both serves and helps to perpetuate a political system; or is its role invariably that of critic and watch-dog? Is its obligation to help preserve individual freedom, as well as free access to information, at variance with its legitimate right to profit in a competitive, mercantile economy? In terms of service to the public, there are still vague areas where the press itself is confronted with the decision of giving the reader every last bit of information, so that the public can come to its own conclusions; or, on the other hand, of yielding to the temptation, as Lippmann seems to suggest, of digesting and distilling the news, and presenting it in such fashion that the reader is both informed and directed. Under such circumstances, the responsibility of the press is formidable, indeed, for it not only reports the events, but leads the reader to suggested modes of thought and action. It becomes not a passive informant, but a dynamic agent in the formation of opinions and of ultimate consensus.

In a government where consent of the governed means a functional, operational concept of public opinion, the function of the media is to gather and disseminate information so that the public itself can absorb the facts and, through the crucible of discussion on the individual and group level, come to conclusions which will be reflected in action. Under the libertarian philosophy, the press as a mass medium protected the citizen from the encroachment of political authority. Under the democratic system, as it developed in America, the theory of a free press was expounded succinctly by Jefferson: "Where the press is free, and every man able to read, all is safe." This implies more than a free press. It assumes a universal system of education where a free press and an intelligent and knowledgeable citizenry combine to establish and preserve the democratic system. But the present system retains from the Eighteenth Century philosophy a sufficient residue to assure that the media have a right to operate at a profit. And this right is neither mutually exclusive nor exhaustive with the obligation to act responsibly and in the public interest. Where monopoly exists, the function of government is to control or regulate. But political authority cannot own or operate the media of communication, for this would lead inevitably to an effort to perpetuate the incumbent power elite. The media operate best when they operate under private auspices, but in the interest of the people.

Critics of such a philosophy of communication believe that unless the media are controlled and directed, at least to some degree, they tend to preserve the status quo and to resist the forces of social change. Furthermore, in the pursuit of profit, they insist that media cannot truly be responsive to the interests of the public. The press has been criticized, for example, for failure to recognize the legitimate need for expression by, and from, racial, economic and religious minorities, of failing to come to grips with urban problems and of perpetuating the status quo. But the recent absorption of the press with racial injustice did not stem from political pressure. It was generated as a result of a recognition by the press that public opinion and changing social dynamics demanded a change in the orientation of the print journalism. The fact is that the media, always keenly aware of public opinion, largely have been in the vanguard of social change. Television, in particular, has probed areas of racial unrest and social deprivation in many public affairs programs dealing with the hungry American, with educational needs, with strife in the cities and with racial disturbances.

Social Responsibility of Media

It is through exposure and discussion in the newspaper and by the electronic media that the social responsibility theory of mass communication proves to be both salutary and pragmatic. It establishes that a free press is essential to a functional democracy, but asserts also that with freedom goes responsibility and obligation. If the media are to be permitted to flourish under the freedom established by the First Amendment, they are expected to serve democratically arrived at ends. Social change, reflected in the urban crisis, the disturbances on the campus, black militancy and the demand for food and health care for all Americans, have changed the whole concept of obligation in mass communication from libertarianism to a strong measure of social, as well as cultural, responsibility. This responsibility is not to any one political, economic, cultural or social group, but to *all* of society, to media audiences everywhere. The media operate at a profit which is not—and must not become—inconsistent with their obligation to preserve the democratic process, to enlighten as well entertain. The liberty of the press is not a natural right, but one which derives from public opinion and consensus. The public, in return, is entitled to expect certain standards of performance from the media.

As early as 1923, when social problems were less complicated, the American Society of Newspaper Editors recognized the need for a free and responsible press by setting up the Canons of Journalism. Analogous codes have been fashioned by the motion picture, publishing and broadcasting industries, although the motion picture and comic book codes stress negative, rather than positive, values. And, in such studies as William Ernest Hocking's *A Free and Responsible Press*, which grew out of the report of the Commission on Freedom of the Press, certain criteria by which the press should serve the public were clearly delineated. The press —in this instance the newspaper—is urged to provide an accurate, truthful, intelligent and comprehensive report of the news to the public. Fact and opinion (editorial and news) must be separated clearly. The press was urged to present all conflicting shades of opinion, similar to the current emphasis in broadcasting on a fair and balanced presentation of all sides of an issue. Stereotyping is to be avoided in favor of an extensional representation of people of all races, creeds and colors. Finally, the press is urged to withhold no news—good or bad—from the people. For, only through a free flow of information can the public interest be protected and enhanced through the instrumentality of mass communication.

This does not mean, however, that reporting must be so utterly objective as to become a sterile revelation of fact. It is recognized that all fact is fact which contains an overlay of opinion. The media cannot operate intelligently if they are to become so disinterested that their function becomes one of sheer recording. The media and society constantly interact, and the media—particularly newspapers and television —can best exercise their function by the kind of reporting which is not only factual, but also interpretative. The media use verbal and visual symbols which are not reality, but a representation of it. Since man cannot experience all events extensionally, nor can he verify all experience empirically, he must depend upon and trust communication to do some of it for him. The degree of responsibility with which the media accomplish this purpose is a criterion of their excellence in serving society, as well as of their limitations as instruments of social control.

All of the major media have set up, at one time or another, parameters of responsibility or codes of conduct similar to the Canons of Journalism of the newspaper publishers. The American Library Association and The American Book Publishers Council, in a statement entitled "Freedom to Read" outlined a set of standards and goals to serve as a modus vivendi for the book publishing industry. It called for the acceptance for publication of books containing every conceivable shade of opinion and ideas, even though the editor or publisher may not be in agreement with the communications content. Books are to be evaluated and judged on their merit as literature, and the political inclination of the author is not relevant to the acceptability of the manuscript for publication. Furthermore, libraries and publishing houses must resist "encroachment" on their freedom to publish by special interest groups and special pleaders who might attempt censorship prior to publication or who attempt to impose a particular point of view. Finally, on the conviction that, while ideas might be dangerous weapons, the regulation of ideas is even more dangerous, it is important that each individual determine for himself his choice of what he reads and that he be able to choose freely.

It is clear that neither the Canons of Journalism nor the publishers' credo deals with matters of morality, sexual license, religion or general questions of taste in journalism and literature. They are, rather, extensions and elaborations of the spirit of the First Amendment, designed to assure that a press that functions freely must also operate responsibly. The various media codes are, however, essentially negative, rather than affirmative, in character. They deal primarily not with what can be done, but with what must be avoided. These strictures are particularly true of the motion picture and comic book codes, far less so of the television code which was devised with the unique responsibilities of a medium as far-reaching as broadcasting in mind. The Canons of Journalism were predicated on the assumption that the newspaper reader, if kept fully informed by a free flow of information, can reach his own conclusions in terms of each individual's value system and orientation. The press is obliged, under free, competitive conditions, to convey the news with candor and integrity. On the other hand, the motion picture code was written as a reaction to scandal and exposé, and it was negative and restrictive from its inception. In the interest of protecting the public, however, the code simply made motion pictures both hypocritical and false in their presentation of the plain facts of everyday life. It condoned sexuality and brutality under a sheen of self-righteousness. Now, in its latest version, the code has realistically—and many believe shockingly—pulled out all stops. In the opinion of many social critics who cannot be called squeamish, the new permissiveness in motion picture making, with its explicit delineation of sex and violence, cannot be glossed over or excused by the fact that the public is warned by symbolic rating designations of films as intended for mature audiences or restricted to those under seventeen. Such as arbitrary code neglects the basic psychology of individual differences and merely opens the door to licentiousness and perversion.

The radio code, as originally constructed, dealt not only with matters of taste and with material which might be considered either moral or immoral, but also with the question of criteria of taste in commercial advertising and with the need for a so-called "balanced schedule" embracing both entertainment and public service programming. It emphasized the importance of news and public affairs programming and also provided that the advertising message be placed only in certain spots in the program structure. Subsequently, the Television Code of the National Association of Broadcasters dealt also with questions of establishing and maintaining high standards of taste and with commercial practices. A balance between news and public affairs and entertainment was essential. All sides of an issue were to be given a fair and adequate presentation. And, in terms of the herculean task of programming for the massive and heterogeneous viewing audiences, the NAB code stressed the need for recognition of the fact that television is a family medium, watched a great deal of the time by young people.

After the vitriolic criticism of Dr. Frederic Wertham and others, the comic book industry decided to establish a code of ethical conduct. The thrust here, too, was negative, emphasizing the need for "taste," but providing a guide toward what must be eschewed, rather than toward the development of a system of affirmative values. The old shibboleths were trotted out once again—justice must triumph, the "good guys" must defeat the bad, the home is sacrosanct, sexuality is permitted if ultimately justified by marriage. But the unfortunate fact is that every rule in the book can be broken along the tortuous road to morality. Nor has the tenet about not accepting advertisements of questionable taste been scrupulously observed, as the permissiveness in comic book advertising clearly reveals.

The codes, in general, have not succeeded in their stated objective. The most forthright is that of the NAB, but even in the broadcasting area, it was possible for CBS to point with pride to the fact that its standards of program practices were even higher than those of the industry code. For, in the long run, the restrictiveness and negativism of the media codes display a basic sophistry and contempt for ethical standards and for the intelligence of the public. Standards in mass communication may be established by the construction of a code of conduct, but freedom and responsibility can only result from effort and initiative on the part of each individual publisher, producer and broadcaster.

A Competitive Economy

The establishment of standards of taste involves the moral and cultural aspects of the mass media. But the communicative arts also operate in a highly competitive economy. Paradoxically, however, even in a competitive economy, the tendency generally has been not toward expansion but toward contraction. This is particularly true in the instance of newspapers and magazines. It has resulted in the oft reiterated charge that all of the media, but newspapers and television in particular, are virtually monopolistic in structure, and this has posed special problems in responsibility and control. The charge is leveled, for example, that, even with the ever-growing and developing audience, mass media prefer perpetuating the status quo to any serious effort at experimentation. The reason attributed is that, as media became standardized, they tended to function as large, conservatively oriented corporate enterprises with no desire to rock the boat of profit and success. Newspaper enterprises became richer, but fewer, as those which could not compete yield to the survival of the fittest. National television service is concentrated in three major networks, with the third network running behind the first two, although critics pass over the highly competitive nature of the medium. Stations hold precious franchises which, until 1969, were rarely challenged.

Part of the problem owes to factors which are purely economic. It was virtually impossible to start a newspaper or magazine in the inflated economy of the 1960's, for the odds are that the investors would never see a return on their capital investment. As a result, newspapers have dwindled, and wire services and syndicated copy have become a staple for many large chains which cannot afford national or international reporting staffs and correspondents. Wire copy, however, tends to become stereotyped, but it has become the most feasible and economic way to run a newspaper enterprise successfully. At the same time, mergers and combines take place as a desperate measure to keep ailing newspapers in business. In New York, which once boasted fourteen papers, the number was reduced to eight, and by 1969, to three daily newspapers. In many important areas of the country, there is only one newspaper available. In others, the morning and evening papers use the same plant as an economy move. Costs of newsprint have increased, and newspaper guilds have not hesitated to call long and erosive strikes in order to stave off automation and insure employment for members. Unfortunately, this has resulted in the demise of more than one major paper with both union and management the inevitable victims.

The magazine has contracted even more vigorously than the newspaper. Many magazines are started, but few survive. The great national periodicals have suffered grievous circulation losses. More and more, the magazine has had to depend on promotional gimickry as well as on a more aggressive and sensational editorial policy. The passing of the once invulnerable *Saturday Evening Post* was as much an economic phenomenon as it was a sign of social and political change. In the publishing world, of books as well as newspapers, the tendency has been toward merger and consolidation. Companies such as Time, Inc., McGraw-Hill, and Meredith

Publishing have ventured into various areas of media cross-pollenization. They own, variously, book companies, magazine units, radio and television stations and even newspapers. Many have invested in teaching machines, record companies and in cable television. Some, such as Random House and Holt, Rinehart and Winston have become part of communications and broadcasting companies, such as RCA and CBS.

Comparable changes have taken place in the motion picture industry since the Consent Decree of 1946 and the successful advent of television in 1948. The big five companies, mentioned earlier, have had to divorce production from exhibition. The studios have made fewer theatrical films, and have devoted time and effort to filmed shows for television. Recently, Warner Bros.-Seven Arts was absorbed by the Kinney Corporation in still another example of the growth of conglomerates, and Paramount became part of the Gulf and Western empire. The earlier plethora of so-called grade B films is gone forever, and has been replaced by fewer films, some genuinely artistic, too many simply exploitative and licentious. The movies, of course, do not exist on advertising revenues, but spend a great deal to advertise their own product in the press and on radio and local television. At the present time, the line of demarcation between movies and television grows thinner, as most stations carry at least one movie each night and as the major television companies establish separate theatrical motion picture subsidiaries and divisions. Still, the television industry remains not only competitive with the motion picture theatre, but the competition exists intramurally as well. Both network and local television are keenly competitive in every area—in their quest for the largest share of audience, for major advertising commitments and for a lion's share of publicity in the nation's press.

If the mass media are to operate freely and responsibly, they must also operate competitively. For competition forces a regard for public opinion and demands an ever-present need to create a successful and acceptable product. Yet, concentration of newspaper enterprises has not interfered with journalistic integrity. Indeed, there are scholars of American journalism who believe profoundly that a lone newspaper operating unilaterally will be scrupulously careful to cover and print the news with a high standard of impartiality. Wire copy may have increased the amount of "canned" news, but it has not restricted the free flow of news. And, in the face of unremitting pressure from many quarters, television news and public affairs programs have covered all of the news impartially and have not flinched from reporting many of the tragic and unpalatable aspects of American society including Vietnam, hunger, air pollution and racial bias. The communications media have managed to maintain cultural and social diversity even in a period where new enterprise is economically impossible in any of the media, with the exception of the still-growing and competitive broadcasting industry.

It is in the area of correction of concentration and monopoly that government intervention has been frequently salutary, rather than in the area of program or content control. For the responsibility of government, in a democratically oriented economy, is to foster competition and to prevent cartelization. It was the application of this philosophy which resulted in the motion picture Consent Decree of 1946, which also forced the Associated Press to permit any reputable and economically solvent buyer to secure AP services and which brought about the divorcement of the Red and Blue Networks.

It may be true that concentration in the newspaper market may tend to reduce the coverage of local news events. But the circumscribed world of the small town meeting no longer exists. The crucible for news has become the large urban community and the international event. It is also true that media depend largely on advertising revenues and that they have obligations to shareholders. Few would deny that media management exercises some degree of editorial control, and that management has a point of view. But this merely underscores the conviction that a medium of mass communication is no better or worse than the responsibility of those who are entrusted with its management. It is not government which can assure and maintain freedom and responsibility, but the media themselves in dynamic interaction with an alert, informed and intelligent public opinion.

Broadcasting: A Regulated Medium

The one officially regulated medium is broadcasting. It is often pointed out that the public is simply unaware of the fact that the people own the air and not any single network or station. At first, the Federal Communications Commission was established to see to it that channels were clear, that spectrum space was allocated so that stations could broadcast, and the audiences received broadcasts, without interference. As broadcasting grew, however, the functions and responsibilities of the Commission multiplied. Although the FCC grants licenses for three years, with renewal dependent upon how well a station has functioned in the public interest, the Commission has been accused of rubber stamping renewals partly because of political pressures and partly because of lack of personnel to carry the enormous and increasing work load. Over the past few years, however, the Commission has taken a much harder look at license renewals and in 1969, for the first time, several challenges were issued to individual stations. The whole question of single ownership of newspaper and television enterprises came under serious scrutiny and evaluation. In Boston, the Commission refused to renew the license of station WHDH-TV and the case will be contested probably for some years in the courts. In New York, a group of citizens have challenged the licensing of station WPIX to the New York *Daily News*. A similar challenge ensued in San Francisco. The ultimate disposition of these cases will affect the entire framework of the broadcasting industry.

Unlike print, the broadcast media operate under various regulatory sections of the Communications Act. It was only the suspension of Section 315—the so-called "equal time" provision, which provided that broadcast time given to one political candidate must also be made available equally to *all* other candidates, however minor the party—which permitted the Kennedy-Nixon appearances on national television and provided a magnificent educational experience in political action for millions of Americans. Failure of the Congress to suspend Section 315 prevented a similar confrontation on television in the 1968 elections.

Unlike print, too, the broadcast media operate what has become known as the Fairness Doctrine, which was most recently elaborated by the Supreme Court in the Red Lion Case of 1969. The Red Lion Case resulted from an attack on the air by the Reverend Billy James Hargis in November of 1964 against a writer named Fred J. Cook in which Hargis accused Cook of having been fired by a newspaper for fabricating charges against public officials, and also of having left-wing affiliations. Cook claimed that this was a personal attack and that, under the Fairness Doctrine, he must be provided with time to reply. The Red Lion Broadcasting Company, of Pennsylvania, refused Cook such time, but was ordered to provide it by the Federal Communications Commission. Various appeals were made to the courts, among them one by the Radio-Television News Directors Association which charged that the FCC rules were unconstitutional because they abridged freedom of speech and the press. It was claimed that the FCC simply substituted its judgment for that of the licensee and that, if every issue were covered exhaustively, the medium would be reduced to a "bland neutrality."

The Supreme Court held, however, that broadcasting was a new and different medium and that a strict interpretation of the First Amendment did not provide sanctuary. Justice Byron White stated that "it is the right of the viewers which is paramount . . . it is the purpose of the First Amendment to preserve an uninhibited market place of ideas in which truth will ultimately prevail, rather than to countenance monopolization of that market, whether it be by government itself or a private licensee . . . it is not inconsistent with the Fairness Doctrine . . . to require broadcasters to permit answers to personal attacks occurring in the course of discussing controversial issues . . . there is no sanctuary in the First Amendment for unlimited private censorship operating in a medium open to all."

Freedom: A Functional Concept

In order that the media of mass communication be permitted to function without undue coercion, interference and control there must obviously be some concept of what is meant by freedom and responsibility.

This concept must not only be a feasible one, but must be structured in extensional terms. On any other basis, one is dealing merely with high level abstractions. The crucial question is not freedom, but freedom to do what; not responsibility in the abstract, but a dynamic, functional definition which can operate in the crucible of experience. These goals can only be arrived at in a spirit of free inquiry, a climate of trial and error, not under prior conditions imposed by an outside authority, governmental or otherwise. Internal censorship, as FCC Commissioner Nicholas Johnson erroneously asserted, is hardly to be equated with the exercise of individual responsibility in an empirical, rather than an authoritarian, environment. Commissioner Johnson's charge that the television networks censor their own programs was refuted point-by-point by CBS News President Richard S. Salant in a rebuttal to Johnson's article in *TV Guide* magazine in September of 1969. Although Mr. Salant's references were to CBS News programs, the principle would apply equally to both NBC and ABC.

It is rare, indeed, despite a belief to the contrary by skeptical observers, that either print or broadcast news media impose internal censorship to avoid unpleasant topics, and it is refuted by the fact that both electronic and print journalism have confronted any number of unpalatable social, political and economic stories which officialdom and special interest groups would prefer to see passed over. The decision of the communicator in confronting controversial problems is not one which should be predicated on what any external sources might like to see printed or aired, but rather on the communicator's judgment of what the public is entitled to know. Freedom of information implies freedom of the right of the public to know and this, in turn, demands that the media take ultimate responsibility for what is communicated. Matters of freedom of access to news, of fairness and balance and of the need to reject special interests in favor of the public interest are concepts which only the communicator can determine in juxtaposition with an intelligent and informed citizenry.

The conflict between officialdom and special interests and the mass media was exemplified clearly in the circumstances of the Democratic National Convention of 1968 in Chicago. The media, particularly television but also the print media, complained that they were not permitted to cover the conflict which took place on the streets and in Grant Park. The city officials asserted that it was the presence of mass media which exacerbated the conflict. The media were accused, in particular, of seeking out the most sensational and of aggrandizing it. The central issues were twofold. In the first place, the controversy highlighted dramatically the whole concept of freedom and control. Secondly, the conflict was never resolved by rational or meaningful dialogue, but became a semantic exercise in which stereotypes, name-calling and black or white alternatives precluded any recourse to reason. In the last analysis, even admitting that the presence of the media may have been implicitly instigatory—a very moot question at best—the basic issue was the right to freedom of information, a right which the media were asserting on behalf of the public. No useful conclusion or solution could have been reached in an atmosphere of controlled news, repression and prohibition. The question of whether all of the media acted responsibly is one which has drawn adherents for both pro and con positions. But the nature of events and the repressive acts of the authorities—along with a generally impartial record of news coverage on the part of both print and electronic journalism—argue strongly for support of the mass media.

What was involved fundamentally in the Chicago situation was a test of the strength and validity of the First Amendment and all that is implied in its application and interpretation. The decision as to the employment of television cameras cannot be imposed by any group, official or otherwise, with an ulterior purpose in mind. However perfectly, or imperfectly, they may perform in the opinion of specially interested parties, the media of communication have a right to access. The public, in turn, has a right to receive the news of the day without restrictive or coercive measures, whether these measures be outright repression or censorship or the application of a "credibility gap" through the catalyst of public relations procedures. The case for a "hands off" policy on the part of government is a strong one when it is applied to mass communication, and this was recognized as early as the Seventeenth Century by the English philosophers and by such Americans as Thomas Jefferson. With the exception of laws against libel, sedition or obscenity—and the last has given the courts considerable difficulty in defining—mass media, if they are to fulfill their function successfully, must be recognized as distinct from other privately operated enterprises. Their ultimate function is to meet the crucial need of the public for information. This function cannot be promulgated successfully unless information is gathered and disseminated freely, beyond the tentacles of *a priori* (or prior) censorship or control, as well as beyond any a *posteriori* effort to punish the media for printing or airing information which may be inimical to special interests. The criterion is not who may be affected, but simply whether the information is true.

One task of the media is obviously a difficult and challenging one—to remain free and yet responsible at the same time; to remain independent of control and yet to be able to call upon government when the circumstances demand; to develop sufficient economic strength to withstand advertiser, sponsor and special interest pressures and sufficient ethical standards to determine what is not only "fit to print," but necessary to print. In the area of the newspaper, the question of government control of the media has presented no major problem. But broadcasting is another matter, because the broadcast spectrum belongs to the people. A newspaper does not exist by license and its franchise, unlike a television station's, is not renewed every three years. It operates under no hazy obligation to function "in the public interest, convenience and necessity." It faces no challenge in the courts from other interested parties who claim that they will perform more capably than the present incumbent. It faces few, if any, investigations of sex and violence, however lurid its stories and pictures may be. Television stations are licensed. Very high frequency channels are precious and limited. The FCC licenses, and renews the licenses of stations, on the basis of how well they have fulfilled their "public interest" obligations over the past three years. The station must be of excellent quality. Its log must be in order. It must serve the community and reflect the needs and aspirations of that community in its over-all program balance. But, significantly, the FCC does not intervene in the specific area of program content. The criticism of programming from Newton Minow and Nicholas Johnson generally has eschewed the delicate area of content control. The FCC, under the Communications Act, may survey the total performance over a three year period in renewing a license, but it may not exert any control over communication (program) content.

Beyond the FCC is the legislative power of the Congress. Over the past twenty years, there have been numerous Congressional hearings on one aspect or another of the broadcasting industry. The equal time provisions of Section 315, for example, could only be suspended—or rescinded—by the Congress, not by the FCC. But the FCC was created by the Congress, and the Congress can add to, or take away from, the scope and powers of the Commission on many major issues affecting broadcasting. The matter of network control over programming, for example, has been one which has been discussed in Washington on more than one occasion over the past fifteen years. The charges were made at one time that, because stations were obliged to take network programs, they were unable to meet local community needs. At one juncture, the networks were accused of relinquishing program control to advertisers and other outside packagers. At another, they were criticized for exerting too much control. These contradictory positions indicate not only the unique nature of the broadcast service, but also the semantic and pragmatic problems involved.

Most stations clearly prefer and value network affiliation, because only a network can supply the quality news and entertainment programming which, along with its local performance, enhances the station's economic and cultural position. And, in the last analysis, if networks are to be held accountable, culturally or morally, for what they put on the air, then only the network can take utimate responsibility for its decisions in both programming and program practices.

The public expects no less from the media of mass communication in a democracy. In the new American republic, freedom of the press meant the right to print any content whatever, without restraint and regardless of the truth, falsity or bias of the report. The Twentieth Century environment would not be favorable to a freedom which was actually a license to indulge in fierce partisanship and even libel. The newspaper of today may incline to support a party or candidate editorially, but there are limits to the extent of partisanship. An editorial position is tempered by the application of standards of truth, honesty and good taste in the coverage of news. Furthermore, both print and electronic journalism make a distinction between editorializing and news, and they label editorial opinion precisely for what it purports to be. The press is, of course, not always beyond reproach in its journalistic techniques. The reporter or photographer who asks that two antagonists shake hands smiling a moment after a bitter verbal altercation, puts a good picture above accurate coverage of the news. There is, too, a temptation, and often a tendency to slant news by omission of relevant data, by adroit handling of headlines or by disproportionate emphasis on the sensational. Drawing the very thin line between interpretation and editorializing is a delicate and controversial process. On the whole, however, the balance is far and away in favor of a press which is as truthful, responsible and accurate as any in the world.

Pressures and Special Interests

But the mass media, despite their crucial demand for independence, are not invulnerable to pressures from special pleaders, persuaders and propagandists. Political, religious, educational, ethnic groups subject the newspaper, and particularly television, to unrelenting pressure to embrace and foster a particular point of view. Failure to accede frequently results in an excoriating attack against the medium as unfair and biased. Now, there are occasions when the citing of areas where the media may be remiss may be both necessary and helpful. The obvious need for a greater representation of blacks is one of these areas. But the demand that *any* group or individual be given air time or newspaper space as a platform or sounding board is neither sound journalism, nor justified under the First Amendment or under any canon of ethical practices. The criteria by which the media must decide are, first, the relevance of the request in terms of news value and, second, the degree to which the public interest will be served by acceding to the request to be heard.

Unfortunately, the rejection of special interest demands either by print or electronic media is not simply disposed of. Pressure from special pleaders can be brutal, trenchant, intense and unremitting—by means of letter writing campaigns, telephone calls, telegrams, delegations of visitors, picketing and even the placement of advertising. The print media tend to be more free of such pressures than radio and television or motion pictures. At one time, for example, the motion picture industry was under enormous pressure from church groups and other special organizations which had set up self-constituted standards of motion picture morality. It was a Supreme Court decision on a film entitled "The Miracle" which finally established that the First Amendment applied to motion pictures as to any other medium. An analogous decision relating to James Joyce's *Ulysses* also established that literature was subsumed under the philosophy of the First Amendment. Over the past several years, the television industry has been subjected to a great deal of pressure from various investigating committees and organizations and other special interest groups. Unfortunately, the criticism is not directed toward the establishing of affirmative values or goals, but toward the recommendation that the industry be regulated and that program content be controlled. Like print media, television must continue to resist such pressures. The standards of independence set by such journalistic enterprises as *The New York Times* and *The St. Louis Post-Dispatch* fortunately is being matched by the resistance to control manifested by the television networks.

Beyond the overt demands of pressure groups, are more subtle efforts to manipulate and influence mass communication by the techniques of persuasion and public relations. The newspapers, the television news rooms and the wire services, of course, receive thousands of press releases daily and are invited to cover innumerable press conferences and special events. Many of these are quite newsworthy and illustrate why the ethical and able public relations practitioner is a source of considerable importance to the operation of the press. The fact that a public relations man, representing a client, directs his energies toward publicizing his client in print is, as such, neither good nor bad. It is the newsworthiness of the story or event that must be the ultimate determinent of what is printed or aired. Under ideal conditions, the reputable publicist is an important adjunct to the journalistic profession. At worst, however, the press relations man can not only distort news, but also can operate to prevent the news from reaching the public. This is not as true of corporate public relations activities as it is of government press secretaries on all levels who frequently create a credibility gap with the press by concealment, distortion and half-truth. This kind of public relations actually tends to subvert truth and restrict the free flow of information. Some special interests have engaged in gigantic advertising campaigns directed toward making the worse appear the better reason.

It is at this juncture that the integrity of the mass media comes under its most severe test, when the distinction between news and propaganda must be made and when advertiser pressure must be resisted. In general, the press has resisted special pleading and persuasion and has refused to be diverted from its main obligation to print the news. Although the broadcasting networks derive a considerable revenue from cigarette advertising, the news divisions have presented broadcasts discussing the relationship between cigarette smoking and cancer and have ventured into many other areas where the program content was not favorable to the interests of important advertisers.

Public relations as propaganda does not serve the media, but subverts them toward ends that are not in the public interest. Consensus is not arrived at through the crucible of interaction between press and public, but through the manipulation or "engineering" of consent. In the interest of freedom and responsibility, the mass media must distinguish between legitimate and newsworthy public relations services and special pleading. Truth must be separated from propaganda, fact from opinion. The best of public relations provides a source of news to the press, particularly in an age of complicated technology where business and its publics are separated by an ever-widening gap. In the last analysis, the media need not reject public relations, but can utilize it to help keep mass communication free of manipulation, coercion and control.

Not all editors have a sacred view of their calling. A newspaper executive on a major metropolitan daily recently admitted that he served as an off-the-record public relations counsel to a company which not only advertised in his newspaper, but which was under investigation in a series of articles appearing in the paper. Many editors in all departments of newspapers, with rare exceptions, accept invitations to junkets, the prime purpose of which is to publicize product. This practice is defended by both the press and the sponsoring company as a perfectly ethical one, for the editors presumably are under no pressure to write favorably. Indeed no less a reputable journalist than John Crosby defended a film junket to Hawaii in *The New York Herald Tribune* by pointing out that the trip did not prevent him from lambasting the presentation. Ideally, the press should pay its own way in covering news events in areas where there may be any possible exerting of influence. As a practical matter it does not, and on the whole—although not invariably—the journalist has remained remarkably immune from influence and pressure. It has become a tacit understanding, a kind of unwritten code between press agent and press, that free tickets or trips are not expected to produce favorable reviews of products unless, in the opinion of the critic, the product is deserving of it. In general, the practice has worked, if only because, as cynics claim, the journalist receives so many invitations that he can afford to remain independent.

Both the print and electronic media are advertiser-supported. Books, cartoons and motion pictures are basically independent of the need for advertising revenues. The question is raised repeatedly, however, of precisely how the media can reconcile the need for advertiser support with the need to be free and responsible. Clearly, advertiser control over content is not in the public interest, nor is it morally justifiable on the part of the newspaper, magazine, radio or television station. Since television and newspapers are totally advertiser supported, there are those critics who assert that neither medium can function without at least some implicit advertiser pressure, with a resultant acquiescence to that pressure. In the formative period of television and radio, the advertiser was intricately involved both in the program format and the commerical. Under the present structure, however, it is accurate to say that the networks, in particular, not only maintain basic control over all programs which they broadcast, even outside "packages," but that the network program practices require that advertising meet network standards of taste. Certainly electronic journalism enjoys, and insists upon having, as much freedom as print. There have been instances when networks have broadcast highly controversial public affairs programs, even though it was evident that the content of the program would prove inimical to the interests of important sponsors. Similarly, the best newspapers have not hesitated to run an unpopular series of articles even though the subject matter may invade areas considered immune from press exposure. A medium which eschews controversy is a medium which does not deserve to operate freely. Unfortunately, too many advertisers are reluctant to risk investment in programs which do not deliver large audiences, and it is usually the institutional sponsor who supports cultural programming on television. Networks, while they have gained greater sponsor support for news programs, still operate their news divisions at a substantial loss which must be compensated for by the entertainment schedule. For, a prime time public affairs programs, if it does not gain a respectable audience, may also limit the audience for the subsequent program.

Just how successful the techniques of persuasion are when applied to mass media is still under investigation by social scientists. Mass communication, except in isolated instances, such as the famous Orson Welles "Invasion From Mars" radio broadcast which some of the public thought was true, do not effect any immediate, overt or drastic change in opinion or behavior. Communication content is modified by the reader's or viewer's attitudes, education, religious training, political orientation and his basic set of value judgments. Furthermore, research has shown that television viewers and newspaper readers tend to select out, and react favorably to, content with which they are in basic agreement. Even controversial data is re-defined so as to cohere with the respondent's point of view. It has been demonstrated further that personal influence may well be a more potent factor in influencing opinion that media content. The media, however persuasive the content, usually do not radically change attitudes. They may modify thinking, but essentially they tend to reinforce attitudes already existent.

Mass media can field the pressure from special interest groups as well as from government, only by performing up to the spirit and letter of a high standard of social responsibility. The media can set up norms or standards which are not merely codes of what not to do, but affirmative ways of acting in the public interest. Codes are negative instruments Responsibility is a positive and dynamic creed. Codes cannot operate to improve the aesthetics of mass communication, nor are they instruments of positive ethical values. The criterion for excellence in mass communication is not to be found in the rule book of the codes, but in an environment of free inquiry, personal responsibility and aesthetic sensitivity.

Media and the Public Interest

But critics of media performance ask what recourse can be taken if the press or television does not function responsibly. The question itself is ambiguous, for a performance which is considered responsible in one quarter may be condemned as utterly irresponsible in another. Much depends upon whose interests are impinged upon and what extensional meaning is given to "responsible" behavior. Clearly, one criteria is that the media operate not in behalf of any special interest, but in the *public* interest. Still, there are many who believe that a medium as large and powerful as television must be subjected to some regulation which will define and delimit the meaning of public interest. Pressure groups have made the point frequently that television can only program in the public interest if content is controlled, i.e. censored. Obviously, there is only one agency which can exert such control and that instrumentality is government. But it is equally obvious that governments tend to perpetuate themselves and their powers, and this is particularly true, as history has shown, when there is any semblance of control over the media of communication. The basic function of government—federal, state or local—is not to censor, suppress, control or regulate, but rather to provide an atmosphere in which media can function freely and can act in the public interest. The courts, recognizing the need to limit government in the area of mass communication, traditionally have inclined to be extremely cautious on the whole question of regulation. In case after case involving motion pictures, books and magazines, the courts have been reluctant to censor or to place obstacles in the path of freedom of communication. The wisdom of the court is simply that suppression today for what may appear to be a valid reason may set a precedent for additional suppression tomorrow for reasons that are totally invalid and inimical to a democratic way of life. Government, however, can open new vistas for mass media by encouraging experimentation and by fostering the development of supplementary services such as the development of the Public Broadcasting Corporation. The function of government is not to impede, but to stimulate the free flow of information and knowledge.

On the whole, both print and electronic journalism have done a superb job of objective and honest reporting. Newspapers which are antagonistic to political candidates on the editorial page generally have made scrupulous efforts to be fair on the news pages. Television has functioned with a notable degree of fairness and balance. The press, of course, is expected to do more than report bald facts. The best news reporting is now recognized as interpretative reporting—that which reports the forces behind the news. News analysis and commentary also enlightens the public about the news. The columnist and the television analyst, such as James Reston or Eric Sevareid, has a distinct place in journalism and offers a unique and valuable service to the reader and viewer. It is true, of course, that all news is slanted to those who do not agree with it, and it is equally true that no newspaper report or television news program can achieve an immaculate degree of fairness and balance. Those who communicate are also subject to normal human frailties. Neither man nor media operates in a vacuum of perfection. The public cannot ask more of mass communication than that it strive for responsibility and integrity as its ultimate goals of excellence. Fairness and balance, carried to extreme, can result in a faceless neutrality, so that the media operate without either color or character. Sheer, quantitative information is not sufficient to meet the public's needs. The media are both social and educational institutions with an obligation to offer a balanced and fair view of the society which they serve and reflect. Newspapers which emphasize the sensational on their front pages to the virtual exclusion of important national and world news are derelict in their responsibility to the reader. For it is not enough to omit news because, in the view of editor or publisher, the public is not interested in it. The public interest is served only by a balanced presentation of what the public appears to want, along with news that is clearly in the public interest. Only in this way can majority and minority interests be successfully accommodated by the mass media.

In order for the mass media to fulfill their obligations responsibly, they must be permitted to function without censorship or control by any group with special interests, be it government or private in origin. Indeed, the very freedom enjoyed by the media under the First Amendment places a unique obligation to operate solely in the public interest. There have been occasions when the reporter, in the urgency of fast breaking news, may violate principles of responsible behavior. The media, print and electronic, came under criticism for the coverage of the shooting of Lee Harvey Oswald, but it should also be pointed out that the authorities had an equal responsibility to see to it that Oswald had adequate protection. Again, the media have been taken to task for their coverage of urban and campus rioting. While there may have been instances where the reporters were intrusive, the fact remains that the obligation to cover the breaking news is a demanding one. The media have been scrupulously careful, in general, to avoid situations which trigger rioting because of their very presence.

All of the media have been accused, at one time or another, of invading the privacy of the individual, or of printing or airing news which the source would prefer to see relegated to limbo. The criterion of what is "fit to print" obviously must be predicated on the public interest. The right to know on the part of the media and the public supersedes, as it should, the demand of any special or parochial interest. At the same time, the right to privacy presents a more complicated problem. For it must be recognized that politicians, as well as motion picture, stage and television stars and authors who enjoy the limelight of publicity are—and tend to make—news. It is precisely because they make news that the media have an obligation to cover their activities when these activities are newsworthy. The marriage of Jacqueline Kennedy to Aristotle Onassis could not have been a private happening, even if the press had wanted to treat it as such. The only criterion by which the press can function is to determine when the importance of the news must be given priority over the right to privacy. Trials and conventions are not established as theatrical events for the benefit of the press, nor would a responsible press want them to be. There have been occasions—fortunately rare—where isolated reporters have obtained information under false pretenses and where a newspaper has given a story a sensational thrust. The majority of newspapers, however, function with a high degree of integrity, and this has increased with better training of journalists and with the growth of college and graduate school programs in mass communication. The reporter depicted in some of the conventional motion pictures and plays of the 30's would be a travesty under the conditions of contemporary journalistic practice.

The responsibilities faced by the mass media go beyond questions of invading the individual's right to privacy. In the public affairs sector, the relationship between government and the press has been a delicate one since the founding of the republic. Although newspapers are no longer licensed, and the only regulated medium is television, government on all levels—federal, state and local—has frequently displayed a tendency to work with the press on favorable news and to avoid a confrontation on news that may not elicit an affirmative public opinion. The media have indicated considerable concern over concealed news, withholding of relevant information, the setting up of the smoke screen of "privileged" material and the bold request that reporters omit newsworthy items as a favor to the individual involved. In a sense, the running battle between the media and officialdom is healthy. It underscores the freedom of the media and the need to operate in the interest of none but the public. Unless there is, indeed, a "clear and present danger," unless delicate problems of security or diplomacy are involved, there is every reason for the mass media to insist that the daily operations of the government be illuminated for the scrutiny of the people through the searchlight of mass communication.

The press has a right to insist that all information not clearly inimical to the interests of the country be open to reporters for newspapers, radio and television. At the same time, the media must also make clear to the officials involved that information will be used judiciously and temperately and solely in the interest of keeping the people informed. Far too much data, in industry as well as in government, is doled out to the press on an "off the record" or a "do not quote" basis. The history of journalism in this country shows clearly that, for the most part, responsible newspapers know when to avoid the publication of news which, however interesting, may *not* be in the public interest. The media, for example, were careful to avoid exacerbating the tense situation in urban communities in the aftermath of the assassination of Martin Luther King, Jr. In another context, the story has been told of the debate which took place on high levels of *The New York Times* over breaking—or holding—the story which *The Times* had discovered about the ill-fated Bay of Pigs invasion. The public interest was involved in both of these situations. It is the public—through its educational and other community institutions, as well as through its expression of opinion by mail and phone—which has a right to demand high standards of performance and judgment by the media. For newspapers and television are instruments of information and education, and their service to the public is in many ways a contribution not only to public opinion, but also to knowledge.

The degree to which public opinion acts to insist on high standards of media performance depends upon the degree to which the public has been oriented to understand the need for free and responsible mass communication. As the public has made its opinions articulate about the schools and other civic agencies, so it can articulate its need for honesty, integrity and efficiency by the mass media. The television industry has a genuine point in its reply to critics when it asserts that the viewer can watch or tune out any given program by the turn of a dial. As educational opportunity increases, discrimination may also be expected to increase. More and more readers and viewers are becoming selective, critical and discriminating in their choice of books, plays, motion pictures and television. In the area of the newspaper, it is doubtful that the personal and flamboyant journalism of Hearst and Pulitzer would flourish in the social climate of today. Through critical discussions in the schools, and the proliferation of courses in mass media in the colleges and universities, through the instrumentality of groups such as the Public Education Association and various citizen committees, the public has developed a sense of involvement in education, civic affairs and mass communication. And the media themselves have engaged in research studies, undertaken by reputable scholars in the social sciences, to determine their effect on the opinions of the public and to evaluate their assets and shortcomings.

These evaluations, by the media themselves, as well as by the public, are critically important in a period when mass media, and particularly television, are subjected to a variety of pressures. At one time, for example, the media were scored for not giving space and time to the dissident and the disenfranchised, and to racial minorities. The result has been a greater degree of exposure of minority opinion, however dissident, in the press and certainly on television. But some believe that this has simply added fuel to the fires of social discontent. However justifiable these discontents may be, the media cannot accede to the request that any and all critiques, regardless of what is involved, be granted time for rebuttal. It is as undemocratic for the media to permit a cacophony of voices to engage in debate and rebuttal as it is to neglect social problems altogether. As Walter Lippmann so wisely pointed out more than three decades ago, the public cannot ferret out, organize and interpret the multiplicity of news events. The press, through the efforts of trained journalists must attempt to accomplish this end for the people. This is even more true in today's complicated world of changing technology.

Vice President Agnew's Critique

The issue of freedom in mass communication as against implicit, or direct, control of the mass media was joined acutely in November of 1969 when the Vice President of the United States made two scathing indictments of both electronic and print journalism. The impact of Vice President Agnew's unprecedented criticism of the media was traumatic. This was probably the first time since the Colonial period in American history that a free press had come under so devastating an indictment from a high official of government. While it is true that Presidents of the United States, beginning with George Washington, had complained about their treatment by the press, no government official had taken the media so vigorously to task as had the Vice President in his two separate addresses, one of which reached millions of viewers by means of national television.

In an address before the Midwest Regional Republican Committee, on November 14, the Vice President accused the television networks of distortion of the news, biased reporting and concentration of power in the hands of a small group of persons, based in the East and isolated from the rest of the country, "and enjoying a monopoly sanctioned and licensed by government." Mr. Agnew invited the public—what the President had called the "silent majority," to verify his point of view by making its own views known to the national networks.

Shortly after his indictment of television news, the Vice President expanded his comments on the communications media and accused many newspapers, particularly *The New York Times* and *The Washington Post*, of unfair handling of the news. One of the basic problems, the Vice President said, was the fact that many newspapers had gone out of business, thus resulting in a virtual monopoly and lack of vigorous competition. In this address, before the Alabama Chamber of Commerce, the Vice President stated that *The New York Times* had distorted the news, had given unfair emphasis to some stories while omiting others, and had gone beyond "fair comment and criticism."

The reaction to both addresses from both electonic and print journalism, after the impact of so vigorous an attack, was one of forthright defense of a free and responsible press and a vigorous demand for the exercise of freedom and responsibility without intimidation, censorship or control—although the Vice President had stated that he was opposed to censorship. Executives of the television industry, in particular, stated that they were deeply concerned that a high official of the government would threaten a medium licensed by that very government. Leonard Goldenson, President of the American Broadcasting Company, insisted that "the performance of ABC News has always been and will continue to be fair and objective." Dr. Frank Stanton, President of CBS, pointed out that, while no institution should be immune to public criticism, "we do not believe, however, that this unprecedented attempt by the Vice President of the United States to intimidate a news medium which depends on its existence for government license represents legitimate criticism." Julian Goodman, President of NBC, termed Vice President Agnew's attack "an appeal to prejudice."

Newspaper officials were equally swift to reply to the Vice President strictures against print journalism. Arthur Ochs Sulzberger, President and Publisher of *The New York Times,* termed some of Mr. Agnew's statements inaccurate and pointed to several examples intended to refute the claim that *The Times* enjoyed any semblance of a monopoly in journalism or that it slanted the news. Mrs. Katharine Graham, President of *The Washington Post* Company, also asserted that the Vice President's remarks "are not supported by the facts" and added that "the voices of public opinion in the Washington area are plentiful and diverse."

Shortly thereafter, Herbert Klein, the President's Director of Communications, spoke before The International Radio and Television Society and, although more conciliatory toward the media, accented the Vice President's demand for a more balanced presentation of what some have termed "the conservative viewpoint in the media." Finally, in an address before the same organization, CBS President Dr. Frank Stanton offered a vigorous refutation of the Vice President's address and a strong and determined defense of freedom and responsibility in mass communication. Pointing out that broadcast journalism was deeply concerned with the opinion of both press and public, as well as of the network's affiliates, Dr. Stanton insisted that, "as we do not propose to leave unreported the views of the Vice President, we cannot in good conscience leave unreported any other significant voice or happening—whether or not it supports government policy, whether or not it conforms with our own views, whether or not is disturbs the persuasions of any political party or bloc. But no healthy society and no governing authorities worth their salt have to fear the reporting of dissenting or even of hostile voices. What a healthy society and a self-respecting government do have to fear—at the price of their vitality if not of their life—is the suppression of such reporting."

It is clear that what was involved in Vice President Agnew's caustic criticism of the media, and the rebuttals which ensued, was the fundamental question of freedom versus control of the media of mass communication. Despite assurances that no censorship of print or electronic journalism was intended, there were many thoughtful observers—in communications, in the academic world and in the Congress—who felt that the attacks were unfair and without adequate substantiation. Many expressed the conviction that they had polarized public opinion in a very dangerous fashion and that the purpose could only be construed as an effort to intimidate a free press. Broadcasters saw the criticism as an implied threat to their licenses. Print journalism, with notable exceptions like *The New York Daily News,* saw the fundamental principle of freedom, and of the press as a time-honored guardian of the public interest, eroded.

The effect of the two addresses, and of subsequent comment by both government officials and the press, inevitably polarized public opinion. Those who were in general agreement with network news commentary and with news coverage by *The New York Times* and *The Washington Post,* came to the defense of the media. Other special interests saw an opportunity to launch a vitriolic, and frequently biased, attack on the media simply *because* their own political viewpoints or objectives were not supported. But the basic issue was not one of choosing a position to the "right" or "left" in a polarized society. The issue was the fundamental right of the press, under the First Amendment, to act freely and responsibly and solely in the interest of the public. To the criticism that the media had too much power there were those who replied that some of the media actually were too restricted and limited in scope. Indeed, it was not the power of the press that was at issue, but the unlimited and awesome power of government. Compared to the effect of governmental control, the power of the press was circumscribed, limited and relatively benign. In fact, the traditional and basic philosophy under challenge was the obligation—indeed the necessity—of the press to operate freely, empirically and in the public interest, even if this meant analysis, interpretation and editorial criticism of government. For in a pluralistic society, a free and responsible press remains the most fundamental hallmark of democracy. The media have no obligation to express any viewpoint by label, whether the label be "conservative" or "liberal" for both are abstract rather than extensional. The sole obligation of a responsible press is to seek and communicate what is newsworthy to the people and to interpret the news in terms of the public interest. Free and responsible media of communication have always constituted—and do so more pointedly in these times—the basic fabric of a free and democratic society.

It is the function of a free press to gather news and information, and to distill this information into sensible and comprehensible form for the benefit of the public. The mass media—in particular television, radio and the newspaper—do not claim omniscience in this exacting assignment, nor do they ask the public to accept uncritically all that the media communicate. Under the First Amendment, however, the media are at the very least free to communicate without restraint. And through this concept the media are also free to operate responsibly to serve the public interest. It is not a perfectly ordered universe of discourse, but it is the best alternative to other systems and it is, above all, pluralistic and democratic in both its means and its ends.

BIBLIOGRAPHY

Berkeley, George. *The Principles of Human Knowledge.* London: G. Routledge and Sons, Ltd., 1907.

Brucker, Herbert. *Freedom of Information.* New York: The Macmillan Company, 1949.

Center for the Study of Democratic Institutions. *Broadcasting and Government Regulation in a Free Society.* Santa Barbara, California. 1959.

Broadcasting in a Free Society: An Occasional Paper on the Role of the Mass Media in a free Society. 1959.

The Great Debates. 1962.

Chafee, Zechariah, Jr. *Government and Mass Communications.* Chicago: University of Chicago Press, 1947.

Columbia Broadcasting System. *Point of View: Equal Time.* New York: Columbia Broadcasting System, 1960.

Commission on Freedom of the Press. *A Free and Responsible Press.* Chicago: University of Chicago Press, 1947.

Coons, John E. *Freedom and Responsibility in Broadcasting.* Evanston, Illinois: Northwestern University Press, 1961.

Cross, Harold L. *The People's Right to Know.* New York: Columbia University Press, 1953.

Emery, Walter B. *Broadcasting and Government.* East Lansing, Michigan: Michigan State University Press, 1961.

Ernst, Morris. *The First Freedom.* New York: The Macmillan Company, 1946.

Ford, Worthington C. *Jefferson and the Newspaper, 1785–1830*. New York: Columbia University Press, 1936.

Flowerman, S. H. "Mass Propaganda in the War Against Bigotry" in *Journal of Abnormal Social Psychology*. Vol. XLII (1947), pp. 429–39.

Gerald, J. Edward. *The Press and the Constitution*. Minneapolis: University of Minnesota Press, 1948.

Hocking, William Ernest. *Freedom of the Press*. Chicago, Illinois: The University of Chicago Press, 1947.

Hume, David. *An Enquiry Concerning the Human Understanding*. Oxford: Clarendon Press, 1894.

Inglis, Ruth. *Freedom of the Movies*. Chicago: University of Chicago Press, 1947.

Jefferson, Thomas. *Democracy*. New York: Appleton Century Company, Inc., 1939.

Kelley, Stanley, Jr. *Public Relations and Political Power*. Baltimore: The Johns Hopkins Press, 1956.

Lacy, Dan *Freedom and Communications*. Urbana, Illinois: University of Illinois Press, 1961.

Levin, Harvey J. *Broadcast Regulation and Joint Ownership of Media*. New York: New York University Press, 1960.

Levy, Leonard W. *Legacy of Suppression*. Cambridge: Harvard University Press, 1960.

Locke, John. *An Eassy Concerning the Understanding, Knowledge opinion and Assent*. Cambridge, Massachusetts: Harvard University Press, 1931.

Luce Commission on the Freedom of the Press. *A Free and Responsible Press*. Chicago, Illinois: The University of Chicago Press, 1947.

Padover, Saul K. *Thomas Jefferson on Democracy*. New York: Penguin Books, Inc., 1939.

Reddick, DeWitt C., ed. *The Rise of the Mass Media in a Democratic Society*. (Papers and discussions from a conference at the University of Texas, February 6 and 7, 1961) University of Texas, 1961.

Schramm, Wilbur. *Responsibility in Mass Communications*. New York: Harper and Brothers, 1957.

Siebert, Fred S., Theodore Peterson, and Wilbur Schramm. *Four Theories of The Press*. Urbana, Illinois: University of Illinois Press, 1956.

Smead, Elmer E. *Freedom of Speech by Radio and Television*. Washington, D.C.: Public Affairs Press, 1959.

Stanton, Frank. *Benjamin Franklin Lecture*. New York: Columbia Broadcasting System, 1961.

Tocqueville, Alexis de. *Democracy in America*. New York: Alfred A. Knopf, Inc., 1945.

17

The Future

As THE United States enters the decade of the 1970's, it is even more apparent than in the past ten years that the revolution in mass communications technology is entering a significant and even crucial phase. Innovations which will affect not only the communications industries, but also the creative artist and the public, are in the process of being devised, interpreted and applied. Decisions which will have enormous effect on the creative resources and the economy of the mass media are being made. Some believe that these decisions are hasty and ill-devised and conceived. Others assert that regulatory and legislative bodies, such as the FCC and the Congress, are dilatory in coming to grips with, and resolving, the varied grabbag of dilemmas that beset the whole television area.

But out of the ferment have come decisions, proposals and a slowly evolving series of solutions to the many problems of electronic communications. Because of, or perhaps in spite of, some of the decisions made, communications technology will continue to develop with greater sophistication than ever before. Communication on what may literally be termed a global scale will become a reality. Video phones, now under experimental study in several countries, will come into active use. Disadvantaged nations finally will acquire that dubious hallmark of social distinction, the telephone. The computer and other techniques of automation will acquire greater refinement. Teaching machines, now used experimentally, will probably become standard equipment in most educational systems. Certainly, the further growth of CATV is inevitable, thus increasing the number of available programming resources. And certainly, satellite communications will bring a new dimension to electronic communications, both on a national and global basis.

In October, 1969, the Federal Communications Commission issued a

Report and Order dealing with community antenna television and opening television program origination to major cities. At the same time, the House Commerce Committee voted 12 to 9 to refer pay-television legislation back to its Communications Subcommittee for further study. The FCC ruling on CATV had extremely important implications for the television industry. In the first place, it permitted CATV operators not only to originate programs, but also—under certain set conditions—to carry commercials. The permission to take commercials was determined in spite of the assertion of the American Civil Liberties Union that commercial programs would hinder service to minority audiences, because sponsors demand large audiences. Secondly, the Commission—following a proposed agreement between cable operators and other broadcast groups by which cable television would not carry entertainment programming in return for certain expansion privileges—declared that it would support the right of CATV systems to interconnect for the purpose of distributing entertainment programs. In short, by January of 1971, the FCC determined that all CATV systems with more than 3,500 subscribers could relay programs as well as commercials of their own origination. Still undetermined were other peripheral problems. The FCC would prohibit multiple ownership of CATV systems along with commercial television stations, just as the Department of Justice has opposed common ownership by publishing interests of newspapers and CATV operations.

But the implication of the FCC ruling was clear. Its purpose was to provide greater programming resources and, therefore, greater diversity of content for majority and minority publics. At the same time, the FCC announced—without any clear explanation of how it would be implemented—that it would take precautionary measures to see to it that other broadcast services could function freely and without restriction or "loss or deterioration."

Other areas of the field of mass communications were equally in ferment. And of particular significance was the question of a domestic satellite system. In a most significant address before the Audio Engineering Society in 1969, Dr. Frank Stanton, President of CBS, proposed a new approach to a domestic satellite system which drew immediate concurrence from Leonard Goldenson, of ABC, and Julian Goodman, of NBC. Stanton proposed that the three major television networks create a consortium to establish and operate a domestic satellite system "with the necessary stations, capable of transmitting television and radio programming to all fifty states and offshore islands." The proposal stated also that channels be made available to the Corporation for Public Broadcasting at no charge.

One of the major features of the program was the matter of cost, which would be far less than what would be charged under a rate increase by AT &T. It was pointed out that such countries as Canada,

India, Japan, Australia, Brazil and Pakistan are creating their own satellite systems, while Russia has a rudimentary system in operation. For five years, Dr. Stanton asserted, discussions yielded no decisions by government on the disposition of a domestic satellite system. Since 1965, the commercial satellite has relayed broadcast signals, telegraph messages, telephone calls and computer data over the oceans. But, despite its international usefulness, its use in the United States has been insignificant, and educational television in particular has not had access to the areas which could be explored by the activation of a domestic satellite system.

There are still questions to be decided in the area of global communications. COMSAT and INTELSAT are both commercial ventures. ITU is concerned primarily with allocation of spectrum space and with the technology of international communications. But the basic problem is economic. Under viable economic conditions, and with a flow of funds available, most countries can—and eventually will—establish a successfully functioning electronic communications system. Despite the fact that ITU received comparatively little money from the United Nations, it has continued to be a positive and constructive force throughout the world, but particularly in areas where there is a poorly developed communications technology.

The problems of "hardware," however difficult and widely debated, are slowly being resolved. Magnificent development in communications technology are in progress and will continue into the 1980's. But no technology, however sophisticated, can resolve the educational, social and ethical problems which arise from the impact of mass communication on modern man. Major areas of concern are the proper application of teaching machines, the effective control and use of the computer and, above all, the need to surmount the always dangerous semantic roadblocks to communication that set social group against social group and nation against nation. The most effective technology cannot resolve the pernicious influence of conflicting ideologies which refuse to be brought out of the stratum of abstraction into the pragmatism of extensional discourse. For these problems, there is no technological solution. They are normative areas which involve value judgments and which require an evolving philosophy of the ethical implications of mass communication. The technical structure eventually will function with a minimum, or total absence, of noise. The goals of the mathematical theoreticians may be realized. But the social and esthetic and ethical problems are those that require the best minds in the mass media and related disciplines.

In the United States, in particular, communications functions responsibly and without imposition of censorship or control. The First Amendment and the courts have seen to that. Yet, there are pressing problems involving widespread criticism of mass media on matters of violence, alleged failure to reach minority publics, challenges on the basis of fairness, monopoly, slanted news and, indeed, overt attacks on the integrity of the media by those who would invoke censorship apparatus because their own views are not advanced. Part of these unfortunate strictures, some believe, are a result of the fact that the media do not always relate to reality. Part is due to the inevitable cultural lag that exists between technological breakthrough and the ability of other social agencies—including the media—to catch up with technology. Some critics assert that the media naturally tend to preserve the status quo, that there are unresolved and deep conflicts between the needs of majority and minority publics. Still others highlight the always present conflict between high culture and "kitsch." Compounding these problems is the fact that, despite the power and reach of mass communication, there are still large pockets of ignorance and of the educationally disadvantaged in the United States. And finally, there is the urgent need to relate communications technology in a meaningful way to the American system of education, on all levels from elementary school to college.

Freedom and Challenge

These are, admittedly, large problem areas. But they reveal a ferment and a continuing discourse which are coming to grips with the problems and which are intent upon finding workable solutions. The social answers may lag behind the technological achievements, but educators and professional communicators are revealing a keen awareness that questions exist and must be answered by empirical means. For the fact is that modern man has more volume of information available than ever before in history. The need exists to separate the wheat from the chaff, to relate abstract ideas to the extensional world. Despite the fact that the advertiser pays the bill, the mass media are as free as in any country in the world, and certainly the antithesis of the controlled systems of Russia and Red China. Despite the fact that the media are said to encourage simplistic thinking and polarization of viewpoint, more opportunities are available to study semantics and communications problems in the colleges and universities. And more and more the universities are insisting that they operate without any control, overt or implicit, over basic research.

The sheer ability to convey information to the people has never been more speedy or more effective. What is needed, therefore, is not speedier technology, but a stress on diversity and pluralism of viewpoint. The mass media are acutely aware of this need, and out of a sense of awareness should come a continuing spirit of free inquiry. But even the most simple solutions are costly. More people read books than ever before, even in this age of electronic competition, but the need for bookstores is evident in any but the largest metropolitan areas. The country's libraries are not only too few, but are woefully inadequate in what they have to offer. The legitimate theatre, the ballet and the opera—despite the growth of small groups and touring companies—are also largely restricted to major cities and are behind the financial reach of many millions of people.

Mass communications, in short, presents a singular paradox of pockets of cultural poverty in the midst of technological excellence. It is clear, however, that these areas are diminishing and will continue to grow smaller as the result of the growth of a domestic satellite system and other developments. Man's need to master the computer and the teaching machine is a recognized one. And, in the long run, the continuous recognition of social responsibility by the media—along with technology—will prove a major factor in bringing education, information and entertainment to all of the people on a scale unanticipated even by the most far-seeing pioneers in mass communication. This recognition of responsibility by the media, along with the growth of mass communications study and research in the schools, colleges and universities, will result in an increasing critical awareness by the people. And, out of this awareness, must come an increasing demand for the kind of excellence in mass communication that this country is poised to achieve.

Appendix

APPENDIX A

CANONS OF JOURNALISM

"CODE OF ETHICS OR CANONS OF JOURNALISM—THE AMERICAN SOCIETY OF NEWSPAPER EDITORS

"THE PRIMARY function of newspapers is to communicate to the human race what its members do, feel and think. Journalism, therefore, demands of its practitioners the widest range of intelligence, or knowledge, and of experience, as well as natural and trained powers of observation and reasoning. To its opportunities as a chronicle are indissolubly linked its obligations as teacher and interpreter.

"To the end of finding some means of codifying sound practice and just aspirations of American journalism, these canons are set forth:

"I. Responsibility

"The right of a newspaper to attract and hold readers is restricted by nothing but considerations of public welfare. The use a newspaper makes of the share of public attention it gains serves to determine its sense of responsibility, which it shares with every member of its staff. A journalist who uses his power for any selfish or otherwise unworthy purpose is faithless to a high trust.

"II. Freedom of the press

"Freedom of the press is to be guarded as a vital right of mankind. It is the unquestionable right to discuss whatever is not explicitly forbidden by law, including the wisdom of any restrictive statute.

"III. Independence

"Freedom from all obligations except that of fidelity to the public interest is vital.

"1. Promotion of any private interest contrary to the general welfare, for whatever reason, is not compatible with honest journalism. So-called news communications from private sources should not be published without public notice of their source or else substantiation of their claims to value as news, both in form and substance.

"2. Partisanship, in editorial comment which knowingly departs from the truth, does violence to the best spirit of American journalism; in the news columns it is subversive of a fundamental principle of the profession.

"IV. Sincerity, Truthfulness, Accuracy

"Good faith with the reader is the foundation of all journalism worthy of the name.

"1. By every consideration of good faith a newspaper is constrained to be truthful. It is not to be excused for lack of thoroughness or accuracy within its control, or failure to obtain command of these essential qualities.

"2. Headlines should be fully warranted by the contents of the articles which they surmount.

"V. *Impartiality*

"Sound practice makes clear distinction between news reports and expressions of opinion. News reports should be free from opinion or bias of any kind.

"1. This rule does not apply to so-called special articles unmistakably devoted to advocacy or characterized by a signature authorizing the writer's own conclusions and interpretation.

"VI. *Fair Play*

"A newspaper should not publish unofficial charges affecting reputation or moral character without opportunity given to the accused to be heard; right practice demands the giving of such opportunity in all cases of serious accusation outside judicial proceedings.

"1. A newspaper should not invade private rights or feelings without sure warrant of public right as distinguished from public curiosity.

"2. It is the privilege, as it is the duty, of a newspaper to make prompt and complete correction of its own serious mistakes of fact or opinion, whatever their origin.

"*Decency*

"A newspaper cannot escape conviction of insincerity if while professing high moral purpose it supplies incentives to base conduct, such as are to be found in details of crime and vice, publication of which is not demonstrable for the general good. Lacking authority to enforce its canons the journalism here presented can but express the hope that deliberate pandering to vicious instincts will encounter effective public disapproval or yield to the influence of a preponderant professional condemnation."

MOTION PICTURES PRODUCTION CODE

Foreword

Motion picture producers recognize the high trust and confidence which have been placed in them by the people of the world and which have made motion pictures a universal form of entertainment.

They recognize their responsibility to the public because of this trust and because entertainment and art are important influences in the life of a nation.

Hence, though regarding motion pictures primarily as entertainment without any explicit purpose of teaching or propaganda, they know that the motion picture within its own field of entertainment may be directly responsible for spiritual or moral progress, for higher types of social life, and for much correct thinking.

On their part, they ask from the public and from public leaders a sympathetic understanding of the problems inherent in motion picture production and a spirit of cooperation that will allow the opportunity necessary to bring the motion picture to a still higher level of wholesome entertainment for all concerned.

The Production Code

General Principles

1. No picture shall be produced which will lower the moral standards of those who see it. Hence the sympathy of the audience shall never be thrown to the side of crime, wrong-doing, evil or sin.

2. Correct standards of life, subject only to the requirements of drama and entertainment, shall be presented.

3. Law—divine, natural or human—shall not be ridiculed, nor shall sympathy be created for its violation.

Particular Applications:

I. CRIME:
1. Crime shall never be presented in such a way as to throw sympathy with the crime as against law and justice, or to inspire others with a desire for imitation.
2. Methods of crime shall not be explicitly presented or detailed in a manner calculated to glamorize crime or inspire imitation.

3. Action showing the taking of human life is to be held to the minimum. Its frequent presentation tends to lessen regard for the sacredness of life.

4. Suicide, as a solution of problems occurring in the development of screen drama, is to be discouraged unless absolutely necessary for the development of the plot, and shall never be justified, or glorified, or used specifically to defeat the ends of justice.

5. Excessive flaunting of weapons by criminals shall not be permitted.

6. There shall be no scenes of law-enforcing officers dying at the hands of criminals, unless such scenes are absolutely necessary to the plot.

7. Pictures dealing with criminal activities in which minors participate, or to which minors are related, shall not be approved if they tend to incite demoralizing imitation on the part of youth.

8. Murder:
   (a) The technique of murder must not be presented in a way that will inspire imitation.
   (b) Brutal killings are not to be presented in detail.
   (c) Revenge in modern times shall not be justified.
   (d) Mercy killing shall never be made to seem right or permissible.

9. Drug addiction or the illicit traffic in addiction-producing drugs shall not be shown in the portrayal:
   (a) Tends in any manner to encourage, stimulate or justify the use of such drugs; or
   (b) Stresses, visually or by dialogue, their temporarily attractive effects; or
   (c) Suggests that the drug habit may be quickly or easily broken; or
   (d) Shows details of drug procurement or of the taking of drugs in any manner; or
   (e) Emphasizes the profits of the drug traffic; or
   (f) Involves children who are shown knowingly to use or traffic in drugs.

10. Stories on the kidnapping or illegal abduction of children are acceptable under the Code only (1) when the subject is handled with restraint and discretion and avoids details, gruesomness and undue horror, and (2) the child is returned unharmed.

II. BRUTALITY:

Excessive and inhumane acts of cruelty and brutality shall not be presented. This includes all detailed and protracted presentation of physical violence, torture and abuse.

III. SEX:

The sanctity of the institution of marriage and the home shall be upheld. No film shall infer that casual or promiscuous sex relationships are the accepted or common thing.

1. Adultery and illicit sex, sometimes necessary plot material, shall not be explicitly treated, nor shall they be justified or made to seem right and permissible.

2. Scenes of passion:
   (a) These should not be introduced except where they are definitely essential to the plot.
   (b) Lustful and open-mouth kissing, lustful embraces, suggestive posture and gestures are not to be shown.
   (c) In general, passion should be treated in such manner as not to stimulate the baser emotions.
3. Seduction or rape:
   (a) These should never be more than suggested, and then only when essential to the plot. They should never be shown explicitly.
   (b) They are never acceptable subject matter for comedy.
   (c) They should never be made to seem right and permissible.
4. The subject of abortion shall be discouraged, shall never be more than suggested, and when referred to shall be condemned. It must never be treated lightly or made the subject of comedy. Abortion shall never be shown explicitly or by inference, and a story must not indicate that an abortion has been performed. The word "abortion" shall not be used.
5. The methods and techniques of prostitution and white slavery shall never be presented in detail, nor shall the subjects be presented unless shown in contrast to right standards of behavior. Brothels in any clear identification as such may not be shown.
6. Sex perversion or any inference of it is forbidden.
7. Sex hygiene and venereal diseases are not acceptable subject matter for theatrical motion pictures.
8. Children's sex organs are never to be exposed. This provision shall not apply to infants.

IV. VULGARITY:

Vulgar expressions and double meanings having the same effect are forbidden. This shall include but not be limited to such words and expressions as chippie, fairy, goose, nuts, pansy, S.O.B., son-of-a. The treatment of low, disgusting, unpleasant, though not necessarily evil, subjects should be guided always by the dictates of good taste and a proper regard for the sensibilities of the audience.

V. OBSCENITY:

1. Dances suggesting or representing sexual actions or emphasizing indecent movements are to be regarded as obscene.
2. Obscenity in words, gesture, reference, song, joke or by suggestion, even when likely to be understood by only part of the audience, is forbidden.

VI. BLASPHEMY AND PROFANITY:

1. Blasphemy is forbidden. Reference to the Deity, God, Lord, Jesus, Christ, shall not be irreverent.
2. Profanity is forbidden. The words "hell" and "damn," while sometimes dramatically valid, will if used without moderation be considered offensive by many members of the audience. Their use shall be governed by the discretion and prudent advice of the Code Administration.

VII. COSTUMES:

1. Complete nudity, in fact or in silhouette, is never permitted, nor shall there be any licentious notice by characters in the film of suggested nudity.
2. Indecent or undue exposure is forbidden.
    (a) The foregoing shall not be interpreted to exclude actual scenes photographed in a foreign land of the natives of that land, showing native life, provided:
        (1) Such scenes are included in a documentary film or travelogue depicting exclusively such land, its customs and civilization, and
        (2) Such scenes are not in themselves intrinsically objectionable.

VIII. RELIGION:

1. No film or episode shall throw ridicule on any religious faith.
2. Ministers of religion, or persons posing as such, shall not be portrayed as comic characters or as villains so as to cast disrespect on religion.
3. Ceremonies of any definite religion shall be carefully and respectfully handled.

IX. SPECIAL SUBJECTS:

The following subjects must be treated with discretion and restraint and within the careful limits of good taste:

1. Bedroom scenes.
2. Hangings and electrocutions.
3. Liquor and drinking.
4. Surgical operations and childbirth.
5. Third degree methods.

X. NATIONAL FEELINGS:

1. The use of the flag shall be consistently respectful.
2. The history, institutions, prominent people and citizenry of all nations shall be represented fairly.
3. No picture shall be produced that tends to incite bigotry or hatred among peoples of differing races, religions or national origins. The use of such offensive words as Chink, Dago, Frog, Greaser, Hunkie, Kike, Nigger, Spig, Wop, Yid, should be avoided.

XI. TITLES:

The following titles shall not be used:
1. Titles which are salacious, indecent, obscene, profane or vulgar.
2. Titles which violate any other clause of this Code.

XII. CRUELTY TO ANIMALS:

In the production of motion pictures involving animals the producer shall consult with the authorized representative of the American Humane Association, and invite him to be present during the staging of such animal action.

There shall be no use of any contrivance or apparatus for tripping or otherwise treating animals in an unacceptably harsh manner.

Reasons Supporting the Code

I. Theatrical motion pictures, that is, pictures intended for the theatre as distinct from pictures intended for churches, schools, lecture halls, educational movements, social reform movements, etc., are primarily to be regarded as entertainment.

> Mankind has always recognized the importance of entertainment and its value in rebuilding the bodies and souls of human beings.
>
> But it has always recognized that entertainment can be of a character either helpful or harmful to the human race, and in consequence has clearly distinguished between:
>
> a. Entertainment which tends to improve the race, or at least to re-create and rebuild human beings exhausted with the realities of life; and
>
> b. Entertainment which tends to degrade human beings, or to lower their standards of life and living.
>
> Hence the moral importance of entertainment is something which has been universally recognized. It enters intimately into the lives of men and women and affects them closely; it occupies their minds and affections during leisure hours; and ultimately touches the whole of their lives. A man may be judged by his standard of entertainment as easily as by the standard of his work.
>
> So correct entertainment raises the whole standard of a nation.
>
> Wrong entertainment lowers the whole living conditions and moral ideals of a race.
>
> Note, too, the effect on ancient nations of gladiatorial combats, the obscene plays the unhealthy reactions to sports like cockfighting, bullfighting, bear baiting, etc.
>
> Note, too, the effect on ancient nations of gladiatorial combats, the obscene plays of Roman times, etc.

II. Motion pictures are very important as art.

> Though a new art, possibly a combination art, it has the same object as the other arts, the presentation of human thought, emotion and experience, in terms of an appeal to the soul through the senses.
>
> Here, as in entertainment,
>
> Art enters intimately into the lives of human beings.
>
> Art can be morally good, lifting men to higher levels. This has been done through good music, great painting, authentic fiction, poetry, drama. Art can be morally evil in its effects. This is the case clearly enough with unclean art, indecent books, suggestive drama. The effect on the lives of men and women is obvious.

Note: It has often been argued that art in itself is unmoral, neither good nor bad. This is perhaps true of the thing which is music, painting, poetry, etc. But the thing is the product of some person's mind, and the intention of that mind was either good or bad morally when it produced the thing. Besides, the thing has its effect upon those who come into contact with it. In both these ways, that is, as a product of a mind and as the cause of definite effects, it has a deep moral significance and an unmistakable moral quality.

Hence: The motion pictures, which are the most popular of modern arts for the masses, have their moral quality from the intention of the minds which produce them and from their effects on the moral lives and reactions of their audiences. This gives them a most important morality.

1. They reproduce the morality of the men who use the pictures as a medium for the expression of their ideas and ideals.

2. They affect the moral standards of those who, through the screen, take in these ideas and ideals.

In the case of the motion picture, this effect may be particularly emphasized because no art has so quick and so widespread an appeal to the masses. It has become in an incredibly short period the art of the multitudes.

III. The motion picture, because of its importance as entertainment and because of the trust placed in it by the peoples of the world, has special moral obligations.

A. Most arts appeal to the mature. This art appeals at once to every class, mature, immature, developed, undeveloped, law abiding, criminal. Music has its grades for different classes; so have literature and drama. This art of the motion picture, combining as it does the two fundamental appeals of looking at a picture and listening to a story, at once reaches every class of society.

B. By reason of the mobility of a film and the ease of picture distribution, and because of the possibility of duplicating positives in large quantities, this art reaches places unpenetrated by other forms of art.

C. Because of these two facts, it is difficult to produce films intended for only certain classes of people. The exhibitors' theatres are built for the masses, for the cultivated and the rude, the mature and the immature, the self-respecting and the criminal. Films, unlike books and music, can with difficulty be confined to certain selected groups.

D. The latitude given to film material cannot, in consequence, be as wide as the latitude given to book material. In addition:

a. A book describes; a film vividly presents. One presents on a cold page; the other by apparently living people.

b. A book reaches the mind through words merely; a film reaches the eyes and ears through the reproduction of actual events.

c. The reaction of a reader to a book depends largely on the keenness of the reader's imagination; the reaction to a film depends on the vividness of presentation.
Hence many things which might be described or suggested in a book could not possibly be presented in a film.

E. This is also true when comparing the film with the newspaper.

a. Newspapers present by description, films by actual presentation.

b. Newspapers are after the fact and present things as having taken place; the film gives the events in the process of enactment and with the apparent reality of life.

F. Everything possible in a play is not possible in a film:

a. Because of the larger audience of the film, and its consequential mixed character. Psychologically, the larger the audience, the lower the moral mass resistance to suggestion.

b. Because through light, enlargement of character, presentation, scenic emphasis, etc., the screen story is brought closer to the audience than the play.

c. The enthusiasm for and interest in the film actors and actresses, developed beyond anything of the sort in history, makes the audience largely sympathetic toward the characters they portray and the stories in which they figure. Hence the audience is more ready to confuse actor and actress and the characters they portray, and it is most receptive of the emotions and ideals presented by its favorite stars.

G. Small communities, remote from sophistication and from the hardening process which often takes place in the ethical and moral standards of groups in larger cities, are easily and readily reached by any sort of film.

H. The grandeur of mass settings, large action, spectacular features, etc., affects and arouses more intensely the emotional side of the audience.

In general, the mobility, popularity, accessibility, emotional appeal, vividness, straightforward presentation of fact in the film make for more intimate contact with a larger audience and for greater emotional appeal.

Hence the larger moral responsibilities of the motion pictures.

REASONS UNDERLYING THE GENERAL PRINCIPLES

I. No picture shall be produced which will lower the moral standards of those who see it. Hence the sympathy of the audience should never be thrown to the side of crime, wrong-doing, evil or sin.

This is done:

1. When evil is made to appear attractive or alluring, and good is made to appear unattractive.

2. When the sympathy of the audience is thrown on the side of crime, wrongdoing, evil, sin. The same thing is true of a film that would throw sympathy against goodness, honor, innocence, purity or honesty.

Note: Sympathy with a person who sins is not the same as sympathy with the sin or crime of which he is guilty. We may feel sorry for the plight of the murderer or even understand the circumstances which led him to his crime. We may not feel sympathy with the wrong which he has done.

The presentation of evil is often essential for art or fiction or drama.

This in itself is not wrong provided:

a. That evil is not presented alluringly. Even if later in the film the evil is condemned or punished, it must not be allowed to appear so attractive that the audience's emotions are drawn to desire or approve so strongly that later the condemnation is forgotten and only the apparent joy of the sin remembered.

b. That throughout, the audience feels sure that evil is wrong and good is right.

II. Correct standards of life shall, as far as possible, be presented.

A wide knowledge of life and of living is made possible through the film. When right standards are consistently presented, the motion picture exercises the most powerful influences. It builds character, develops right ideals, inculcates correct principles, and all this in attractive story form. If motion pictures consistently hold up for admiration high types of characters and present stories that will affect lives for the better, they can become the most powerful natural force for the improvement of mankind.

III. Law—divine, natural or human—shall not be ridiculed, nor shall sympathy be created for its violation.

By natural law is understood the law which is written in the hearts of all mankind, the great underlying principles of right and justice dictated by conscience.

By human law is understood the law written by civilized nations.

1. The presentation of crimes against the law is often necessary for carrying out of the plot. But the presentation must not throw sympathy with the crime as against the law with the criminal as against those who punish him.

2. The courts of the land should not be presented as unjust. This does not mean that a single court may not be represented as unjust, much less that a single court official must not be presented this way. But the court system of the country must not suffer as a result of this presentation.

REASONS UNDERLYING PARTICULAR APPLICATIONS

I. Sin and evil enter into the story of human beings and hence in themselves are valid dramatic material.

II. In the use of this material, it must be distinguished between sins which repel by their very nature, and sins which often attract.

    a. In the first class come murder, most theft, many legal crimes, lying, hypocrisy, cruelty, etc.

    b. In the second class come sex sins, sins and crimes of apparent heroism, such as banditry, daring thefts, leadership in evil, organized crime, revenge, etc.

The first class needs less care in treatment, as sins and crimes of this class are naturally unattractive. The audience instinctively condemns all such and is repelled.

Hence the important objective must be to avoid the hardening of the audience, especially of those who are young and impressionable, to the thought and fact of crime. People can become accustomed even to murder, cruelty, brutality, and repellent crimes, if these are too frequently repeated.

The second class needs great care in handling, as the response of human nature to their appeal is obvious. This is treated more fully below.

III. A careful distinction can be made between films intended for general distribution, and films intended for use in theatres restricted to a limited audience. Themes and plots quite appropriate for the latter would be altogether out of place and dangerous in the former.

Note: The practice of using a general theatre and limiting its patronage during the showing of a certain film to "Adults Only" is not completely satisfactory and is only partially effective.

However, maturer minds may easily understand and accept without harm subject matter in plots which do younger people positive harm.

Hence: If there should be created a special type of theatre, catering exclusively to adult audience, for plays of this character (plays with problem themes, difficult discussions and maturer treatment) it would seem to afford an outlet, which does not now exist, for pictures unsuitable for general distribution but permissible for exhibitions to a restricted audience.

I. CRIMES AGAINST THE LAW

The treatment of crimes against the law must not:

1. Teach methods of crime.

2. Inspire potential criminals with a desire for imitation.

3. Make criminals seem heroic and justified.

Revenge in modern times shall not be justified. In lands and ages of less developed civilization and moral principles, revenge may sometimes be presented. This would be the case especially in places where no law exists to cover the crime because of which revenge is committed.

Because of its evil consequences, the drug traffic should not be presented except under careful limitations.

II. BRUTALITY

Excessive and inhumane acts of cruelty and brutality have no proper place on the screen.

III. SEX

Out of regard for the sanctity of marriage and the home, the triangle, that is, the love of a third party for one already married, needs careful handling. The treatment should not throw sympathy against marriage as an institution.

Scenes of passion must be treated with an honest acknowledgment of human nature and its normal reactions. Many scenes cannot be presented without arousing dangerous emotions on the part of the immature, the young or the criminal classes.

Even within the limits of pure love, certain facts have been universally regarded by lawmakers as outside the limits of safe presentation.

In the case of impure love, the love which society has always regarded as wrong and which has been banned by divine law, the following are important:

1. Impure love must not be presented as attractive and beautiful.

2. It must not be the subject of comedy or farce, or treated as material for laughter.

3. It must not be presented in such a way as to arouse passion or morbid curiosity on the part of the audience.

4. It must not be made to seem right and permissible.

5. In general, it must not be detailed in method and manner.

6. Certain places are so closely and thoroughly associated with sexual life or with sexual sin that their use must be carefully limited.

IV. VULGARITY

This section is intended to prevent not only obviously vulgar expressions but also double meanings that have the same effect.

V. OBSCENITY

Dances which suggest or represent sexual actions, whether performed solo or with two or more; dances intended to excite the emotional reaction of an audience; dances with movement of the breasts, excessive body movements while the feet are stationary, violate decency and are wrong.

This section likewise applies to obscene words, gestures, references, songs, jokes and gags.

VI. BLASPHEMY AND PROFANITY

It is clear that neither blasphemy nor profanity should be permitted on the screen.

VII. COSTUMES

General principles:

1. The effect of nudity or semi-nudity upon the normal man or woman, and much more upon the young and upon immature persons, has been honestly recognized by all lawmakers and moralists.

2. Hence the fact that the nude or semi-nude body may be beautiful does not make its use in the films moral. For, in addition to its beauty, the effect of the nude or semi-nude body on the normal individual must be taken into consideration.

3. Nudity or semi-nudity used simply to put a "punch" into a picture comes under the head of immoral actions. It is immoral in its effect on the average audience.

4. Nudity can never be permitted as being necessary for the plot. semi-nudity must not result in undue or indecent exposures.

5. Transparent or translucent materials and silhouette are frequently more suggestive than actual exposure.

VIII. RELIGION

The reason why ministers of religion may not be portrayed as comic characters or as villains so as to cast disrespect on religion is simply because the attitude taken toward them may easily become the attitude taken toward religion in general. Religion is lowered in the minds of the audience because of the lowering of the audience's respect for a minister.

IX. SPECIAL SUBJECTS

Such subjects are occasionally necessary for the plot. Their treatment must never offend good taste nor injure the sensibilities of an audience.

The use of liquor should never be excessively presented. In scenes from American life, the necessities of plot and proper characterization alone justify its use. And in this case, it should be shown with moderation.

X. NATIONAL FEELINGS

The just rights, history, and feelings of peoples and nations are entitled to most careful consideration and respectful treatment.

XI. TITLES

As the title of a picture is the brand on that particular type of goods, it must conform to the ethical practices of all such honest business.

XII. CRUELTY TO ANIMALS

The purpose of this provision is to prevent the treatment of animals in films in any unacceptably harsh manner.

APPENDIX C

NEW CODE OF SELF-REGULATION

MOTION PICTURE ASSOCIATION OF AMERICA

The Code of Self-Regulation of the Motion Picture Association of America shall apply to production, to advertising, and to titles of motion pictures.

The Code shall be administered by an office of Code Administration, headed by an Administrator.

There shall also be a Director of the Code for Advertising, and a Director of the Code for Titles.

Nonmembers are invited to submit pictures to the Code Administrator on the same basis as members of the Association.

• • •

DECLARATION OF PRINCIPLES OF THE CODE OF SELF-REGULATION OF THE MOTION PICTURE ASSOCIATION

This revised Code is designed to keep in closer harmony with the mores, the culture, the moral sense and the expectations of our society.

The revised Code can more completely fulfill its objectives, which are:

1. To encourage artistic expression by expanding creative freedom

and

2. To assure that the freedom which encourages the artist remains responsible and sensitive to the standards of the larger society.

Censorship is an odious enterprise. We oppose censorship and classification-by-law (or whatever name or guise these restrictions go under) because they are alien to the American tradition of freedom.

Much of this nation's strength and purpose is drawn from the premise that the humblest of citizen has the freedom of his own choice. Censorship destroys this freedom of choice.

It is within this framework that the Motion Picture Association continues to recognize its obligation to the society of which it is an integral part.

In our society the parents are the arbiters of family conduct.

Parents have the primary responsibility to guide their children in the kind of lives they lead, the character they build, the books they read, and the

> The new Code of Self Regulations presented herewith as approved by the board of directors of the Motion Picture Association of America, was effective September 20, 1966, and supplants the original Motion Picture Code, operative since 1930. Text of the original Code will be found in the 1966 Edition of Motion Picture Almanac.

movies and other entertainment to which they are exposed.

The creators of motion pictures undertake a responsibility to make

337

available pertinent information about their pictures which will enable parents to fulfill their function.

An important addition is now being made to the information already provided to the public in order to enable parents better to choose which motion pictures their children should see.

As part of the revised Code, there is a provision that producers in co-operation with the Code Administration, will identify certain pictures as SUGGESTED FOR MATURE AUDIENCES.

Such information will be conveyed by advertising, by displays at the theatre and by other means.

Thus parents will be alerted and informed so that they may decide for themselves whether a particular picture because of theme, content or treatment, will be one which their children should or should not see, or may not understand or enjoy.

We believe self-restraint, self-regulation, to be in the tradition of the American purpose. It is the American society meeting its responsibility to the general welfare. The results of self-discipline are always imperfect because that is the nature of all things mortal. But this Code, and its administration, will make clear that freedom of expression does not mean toleration of license.

The test of self-restraint . . . the rule of reason . . . lies in the treatment of a subject for the screen. The Seal of the Motion Picture Association on a film means that the picture has met the test of self-regulation.

All members of the Motion Picture Association, as well as many independent producers cooperate in this self-regulation. Not all motion pictures, however, are submitted to the Production Code Administration of the MPA, and the presence of the Seal is the only way the public can know which pictures have come under the Code.

We believe in and pledge our support to these deep and fundamental values in a democratic society:

Freedom of choice . . .

The right of creative man to achieve artistic excellence . . .

The role of the parent as the arbiter of the family's conduct.

The men and women who make motion pictures under this Code value their social responsibility as they value their creative skills. The Code, and all that is written and implied in it, aims to strengthen both those values.

STANDARDS FOR PRODUCTION

In furtherance of the objectives of the Code to accord with the mores, the culture, and the moral sense of our society, the principles stated above and the following standards shall govern the Administrator in his consideration of motion pictures submitted for Code approval:

● ● ●

The basic dignity and value of human life shall be respected and upheld.

Restraint shall be exercised in portraying the taking of life.

● ● ●

Evil, sin, crime and wrong-doing shall not be justified.

● ● ●

Special restraint shall be exercised in portraying criminal or anti-social activities in which minors participate or are involved.

• • •

Detailed and protracted acts of brutality, cruelty, physical violence, torture and abuse, shall not be presented.

• • •

Indecent or undue exposure of the human body shall not be presented.

• • •

Illicit sex relationships shall not be justified. Intimate sex scenes violating common standards of decency shall not be portrayed.

• • •

Restraint and care shall be exercised in presentations dealing with sex aberrations.

Obscene speech, gestures or movements shall not be presented. Undue profanity shall not be permitted.

Religion shall not be demeaned.

• • •

Words or symbols contemptuous of racial, religious or national groups, shall not be used so as to incite bigotry or hatred.

• • •

Excessive cruelty to animals shall not be portrayed and animals shall not be treated inhumanely.

STANDARDS FOR ADVERTISING

The principles of the Code cover advertising and publicity as well as production. There are times when their specific application to advertising may be different. A motion picture is viewed as a whole and may be judged that way. It is the nature of advertising, however, that it must select and emphasize only isolated portions and aspects of a film. It thus follows that what may be appropriate in a motion picture may not be equally appropriate in advertising. This must be taken into account in applying the Code standards to advertising. Furthermore, in application to advertising, the principles and standards of the Code are supplemented by the following standards for advertising:

• • •

Illustrations and text shall not misrepresent the character of a motion picture.

• • •

Illustrations shall not depict any indecent or undue exposure of the human body.

• • •

Advertising demeaning religion, race, or national origin shall not be used.

• • •

Salacious postures and embraces shall not be shown.

• • •

Censorship disputes shall not be exploited or capitalized upon.

Standards for Titles

A salacious, obscene, or profane title shall not be used on motion pictures.

Production Code Regulations

I. Operations

A. Prior to commencement of production of a motion picture, the producer shall submit a shooting, or other, script to the Office of Code Administration. The Administrator of the Code shall inform the producer in confidence whether a motion picture based upon the script appears to conform to the Code. The final judgment of the Administrator shall be made only upon reviewing of the completed picture.

B. The completed picture shall be submitted to the Code Office and if it is approved by the Administrator, the producer or distributor shall upon public release of the picture place upon an introductory frame of every print distributed for exhibition in the United States the official Seal of the Association with the word "Approved" above the Seal, and below, the words "Certificate Number," followed by the number of the Certificate of Approval. All prints bearing the Code Seal shall be identical.

C. The Administrator, in issuing a Certificate of Approval, shall condition the issuance of the Certificate upon agreement by the producer or distributor that all advertising and publicity to be used for the picture shall be submitted to and approved by the Director of the Code for Advertising.

D. The Administrator, in approving a picture under the Code, may recommend that advertising for the picture carry the informational line SUGGESTED FOR MATURE AUDIENCES. If the Administrator so determines, the distributing company shall carry the line SUGGESTED FOR MATURE AUDIENCES in its advertising. The Administrator shall notify the Director of the Code for Advertising of all such pictures.

E. The title of an approved motion picture shall not be changed without prior approval of the Director of the Code for Titles.

F. Nonmembers of the Association may avail themselves of the services of the Office of Code Administration in the same manner and under the same conditions as members of the Association.

G. The producer or distributor, upon receiving a Certificate of Approval for a picture, shall pay to the Office of Code Administration of fee in accordance with the uniform schedule of fees approved by the Board of Directors of the Association.

II. Motion Picture Code Board

A. A Motion Picture Code Board is established with these two principal functions:

—To hear appeals from decisions of the Code Administrator.

—To act as an advisory body on Code matters.

1. The Code Board shall be composed of the following:

    (a) The President of the Motion Picture Association of America, and nine other directors of the Association appointed by the President;

    (b) Six exhibitors appointed by the President upon nomination by the National Association of Theatre Owners; and

    (c) Four producers appointed by the President upon nomination by the Screen Producers Guild.

2. The President of the Motion Picture Association of America shall be Chairman of the Code Board, and the Association shall provide the secretariat.

3. The President may designate not more than two pro tempore members for each category as substitutes for members unable to attend a particular Board meeting or a hearing.

4. The presence of ten members shall constitute a quorum of the Board for meetings and hearings.

5. The members of the Board required to travel to attend a meeting shall be reimbursed for transportation and subsistence expenses, which shall be paid to them from funds of the Office of Code Administration.

B. Advisory

The procedures governing meetings of the Board in its advisory function shall be as follows:

1. The Board shall meet upon call of the Chairman at a time and place he may designate.

2. Members may submit suggestions for an agenda, which shall be prepared and circulated by the Chairman in advance of meetings. Upon majority vote, additional items may be submitted and brought up for discussion at meetings.

3. The Board through the Chairman may request the presence of the Code Administrator at meetings; may request oral and written reports from its distributors exhibitor and producer members on the status of the Code; may call for advice and reports upon others in a position to contribute to a better understanding and more efficacious operation of the system of self-regulation; and may perform such other functions of an advisory nature as may redound to the benefit of the Code.

C. Appeals

1. Any producer or distributor whos picture has not been approved by the Code Administrator may appeal the decision to the Motion Picture Code Board by filing a notice of appeal to the Chairman of the Board.

2. The procedures governing appeals before the Code Board shall be as follows:

    (a) The Board, upon being called into meeting by the Chairman, shall view an identical print of the picture denied a Certificate of Approval by the Code Administrator.

    (b) The producer or the distributor and the Code Administrator, or their representatives, may present oral or written statements to the board.

    (c) The Board shall decide the appeal by majority vote of the members present and its decision shall be final.

    (d) No member of the Board shall participate in an appeal involving a picture in which the member has a financial interest.

3. The jurisdiction of the Board is limited to hearing the appeal and it is without power to change or amend the Code.

4. The Code Board, if it authorizes the issuance of a Certificate of Approval, may do so upon such terms and conditions as it may prescribe.

Advertising Code Regulations

1. These regulations are applicable to all members of the Motion Picture Association of America, and to all producers and distributors of motion pictures with respect to each picture for which the Association has granted its Certificate of Approval.

2. The term "advertising" and used herein shall be deemed to mean all forms of motion picture advertising and exploitation, and ideas therefore, including the following; pressbooks; still photographs; newspaper, magazine and trade paper advertising; publicity copy and art intended for use in pressbooks or otherwise intended for general distribution in printed form or for theatre use; trailers; posters, lobby displays, and other outdoor displays; advertising accessories, including heralds and throw-aways; novelties; copy for exploitation tieups; and all radio and television copy and spots.

3. All advertising shall be submitted to the Director of the Code for Advertising for approval before use, and shall not be used in any way until so submitted and approved. All advertising shall be submitted in duplicate with the exception of pressbooks, which shall be submitted in triplicate.

4. The Director of the Code for Advertising shall proceed as promptly as feasible to approve or disapprove the advertising submitted.

The Director of the Code for Advertising shall stamp "Approved" on one copy of all advertising approved by him and return the stamped copy to the Company which submitted it. If the Director of the Code for Advertising disapproves of any advertising, the Director shall stamp the word "Disapproved" on one copy and return it to the Company which submitted it, together with the reasons for such disapproval; or, if the Director so desires, he may return the copy with suggestions for such changes or corrections as will cause it to be approved.

5. All pressbooks approved by the Director of the Code for Advertising shall bear in a prominent place the official seal of the Motion Picture Association of America. The word "Approved" shall be printed under the seal. Pressbooks shall also carry the following notice:

All advertising in this pressbook, as well as all other advertising and publicity materials referred to therein, has been approved under the Standards for Advertising of the Code of Self-Regulation of the Motion Picture Association of America. All inquiries on this procedure may be addressed to:

Director of Code for Advertising
Motion Picture Association of America
522 Fifth Avenue
New York, New York 10036

6. When the Code Administrator determines that any picture shall carry the informational line SUGGESTED FOR MATURE AUDIENCES, the

Director of the Code for Advertising shall require this line to appear in such advertising for that picture as the Director may specify. When the advertisement is limited in size, the Director may authorize the initials SMA to stand for SUGGESTED FOR MATURE AUDIENCES.

7. Appeals. Any Company whose advertising has been disapproved may appeal from the decision of the Director of the Code for Advertising, as follows:

It shall serve notice of such appeal on the Director of the Code for Advertising and on the President of the Association. The President, or in his absence a Vice President designated by him, shall thereupon promptly and within a week hold a hearing to pass upon the appeal. Oral and written evidence may be introduced by the Company and by the Director of the Code for Advertising, or their representatives. The appeal shall be decided as expeditiously as possible and the decision shall be final.

8. Any Company which uses advertising without prior approval may be brought up on charges before the Board of Directors by the President of the Association. Within a reasonable time, the Board may hold a hearing, at which time the Company and the Director of the Code for Advertising, or their representatives, may present oral or written statements. The Board, by a majority vote of those present, shall decide the matter as expeditiously as possible.

If the Board of Directors finds that the Company has used advertising without prior approval, the Board may direct the Administrator of the Code to void and revoke the Certificate of Approval granted for the picture and require the removal of the Association's seal from all prints of the picture.

9. Each Company shall be responsible for compliance by its employees and agents with these regulations.

CODE OF THE COMICS MAGAZINE ASSOCIATION
OF AMERICA

PREAMBLE

The comic book medium, having come of age on the American cultural scene, must measure up to its responsibilities.

Constantly improving techniques and higher standards go hand in hand with these responsibilities.

To make a positive contribution to contemporary life, the industry must seek new areas for developing sound, wholesome entertainment. The people responsible for writing, drawing, printing, publishing and selling comic books have done a commendable job in the past, and have been striving toward this goal.

Their record of progress and continuing improvement compares favorably with other media in the communications industry. An outstanding example is the development of comic books as a unique and effective tool for instruction and education. Comic books have also made their contribution in the field of letters and criticism of contemporary life.

In keeping with the American tradition, the members of this industry will and must continue to work together in the future.

In the same tradition, members of the industry must see to it that gains made in this medium are not lost and that violations of standards of good taste, which might tend toward corruption of the comic book as an instructive and wholesome form of entertainment, will be eliminated.

Therefore, the Comics Magazine Association of America, Inc. has adopted this Code, and placed strong powers of enforcement in the hands of an independent Code Authority.

Further, members of the Association have endorsed the purpose and spirit of this Code as a vital instrument to the growth of the industry.

To this end, they have pledged themselves to conscientiously adhere to its principles and to abide by all decision based on the Code made by the Administrator.

They are confident that this positive and forthright statement will provide an effective bulwark for the protection and enhancement of the American reading public, and that it will become a landmark in the history of self-regulation for the entire communications industry.

Code for Editorial Matter

GENERAL STANDARDS PART A

1—Crimes shall never be presented in such a way as to create sympathy for the criminal, to promote distrust of the forces of law and justice, or to inspire others with a desire to imitate criminals.

2—No comics shall explicitly present the unique details and methods of a crime.

3—Policemen, judges, government officials and respected institutions shall never be presented in such a way as to create disrespect for established authority.

4—If crime is depicted it shall be as a sordid and unpleasant activity.

5—Criminals shall not be presented so as to be rendered glamorous or to occupy a position which creates a desire for emulation.

6—In every instance good shall triumph over evil and the criminal punished for his misdeeds.

7—Scenes of excessive violence shall be prohibited. Scenes of brutal torture, excessive and unnecessary knife and gun play, physical agony, gory and gruesome crime shall be eliminated.

8—No unique or unusual methods of concealing weapons shall be shown.

9—Instances of law enforcement officers dying as a result of a criminal's activities should be discouraged.

10—The crime of kidnapping shall never be portrayed in any detail, nor shall any profit accrue to the abductor or kidnapper. The criminal or the kidnapper must be punished in every case.

11—The letters of the word "crime" on a comics magazine cover shall never be appreciably greater in dimension than the other words contained in the title. The word "crime" shall never appear alone on a cover.

12—Restraint in the use of the word "crime" in titles or sub-titles shall be exercised.

GENERAL STANDARDS PART B

1—No comic magazine shall use the word horror or terror in its title.

2—All scenes of horror, excessive bloodshed, gory or gruesome crimes, depravity, lust, sadism, masochism shall not be permitted.

3—All lurid, unsavory, gruesome illustrations shall be eliminated.

4—Inclusion of stories dealing with evil shall be used or shall be published only where the intent is to illustrate a moral issue and in no case shall evil be presented alluringly nor so as to injure the sensibilities of the reader.

5—Scenes dealing with, or instruments associated with walking dead, torture, vampires and vampirism, ghouls, cannibalism and were-wolfism are prohibited.

GENERAL STANDARDS PART C

All elements or techniques not specifically mentioned herein, but which are contrary to the spirit and intent of the Code, and are considered violations of good taste or decency, shall be prohibited.

DIALOGUE

1—Profanity, obscenity, smut, vulgarity, or words or symbols which have acquired undesirable meanings are forbidden.

2—Special precautions to avoid references to physical afflictions or deformities shall be taken.

3—Although slang and colloquialisms are acceptable, excessive use should be discouraged and wherever possible good grammar shall be employed.

RELIGION

1—Ridicule or attack on any religious or racial group is never permissible.

COSTUME

1—Nudity in any form is prohibited, as is indecent or undue exposure.
2—Suggestive and salacious illustration or suggestive posture is unacceptable.
3—All characters shall be depicted in dress reasonably acceptable to society.
4—Females shall be drawn realistically without exaggeration of any physical qualities.

NOTE: It should be recognized that all prohibitions dealing with costume, dialogue or artwork applies as specifically to the cover of a comic magazine as they do to the contents.

MARRIAGE AND SEX

1—Divorce shall not be treated humorously nor represented as desirable.
2—Illicit sex relations are neither to be hinted at or portrayed. Violent love scenes as well as sexual abnormalities are unacceptable.
3—Respect for parents, the moral code, and for honorable behavior shall be fostered. A sympathetic understanding of the problems of love is not a license for morbid distortion.
4—The treatment of love-romance stories shall emphasize the value of the home and the sanctity of marriage.
5—Passion or romantic interest shall never be treated in such a way as to stimulate the lower and baser emotions.
6—Seduction and rape shall never be shown or suggested.
7—Sex perversion or any inference to same is strictly forbidden.

Code for Advertising Matter

These regulations are applicable to all magazines published by members of the Comics Magazine Association of America, Inc. Good taste shall be the guiding principle in the acceptance of advertising.

1—Liquor and tobacco advertising is not acceptable.
2—Advertisement of sex or sex instruction books are unacceptable.
3—The sale of picture postcards, "pin-ups," "art studies," or any other reproduction of nude or semi-nude figures is prohibited.
4—Advertising for the sale of knives, concealable weapons, or realistic gun facsimiles is prohibited.
5—Advertising for the sale of fireworks is prohibited.
6—Advertising dealing with the sale of gambling equipment or printed matter dealing with gambling shall not be accepted.
7—Nudity with meretricious purpose and salacious postures shall not be permitted in the advertising of any product; clothed figures shall never

be presented in such a way as to be offensive or contrary to good taste or morals.

8—To the best of his ability, each publisher shall ascertain that all statements made in advertisements conform to fact and avoid misrepresentation.

9—Advertisement of medical, health, or toiletry products of questionable nature are to be rejected. Advertisements for medical, health or toiletry products endorsed by the American Medical Association, or the American Dental Association, shall be deemed acceptable if they conform with all other conditions of the Advertising Code.

APPENDIX E

THE NATIONAL ASSOCIATION OF BROADCASTERS

PREAMBLE

TELEVISION is seen and heard in every type of American home. These homes include children and adults of all ages, embrace all races and all varieties of religious faith, and reach those of every educational background. It is the responsibility of television to bear constantly in mind that the audience is primarily a home audience, and consequently that television's relationship to the viewers is that between guest and host.

The revenues from advertising support the free, competitive American system of telecasting, and make available to the eyes and ears of the American people the finest programs of information, education, culture and entertainment. By law the television broadcaster is responsible for the programming of his station. He, however, is obligated to bring his positive responsibility for excellence and good taste in programming to bear upon all who have a hand in the production of programs, including networks, sponsors, producers of film and of live programs, advertising agencies, and talent agencies.

The American businesses which utilize television for conveying their advertising messages to the home by pictures with sound, seen free-of-charge on the home screen, are reminded that their responsibilities are not limited to the sale of goods and the creation of a favorable attitude toward the sponsor by the presentation of entertainment. They include, as well, responsibility for utilizing television to bring the best programs regardless of kind, into American homes.

Television and all who participate in it are jointly accountable to the American public for respect for the special needs of children, for community responsibility, for the advancement of education and culture, for the acceptability of the program materials chosen, for decency and decorum in production, and for propriety in advertising. This responsibility cannot be discharged by any given group of programs, but can be discharged only through the highest standards of respect for the American home, applied to every moment of every program presented by television.

In order that television programming may best serve the public interest, viewers should be encouraged to make their criticisms and positive suggestions known to the television broadcasters. Parents in particular should be urged to see to it that out of the richness of television fare, the best programs are brought to the attention of their children.

I. ADVANCEMENT OF EDUCATION AND CULTURE

1. Commercial television provides a valuable means of augmenting the educational and cultural influence of schools, institutions of higher learning, the home, the church, museums, foundations, and other institutions devoted to education and culture.

348

2. It is the responsibility of a television broadcaster to call upon such institutions for counsel and cooperation and to work with them on the best methods of presenting educational and cultural materials by television. It is further the responsibility of stations, networks, advertising agencies and sponsors consciously to seek opportunities for introducing into telecasts factual materials which will aid in the enlightenment of the American public.

3. Education via television may be taken to mean that process by which the individual is brought toward informed adjustment to his society. Television is also responsible for the presentation of overtly instructional and cultural programs, scheduled so as to reach the viewers who are naturally drawn to such programs, and produced so as to attract the largest possible audience.

4. The television broadcaster should be thoroughly conversant with the educational and cultural needs and desires of the community served.

5. He should affirmatively seek out responsible and accountable educational and cultural institutions of the community with a view toward providing opportunities for the instruction and enlightenment of the viewers.

6. He should provide for reasonable experimentation in the development of programs specifically directed to the advancement of the community's culture and education.

7. It is in the interest of television as a vital medium to encourage and promote the broadcast of programs presenting genuine artistic or literary material, valid moral and social issues, significant controversial and challenging concepts and other subject matter involving adult themes. Accordingly, none of the provisions of this Code, including those relating to the responsibility toward children, should be construed to prevent or impede their broadcast. All such programs, however, should be broadcast with due regard to the composition of the audience. The highest degree of care should be exercised to preserve the integrity of such programs and to ensure that the selection of themes, their treatment and presentation are made in good faith upon the basis of true instructional and entertainment values, and not for the purposes of sensationalism, to shock or exploit the audience or to appeal to prurient interests or morbid curiosity.

II. Responsibility Toward Children

1. The education of children involves giving them a sense of the world at large. It is not enough that only those programs which are intended for viewing by children shall be suitable to the young and immature. In addition, those programs which might be reasonably expected to hold the attention of children and which are broadcast during times of the day when children may be normally expected to constitute a substantial part of the audience should be presented with due regard for their effect on children.

2. Such subjects as violence and sex shall be presented without undue

emphasis and only as required by plot development or character delineation. Crime should not be presented as attractive or as a solution to human problems, and the inevitable retribution should be made clear.

3. The broadcaster should afford opportunities for culture growth as well as for wholesome entertainment.
4. He should develop programs to foster and promote the commonly accepted moral, social and ethical ideals characteristic of American life.
5. Programs should reflect respect for parents, for honorable behavior, and for the constituted authorities of the American community.
6. Exceptional care should be exercised with references to kidnapping or threats of kidnapping of children in order to avoid terrorizing them.
7. Material which is excessively violent or would create morbid suspense, or other undesirable reactions in children, should be avoided.
8. Particular restraint and care in crime or mystery episodes involving children or minors should be exercised.

III. COMMUNITY RESPONSIBILITY

1. A television broadcaster and his staff occupy a position of responsibility in the community and should conscientiously endeavor to be acquainted fully with its needs and characteristics in order better to serve the welfare of its citizens.
2. Requests for time for the placement of public service announcements of programs should be carefully reviewed with respect to the character and reputation of the group, campaign or organization involved, the public interest content of the message, and the manner of its presentation.

IV. GENERAL PROGRAM STANDARDS

1. Program materials should enlarge the horizons of the viewer, provide him with wholesome entertainment, afford helpful stimulation, and remind him of the responsibilities which the citizen has towards his society. The intimacy and confidence placed in television demand of the broadcaster, the network and other program sources that they be vigilant in protecting the audience from deceptive program practices.
2. Profanity, obscenity, smut and vulgarity are forbidden, even when likely to be understood only by part of the audience. From time to time, words which have been acceptable, acquire undesirable meanings, and telecasters should be alert to eliminate such words.
3. Words (especially slang) derisive of any race, color, creed, nationality or national derivation, except wherein such usage would be for the specific purpose of effective dramatization such as combating prejudice, are forbidden, even when likely to be understood only by part of the audience. From time to time, words which have been acceptable, acquire undersirable meanings, and telecasters should be alert to eliminate such words.

4. Racial or nationality types shall not be shown on television in such a manner as to ridicule the race or nationality.

5. Attacks on religion and religious faiths are not allowed. Reverence is to mark any mention of the name of God, His attributes and powers. When religious rites are included in other than religious programs the rites shall be accurately presented. The office of minister, priest or rabbi shall not be presented in such a manner as to ridicule or impair its dignity.

6. Respect is maintained for the sanctity of marriage and the value of the home. Divorce is not treated casually as a solution for marital problems.

7. In reference to physical or mental afflictions and deformities, special precautions must be taken to avoid ridiculing sufferers from similar ailments and offending them or members of their families.

8. Excessive or unfair exploitation of others or of their physical or mental afflictions shall not be presented as praiseworthy.
The presentation of cruelty, greed and selfishness as worthy motivations is to be avoided.

9. Law enforcement shall be upheld and, except where essential to the program plot, officers of the law portrayed with respect and dignity.

10. Legal, medical and other professional advice, diagnosis and treatment will be permitted only in conformity with law and recognized ethical and professional standards.

11. The use of animals both in the production of television programs and as part of television program content, shall at all times, be in conformity with accepted standards of humane treatment.

12. Care should be exercised so that cigarette smoking will not be depicted in a manner to impress the youth of our country as a desirable habit worthy of imitation.

13. Criminality shall be presented as undesirable and unsympathetic. The condoning of crime and the treatment of the commission of crime in a frivolous, cynical or callous manner is unacceptable.
The presentation of techniques of crime in such detail as to invite imitation shall be avoided.

14. The presentation of murder or revenge as a motive for murder shall not be presented as justifiable.

15. Suicide as an acceptable solution for human problems is prohibited.

16. Illicit sex relations are not treated as commendable.
Sex crimes and abnormalities are generally unacceptable as program material. The use of locations closely associated with sexual life or with sexual sin must be governed by good taste and delicacy.

17. Drunkenness should never be presented as desirable or prevalent. The use of liquor in program content shall be de-emphasized. The consumption of liquor in American life, when not required by the plot or for proper characterization, shall not be shown.

18. Narcotic addiction shall not be presented except as a vicious habit. The administration of illegal drugs will not be displayed. The

use of hallucinogenic drugs shall not be shown or encouraged as desirable or socially acceptable.

19. The use of gambling devices or scenes necessary to the development of plot or as appropriate background is acceptable only when presented with discretion and in moderation, and in a manner which would not excite interest in, or foster, betting nor be instructional in nature.

20. Telecasts of actual sports programs at which on-the-scene betting is permitted by law should be presented in a manner in keeping with Federal, state and local laws, and should concentrate on the subject as a public sporting event.

21. Program material pertaining to fortune-telling, occultism, astrology, phrenology, palm-reading, numerology, mind-reading, or character-reading, is unacceptable when presented for the purpose of fostering belief in these subjects.

22. Quiz and similar programs that are presented as contests of knowledge, information, skill or luck must, in fact, be genuine contests and the results must not be controlled by collusion with or between contestants, or any other action which will favor one contestant against any other.

23. No program shall be presented in a manner which through artifice or simulation would mislead the audience as to any material fact. Each broadcaster must exercise reasonable judgment to determine whether a particular method of presentation would constitute a material deception, or would be accepted by the audience as normal theatrical illusion.

24. The appearances or dramatization of persons featured in actual crime news will be permitted only in such light as to aid law enforcement or to report the news event.

25. The use of horror for its own sake will be eliminated; the use of visual or aural effects which would shock or alarm the viewer, and the detailed presentation of brutality or physical agony by sight or by sound are not permissible.

26. Contests may not constitute a lottery.

27. The costuming of all performers shall be within the bounds of propriety and shall avoid such exposure or such emphasis on anatomical detail as would embarrass or offend home viewers.

28. The movements of dancers, actors, or other performers shall be kept within the bounds of decency, and lewdness and impropriety shall not be suggested in the positions assumed by performers.

29. Camera angles shall avoid such views of performers as to emphasize anatomical details indecently.

30. The use of the television medium to transmit information of any kind by the use of the process called "subliminal perception," or by the use of any similar technique whereby an attempt is made to convey information to the viewer by transmitting messages below the threshold of normal awareness, is not permitted.

31. The broadcaster shall be constantly alert to prevent activities that

may lead to such practices as the use of scenic properties, the choice and identification of prizes, the selection of music and other creative program elements and inclusion of any identification of commercial products or services, their trade names or advertising slogans, within a program dictated by factors other than the requirements of the program itself. The acceptance of cash payments or other considerations in return for including any of the above within the program is prohibited except in accordance with Sections 317 and 508 of the Communications Act.

32. A television broadcaster should not present fictional events or other non-news material as authentic news telecasts or announcements, nor should he permit dramatizations in any program which would give the false impression that the dramatized material constitutes news. Expletives (presented aurally or pictorially), such as "flash" or "bulletin" and statements such as "we interrupt this program to bring you . . ." should be reserved specifically for news room use. However, a television broadcaster may properly exercise discretion in the use in non-news programs of words or phrases which do not necessarily imply that the material following is a news release.

33. Program content should be confined to those elements which entertain or inform the viewer and to the extent that titles, teasers and credits do not meet these criteria, they should be restricted or eliminated.

34. The creation of a state of hypnosis by act or demonstration on the air is prohibited and hypnosis as an aspect or "parlor game" antics to create humorous situations within a comedy setting cannot be used.

V. Treatment of News and Public Events

News

1. A television station's news schedule should be adequate and well-balanced.

2. News reporting should be factual, fair and without bias.

3. A television broadcaster should exercise particular discrimination in the acceptance, placement and presentation of advertising in news programs so that such advertising should be clearly distinguishable from the news content.

3. At all times, pictorial and verbal material for both news and comment should conform to other sections of these standards, wherever such sections are reasonably applicable.

5. Good taste should prevail in the selection and handling of news: Morbid, sensational or alarming details not essential to the factual report, especially in connection with stories of crime or sex, should be avoided. News should be telecast in such a manner as to avoid panic and unnecessary alarm.

6. Commentary and analysis should be clearly identified as such.

7. Pictorial material should be chosen with care and not presented in a misleading manner.

8. All news interview programs should be governed by accepted standards of ethical journalism, under which the interviewer selects the questions to be asked. Where there is advance agreement materially restricting an important or newsworthy area of questioning, the interviewer will state on the program that such limitation has been agreed upon. Such disclosure should be made if the person being interviewed requires that questions be submitted in advance or if he participates in editing a recording of the interview prior to its use on the air.

9. A television broadcaster should exercise due care in his supervision of content, format, and presentation of newscasts originated by his station, and in his selection of newscasters, commentators, and analysts.

Public Events

1. A television broadcaster has an affirmative responsibility at all times to be informed of public events, and to provide coverage consonant with the ends of an informed and enlightened citizenry.

2. The treatment of such events by a television broadcaster should provide adequate and informed coverage.

VI. Controversial Public Issues

1. Television provides a valuable forum for the expression of responsible views on public issues of a controversial nature. The television broadcaster should seek out and develop with accountable individuals, groups and organizations, programs relating to controversial public issues of import to his fellow citizens; and to give fair representation to opposing sides of issues which materially affect the life or welfare of a substantial segment of the public.

2. Requests by individuals, groups or organizations for time to discuss their views on controversial public issues, should be considered on the basis of their individual merits, and in the light of the contribution which the use requested would make to the public interest, and to a well-balanced program structure.

3. Programs devoted to the discussion of controversial public issues should be identified as such. They should not be presented in a manner which would mislead listeners or viewers to believe that the program is purely of an entertainment, news, or other character.

4. Broadcasts in which stations express their own opinions about issues of general public interest should be clearly identified as editorials. They should be unmistakably identified as statements of station opinion and should be appropriately distinguished from news and other program material.

VII. Political Telecasts

1. Political telecasts should be clearly identified as such. They should not be presented by a television broadcaster in a manner which would mislead listeners or viewers to believe that the program is of any other character.

(Ref.: Communications Act of 1934 as amended, Secs. 315 and 317, and FCC Rules and Regulations, Secs. 3.654, 3.657, 3.663, as discussed in NAB's "A Political Catechism.")

VIII. Religious Programs

1. It is the responsibility of a television broadcaster to make available to the community appropriate opportunity for religious presentations.
2. Telecasting which reaches men of all creeds simultaneously should avoid attacks upon religion.
3. Religious programs should be presented respectfully and accurately and without prejudice or ridicule.
4. Religious programs should be presented by responsible individuals, groups and organizations.
5. Religious programs should place emphasis on broad religious truths, excluding the presentation of controversial or partisan views not directly or necessarily related to religion or morality.
6. In the allocation of time for telecasts of religious programs the television station should use its best efforts to apportion such time fairly among the representative faith groups of its community.

IX. General Advertising Standards

1. This Code establishes basic standards for all television broadcasting. The principles of acceptability and good taste within the Program Standards section govern the presentation of advertising where applicable. In addition, the Code establishes in this section special standards which apply to television advertising.
2. A commercial television broadcaster makes his facilities available for the advertising of products and services and accepts commercial presentations for such advertising. However, a television broadcaster should, in recognition of his responsibility to the public, refuse the facilities of his station to an advertiser where he has good reason to doubt the integrity of the advertiser, the truth of the advertising representations, or the compliance of the advertiser with the spirit and purpose of all applicable legal requirements.
3. Identification of sponsorship must be made in all sponsored programs in accordance with the requirements of the Communications Act of 1934, as amended, and the Rules and Regulations of the Federal Communications Commission.
4. Representations which disregard normal safety precautions shall be avoided.
   Children shall not be represented, except under proper adults supervision, as being in contact with, or demonstrating a product recognized as potentially dangerous to them.
5. In consideration of the customs and attitudes of the communities served, each television broadcaster should refuse his facilities to the advertisement of products and services, or the use of advertising scripts, which the station has good reason to believe would be objectionable to a substantial and responsible segment of the community. These standards should be applied with judgment and

flexibility, taking into consideration the characteristics of the medium, its home and family audience, and the form and content of the particular presentation.

6. The advertising of hard liquor (distilled spirits) is not acceptable.
7. The advertising of beer and wines is acceptable only when presented in the best of good taste and discretion, and is acceptable only subject to Federal and local laws. (*See Television Code Interpretation No. 5*)

   The advertising of cigarettes shall not state or imply claims regarding health and shall not be presented in such a manner as to indicate to youth that the use of cigarettes contributes to individual achievement, personal acceptance or is a habit worthy of imitation.
9. Advertising by institutions or enterprises which in their offers of instruction imply promises of employment or make exaggerated claims for the opportunities awaiting those who enroll for courses is generally unacceptable.
10. The advertising of firearms/ammunition is acceptable provided it promotes the product only as sporting equipment and conforms to recognized standards of safety as well as all applicable laws and regulations. Advertisements of firearms/ammunition by mail order are unacceptable. The advertising of fireworks is acceptable subject to all applicable laws.
11. The advertising of fortune-telling, occultism, astrology, phrenology, palm-reading, numerology, mind-reading, character reading or subjects of a like nature is not permitted.
12. Because all products of a personal nature create special problems, such products, when accepted, should be treated with especial emphasis on ethics and the canons of good taste. Such advertising of personal products as is accepted must be presented in a restrained and obviously inoffensive manner.

    The advertising of particularly intimate products which ordinarily are not freely mentioned or discussed is not acceptable. (*See Television Code Interpretation No. 3*)
13. The advertising of tip sheets, race track publications, or organizations seeking to advertise for the purpose of giving odds or promoting betting or lotteries is unacceptable.
14. An advertiser who markets more than one product should not be permitted to use advertising copy devoted to an acceptable product for purposes of publicizing the brand name or other identification of a product which is not acceptable.
15. "Bait-switch" advertising, whereby goods or services which the advertiser has no intention of selling are offered merely to lure the customer into purchasing higher-price substitutes, is not acceptable.
16. Personal endorsements (testimonials) shall be genuine and reflect personal experience. They shall contain no statement that cannot be supported if presented in the advertiser's own words.

X.   PRESENTATION OF ADVERTISING

1. Advertising messages should be presented with courtesy and good taste; disturbing or annoying material should be avoided; every effort should be made to keep the advertising message in harmony with the content and general tone of the program in which it appears.

2. The role and capability of television to market sponsors' products are well recognized. In turn, this fact dictates that great care be exercised by the broadcaster to prevent the presentation of false, misleading or deceptive advertising. While it is entirely appropriate to present a product in a favorable light and atmosphere, the presentation must not, by copy or demonstration, involve a material deception as to the characteristics, performance of appearance of the product.

3. The broadcaster and the advertiser should exercise special caution with the content and presentation of television commercials placed in or near programs designed for children. Exploitation of children should be avoided. Commercials directed to children should in no way mislead as to the product's performance and usefulness.
   Appeals involving matters of health which should be determined by physicians should not be directed primarily to children.

4. Appeals to help fictitious characters in television programs by purchasing the advertiser's product or service or sending for a premium should not be permitted, and such fictitious characters should not be introduced into the advertising message for such purposes.

5. Commercials for services or over-the-counter products involving health considerations are of intimate and far-reaching importance to the consumer. The following principles should apply to such advertising:
   a. Physicians, dentists or nurses, or actors representing physicians, dentists or nurses shall not be employed directly or by implication. These restrictions also apply to persons professionally engaged in medical services (e.g., physical therapists, pharmacists, dental assistants, nurses' aides).
   b. Visual representations of laboratory settings may be employed, provided they bear a direct relationship to bona fide research which has been conducted for the product or service. (*See Television Code, X, 10*). In such cases, laboratory technicians shall be identified as such and shall not be employed as spokesmen or in any other way speak on behalf of the product.
   c. Institutional announcements not intended to sell a specific product or service to the consumer and public service announcements by non-profit organizations may be presented by accredited physicians, dentists or nurses, subject to approval by the broadcaster. An accredited professional is one who has met required qualifications and has been licensed in his resident state.

6. Advertising should offer a product or service on its positive merits

and refrain by identification or other means from discrediting, disparaging or unfairly attacking competitors, competing products, other industries, professions or institutions.

7. A sponsor's advertising messages should be confined within the framework of the sponsor's program structure. A television broadcaster should avoid the use of commercial announcements which are divorced from the program either by preceding the introduction of the program (as in the case of so-called "cow-catcher" announcements) or by following the apparent sign-off of the program (as in the case of so-called trailer or "hitch-hike" announcements). To this and, the program itself should be announced and clearly identified, both audio and video, before the sponsor's advertising material is first used, and should be signed off, both audio and video, after the sponsor's advertising material is last used.

8. Since advertising by television is a dynamic technique, a television broadcaster should keep under surveillance new advertising devices so that the spirit and purpose of these standards are fulfilled.

9. A charge for television time to churches and religious bodies is not recommended.

10. Reference to the results of bona fide research, surveys or tests relating to the product to be advertised shall not be presented in a manner so as to create an impression of fact beyond that established by the work that has been conducted.

XI. Advertising of Medical Products

1. The advertising of medical products presents considerations of intimate and far-reaching importance to the consumer because of the direct bearing on his health.

2. Because of the personal nature of the advertising of medical products, claims that a product will effect a cure and the indiscriminate use of such words as "safe," "without risk," "harmless," or terms of similar meaning should not be accepted in the advertising of medical products on television stations.

3. A television broadcaster should not accept advertising material which in his opinion offensively describes or dramatizes distress or morbid situations involving ailments, by spoken words, sound or visual effects.

XII. Contents

1. Contests shall be conducted with fairness to all entrants, and shall comply with all pertinent laws and regulations. Care should be taken to avoid the concurrent use of the three elements which together constitute a lottery—prize, chance and consideration.

2. All contest details, including rules, eligibility requirements, opening and termination dates should be clearly and completely announced and/or shown, or easily accessible to the viewing public, and the winners' names should be released and prizes awarded as soon as possible after the close of the contest.

3. When advertising is accepted with requests contestants to submit items of product identification or other evidence of purchase of

products, reasonable facsimiles thereof should be made acceptable unless the award is based upon skill and not upon chance.

4. All copy pertaining to any contest (except that which is required by law) associated with the exploitation or sale of the sponsor's product or services, and all references to prizes or gifts offered in such connections should be considered a part of and included in the total time allowances as herein provided. (*See Television Code, XIV*)

XIII. Premiums and Offers

1. Full details of proposed offers should be required by the television broadcaster for investigation and approved before the first announcement of the offer is made to the public.

2. A final date for the termination of an offer should be announced as far in advance as possible.

3. Before accepting for telecast offers involving a monetary consideration, a television broadcaster should satisfy himself as to the integrity of the advertiser and the advertiser's willingness to honor complaints indicating dissatisfaction with the premium by returning the monetary consideration.

4. There should be no misleading descriptions or visual representations of any premiums or gifts which would distort or enlarge their value in the minds of the viewers.

5. Assurances should be obtained from the advertiser that premiums offered are not harmful to person or property.

6. Premiums should not be approved which appeal to superstition on the basis of "luck-bearing" powers or otherwise.

XIV. Time Standards for Non-Program Material

In order that the time for non-program material and its placement shall best serve the viewer, the following standards are set forth in accordance with sound television practice:

1. Non-Program Material Definition: Non-program material, in both prime time and all other time, includes billboards, commercials, all credits in excess of 30 seconds and promotional announcements. Public service announcements and promotional announcements for the same program are excluded from this definition.

2. Allowable Time for Non-Program Material.
   a. In prime time, non-program material shall not exceed 10 minutes in any 60-minute period.
      Prime time is a continuous period of not less than three consecutive evening hours per broadcast day as designated by the station between the hours of 6:00 PM and Midnight.
   b. In all other time, non-program material shall not exceed 16 minutes in any 60-minute period.

3. Program Interruptions.
   a. Definition: A program interruption is any occurrence of non-program material within the main body of the program.
   b. In prime time, the number of program interruptions shall not

exceed two within any 30-minute program, or four within any 60-minute program.

Programs longer than 60 minutes shall be pro-rated at two interruptions per half-hour.

The number of interruptions in 60-minute variety shows shall not exceed five.

c. In all other time, the number of interruptions shall not exceed four within any 30-minute program period.

d. In both prime time and all other time, the following interruption standard shall apply within programs of 15 minutes or less in length:

5-minute program—1 interruption;
10-minute program—2 interruptions;
15-minute program—2 interruptions.

e. News, weather, sports and special events programs are exempt from the interruption standard because of the nature of such programs.

4. No more than four commercial announcements shall be scheduled consecutively within programs, and no more than three commercial announcements shall be scheduled consecutively during station breaks. The consecutive commercial message limitation shall not apply to a single sponsor who wishes to further reduce the number of interruptions in the program.

5. A multiple product announcement is one in which two or more products or services are presented within the framework of a single announcement.

A multiple product announcement shall be counted as a single announcement provided the products or services are so treated in audio and video throughout the announcement as to appear to the viewer as a single unit. Multiple product announcements not meeting this definition shall be counted as two or more announcements under this section of the Code. This provision shall not apply to retail or service establishments.

6. The use of billboards, in prime time and all other time, shall be confined to programs sponsored by a single or alternate week advertiser and shall be limited to the products advertised in the program.

7. Reasonable and limited identification of prizes and donors' names where the presentation of contest awards or prizes is a necessary part of program content shall not be included as non-program material as defined above.

8. Programs presenting women's service features, shopping guides, fashion shows, demonstrations and similar material provide a special service to the public in which certain material normally classified as non-program is an informative and necessary part of the program content. Because of this, the time standards may be waived by the Code Authority to a reasonable extent on a case-by-case basis.

9. Gratuitous references in a program to a non-sponsor's product or service should be avoided except for normal guest identification.

10. Stationary backdrops or properties in television presentations show-

ing the sponsor's name or product, the name of his product, his trade-mark or slogan should be used only incidentally and should not obtrude on program interest or entertainment.

Interpretations of the Television Code

INTERPRETATION No. 1

June 7, 1956, Revised June 9, 1958
"Pitch" Programs

The "pitchman" technique of advertising on television is inconsistent with good broadcast practice and generally damages the reputation of the industry and the advertising profession.

Sponsored program-length segments consisting substantially of continuous demonstrations or sales presentation, violate not only the time standards established in the Code but the broad philosophy of improvement implicit in the voluntary Code operation and are not acceptable.

INTERPRETATION No. 2

June 7, 1956
Hollywood Film Promotion

The presentation of commentary or film excerpts from current theatrical releases in some instances may constitute commercial material under the Time Standards for Advertising. Specifically, for example, when such presentation, directly or by inference, urges viewers to attend, it shall be counted against the commercial allowance for the program of which it is a part.

INTERPRETATION No. 3

June 7, 1956
Non-Acceptability of Particularly Intimate Products

Paragraph 12 of the General Advertising Standards reads in part, "The advertising of particularly intimate products which ordinarily are not freely mentioned or discussed is not acceptable."

Products for the treatment of hemorrhoids and for use in connection with feminine hygiene are not acceptable under the above stated language.

INTERPRETATION No. 4

January 23, 1959
Prize Identification

Aural and/or visual prize identification of up to ten seconds duration may be deemed "reasonable and limited" under the language of Paragraph 7 of the Time Standards for Advertising. Where such identification is longer than ten seconds, the entire announcement or visual presentation will be charged against the total commercial time for the program period.

INTERPRETATION No. 5

March 4, 1965
Drinking on Camera

Paragraph 7, Section IX, General Advertising Standards, states that the "advertising of beer and wine is acceptable only when presented in the best of good taste and discretion." This requires that commercials involving beer and wine avoid any representation of on-camera drinking.

> *Note: From time to time the Code Authority issues advertising guidelines and clarifications expanding on provisions of the Code. Among areas covered are alcoholic beverages, acne products, arthritis and rheumatism remedies, bronchitis products, cigarettes, disparagement, men-in-white, testimonials, toys and weight reducing products. Copies may be obtained from any NAB Code, Authority Office.*

INDEX